On
Unders  Religion

Joseph M. Kitagawa

PRINCETON UNIVERSITY PRESS, PRINCETON, NEW JERSEY

Published by Princeton University Press, 41 William Street, Princeton,
New Jersey 08540
In the United Kingdom: Princeton University Press, Guildford, Surrey

Library of Congress Cataloging in Publication Data will be found on the last
printed page of this book

For information on the previous publication of essays contained
in this book, see page xxiii.

ISBN 0-691-07313-9   0-691-10229-5 (LPE)

This book has been composed in Linotron Galliard type

Clothbound editions of Princeton University Press books are printed on acid-free
paper, and binding materials are chosen for strength and durability. Paperbacks,
although satisfactory for personal collections, are not usually suitable
for library rebinding

Printed in the United States of America by Princeton University Press,
Princeton, New Jersey

For Evelyn and Anne Rose

Contents

CONTENTS

Preface

THERE ARE MANY reasons for the publication of this volume, not the least of which is its aim to draw together in a single volume articles which originally appeared in disparate sources, many of them hard to obtain now. That fact may partially explain why the collection as it stands seems to betray a certain lack of balance and why it occasionally repeats the same theme. On the other hand, there may be some good reason to have studies in Japanese religion seen primarily from the perspective of the history of religions collected and available to students.

By training and profession, I am both a historian of religions and an Orientalist. Contrary to those who believe that the history of religions (*Religionswissenschaft*) is nothing but an umbrella term for all kinds of inquiries into specialized phenomena, I am persuaded that the history of religions is a discipline with its own coherent methodology and objectives.[1] Just as a student of linguistics from time to time feels called upon to deal with specific languages—not so much to get to know those languages as to advance his or her research in linguistics—the historian of religions often takes up the study of specific preliterate, classical, or modern religions. This is even more true in my case, as I have tried to remain both a historian of religions and a specialist in Japanese religion. I have thus studied Japanese religion and Buddhism for what the richness of these traditions might contribute to my understanding of the history of religions; but, conversely, I have also tried to bring the perspective and methodology of the history of religions to bear on my studies of Japanese religion and Buddhism. (It of course must be admitted that even though anyone studying Japanese religion must be sufficiently informed about Buddhism, Buddhist studies are obviously a legitimate area quite apart from studies of Japanese religion as such.)

In retrospect, it becomes more evident that my aspiration to become both a historian of religions and a student of Japanese religion was

---

[1] For my understanding of the perspective and methodology, see my articles in M. Eliade and J. M. Kitagawa, eds., *The History of Religions: Essays in Methodology* (Chicago: University of Chicago Press, 1959); J. M. Kitagawa, ed., *The History of Religions: Essays on the Problem of Understanding* (Chicago: University of Chicago Press, 1967); and idem, ed., *The History of Religions: Retrospect and Prospect* (New York: Macmillan, 1985).

not so easily fulfilled, partly because of my upbringing. During the better part of my childhood, my father—a Confucianist-turned-Christian minister—was the pastor of a church in Kashiwara City, where the legendary first emperor of Japan was said to have founded the Japanese nation. Being brought up in the Kashiwara area with children of Shinto and Buddhist clerics among my playmates, and attending the Unebi Middle School, at which a series of eminent Japanese historians had taught, made me early on deeply appreciative of ancient Japanese culture. I could walk to many of the places mentioned in the *Kojiki* (Records of Ancient Matters), in the *Nihongi* (Chronicles of Japan), and in the early collection of verses called the *Man'yōshū*. Education was conducted according to the directives of the government, which was attempting to impose both the cult of the emperor and State Shinto on the Japanese people. My classes were thus required to make numerous trips to the Kashiwara Shrine, the legendary birthplace of the Japanese nation, and to the Unebi Imperial Mausoleum, where the first emperor presumably was buried. Our art teachers obliged us to visit old Buddhist temples to see famous Japanese, Korean, and Chinese paintings and other works of art. From my childhood experiences, then, I gained the strong impression that Japanese religion is a composite of different religious traditions, each with its own dynamics, and that the way to study Japanese religion is to study these traditions separately.

Even today I feel the importance of learning in depth the different strands of Japanese religion, to which many of the articles in this volume can attest. I would like to resist, however, the temptation to look at the whole of Japanese religion through the mental window of just one of its constituent elements. For example, some of my Shinto friends tend to feel that the most enduring thread within Japanese religion has been Shinto, which has managed to "indigenize" Confucianism and Taoism as well as Buddhism. Some of my Buddhist friends (who readily acknowledge the foreign origin of Buddhism) feel that the pre-Buddhist Japanese religion lacked sophistication in cosmology and epistemology, and that it was primarily Buddhism which elevated the religious standards of the Japanese people. Perhaps less surprisingly, Confucian diehards assert that from the seventh century onward, it was Confucianism which provided an invisible framework for both Shinto and Buddhism, and that the best way to understand Japanese religion is to see how Confucianism has penetrated every corner of Japanese life. Interestingly, I have met many Western observers and scholars who reflect these disparate views.

In college, I learned of two other ways to look at Japanese religion.

The first comprises a "religion and . . ." approach. Religion in Japan, as elsewhere, is closely related to other aspects of human life; thus, it is understandable that scholars in the fields of art, polity, sociology, economics, psychology, and so forth explore the meaning of Japanese religion in order to gain a better understanding of their respective subjects. And, not infrequently, these studies of nonreligious subjects illuminate aspects of religious meaning that have been overlooked by scholars of religion(s). This is particularly true in the areas of art and polity because of the proximity of religious and aesthetic experiences and of religion and state in Japan.

I also learned to appreciate the relevance of religion's influence on the *Zeitgeist*. Certainly it would be impossible to discuss the ethos of early Japan without considering the influence of religious and semi-religious systems such as Confucianism, Taoism, and Buddhism on Japanese culture and society. How could one explicate the medieval mood of Japan, especially during the thirteenth century, without some appreciation of the heightened religious consciousness stimulated by leaders in the Pure Land, Zen, Nichiren, and Ise Shinto movements? Here again, studies of the *Zeitgeist* (prehistoric, early, medieval, pre-modern, and modern) might uncover some of the hitherto neglected aspects of Japanese religion. Important as the "religion and . . ." approach and studies of the *Zeitgeist* are, however, I am persuaded that they will not replace the study of Japanese religion any more than do studies of the specific features of Shinto, Buddhism, and Confucianism.

THROUGHOUT my thirty-odd years of teaching at the University of Chicago, I have encountered students with various motivations. Many students of the history of religions approach Japanese religion as a part of the religious experience of the human race and go on to explore the meaning and purpose of religion in human life. Among students of Far Eastern languages and civilizations, some are interested in the study of Japanese religion per se; others are attracted to specific religious systems—Shinto, Buddhism, Confucianism, Japanese folk religion, and so forth; still others are motivated to study religious influences on a variety of subjects, including art, the state, literature, economics, and the *Zeitgeist*. And as is so often the case, I have learned much in teaching these graduate students.

In 1962-63, I was asked to give five lectures under the general title of "Religion in Japanese History" in the American Council of Learned Societies' Lectures on the History of Religions. These lectures were

later published under the same title, and in the preface to that volume
I stated:

The complexity of the historic interaction of various religious systems in Japan
is such that it would have been safer, for readers as well as for the author, if
the study concentrated either on the religious development of one historic
period or on one of the major religious systems, such as Shinto, Buddhism,
or Japanese Confucianism. However, the scarcity of works, especially in Western languages, dealing with Japanese religion as a whole challenged me to
undertake the present task.[2]

I went on to say:

I shall approach Japanese religion historically, not only in the sense of studying
its involvement in the social and political life of the nation . . . but also to
show how the universal phenomenon called "religion" has unfolded itself in
the drama of Japanese history.[3]

Basically, I am persuaded that Japanese religion has been singularly
preoccupied with *this* world, with its emphasis on finding ways to
cohabit with the *kami* (sacred) and with other human beings. Also,
Japanese religion, like other nonrevelatory religions, ultimately seeks
an "immanental theocratic model" from a synthesis of polity, religion,
society, and culture, just as religions based on a transcendental deity
and its revelation often seek a "theocratic principle." In the course of
the Japanese experience, there have been three major syntheses: the
Ritsuryō (imperial rescript) of the seventh and eighth centuries A.D.,
the Tokugawa (1603-1868), and the Meiji (1868-1945).

The Ritsuryō synthesis. Briefly stated, the Ritsuryō synthesis was primarily based on three principles: (1) the mutual dependence of Emperor's Law and Buddha's Law (*Ōbō-Buppō*), (2) Shinto-Buddhist institutional syncretism (*Shin-Butsu Shūgō*), and (3) the belief in
Japanese deities as manifestations of the Buddhas and Bodhisattvas of
India (*honji suijaku*). Saicho, called posthumously Dengyō Daishi (A.D.
767-822), described himself in his famous vow as "the greatest among
all fools, and the least worthy among men, having violated the teaching of the Buddha and the laws of the sovereign, and failed in filial
piety and propriety. . . ."[4] Thus he portrayed himself as both a firm

[2] J. M. Kitagawa, *Religion in Japanese History* (New York: Columbia University Press,
1966), p. vi.
[3] Ibid., p. 3.
[4] His "Vow" was translated in Wing-tsit Chan, I. R. al-Fārūqī, J. M. Kitagawa, and
P. T. Raju, comps., *The Great Asian Religions: An Anthology* (New York: Macmillan,
1969), pp. 266-267.

believer in *Ōbō-Buppō* mutual dependence and a practitioner of the Shinto-Buddhism-Confucianism combination which was the main tenet of the Ritsuryō system. Clearly, Ritsuryō Japan followed the model of Emperor Wen Ti of Sui China (r. 581-604), who unified races, cultures, and diverse areas of his empire by subordinating Confucianism, Buddhism, and, to a lesser degree, Taoism to the throne. Likewise the architects of the Ritsuryō system did not hesitate to equate the sacred modalities of Buddhism with those of native Shinto traditions. Shinto-Buddhist institutional syncretism precipitated the establishment of Jingū-ji (Buddhist chapels dedicated to Shinto *kami*) and Shinto chapels within the Buddhist temple compounds. This synthesis furthered popular acceptance of the theory of *honji suijaku* because it was articulated not by Shinto theoreticians but by Tendai and Shingon esoteric masters in terms of *Sannō-ichijitsu-Shinto* or *Ryōbu-Shinto*.[5]

As I pointed out in "Monarchy and Government: Traditions and Ideologies in Pre-Modern Japan," which appears in this volume, the Ritsuryō system was destined to undergo some formal changes, but its ideology persisted until the Ōnin War (1467-1477), which ushered in the age of Sengoku (incessant wars among feudal lords). It took three strongmen—Oda Nobunaga (1534-1582), Toyotomi Hideyoshi (1536-1598), and Tokugawa Iyeyasu (1542-1616)—to unify Japan under a new ideological synthesis. The first two, Nobunaga and Hideyoshi, gave lip service to *Ōbō* (the Sovereign's Law) but rejected the first cardinal principle of the Ritsuryō synthesis: that *Ōbō* needed *Buppō* (Buddha's Law) for the sake of the nation.[6] Both men thus campaigned against the rich and powerful Buddhist institutions on Mount Hi'ei and Mount Kōya and against the Hongan-ji, the main temple of True Pure Land Buddhism.

The Tokugawa synthesis. In 1603, Iyeyasu established the Tokugawa feudal regime (*bakufu* or shogunate). A new type of "immanental theocracy," it was a comprehensive political, social, legal, philosophical, religious, and moral order under the Tokugawa *shōgun* (generalissimo). In sharp contrast to the Ritsuryō system, which was based on

[5] See Noboru Miyata, ed., *Kami to Hotoke* (*Kami* and the Buddha) (Tokyo: Shogakkan, 1983) and Ichiro Ishida, *Kami to Nihon bunka* (*Kami* and Japanese Civilization) (Tokyo: Perikan-sha, 1983). On the technical Shingon debates on *honji* and *kami*, see Minoru Kiyota, *Shingon Buddhism: Theory and Practice* (Los Angeles and Tokyo: Buddhist Books International, 1978), pp. 74-80.

[6] On Nobunaga's religious policy, see Neil McMullin, *Buddhism and State in Sixteenth-Century Japan* (Princeton: Princeton University Press, 1984).

a Shinto version of sacred kingship, the Tokugawa synthesis was based on the Neo-Confucian principles of natural laws and natural norms implicit in human, social, and political order, all grounded in the Will of Heaven.

Although the Tokugawa regime considered Neo-Confucianism the official and guiding principle for the nation, it used Buddhist institutions to fortify its claims. In fact, Tokugawa shoguns skillfully maneuvered the Buddhist schools into serving as the bulwark of the regime. But the second cardinal principle of the Ritsuryō system, the institutional synthesis of Shinto and Buddhism, was still operative. Reared in the tradition of the Pure Land (Jōdo) School, Iyeyasu honored this Buddhist denomination by building an impressive edifice for the Zōjō-ji (temple) in Edo. At the same time, he catered to his adviser Tenkai's Sannō-ichijitsu-Shinto (the so-called Tendai Shinto); in return, Tenkai declared Iyeyasu the "Sun God of the East," to contrast with the "Sun God of the West," the emperor.

The Tokugawa system preserved as well the third basic principle of the Ritsuryō synthesis, the theory of Japanese deities as manifestations of the Buddhas and Bodhisattvas of India (*honji suijaku*). A passage in the edict banning Christianity and revealing Iyeyasu's understanding of the belief in *honji suijaku* reads: "Japan is called the land of the Buddha and not without reason ... [*kami*] and Buddha differ in name, but their meaning is one."[7]

In short, the Tokugawa feudal regime had no room for Ōbō or Ōbō-Buppō mutual dependence (the first principle of the Ritsuryō system), was surprisingly supportive of Shinto-Buddhist institutional syncretism (the second principle), and openly affirmed the doctrine of *honji suijaku* (the third principle).

The Meiji synthesis. The combined effect of internal and external pressures resulted in the dissolution of the Tokugawa feudal regime and fostered direct monarchical rule under the boy emperor, Meiji, in 1868. The architects of the new regime were a group of ambitious warriors and lower courtiers who agreed on pragmatic policies and attempted to combine the earlier Ritsuryō and Tokugawa syntheses. They were aware that there was no room for the mutual dependence of Ōbō-Buppō and they dissolved Shinto-Buddhist institutional syncretism by proclaiming the separation of Shinto from Buddhism (*Shin-Butsu Hanzen-rei*). Instead, the Meiji regime concocted the hitherto

[7] Quoted in Sir Charles Eliot, *Japanese Buddhism* (New York: Barnes and Noble, 1959), p. 309.

unknown State Shinto as a "nonreligious" (the term used by the government) national cult closely related to the cult of the emperor. The new regime did nothing, however, to interfere with the belief in *honji suijaku*. The precarious attempt to incorporate elements of the modern West and features of the Ritsuryō and Tokugawa syntheses into a new system could not halt so persistent a religious pattern as *honji suijaku*.

The belief in *honji suijaku* was kept alive through the reigns of Meiji (1868-1912), Taishō (1912-1926), and Shōwa (1926-) until 1945. Since then, Japan has become a modern, secular industrial nation in which there is no room for "immanental theocracy" in any form, as I point out in "The Religious Ethos of Present-Day Japan," which is included in this volume. Nowadays, the Japanese people have no use for the principles of mutually dependent "sovereign's law and Buddha's law" (*Ōbō-Buppō*) or Shinto-Buddhist institutional syncretism (*Shin-Butsu Shūgō*). Yet an amazing number of Japanese continue to affirm the simplistic equation of *kami* and the Buddha.

THE ESSAYS of the present volume were selected from diverse articles I have written, mostly in English, over nearly three decades. Some of them, therefore, do not have up-to-date references, although it is hoped that their theses are still important and defensible. (It may be useful to mention my contribution, entitled "The Japanese Religion," to *A Reader's Guide to the Great Religions*, edited by C. J. Adams, for the benefit of those who need more current bibliographical data.[8]) For the same reason, the present volume does not pretend to present a well-balanced portrayal of all aspects of Japanese religion. Thus the book is unevenly divided into five parts: Prehistory, Historic Development of Japanese Religion, Shinto Tradition, Buddhist Tradition, and the Modern Phase of the Japanese Religious Tradition. An appended section, on Buddhism in this country, rounds out the book.

Prehistory. No one is certain how far back we can trace human habitation in the Japanese islands, for future archaeological discoveries could easily change our views on this problem. But as far as we now know, stone implements that belonged to early inhabitants can be traced to the so-called Tachikawa loam bed, a deposit of volcanic ash laid down on the Kantō plain in mid-Pleistocene times, some four to five hundred thousand years ago. The existence of such stone implements indicates that, although these early people did not yet possess pottery, they had passed the stage of scraping out a livelihood with

[8] Published by The Free Press, New York, N.Y., 1965 and 1977.

their bare hands. It is estimated that this "pre-ceramic" period lasted for at least ten to twenty thousand years and can be divided into three stages based on developments in stone tool technology:

The first dates back thirty thousand years to a time preceding the diffusion of knife-shaped tools. The second stage was about twenty thousand years ago when knife-shaped tools of all kinds were extensively used. In the third and last stage, knife-shaped tools were eclipsed by thin stone blades known as microliths.[9]

These early Japanese soon began to use fire, which fostered the production of pottery, and which, in turn, ushered in the Jōmon period described in the first article, "Prehistoric Background of Japanese Religion." In recent years, archaeologists have been joined by scholars from other disciplines—history, anthropology, mythology, linguistics, art, and religion—in exploring the pre-ceramic and archaeological stages of life in Japan.

Historic Development of Japanese Religion. In my book, *Religion in Japanese History,* I dwelt chiefly on the last two of the three syntheses in Japanese experience, those of the Tokugawa and the Meiji. Certain articles in this volume, however, demonstrate my keen interest in the first, the Ritsuryō, synthesis, which is the paradigmatic form of "immanental theocracy." In two articles, " 'A Past of Things Present': Notes on Major Motifs of Early Japanese Religions" and "Some Remarks on the Study of Sacred Texts," I attempt to show that the so-called chronicles—the *Kojiki* and the *Nihongi*—were not unbiased ancient histories but were written from the perspective of the Ritsuryō synthesis of the seventh and eighth centuries. These chronicles contain mythologies of the old "imperial ideology," as N. Saigō has phrased it.[10] Even the *Man'yōshū*, which has been considered by many to be a collection of primarily nonideological nature poems, contains in fact many verses attributed to official "court reciters" (*kataribe*). One such poet laureate was the celebrated Kakinomoto Hitomaro, who, as a composer "of poems of praise and lament of the imperial family," crafted "iconic images which 'prove' the divinity of the imperial family."[11] The verses of the *kataribe* were intimately related to the political

[9] *The History of Kanagawa* (Yokohama: Kanagawa Prefectural Government, 1985), p. 5.

[10] Nobutsuna Saigō, *Kojiki* (Tokyo: Nihon Hyoron-sha, 1947), p. 291.

[11] Ian Hideo Levy, *The Ten Thousand Leaves*, vol. 1 (Princeton: Princeton University Press, 1981), p. 14. According to Nakanishi, the age of the *Man'yō* may be divided into four periods. During the first period (A.D 645-672), there were a number of female court poets (*o'una*). During the second period (A.D. 672-702), these female court poets

and religious developments of the seventh and eighth centuries; they particularly reflected the growth of the Ritsuryō system.

Religiously motivated and religiously inspired political ideologies were key elements of the Ritsuryō, Tokugawa, and Meiji syntheses. In the final analysis, however, it is difficult to determine whether these ideologies were more religious or more political. I emphasize the religious aspect in "Stages of the Japanese 'Religious Universe' " and the political aspect in "Monarchy and Government: Traditions and Ideologies in Pre-Modern Japan." Yet the three syntheses arose not only from the importance of religious traditions, value systems, and ideologies; they also concerned the well-being of human beings—their hopes, dreams, ambitions, and disappointments. Thus my article, "The Shadow of the Sun," treats the concerns and destinies of the Fujiwaras and the imperial family, whose paths crossed throughout Japanese history from the seventh century onward. Both families supported, sometimes modified, and often were supported by, the different modes of synthesis. It is virtually impossible to explain the history of the Fujiwara family—why it was content to support and not to supplant the imperial family, for example—to non-Japanese, with the possible exception of the Nepalese who, in the Fujiwara family, may see reproduced a lineage similar to the hereditary family of their prime minister. If one can understand the mystery of the Fujiwara family as the "shadow of the sun," however, one can very likely understand many facets of Japanese society, culture, and religion.

A well-known salient feature of Japanese religion has been its affirmation of the principle of *saisei-itchi* (unity of church and state, or of religious affairs and political administration). It is undeniably difficult for those raised in the tradition of the separation of church and state to understand this principle. In my article, "*Matsuri* and *Matsuri-goto*: Religion and State in Early Japan," I have explicated the ancient religious rationale for this principle.[12] Another salient feature of Japanese

---

were overshadowed by male court reciters (*kataribe*). (Nakanishi thinks that Kakinomoto Hitomaro was the last major *kataribe*.) During the third period (A.D. 702-729), the *Man'yō* poems included an increasing number of noncourt themes. Finally, during the fourth period (A.D. 729-759), ritual functions traditionally performed by court poets, female or male, were gradually taken over by the new "religious leaders," that is, Buddhist or Shinto clerics. (Susumu Nakanishi, *Man'yō no sekai* [The World of the *Man'yō*] [Tokyo, n.p., 1973], pp. 19-42.)

[12] How to square the tradition of the unity of religion and state with the postwar constitutional guarantee of religious liberty is a very difficult question. When the emperor visits the Grand Shrine of Ise, the tutelary shrine of the imperial family, questions have been raised as to whether he visits Ise as a private individual or as the emperor; for, since 1959, important national ceremonies have been officially required to be conducted according to Shinto rites and, since 1960, the *shintai* (literally, "*kami* body") of

religion throughout its history has been the crucial importance of pilgrimage. My essay, "Three Types of Pilgrimage in Japan," therefore disagrees with those who define religion primarily in terms of doctrine, ethics, or cultic practices.

Shinto Tradition. I cannot explain why I have published several articles on the Shinto tradition in Japanese, German, and Italian, but only one in English.[13] The article, "Shinto," in the present volume was written for Italian publication and has not previously appeared in English. There are two diametrically opposed approaches to Shinto. The first is espoused by leaders and adherents of Shinto. A major Shinto theorist, Sokyō Ono, states:

> From time immemorial the Japanese people have believed in and worshipped *kami* [an honorific term for the sacred and the sacred spirits that permeate everything in the universe] *as an expression of their native racial faith* which arose in the mystic days of remote antiquity. *To be sure, foreign influences are evident.* This *kami*-faith cannot be fully understood without some reference to them. *Yet it is as indigenous as the people* that brought the Japanese nation into existence and ushered in its new civilization; and like that civilization, the *kami*-faith has progressively developed throughout the centuries and still continues to do so in modern times.[14]

The second view is represented by Ichirō Ishida, a well-known intellectual historian, who insists that Shinto has been transformed several times during the course of Japan's history by allying itself with—or by surrendering to—alien religious traditions (Buddhism and Confucianism) or native ideologies (the National Learning of the family-based State-ism).[15] There is truth to both views. Ironically, those who hold the first view often exaggerate the importance of Shinto, thus making it almost a synonym for the whole of Japanese religion, while those who hold the second view often minimize Shinto's importance. Immediately following World War II, Shinobu Origuchi caused a heated controversy in Shinto circles by advocating a change from the tribal ethos of Shinto to the ethos of a global religion through a separation of the belief in the imperial system from Shinto itself.[16] Is the

---

the Ise shrine has been declared to belong to the imperial family. There also does not seem to be a good solution to the current debate on whether the prime minister can officially visit the Yasukuni shrine for deceased soldiers.

[13] J. M. Kitagawa, "Shinto," *Encyclopaedia Britannica*, vol. 12 (1961).

[14] Sokyō Ono, *The "Kami" Way: An Introduction to Shrine Shinto* (Tokyo and Rutland, Vermont: Bridgeway Press, 1959), p. 1. (Emphasis mine.)

[15] Ichirō Ishida, *Kami to Nihon-Bunka* (*Kami* and Japanese Civilization) (Tokyo: n.p., 1983), p. 10.

[16] Referred to in Nanzan shūkyō-kenkyūjo, *Shinto to Kirisuto-kyo* (Shinto and Christianity) (Tokyo: Shunjū-sha, 1984), p. 32.

imperial system *esse, bene esse,* or accidental to Shinto? What other institutions or qualities are necessary for Shinto? Unfortunately, I have more questions than answers about the Shinto tradition as a part of Japanese religion.[17]

Buddhist Tradition. I hope it is clear that my having written more on Buddhism than on Shinto in English is purely accidental. The article, "The Saṃgha and the Ecclesia," stresses the importance of the *saṃgha* not only as the institutional form of Buddhist faith but also as its object, since all adherents must take refuge in the three treasures (the *Buddha,* the *dharma,* and the *saṃgha*). I wrote "Master and Saviour" about the charismatic figure, Kūkai (774-835), who established the Esoteric School (*Mikkyō*) of Buddhism in Japan. After his death he was deified, an act that reflects the characteristic tendency of Japanese religion to depend on the charisma of the holy man as an efficacious aid to salvation. As I have also noted in the article, "The Buddhist Transformation in Japan," the uniqueness of Japanese Buddhism owes a great deal to the Esoteric School—also known as Tantrayāna, Mantrayāna, or Vajrayāna—which originally developed in India several centuries after the rise of the Mahāyāna tradition. The Esoteric School penetrated China significantly later than the introduction of the Mahāyāna tradition there; but in Japan, the introduction of Mahāyāna in the mid-sixth century was followed very quickly by the penetration of Esoteric deities and scriptures.

One of the two Esoteric Buddhist schools in Japan was the Shingon (Chên-yen in Chinese) School, introduced by Kūkai. It is usually called Tō-Mitsu, meaning *Mikkyō* (Esoteric School) connected with the Tō-ji, an important Shingon temple in Kyoto. A second school was the Tendai (T'ien T'ai in Chinese) School, which was founded by Saichō (Dengyō Daishi, 767-822) and is usually called Tai-Mitsu, meaning *Mikkyō* connected with the Tendai monastic center at Mount Hi'ei. Saichō was attracted by the Chinese T'ien T'ai system, which attempted to combine moral precepts, monastic discipline, Zen (Ch'an) meditation, and Esoteric cult practices within the framework of the *Lotus Sūtra.* The religious ideas associated with Kūkai's Tō-Mitsu and Saichō's Tai-Mitsu dominated the Japanese religious scene, particularly after the time of Ennin (792-862), chief priest of the Tendai School and an advocate of the *Nembutsu* (recitation of the name of Amida Buddha). In fact, most of the prominent Buddhist figures in Japan—

---

[17] Many pertinent questions on Shinto were raised in the *Proceedings of the Second International Conference for Shinto Studies: Continuity and Change* (Tokyo: Kokugakuin University, 1968).

Yōsai (or Eisai, 1141-1215), Hōnen (1133-1212), Shinran (1173-1262), Nichiren (1222-1282), and Dōgen (1200-1253)—were trained in the Tai-Mitsu tradition, and they were strongly conscious of the transmission of *dharma* through patriarchal lineage and sacred scriptures. I believe that it was this strong impact of Esoteric insights that later enabled the Japanese Buddhist tradition to be integrated so smoothly into the mainstream of Japanese religion.

Strangely enough, Japanese Buddhism, which became a self-conscious feature of Japanese religion, always looked not to India but to China for its source of legitimacy. As I discuss in the article, "Buddhist Translation in Japan," this focus is without doubt the underlying psychological reason for the absence of Japanese translations of the Indian Buddhist scriptures until our time. Yet, as I explicate in "The Career of Maitreya, with Special Reference to Japan," Maitreya, who inspired political revolutions in China as well as in South and Southeast Asia and who was the eschatological symbol of the Buddhist tradition, completely lost eschatological meaning in the context of Japanese religion, preoccupied as it is with existence in the "here and now" of this world.

In my article, "Paradigm Change in Japanese Buddhism," I compare the ideals of Japanese Buddhism to those of the Indian, South Asian, and Chinese Buddhist traditions. Contrary to those who uphold the "plural belonging theory"—that the Japanese belong simultaneously to Shinto, Buddhist, Confucian, folk religious, and other traditions—I believe that Japanese Buddhists are self-consciously heirs of both historic Buddhism and Japanese religion.[18]

The Modern Phase of the Japanese Religious Tradition. We suffer today from a strange cultural tendency which divides history into two components—traditional and modern—with the implication that whatever is not modern is traditional and so worthless. The author of this volume does not subscribe to that view. Irving Kristol's observation that "the twentieth century began in 1945"[19] is, however, applicable to Japan: in losing World War II, Japan was subjected for the first time in her history to occupation by foreign forces. The year 1945 thus marked the end of the Meiji synthesis.

There is real wisdom in placing postwar Japan in the larger context of modern history as I try to do in "The Religious Ethos of Present-Day Japan." On examination of this essay, one finds that modern Ja-

---

[18] This is taken for granted in *Understanding Japanese Buddhism* (Tokyo: Twelfth WFB Confab Japan Committee, Japan Buddhist Federation, 1978).

[19] In the Magazine section of the Sunday *New York Times*, 2 May 1965, p. 25.

pan is a peculiar mixture of external forces and internal dynamics. Westernization, for example, was not imposed by outsiders but was the conscious policy of the architects of modern Japan. They were willing to welcome things Western because of their secure grounding in the Eastern ethos, particularly in the Confucian tradition. One realizes as well that Westernization was inevitably instrumental in the modernization of Japan. These two trends, Westernization and modernization, confused both insiders and outsiders. Elements of this knotty issue are discussed in my article, "Some Reflections on Foreign Scholars' Understanding of Japanese Culture and Shinto."[20]

While many Japanese and Westerners equated Westernization with modernization, there were some scholars—as I indicate in my article, "Buddhism and Modern Japanese Thought"—who perceived their own cultural experiences in modern, global terms. A group of thinkers often called the Kyoto School is a case in point. Their pioneers were Kitarō Nishida (1870-1945) and his junior colleague at Kyoto University, Hajime Tanabe (1885-1962). Concerning this school, Y. Takeuchi has written:

Adopting Western methods, utilizing Western categories, and at the same time criticizing both, they endeavour to find a new way to express their original philosophical insights and often, in view of the results so far achieved, their own life and world views, nurtured in the tradition of Oriental thought.[21]

Usually not identified with the Kyoto School were thinkers such as D. T. Suzuki (1870-1960), Nishida's childhood friend;[22] Seichi Hatano (1877-1950), author of *A Study of Spinoza* (1910); Tetsurō Watsuji (1899-1960); and Satomi Takahashi (1886-1964). All addressed themselves neither to the East nor to the West but to the world. Many members of the Kyoto School have been influenced by the Zen or Amida traditions, as well as by the Confucian element of Japanese religion. This is evidenced in the contrast between Western thinkers, who defined thinking as being, substance, the individual, and self-awareness, and these modern Japanese thinkers, who dug into their religio-philosophical-cultural tradition until they reached the con-

[20] See also the introduction to J. M. Kitagawa, ed., *Understanding Modern China* (Chicago: Quadrangle Books, 1969), pp. 21-41.

[21] Yoshinori Takeuchi, "Japanese Philosophy," *Encyclopaedia Britannica*, 1968 ed., 12:958J-959.

[22] To date, D. T. Suzuki has been known primarily as the interpreter of Zen to the West. It is my feeling, however, that in the future, Suzuki's contribution to Nishida's thinking and his reflection of Nishida's religio-cultural background will be better understood.

cept of "nothingness."[23] All of these men are indebted to Nishida's view that religion is made manifest through "disjunction-conjunction" between God (the Absolute) and man (the relative). "God stands against man as Will to will. He is transcendent to man. At the same time, he is immanent. . . . He is Absolute Being and Absolute Nothingness in his true identity of contradiction."[24] These Japanese thinkers feel that the experience of reconciling Zen with faith in Amida gives them the unique ability to reconcile Eastern and Western thought patterns. Such a reconciliation, which they consider their responsibility, is essential for a world which must integrate East and West, North and South. With this in mind, I have added my article, "Buddhism in America," as the appendix because this phenomenon cannot be overlooked in any discussion of Japanese religion and because it demonstrates the extent to which this reconciliation has taken place.

IT IS MY pleasant duty to thank Miriam Brokaw, Margaret Case, Cathie Brettschneider, and Andrew Mytelka of Princeton University Press for their advice and assistance in bringing together this collection.

Thanks also are due to Dean Franklin I. Gamwell and my colleagues in both the History of Religions and the Department of Far Eastern Languages and Civilizations at the University of Chicago for their encouragement and support. I also want to thank my secretary, Ms. Martha Morrow-Vojacek, and my research assistant, Mr. Peter Chemery, upon whose extensive care and attention my recent work has depended.

In 1983 my wife and daughter were able to join me for a visit to Japan. I dedicate this volume to them in hopes that it will be possible for us to visit Japan again.

University of Chicago   Joseph M. Kitagawa
July 1986

---

[23] Takeuchi insists that "Absolute nothingness or non-being—'mu' in Japanese—is not the '*me on*' of Platonism. Neither is it by any means limited to the meaning of the so-called 'annihilating nothingness' of existentialism. It includes, of course, this negative meaning, but by means of a thoroughgoing negativity the very negation turns itself into the most positive activity. The closest approximation which Western thought offers to our Oriental view is, I believe, the Hegelian notion of 'absolute negativity' or 'negation of negation.' " (Y. Takeuchi, "Buddhism and Existentialism," in *Religion and Culture: Essays in Honor of Paul Tillich*, ed. W. Leibrecht [New York: Harper, 1959], p. 292.)

[24] Takeuchi, "Japanese Philosophy," p. 961.

Publishing History

CHAPTER 1. *History of Religions* 2, no. 2 (Winter 1963): 292-328.

CHAPTER 2. *History of Religions* 20, nos. 1 and 2 (August-November 1980): 27-42.

CHAPTER 3. *The Critical Study of Sacred Texts*, ed. Wendy D. O'Flaherty (Berkeley: Graduate Theological Union, 1979), 231-242.

CHAPTER 4. *Studi e Materiali di Storia delle Religioni* 7, no. 1 (1983): 61-73.

CHAPTER 5. *Kingship in Asia and Early America*, ed. A. L. Basham (Thirtieth International Congress of Human Sciences in Asia and North Africa) (Mexico: El Colegio de México, 1981), 217-232.

CHAPTER 6. *Austrina: Essays in Commemoration of the Twenty-Fifth Anniversary of the Founding of the Oriental Society of Australia*, ed. A. R. David and A. D. Stefanowska (Sydney: Oriental Society of Australia, 1982), 422-438.

CHAPTER 7. *Religious Traditions* 2, no. 1 (April 1979): 30-37.

CHAPTER 8. *Studies in Mysticism and Religion*, presented to Gershom G. Scholem, ed. E. E. Urbach et al. (Jerusalem: Magnes Press, Hebrew University, 1967), 155-164.

CHAPTER 9. *Storia delle Religioni*, ed. Giuseppe Castellani, 6th ed. (Turin: Unione Tipografico-Editrice Torinese, 1970), 5:799-852. (In Italian.)

CHAPTER 10. *Proceedings of the Ninth International Congress for the History of Religions* (Tokyo: Maruzen, 1960), 550-555.

CHAPTER 11. *Studies of Esoteric Buddhism and Tantrism* (Kōyasan: Kōyasan University, 1965), 1-26.

CHAPTER 12. *History of Religions* 4, no. 2 (Winter 1965): 319-336.

CHAPTER 13. *Babel*, nos. 1 and 2 (1963): 53-59.

CHAPTER 14. *History of Religions* 21, no. 2 (November 1981): 107-125.

CHAPTER 15. *Japanese Journal of Religious Studies* 11, nos. 2 and 3 (June-September 1984): 115-142.

CHAPTER 16. Public lecture given at the University of Tennessee, 1983.

CHAPTER 17. *Proceedings of the Second International Conference for Shinto Studies* (Tokyo: Kokugakuin University, 1968), 122-134.

CHAPTER 18. Expanded version of a lecture given at the University of Chicago in 1984. Original title was "Buddhist Philosophy in Japan."

APPENDIX. *Japanese Religions* 5, no. 1 (July 1967): 32-57.

Professor Kitagawa has prepared the Chronology of Japanese Religion and the Glossary especially for this collection.

Each of the reprinted essays has received limited editing. As the differences in transliteration, dating, and name order indicate, however, the reprints appear essentially as they were originally published.

Chronology of Japanese Religion

Pre-Ceramic Period

Jōmon Period (ca. 2500 B.C.-250 B.C.)

Yayoi Period (ca. 250 B.C.-A.D. 250)

A.D. 57	Japanese envoy from the State of Nu pays tribute to the Han court in China
239	Envoy of Queen Himiko dispatched to the Wei court in China

Kofun ("Tumulus") Period (ca. 250-550)

369	Japanese forces occupy southern tip of Korea

Asuka Period (ca. 550-710)

538 (or 552)	Official introduction of Buddhism from the Paekche court in Korea to the Yamato court
562	Kingdom of Silla (Shilla) destroys Mimana, Japan's foothold in Korea
589	Unification of China by the Sui dynasty
593-621	Regency of Prince Shōtoku (573-621)
604	Seventeen-Article Constitution proclaimed
618	Establishment of T'ang dynasty in China
645	Taika Reform begins
701-702	Taihō Reform Code promulgated

Nara Period (710-781)

710	Establishment of the first permanent capital, Heijō-kyō, at Nara
712	The *Kojiki* (Records of Ancient Matters) compiled
720	The *Nihongi* (Chronicles of Japan) compiled
735	Unification of Korea under Kingdom of Silla
752	Dedication of the Great Buddha statue at Tōdai-ji in Nara

Heian Period (781-1191)

794	Establishment of the second permanent capital, Heian-kyō, at Kyoto
805	Saichō (767-822) returns from China and founds the Tendai Buddhist School
806	Kūkai (774-835) returns from China and founds the Shingon Buddhist School
815	New compilation of the *Register of Families* (*Shinsen shōjiroku*) completed

822	Ordination hall (*kaidan*) established at Mount Hi'ei
847	Ennin (792-862) popularizes Tendai Esoterism (Tai-mitsu)
858	Beginning of *de facto* rule by the Fujiwara oligarchy (Fujiwara regency)
907	End of the T'ang dynasty in China
927	*Institutes of the Engi Era* (*Engi-shiki*) completed
960	Sung dynasty established in China
1017	Death of Genshin (b. 942), author of *Essentials of Salvation* (*Ōjō yōshū*)
1086	Beginning of the "Cloister Rule" (*Insei*)
1132	Death of Ryōnin (b. 1071), forerunner of Pure Land Buddhism in Japan
1156	The *Hogen no Ran* insurrection, led by ex-Emperor Sutoku and others
1175	Hōnen (1133-1212) founds the Pure Land (Jōdo) sect
1191	Yōsai (or Eisai, 1141-1215) introduces the Rinzai (Lin-chi) School of Zen

Kamakura Period (1192-1333)

1192	Minamoto Yoritomo establishes the Kamakura *bakufu* or shogunate
1205	Hōjō Yoshitoki becomes shogun's regent; beginning of Hōjō regency in Kamakura shogunate
1220	The *Gukanshō* (a Buddhist philosophy of history) written
1222	Kamakura regime banishes three retired monarchs (Go-Toba, Tsuchimikado, and Juntoku) from the capital
1224	Shinran (1173-1262) founds the True Pure Land (Jōdo Shin or Ikkō) sect
1227	Dōgen (1200-1253) introduces Sōtō (Ts'ao-tung) Zen
1238	Great statue of Amida Buddha constructed at Kamakura
1253	Nichiren (1222-1282) founds the Nichiren (then called the Hokke or Lotus) sect
1274	First Mongol invasion
1275	Ippen (1239-1289) founds the Ji ("Time") sect
1281	Second Mongol invasion
1333	End of the Kamakura shogunate

Ashikaga (or Muromachi) Period (1338-1573)

1338	Beginning of the Ashikaga shogunate
1339	The *Jinnō-shōtō-ki* (*Records of the Legitimate Succession of the Divine Sovereigns*) by Kitabatake Chikafusa (1293-1354) completed
1368	End of the Mongol (Yuan) dynasty and establishment of the Ming dynasty in China
1392	Establishment of the Yi dynasty in Korea
1401	Ashikaga shogunate requests diplomatic relations with the Ming court

1443	Death of Zeami (b. 1363), master of the *Nō* drama
1467	Beginning of the Ōnin War; beginning of nationwide civil wars
1477	End of the Ōnin War
1479	Rennyo (1415-1499) builds the Hongan-ji, the main temple of the True Pure Land or Ikkō sect, at Yamashina
1511	Death of Yoshida Kanetomo (b. 1435), advocate of Yuiitsu Shinto
1532	Armed conflicts between the Nichiren and the Ikkō sects
1541	Oda Nobunaga (1534-1582), strongman of Japan, helps rebuild the Grand Shrine of Ise
1542 or 1543	Portuguese merchants arrive at Kyushu
1549	Francis Xavier (1506-1552) arrives at Kagoshima
1551	Xavier leaves Japan; Roman Catholic (*Kirishitan*) activities continue
1571	Oda Nobunaga's forces attack Mount Hi'ei monastic center
1573	End of the Ashikaga shogunate

Azuchi-Momoyama Period (1574-1600)

1582	Death of Oda Nobunaga; Toyotomi Hideyoshi (1536-1598) succeeds to power
1587	First persecution of *Kirishitan* (Roman Catholic) faithful
1592	Hideyoshi's first Korean expedition
1597	Hideyoshi's second Korean expedition
1598	Death of Hideyoshi; Tokugawa Iyeyasu (1542-1616) rises to power

Tokugawa Period (1600-1867)

1603	Tokugawa Iyeyasu establishes the Tokugawa shogunate in Edo (Tokyo)
1608	Hayashi Razan (1583-1657) appointed Confucian tutor to shogun
1614	Anti-*Kirishitan* edict issued
1615	*Buke Shohatto* (*Ordinances for the Military Houses*) issued
1619	Death of Fujiwara Seika (b. 1561), noted Confucianist
1624	Spaniards expelled from Japan
1637-1638	The so-called *Kirishitan* uprising in Shimabara, Kyushu
1639-1640	Portuguese and other Europeans expelled from Japan
1641	National exclusion (*sakoku*) begins; only Dutch allowed to remain, but are restricted to Nagasaki
1648	Death of Nakaya Tōju (b. 1608), noted Confucianist
1654	Chinese Zen master Ingen (Tin-yüan, 1592-1673) establishes the Ōbaku sect of Zen Buddhism in Japan
1657	*Dai-Nihon-shi* (*History of Great Japan*) commenced
1661	Manchu dynasty established in China
1682	Death of Yamazaki Ansai (b. 1618), scholar of the Chu Hsi School

1685	Death of Yamaga Sokō (b. 1622), advocate of Bushi-dō
1688-1703	Genroku period, known for exuberance in novels, plays, poems, and paintings
1690	Death of Deguchi (Watarai) Nobuyoshi (b. 1614), Shinto theorist; Confucian temple moved to Yushima section of Edo
1691	Hayashi Hōkō (1644-1732) named hereditary head of the state (Confucian) university; Kumazawa Banzan (b. 1644), Confucian reformer, dies
1694	Death of Matsuo Bashō (b. 1644), Zen master; death of Yoshikawa Koretaru (b. 1615), Shinto theorist
1701	Death of Keichū (b. 1640), Buddhist priest and pioneer in National Learning
1702	Incident of the forty-seven *rōnin*
1705	Death of Itō Jinsai (b. 1627), Confucian scholar
1708	Arrival of Giovanni Battista Sidotti (1668-1715), Italian priest
1709	Arai Hakuseki (1657-1725) appointed Confucian consultant to shogun
1714	Death of Kaibara Ekken (b. 1630), Confucian scholar
1716	Muro Kyūsō (1688-1734) appointed Confucian consultant to shogun
1728	Death of Ogyū Sorai (b. 1666), Confucian scholar
1736	Death of Kada Azumamaro (b. 1669), advocate of National Learning; death of Itō Tōgai (b. 1670), Confucian scholar
1744	Death of Ishida Baigan (b. 1685), founder of the Shingaku movement
1746	Death of Tominaga Nakamoto (b. 1715), rationalist philosopher
1757	Sugita Gempaku (1733-1817) studies Dutch surgery
1768	Death of Rinzai Zen master, Hakuin (b. 1685)
1769	Death of Kamo Mabuchi (b. 1697), Neo-Shintoist
1774	Dutch book, *Tavel Anatomia*, translated into Japanese
1776	Hiraga Gennai (1728-1779) produces frictional electricity machine
1789	Death of Miura Baien (b. 1723), rationalist philosopher
1790	Edict suppressing heterodox learning issued; Chu Hsi school (Shushi-gaku) precepts become official dogma
1795	Ban issued against both the Fuji-kō, a devotional association of Mount Fuji, and the principle of Fuju-fuse ("not receiving from outsiders") of Nichiren Buddhism
1798	Motoori Norinaga (1730-1801) completes the *Kojiki-den* (*Commentary on the "Kojiki"*)
1825	Shogunate issues edict to destroy foreign ships

1829	Fukuoka Mitsugu and other Christians executed
1843	Death of Hirata Atsutane (b. 1776), a Neo-Shintoist
1850	Death of Kurozumi Munetada (b. 1780), founder of the Kurozumi-kyō
1853	First mission of Commodore Matthew Perry to Japan
1854	Perry returns; treaty between Japan and United States concluded
1855	Shogunate establishes School of Western Learning (*Yōgaku-sho*)
1856	Townsend Harris (1804-1878), first American consul-general, arrives; death of Ninomiya Sontoku (b. 1787), religious reformer
1865	Fukuzawa Yukichi (1834-1901) founds a private school later named the Keiō Gijuku

Meiji Synthesis (1867-1945)

Meiji Era (1867-1912)

1868	Charter Oath proclaimed; capital moved to Edo, renamed Tokyo; Separation Edict of Shinto and Buddhism (*Shin-Butsu Hanzen-rei*) issued; Department of Shinto reestablished
1871	The *haibutsu kishaku* ("exterminate Buddhism") movement reaches its climax
1872	Conscription ordinance issued; edict issued that permits Buddhist priests to eat meat, to marry officially, to grow hair, and to take on a family name, but begging for food (*takuhatsu*) no longer allowed
1873	Edict against Christianity remaining from Tokugawa regime removed; edict permitting Buddhist nuns to eat meat and to grow hair issued
1875	Niijima Jō (1843-1890) founds a Christian school, called Dōshisha, in Kyoto
1876	Sundays declared holidays; Kasahara Kenju and Nanjō Bunyū begin studies under F. Max Müller
1877	Tokyo Imperial University established
1878	Ernest Fenollosa (1853-1908) appointed teacher
1881	1872 edict prohibiting begging rescinded
1882	Tokyo Semmon Gakkō (later renamed Waseda University) established
1884	Yayoi period pottery discovered
1889	Constitution permitting a measure of religious freedom adopted
1890	Imperial Rescript on Education promulgated
1893	Japanese delegates attend the World's Parliament of Religions in Chicago
1894-1895	Sino-Japanese War

1898	Hawaii annexed to United States
1899	Extra-territorialities eliminated
1902	Anglo-Japanese alliance concluded
1904-1905	Russo-Japanese War
1909	D. T. Suzuki (1870-1960) returns from the United States
1910	Annexation of Korea
1912	Republican government established in China

Taishō Era (1912-1926)

1914-1918	World War I
1915	Japan presents the Twenty-One Demands to China
1920	First May Day celebrated
1924	Quota Act ends Japanese immigration to United States

Shōwa Era (1926-)

1931	Manchurian incident
1933	Japan withdraws from the League of Nations
1937	Beginning of Japan's war on China
1939-1945	World War II
1940	Rome-Berlin-Tokyo axis concluded

Postwar Period (1945-)

1945	General Douglas MacArthur appointed Supreme Commander of the Allied Powers (SCAP); State Shinto disestablished; death of Kitarō Nishida (b. 1870), religious philosopher
1946	New constitution promulgated; religious liberty assured; Emperor renounces his divinity; establishment of Jinja honchō; renewal of the Sōka Gakkai, Ōmoto-kyō, Honmichi, PL Kyōdan, and other "new religions"
1947	New constitution goes into effect; renewal of World Messianity (Sekai Kyūsei-kyō)
1950	Korean War begins
1951	Matthew Ridgeway succeeds MacArthur as SCAP; San Francisco Peace Conference; formation of Association of New Religions (*Shin-Shū-ren*); Religious Persons Law (*Shūkyō-hōjin-hō*) issued
1952	Second World Buddhist Conference held in Tokyo
1955	Bandung Conference of Asian and African nations held
1961	World Religionists' Peace Conference held in Kyoto
1962	Death of Hajime Tanabe (b. 1885), religious philosopher
1964	Komeito (political wing of the Sōka Gakkai) formed
1965	Second Vatican Council advocates religious liberty
1966	Cultural Revolution begins in China; National Foundation Day (February 11) restored

1972	Sun Myung Moon's Unification Church begins activities in Japan; President Richard Nixon visits China; Okinawa returned to Japan; Twelfth World Buddhist Conference held in Japan
1973	United States withdraws from Vietnam
1974	Richard Nixon resigns American presidency
1976	Death of Mao Tse-tung (b. 1893) in China
1981	First papal visit to Japan
1985	Prime Minister Y. Nakasone pays official visit to Yasukuni Shrine (Shinto shrine for soldiers killed in wars)

PART I

Prehistory

1. Prehistoric Background of Japanese Religion

INTRODUCTION

MUCH HAS been speculated but very little is actually known about the origins of Japan and the Japanese people.* Geologists tell us that the Japanese islands constitute a part of the circum-Pacific organic zone. Sometime between the latter part of the Paleozoic and the early Mesozoic periods, a series of crustal movements resulted in the appearance of large sections of what later became the Japanese islands above the surface of the sea. During the Cenozoic or Tertiary period crustal movements, partial submergence of land areas, and volcanic eruptions took place. The present arrangement of the Japanese archipelago, with four main islands—Honshu, Kyushu, Shikoku, and Hokkaido—and about one thousand smaller islands, was formed during the Pleistocene period or the Great Ice Age.[1]

Needless to say, one of the important factors in the development of Japan was her geographical position. Japan is surrounded by the Sea of Okhotsk in the north, the Sea of Japan in the northwest, the Pacific Ocean in the east and south, and the East China Sea in the southwest. This island setting does not mean, however, that she has been totally

* This article issues from studies undertaken by the author in the course of preparing his book *Religion in Japanese History* (New York: Columbia University Press, 1966). The following abbreviations are used in the notes:

JGZ—Jinrui-gaku Zasshi (Journal of Anthropology), first published in February 1886, by the Anthropological Institute, Faculty of Science, Tokyo Imperial University.

NMT—Nihon Minzokugaku Taikei (Encyclopedia of Japanese Ethnology) (13 vols.; Tokyo: Heibon-sha, 1958–).

NMZ—Nihon Minzokugaku Zenshu (Collected Works on Japanese Folklore) (Tokyo: Akane Shobo, 1961–).

SKT—Sekai Kōkogaku Taikei (Encyclopedia of World Archeology) (16 vols.; Tokyo: Heibon-sha, 1959–).

TASJ—Transactions of the Asiatic Society of Japan.

ZNBT—Zusetsu Nihon Bunkashi Taikei (Illustrated Encyclopedia of Japanese Cultural History) (Tokyo: Shōgakkan, 1956–).

ZNR—Zusetsu Nihon Rekishi (Illustrated History of Japan) (Tokyo: Chūō-kōron-sha, 1960–).

ZSBT—Zusetsu Sekai Bunkashi Taikei (Illustrated Encyclopedia of World Culture) (20 vols.; Tokyo: Kadokawa Shoten, 1959–).

[1] Cf. Takai Fuyuji, "Nihon-retto no Seiritsu," *ZNBT*, Vol. I: *Jōmon Yayoi Kofun Jidai* (The Jōmon, Yayoi, and Kofun Periods), pp. 64-77.

isolated from events on the Eurasian mainland. A glance at the map will show that the northwestern tip of Hokkaido is only about 150 miles from the Siberian coast, and also that it is not difficult to reach Japan from Siberia by way of Sakhalin. The islands of Iki and Tsushima provide natural steppingstones between Kyushu and the southern coast of the Korean peninsula. Furthermore, a warm current from the south seas passes close to the southeastern coast of Japan, and an offshoot of it runs into the Sea of Japan in skirting around Kyushu Island. From the north, cold currents of the Sea of Okhotsk and the Bering Sea descend southward. On account of the natural pull of these oceanic currents, Japan was destined to receive peoples and cultural influences from various surrounding areas.

Scholars have not agreed as to the origins of human culture on the islands of Japan. The much publicized discovery of a fragmentary human bone, now referred to as *Nipponanthropus akashiensis*, has led a few scholars in recent years to propose the hypothesis that an extremely early member of the human race had lived in Japan before the Japanese islands were separated physically from the continent.[2] But this view has not received wide acceptance so far because of the fragmentary character of the bone in question and the lack of other evidence to support such a theory.

More important was a chance discovery of stone implements at Iwajuku, Gumma Prefecture, in 1949. Up to that time many scholars were inclined to feel that paleolithic sites, if they had ever existed, must have sunk into the ocean.[3] At Iwajuku, however, stone implements were unearthed not only from the yellowish clay of the so-called Kanto loam that lies beneath the humus but also from the blackish clay layer that lies below the bottom layer of the Kanto loam. These implements were subsequently identified as tools belonging to a "prepottery" period.[4]

---

[2] In 1948, a noted anthropologist, Hasebe Kotondo, published an article regarding a fragmentary human bone found some years earlier in the Hyōgo Prefecture by Naora Nobuo, asserting that the bone can be traced to hominids as old as *Pithecanthropus erectus* of Java and *Sinanthropus pekinensis* of China. Cf. Naora Nobuo, "Harima no Kuni Nishiyagi Kaigan Kosekisō-chū Hakken no Jinrui Ibutsu," Parts I & II, *JGZ*, Vol. XLVI, Nos. 5 and 6 (1931); Hasebe Kotondo, "Akashi-shi-fukin Nishiyagi Saishinsei-zenki Suisekishutsudō Jinrui Yōkotsu (Sekkōgata) no Genshisei ni tsuite," *JGZ*, Vol. LX, No. 1 (1948). See also *ZNR*, Vol. I: *Nihon Bunka no Akebono* (The Dawn of Japanese Civilization) by Wakamori Taro, pp. 5-6.

[3] Cf. Gerald J. Groot, *The Prehistory of Japan*, ed. Bertram S. Kraus (New York, 1951), p. 5. In Groot's opinion, the deer bone discovered by Tokunaga and Naora in 1936 in a cave on the island of Iyejima, west of Okinawa, belonged to the "third type of paleolithic culture"—a category suggested by O. Menglin in his *Weltgeschichte der Steinzeit* (Vienna, 1931), pp. 119-129.

[4] Sugihara Shōsuke, "Iwajuku no Kyūsekki," *Kagaku Asahi*, Vol. X, No. 7 (July 1960); J. Edward Kidder, "Reconsideration of the 'Pre-Pottery' Culture of Japan," *Ar-*

Since then an increasing number of archeologists has begun to take seriously the possibility of the existence of a paleolithic period in Japan, and their cause has been enhanced by further discoveries of hand axes and other stone tools in nearly one hundred spots scattered from Hokkaido to Kyushu. In this connection, Maringer has expressed the view that the stone implements unearthed at Gongenyama, Gumma Prefecture, have affinities with those of the Lower Paleolithic Patjitan-ian culture of Java.[5] Others have pointed out the typological affinities between the stone tools of the prepottery period in Japan and those discovered in Siberia or in Indo-China.[6] If the Kanto loam belongs to the Middle Pleistocene epoch, when Japan was integral with the Asian continent, as some geologists now contend, it is not impossible that these stone implements discovered in the Kanto plain could have come to Japan from the continent of Asia without the benefit of sea transport.

As far as we are concerned, we can accept the possibility that stone tools of the prepottery period in Japan might have been linked to their counterparts in northern East Asia, but we have to bear in mind that the prepottery "culture" in Japan was, as Beardsley maintains, more recent than microlith-bearing culture on the continent.[7] We are also told that "as Japanese sites are shallow and earth movements have been frequent, one can hardly place full confidence in these implied relationships."[8] Nevertheless, the discovery at Iwajuku started a chain of feverish archeological research activities which we hope will throw some light before long on the question of the Paleolithic period in Japan.

tibus Asiae, XVII (1954), 135-143, his *The Jōmon Pottery of Japan* (Ascona, 1957), and his *Japan before Buddhism* (London, 1959), pp. 27-33; Yawata Ichiro, *Nihon-shi no Rei-mei* (The Dawn of Japanese History) (Tokyo, 1953), pp. 13-24.

[5] J. Maringer, "A Core and Flake Industry of Palaeolithic Type from Central Japan," *Artibus Asiae*, XIX, No. 2 (1956), 111-125, and "Einige faustkeilartige Geräte von Gongenyama [Japan] und die Frage des japanischen Paläolithikums," *Anthropos*, Vol. LI (1956).

[6] See Groot's view in *Prehistory of Japan*, pp. 25-35. See also Oka Masao's view on this question in Oka Masao et al., *Nihon Minzoku no Kigen* (The Origin of the Japanese People) (Tokyo, 1958), pp. 293-294.

[7] Richard K. Beardsley, "Japan before History: A Survey of the Archaeological Record," *Far Eastern Quarterly*, XIX, No. 3 (May 1955), 322.

[8] Kidder, *Japan before Buddhism*, p. 31. According to Yawata Ichiro, it is difficult to reach a definitive conclusion about human habitation or culture in the prepottery period, since no skeleton of this period has been unearthed thus far. Some fossils of elephants have been discovered, however, and many scholars believe that the *Elephas nomadicus* was living in Japan at the end of the Diluvial epoch. Cf. Japanese National Commission for UNESCO, *Japan: Its Land, People and Culture* (referred to as "UNESCO, Japan" hereinafter) (Tokyo, 1958), p. 117.

FROM PREHISTORY TO EARLY HISTORY

The appearance of pottery marks, for all intents and purposes, the beginning of the prehistory of Japan. Usually, the prehistoric period is divided into (1) the Jōmon period (literally, "code pattern," used for pottery decoration), (2) the Yayoi period (so named because of pottery of this period that was unearthed in the Yayoi district of Tokyo), and (3) the Kofun ("Tomb") period. The Jōmon period corresponds very roughly to the New Stone Age in Eurasia, and the latter half of the Kofun period overlaps the early part of the historic period in Japan. The use of these "culture names" as designations for archeological periods is not altogether satisfactory, and Beardsley's suggestion of employing a scheme such as "Middle Prehistoric Period" for the Jōmon period, "Late Prehistoric and Protohistoric Periods" for the Yayoi period, and the "Semihistoric and Early Historic Periods" for the Kofun period may eventually prove to be less confusing.[9] We will, however, follow the current use of "Jōmon, Yayoi, and Kofun" as designations for the three epochs of the prehistoric period in Japan, periods largely determined on the basis of archeological research.

1. The Jōmon period

There are a number of unresolvable problems in connection with the Jōmon period. One is the ambiguity of its chronology. The crucial question as to when the Jōmon period began cannot be settled until and unless we know a little more about the pre-Jōmon—that is, the prepottery—period. In general, it is assumed that the Pacific Ocean reached far inland during the early Jōmon period and that it receded in the later Jōmon period, such that many scholars reconstruct a relative chronology for this period by studying the shell mounds that lie along the Pacific coast of Japan.[10] Kidder follows a widely accepted span of dates for the Jōmon period of from *circa* 4500-3700 B.C. to *circa* 1000-250 B.C., while Beardsley allows a much shorter span of time to the "Middle Prehistoric Period" (which corresponds to the Jōmon period), namely, *circa* 2500 B.C. to 250 B.C. Some Japanese archeologists assert that the beginning of the Jōmon period can be traced as far back as 6000, 7000, or even 8000 B.C. On this question, Groot seems to be on safe ground when he states that the earliest date

---

[9] Beardsley, "Japan before History" p. 320. On the other hand, the use of "culture names" is defended in *ZNR*, Vol. I: *Nihon Bunka no Akebono*, by Wakamori, pp. 11-12.

[10] A list of Jōmon period sites is given in Groot, *Prehistory of Japan*, Appendix E, and *SKT*, Vol. I: *Nihon*, Part I (Tokyo, 1959), Appendix. See also Sakazume Nakao, "Hennenjō yori mita Kaizuka (Gaisetsu)," in Nihon Jinruigaku-kai (ed.), *Nihon Minzoku* (Japanese Race), 1952 and 1961, pp. 58-82.

of the Jōmon period cannot possibly be dated much before 3000 B.C. on the ground that "the Proto-Jōmon cultures reached Japan as a result of pressure exerted upon the mesolithic peoples of Asia by the eastward-migrating neolithic peoples of Europe."[11] Many scholars divide the Jōmon period into five subperiods, but we will follow the looser usage of three subdivisions, that is, the early, middle, and later Jōmon periods.

In our study of the Jōmon period the importance of shell mounds as the repository of archaic remains cannot be exaggerated. "Not only did the kitchen refuse accumulate," says Kidder, "but broken and unusable objects were discarded there, burials were frequently cut right into them, and pits of dwellings located below them," so that in effect the shell mounds furnish us "the ingredients of stratigraphy."[12] The implements of the early Jōmon period are mostly fishing and hunting tools such as bone harpoons, fishhooks, stone axes and clubs, wooden and stone swords, as well as primitive pottery. Evidently, dogs were domesticated for hunting purposes, and the people engaged in fishing in sea and river as much as in shellfish gathering. Judging from their pit houses people must have lived in small family groups, preferring to reside in the foothills where wild game was easily accessible, or along the seashore. Rings and bracelets made of small shells and the tusks of the wild boar were used for ornaments.

There is much truth in Beardsley's characterization of the cultural level of the Jōmon period as "sub-Neolithic."[13] A useful device in studying the cultural development of the prehistoric period in Japan is to analyze the shapes and designs of the pottery. Scholars unfortunately have not agreed on how to classify Jōmon pottery, typologically, because of the wide variety of local styles.[14] Yawata is inclined to feel that there were at least two distinct pottery cultures in the very early stage of the Jōmon period.[15]

[11] Groot, *Prehistory of Japan*, Appendix A. He also thinks that the "Final-Jōmon period" in most of Japan came to an end before the present era.

[12] Kidder, *Japan before Buddhism*, p. 40.

[13] Beardsley, "Japan before History," p. 322. We might add that, while many Japanese scholars loosely use the term *Jōmon Bunka* (culture), we agree with Groot's statement: "this term, conveying as it does a sense of homogeneity of culture in the former translation and a sense of generic relationship in the latter is misleading" (*Prehistory of Japan*, p. 3).

[14] E.g., among the very early Jōmon pottery there are at least three types: the *Yori-ito* (pottery with a simple cord design) unearthed in the southern part of the Kanto plain, *Oshigata* (pottery with a printed design), scattered in Kanto as well as western parts of Japan; and *Tado-shiki* (pottery with a design resembling that of the Kam Kermakik of Siberia), found in a wide area extending between Kanto and Hokkaido (cf. UNESCO, *Japan*, pp. 10-11).

[15] Yawata, *Nihon-shi no Reimei*, pp. 44-45.

The transition from the early to the middle stages of the Jōmon period was marked by the appearance of spirals in ceramic patterns, stone axes of the pestle shape or with pointed head, spherical grinding stones, and the ornamental use of nephrites, especially those of green color. Some of the stone implements appear to have been used as hoes or mattocks, while others might have been used for woodcutting. Undoubtedly hunting and fishing continued, but there is also a strong intimation that taro and some vegetables began to be cultivated at this time.[16] Many human bones, belonging to the middle Jōmon period, have also been unearthed.[17] The dwelling places of this period show some improvement over those of the previous age, in that they are equipped with fireplaces. Many of the middle Jōmon dwelling units are found in groups of ten or more, and in one instance over seventy of them are grouped together.[18] As yet, there is no definitive theory as to why marked changes took place between the early and the middle stages of the Jōmon period.[19]

Local variation seems to have become much more accentuated in the later Jōmon period so that some scholars believe that there were several "cultural centers," such as Kamegaoka on the northern tip of Honshu, Shōnohata in the present Nagano Prefecture, and Angyo in the eastern part of the Kanto plain. Besides, there were at least two late Jōmon cultural centers in Kyushu alone. To make the picture more complex, Kyushu entered the Yayoi culture ahead of other parts of Japan. In some parts of Hokkaido, as well as in the Kuriles and Sakhalin, a special type of pottery has been unearthed, and some archeologists speculate about the existence of an Okhotsk culture on these islands.[20] The existence of such a variety of local cultures makes it exceedingly difficult to give general statements about the late Jōmon period. In the main it is safe to state that many of the late Jōmon communities seem to be located in the plain and that their dwelling places are much more substantial than those of earlier periods. Stone implements, as well as ornaments and tools made of bone and horn,

---

[16] Oka's view on this problem is quoted in ibid., p. 68. Many other scholars feel, however, that any kind of food production did not begin until the Yayoi period.

[17] *SKT*, Vol. I: *Nihon*, Part I, pp. 96-97.

[18] *ZSBT, Nihon*, Part I (Tokyo, 1960), p. 65.

[19] According to Yawata, archeological research has been so far preoccupied with the eastern parts of Japan at the expense of the western parts, so that the degree of impact exerted by the western side over the eastern side has not been ascertained with any amount of accuracy. See his view in Oka et al., *Nihon Minzoku no Kigen*, pp. 160-161.

[20] Cf. K. Komai, "The Okhotsk Culture and the Scythian Culture," in Japanese National Commission for UNESCO (ed.), *International Symposium on History of Eastern and Western Cultural Contacts* (Tokyo, 1959), pp. 77-79. On the Jōmon culture in Hokkaido, see *ZNR*, Vol. I: *Nihon Bunka no Akebono*, by Wakamori, pp. 78-80.

are more refined, and the pottery, too, is of better quality. Evidently it was the use of intense heat that enabled the people of this period to make their aesthetically pleasing ceramics. Many bowls with lids, as well as figurines, especially those portraying females, and a variety of utensils, bows, swords, and wooden ornaments have been unearthed. Several types of jars, used as coffins, have also been discovered.[21]

Toward the end of the Jōmon period, a general decline of the Jōmon type of culture seems to have set in, as evidenced by the deterioration of artistic qualities in pottery-making. Instead, a more practical pottery began to make its appearance, anticipating the coming of the Yayoi culture.[22] Nevertheless, it is a matter of considerable interest that the Jōmon culture, based on such a low economic level, lasted as long as it did, considering the fact that great civilizations already had been well established for centuries in other parts of Asia.

2. The Yayoi period

By the very nature of the case, there is no convenient date for dividing the end of the Jōmon period from the beginning of the Yayoi period. Here, we accept the view that the Yayoi period covers roughly the five hundred years between 250 B.C. and A.D. 250. For our purposes, it is not too important to subdivide it into three stages—early, middle, and later Yayoi periods—except in a general way, since these subperiods were characterized by different degrees of cultural development between the eastern and the western parts of Japan.[23]

The heated controversy regarding continuity versus discontinuity between the cultures of the Jōmon and Yayoi periods has been going on for some time, and it is not likely to be solved easily. Some scholars feel that Yayoi pottery was nothing but the natural development of Jōmon pottery, and that both were made by a people who belonged to the same ethnic group. Others feel that the change between the two was so marked and rapid that the only way to explain it is by postulating the migration of an ethnic group to Japan from outside toward the end of the Jōmon period.[24]

[21] *SKT*, Vol. I: *Nihon*, Part I, pp. 98-124.

[22] Yawata, *Nihon-shi no Reimei*, pp. 96-97.

[23] Ibid., p. 178. As mentioned earlier, the first Yayoi pottery, which is of a neckless kind, was discovered at Yayoi-chō, at the Mukōgaoka shell mound in Tokyo. The first discovery of the pottery of this period in Kyushu was made along the Onga or Enga River, and thus it is called the Ongagawa type. The middle Yayoi culture is often referred to as the Sugu type, named after the cemetery site of this designation. The late Yayoi is called the Takamitsuma type, also for a similar reason (cf. Kidder, *Japan before Buddhism*, p. 123). We are avoiding the use of these confusing names, however.

[24] Holders of the latter view acknowledge the fact that there is a greater difference between the Yayoi pottery and Korean pottery of the same period than between the

There is no question that Yayoi culture is characterized by many new features that had been unknown in the Jōmon period. Yayoi pottery is different from that of the previous period in its shapes, patterns, and techniques of manufacture. It has far less surface decoration and seems to be much more utilitarian than the Jōmon ware. In comparison with Jōmon ware, used primarily to preserve water and raw food items, Yayoi jugs, jars, and pots were used for cooking as much as preserving food.[25] Evidently hunting and fishing continued to be practiced, but what characterized the Yayoi way of life was paddy-field rice cultivation, employing a considerable number of hydraulic facilities. This fact explains the establishment of communities of this period in places of low altitude.[26] Many of the farmhouses have storehouses built close by. Farmers used various kinds of spades, rakes, hoes, and crescent-shaped stone knives. That spinning and weaving were practiced is evident from the discovery of cloth in the burial jars of this period. These hunting people used bows and arrows, while arrowheads were made of bone, stone, and sometimes bronze. To what extent the people practiced fishing is not clear, but some dugout canoes and other fishing tools have been unearthed.[27]

There is no question that iron was introduced during the Yayoi period. According to some scholars, iron was introduced from the continent prior to, or at least simultaneously with, bronze and copper.[28] Discovery of many bronze weapons as well as mirrors from the

---

Yayoi and Jōmon potteries. They resort to the theory that the bearers of the new culture came from some part of the Asiatic continent to Japan through Korea, but that their new culture was greatly influenced by that of the earlier residents in Japan. On this question, Beardsley seems to take a safe middle course by holding that the Jōmon culture continued to last and was overlapped for several centuries by the establishment of the Yayoi culture that began in the western region. Furthermore, he says that "it seems hardly risky to postulate survival of Jōmon ways of life even after Yayoi culture had in turn been overrun farther south by iron-using people" ("Japan before History," p. 329).

[25] Morimoto Rokuji, "Yayoishiki Daki ni okeru Nisha," *Kōkogaku*, Vol. V, No. 1 (1934); Kobayashi Yukio, "Doki no Yoshiki Kozo," *Kōkogaku Hyōron*, Vol. I, No. 2 (1935).

[26] See Yawata's view on this subject in Oka et al., *Nihon Minzoku no Kigen*, pp. 169-172. As far as we can gather, farming was practiced at first on Kyushu early in the Yayoi period, if not before; it reached as far east as the Ise district in less than a century. In a middle or late Yayoi community, discovered in 1943 at Toro, south of Shizuoka City, thirty-three paddies had been plotted. "Nine of these Toro fields were 1,580 square yards, the average size, but one was as large as 2,765, another as small as 790" (Kidder, *Japan before Buddhism*, p. 98).

[27] Opinions vary as to the technique of navigation known by the people during the Yayoi period. On the question of the boat, see Matsumoto Nobuhiro, "Kodai Nihonjin to Fune," in Nihon Jinruigaku-kai, *Nihon Minzoku*, pp. 48-57.

[28] *ZSBT, Nihon*, Part I, pp. 130-131; a broken piece of what might be a carpenter's tool, made of iron, was discovered in a shell mound at Saitō-yama, Kumamoto Prefecture. This is said to be the oldest piece of iron found in Japan.

Han dynasty, China, indicates that continental immigrants were coming in, sporadically at any rate, toward the end of the first century B.C.[29] One of the unsolvable mysteries is the discrepancy between the western zone (Kyushu, western parts of Honshu, and parts of Shikoku) in which most bronze swords, spears, and other weapons have been unearthed and the central zone (Tōkaido, Kinki, and the eastern Inland Sea area) in which most bronze bells (*dō-taku*) have been found.[30] Leaving aside this question, it is still evident that Chinese civilization infiltrated Japan during the Middle and later Yayoi periods. In so doing, it provided new impetus to cultural development.

It has often been said that the so-called Yayoi culture was really a "culture complex," consisting of the residue of the Jōmon tradition together with northeast Asian, Korean, Chinese, and other cultural streams. Also the existence of grooved adzes, dolmens, stone cists, and funeral urns during this period betrays some kind of influence from southeast Asia. And yet, after all is said and done, Yayoi culture has distinctly Japanese cultural traits. Indeed, as Beardsley astutely observes: "What is most striking about the way of life in the late Prehistoric Period is that it was so much like the way of life in Japanese villages fifteen centuries later."[31]

3. The Kofun period

What is called the Kofun period in archeology, roughly covering the period A.D. 250 or 300 to A.D. 600, corresponds to the early period of Japanese history. Pottery-making continued, of course, and a number of wares known as "*Haji*" and "*Suye*" have been unearthed from the Kofun period sites.[32] Evidently, there was not a marked change

---

[29] Takahashi Kenji, *Dō-hoko Dō-ken no Kenkyu* (Studies on Bronze Spears and Swords) (Tokyo, 1925). According to Kidder, bronze weapons entered Kyushu, preceding the bulk of Han dynasty mirrors by a century and a half. It is significant to note that the flow of weapons ceased around A.D. 50, but mirrors increased. He thinks that by the end of the first century B.C. weapons were cast in Japan either by immigrants or by native artisans (cf. Kidder, *Japan before Buddhism*, p. 113; see also *SKT*, Vol. II: *Nihon*, Part II, 78-91).

[30] *ZNBT*, Vol. I: *Jōmon Yayoi Kofun Jidai* (The Jōmon, Yayoi, and Kofun Periods) (Tokyo, 1956), pp. 203-211; *SKT*, Vol. II: *Nihon*, Part II, 92-104. On the possible political implications of these two zones see Enoki Kazuo, *Yamataikoku* (The Yamatai Nation) (Tokyo, 1960), pp. 147-152; see also Tōma Seita, *Nihon Minzoku no Keisei* (Formation of Japanese Race) (Tokyo, 1951 and 1961), pp. 51-63. Tōma also cites the view of Gotō Morikazu who holds that, contrary to the opinion of many scholars, the bronze bells that made their appearance during the early Yayoi period continued to be manufactured until the Kofun period (pp. 69-70 [n. 1]).

[31] Beardsley, "Japan before History," p. 333.

[32] *Haji* is red pottery, frequently round-bottomed. Much of the pottery of this type belongs to the fifth century. *Suye* is ceremonial ware, often regarded as the funeral

between the pottery of the Yayoi and that of the Kofun periods; rather, the dramatic appearance of huge mounds is such that this period has come to be known as the Kofun or Tumulus period, no particular distinctive pottery being at hand to name it. Here let us briefly examine the archeological evidence, leaving the discussion of the complex historical problems of this period until later.

During this period, Sino-Korean civilization exerted tremendous influence on Japan, while its political influence reached to the southern tip of Korea. It is understandable, therefore, that many new features were added to the cultural and social life of the Japanese. A stratification of society that had been going on gradually for centuries became accentuated, as evidenced by elaborate cemeteries constructed for aristocrats. To be sure, already during the Yayoi period tombs for influential people were built in the dolmen form, but they were located in the midst of cemeteries for common people. In the Kofun period, however, gigantic mausoleums were constructed either on the hilltops or in the plain, away from the cemetery sites of common folk. Scholars classify these Kofun according to their shape, location, inner structure, and accompanying objects.[33] In the main, in the early stage of the Kofun period, dome-shaped and semispherical mausoleums were frequently built, while later a circular mound with rectangular projections appeared on the scene. In the later stage of the Kofun period, quadrate mausoleums became the dominant pattern. By far the most elaborate is the mausoleum, supposed to be the grave of the Emperor Nintoku, that occupied 80 acres, having a total length of 2,695 feet from the outer edges of its three moats.[34] Many of these elaborate mausoleums are found in the present Nara and Osaka prefectures, which coincide roughly with the "bronze-bell zone" of the Yayoi period. In short these great tombs are the archeological remains of what historians call the Yamato kingdom.

It goes without saying that only those of the ruling class were buried in such a grand style. The construction of great tombs must have required a considerable labor force, which implies the existence of serfs or peasants. Also, judging from the items discoverd in burial chambers, there must have been professional artisans who produced them. Thus, while the Kofun was meant to be a monument for the ruling

---

pottery originally introduced from Korea. Its use was widespread in the sixth century (cf. Kidder, *Japan before Buddhism*, pp. 188-190).

[33] Cf. Umehara Suyeji, "Jōdai no Koshiki-fun ni tsuite," in Nihon Jinruigaku-kai, *Nihon Minzoku*, pp. 100-112; Kobayashi Yukio, "Kofun-jidai Bunka no Seiin ni tsuite," ibid., pp. 113-129; *ZNBT*, Vol. I: *Jōmon Yayoi Kofun Jidai*, p. 238; *SKT*, Vol. III, pp. 11-50.

[34] Kidder, *Japan before Buddhism*, p. 151.

class it also provides us with insights into the social and cultural conditions of people in the lower strata of Japanese society in the early historic period.[35] Among the items found in burial chambers are caps, tailored clothes, shoes, jewelry made of silver or gold, glass beads, spears, swords with ring-pommels, recurved bows, arrowheads, slat armor, horseback riding equipment, eating utensils, and agricultural tools.[36] Another important discovery in and around the mausoleums is a series of *haniwa* (literally, "clay cylinders"). While earlier *haniwa* were mostly cylindrical, later ones are earthen images of humans, animals, and birds. Many human figures are of warriors with swords and shields, while others portray musicians, dancers, female diviners, or ordinary housewives. Among animal figures are dogs, chickens, monkeys, deer, and horses.[37] The sudden popularity of horseback riding in the second half of the fifth century has aroused many speculations concerning the possible migration of an ethnic group which brought this custom from the continent. But a definite answer to this problem must await other supporting evidence. At any rate, the practice of constructing elaborate mausoleums began to decline in the seventh century, probably due to a change in burial customs under the influence of Buddhism.

PEOPLE IN PREHISTORIC JAPAN

It has often been said that a people can be identified on the basis of the combination of ethnic affiliation, language, culture, and religion. Such a neat scheme, however, is not applicable to the situation in prehistoric Japan. Even a brief survey of archeological evidence as attempted in the previous section makes it clear that any one of the cultural influences could have penetrated Japan from any part of the Asiatic continent without necessarily enforcing its own language or religion. The movement of peoples in the prehistoric period was not

[35] Kobayashi Yukio, *Kofun-jidai no Kenkyu* (A Study of the Kofun Period) (Tokyo, 1961), pp. 137-159.

[36] UNESCO, *Japan*, p. 564: "Also found in the graves were curved jewels (*magatama*), tubular jewels (*kudatama*), hexahedral gems (*kiritama*), round gems (*marutama*) and small jewels (*kotama*) made of such material as jasper, agate, quartz and glass." It is to be noted that curved jewels (*magatama*) were later used as one of the three symbols of the imperial authority.

[37] According to legend, the Emperor Suinin, upon the death of one of his daughters, asked his ministers to revise the custom of burying a deceased person's servants alive. One of the ministers proposed that clay figures be substituted for the living sacrifice. The emperor accepted this suggestion and thus *haniwa* were created. This legend, however, is not to be taken seriously (cf. Noma Seiroku, "Introduction," *Haniwa: A Catalogue of the Haniwa Exhibition in Four American Museums, 1960* (New York: Asia Society, 1960).

bound by the national boundaries of the present world, and there are good reasons to believe that migrations of people to Japan were only insignificant parts of larger movements of archaic peoples covering a wide territory including the continents of Eurasia and North America.

This does not mean, however, that we should not take seriously the evidence presented by archeologists. Indeed, archeological discoveries of human bones, for example, throw much light on the subject, even though bones do not tell us where they came from and to which ethnic group they belonged. For example, a skeleton of the early Jōmon period was discovered not long ago in shell mounds at Hirasaka, within the city boundary of Yokosuka. This human skeleton belonged to the "Hirasaka Shell Mound Man," who is estimated to have been about 163 centimeters tall—slightly taller than the average of the present-day Japanese or Ainu. This man's head was small, but his mastication muscles were well developed. His dental formation would seem to indicate that he ate raw flesh and/or tanned hide with his teeth. His bone formation indicates that he must have squatted down habitually and that he had suffered from malnutrition over a period of years. He also seems to show signs of premature old age.[38] Useful though this information is, we cannot reconstruct the identity of the early Jōmon man on it alone.

Equally uncertain is the identity of the people who lived in the Yayoi period. Some scholars, who have investigated the three human bones which are considered to belong to the middle Yayoi period, feel that the three men concerned were slightly taller than the Jōmon people or the present-day people of North Kyushu. They further suggest that there is not much marked difference between these three men and the people of the Kofun period, and that there is some affinity between them and the southern Koreans of present time.[39] In spite of the lack of conclusive evidence, or perhaps because of it, various theories have been advanced by scholars about the identity of prehistoric man in Japan.

1. The Ainu controversy

One of the most persistent controversies in recent decades regarding the origin of the Japanese people has been that centering around the Ainu. Japanese chronicles are full of accounts of the Ainu who have

[38] Suzuki Hisashi, "Sagami Hirasaka Kaizuka (Sōki-Jōmon-shiki Iseki) no Jinkotsu ni tsuite," *JGZ*, Vol. LXI, No. 3 (1950); see also Yawata, *Nihon-shi no Reimei*, pp. 39-42.

[39] Cf. ZNR, Vol. I: *Nihon Bunka no Akebono*, by Wakamori, pp. 88-89. See also Matsumura Takeo, "On the Cephalic Index and Stature of Japanese and Their Local Differences," *Journal of the Faculty of Science* (Tokyo Imperial University), Vol. I, Part I, Section V (Anthropology).

lived so close geographically to the Japanese people and yet have never been assimilated to the prevailing cultural life of Japan. But no Japanese scholar ever thought of the Ainu as the "original people" of that area. This idea was first suggested by Philip Franz von Siebold (d. 1866) and was later articulated by his son, Heinrich von Siebold.[40] According to the two Siebolds, the Ainus who were the original inhabitants of the Japanese islands were driven north toward Hokkaido and Sakhalin by the Mongoloid (Japanese) race which invaded Japan from the Asiatic continent. This theory influenced many European and American scholars, including J. Milne, Romyn Hitchcock, John Batchelor, and Basil Hall Chamberlain.[41]

Meanwhile, Edward S. Morse advocated a theory to the effect that even before the coming of the Ainus and the Japanese there was a still earlier people, residing in Japan, who were probably cannibalistic.[42] In 1886, Watanabe Shōzaburo suggested that the earliest inhabitants of Japan, whom Morse talked about, were what Ainu legends refer to as *Koropok-guru* (literally, "men who can walk under the leaves of a butterbur plant") or "Little People." Watanabe's theory was enthusiastically supported by Tsuboi Shōgoro but was rejected by Koganei Yoshikiyo, an anatomist, who held that the ancestors of the present-day Ainus were the original inhabitants of Japan.[43] The Tsuboi-Koganei controversy lasted until 1900 when Tsuboi's disciple, Torii Ryūzo, was sent to the Kurile Islands and the Kamchatka peninsula. Upon his return, Torii rejected his teacher's theory and identified the Ainus as the oldest inhabitants of the Japanese islands.[44]

[40] Philip Franz von Siebold lived in Nagasaki from 1823 to 1829 where he taught medicine to Japanese physicians. His son, Heinrich, later lived in Japan as a diplomat and continued to develop his father's theory with some clarification and documentation. His article, "Notes on Japanese Archaeology with Special Reference to the Stone Age" (Yokohama, 1879), has not been available to this author.

[41] Cf. J. Milne, "The Stone Age in Japan," *Journal of the Anthropological Institute of Great Britain and Ireland*, X, 389-423; Romyn Hitchcock, "The Ainos of Yezo, Japan," *Report of the U.S. National Museum, 1889-1890* (Washington, D.C., 1891), pp. 429-502. Among many works by John Batchelor, the most representative is *The Ainu and Their Folk Lore* (London, 1901). B. H. Chamberlain's chief contribution on the Ainu study is "The Language, Mythology and Geographical Nomenclature of Japan Viewed in the Light of Aino Studies," *Memoirs of the Literature College*, No. 1 (Tokyo Imperial University, 1887).

[42] "Shell Mounds of Ōmori," *Memoirs of the Science Department* (Tokyo Imperial University), Vol. I, Part I (1879), and "Traces of an Early Race in Japan," *Popular Science Monthly*, XIX (1879), 257-266.

[43] Koganei compared the Jōmon period human bone with the bones of the Ainus and concluded that there is a great similarity between the physical features of the prehistoric man and those of the present-day Ainus. For a detailed description of Koganei's theory see N. C. Munro, *Prehistoric Japan* (Yokohama, 1908).

[44] Torii Ryūzo, "Études archéologiques de la Mandchourie meridionale," *Journal of the College of Science* (Tokyo Imperial University), Vol. XXXVI (1915), and "Études archéologiques et ethnologiques des Ainu des Îles Kouriles," ibid., Vol. XLII (1919).

Although Torii pronounced the death sentence on the *Koropok-guru* theory, the Ainu controversy continued. Matsumoto Hikoshichiro, the advocate of the "Pan-Ainu theory," suggested that the Jōmon people may not have been the ancestors of the present-day Ainus but that they were not unrelated because the Caucasoids, Austroids, and Ainus came out of one great human stock which originally lived in Central Asia.[45] Kiyono Kenji, while acknowledging possible interbreeding among various ethnic groups, including the Ainus, nevertheless held that interbreeding did not substantially change the physical type of the original inhabitants of Japan. According to him, the people who lived during the Jōmon period are the direct ancestors of the present-day Japanese.[46] Hasebe Kotondo goes still further than Kiyono and speculates on the possibility that the ancestors of the present Japanese migrated to Japan before the Japanese islands were separated from the continent. He believes that the Ainu lived in Hokkaido as early as the Jōmon period, but that there has never been any significant amount of interbreeding between the Ainus and the Japanese.[47] The clear distinction between the Ainu and the Japanese, as suggested by Hasebe, has been subsequently rejected by Y. Koya's research on racial biology.[48]

Who, then, were the ancestors of the Ainu, and where did they come from and when? Opinions still vary on each of these questions. Also debate still continues on possible Ainu influence on Japanese cul-

---

See also his "Chishima ni sonzai seru Sekki-jidai Ibutsu-iseki wa somosomo Nani-shu-zoku no nokoseshi-monoka," *JGZ*, Vol. XVIII (1901), and *Yūshi Izen no Nihon* (Japan before History) (Tokyo, 1918).

[45] Matsumoto Hikoshichiro, "Nihon Senshi Jinrui-ron," *Rekishi to Chiri* (History and Geography), Vol. III, No. 5 (1919), and "Notes on the Stone Age People of Japan," *American Anthropologist*, XXIII, No. 1 (1921), 50-76.

[46] Kiyono Kenji, "Nihon Sekki-jidai Jinrui," *Seibutsugaku Kōza* (Studies in Biology) (Tokyo, 1930); *Nihon Minzoku Seisei-ron* (Development of the Japanese Race) (Tokyo, 1937); and *Kodai Jinkotsu no Kenkyu ni motozuku Nihon Jinshuron* (A Theory about the Japanese Race Based on the Study of Archaic Human Bones) (Tokyo, 1949).

[47] Hasebe tells us that the correct spelling is *Aino*, not *Ainu*. The latter was invented by John Batchelor. Cf. Hasebe Kotondo, "Ezo," in Nihon Jinruigaku-kai, *Nihon Minzoku*, p. 140. He also suggests that the "Ezo" of Northern Honshu, mentioned in the Japanese chronicles, were really Japanese, whereas the "Ezo" in Hokkaido were the Ainus (pp. 130-145). Kindaichi Kyōsuke, on the other hand, holds that the "Ezo" of Northern Honshu were the descendants of the Ainus. See his "Ainu Bunka to Nihon Bunka tono Kosho," *Nihonbunka-Kenkyūjo-Kiyō* (Kokugakuin University, Tokyo), No. 2 (March 1958), pp. 16-39.

[48] According to Koya, the Japanese people living in remote mountain areas of Honshu today share a considerable amount of affinity in physical type with the Ainu living in Hokkaido. His analysis also indicates that the Jōmon people had no strong physical links with the Tungusic tribes, such as the Gilyaks, Buryats, Kalmyks, and Manchurians (cf. "Comparisons of the Ainu of Hokkaido with Other Groups in Nine Physical Traits," by Koya et al., *Rassenkunde der Aino*, cited in Groot, *Prehistory of Japan*, p. 78).

ture and religion, and vice versa.[49] The problem of the Ainu, their religion and culture, however, requires a special study.[50] We can only say at this point that the great mystery of the Ainu remains in our investigation of the people in prehistoric Japan.

2. Identity of the Jōmon and Yayoi peoples

Today, most scholars agree that during the early Jōmon period, if not slightly before, a number of ethnic groups began infiltrating into Japan from the Asiatic continent, bringing with them various cultural elements, and this migration of peoples continued until the early phase of the historic period. It is, therefore, quite plausible that the study of cultural traits might throw some light on the question of identity of peoples, and indeed such efforts have been made by scholars of different disciplines.

No one has yet answered the question as to whether the early Jōmon "culture" developed out of the legacy of the prepottery period or came from outside. But assuming that it came from outside, the cultural features of the early Jōmon period betray strong Siberian influences. In the words of Groot: "The rich bone industry, the fishhooks, the domesticated dogs and the cylindrical axe—all point north to Siberia. The flat-bottomed, cord-impressed pottery seems to suggest the south Siberian Angara culture as the point of origin."[51] While there is wide acceptance of this view, there is no agreement as to who or which ethnic group or groups might have brought the Siberian culture to Japan, for many of the Paleo-Asian tribes were equally possible bearers of such a culture at that time. Regarding the middle Jōmon period, some scholars hold that there was only an indirect cultural influence from outside, while others are inclined to postulate the migration of a new ethnic group. On this question, Groot suggests that the new cultural impetus again came from the south Siberian Angara culture.[52]

[49] John Batchelor, "On the Ainu Term 'Kamui,' " *TASJ*, XVI (1888), 17-32; Basil Hall Chamberlain, "Reply to Mr. Batchelor on the Words 'Kamui' and 'Aino,' " *TASJ*, XVI (1888), 33-38; Origuchi Shinobu, "Tokoyo oyobi Marebito," *Minzoku*, IV, No. 2, 1-62; Alexander Slawik, "Zur Etymologie des japanischen Terminus marebito 'Sakraler Besucher,' " *Wiener Völkerundliche Mitterlungen*, 2d Yearbook, No. 1 (Vienna, 1954), pp. 44-58.

[50] Cf. J. M. Kitagawa, "Ainu Bear Festival (Iyomante)," *History of Religions*, I, No. 1 (Summer 1961), 95-151.

[51] Groot, *Prehistory of Japan*, p. 42.

[52] According to Groot, the spiral designs of middle Jōmon pottery resemble more the Angara spiral design than those of Chinese, Austronesian, or Bessarabian types. He realizes that pottery of the middle Jōmon type is also found in Mindanao and Melanesia but speculates that it was brought southward from Japan and not the other way around (cf. ibid., p. 56).

Many Japanese scholars today, however, tend to look toward the southern Pacific area as the place of origin of the cultural influence that penetrated Japan during the middle Jōmon period.[53] Involved in this debate is the problem of the four-cornered axe (*Vierkantbeil*) that made its appearance in Japan during the middle Jōmon period. Some scholars claim a northern origin, but many people trace it to the Austroasian culture.[54] In either case, no one is as yet certain as to which culture was instrumental in bringing new cultural influences to Japan during the middle Jōmon period.

We have already noted marked cultural changes that took place in the early Yayoi period, such as the introduction of paddy-field rice cultivation and the use of copper, bronze, and iron. As far as paddy-field cultivation is concerned, it can be easily traced to Southeast Asia and Indonesia, but whether it was brought by any one of the Southeast Asian peoples directly to Japan or whether it came via South Korea, where one of the northern tribes might have learned this farming method, remains to be clarified. Yawata proposes a plausible theory that a group of people who lived in the outer edge of Han Chinese culture, possibly in south China or Indochina, "came up northward with the sea current or seasonal wind or along the coast-line into the East China Sea and finally reached South Korea and Western Japan."[55] The beauty of this broad theory is that it manages to explain the introduction of rice, beans, melons, wheat, mulberry, hemp, domestic animals, as well as dolmen-type stone graves and metallic tools that had been unknown in Japan before the Yayoi period. On close examination, however, it is not easy to establish direct relationships between the bronze spears, swords, and bells of this period and those discovered in Korea and China.[56] Besides, the number and geographical distribution of Chinese and Koreans who migrated to Japan during the Yayoi period cannot be easily ascertained.[57] A number of other knotty problems remain unsolved as well. Nevertheless, those who lived in Japan during this period seem to have attained a degree of self-consciousness as one people sharing a common culture in forma-

[53] Yawata, *Nihon-shi no Reimei*, p. 70.

[54] R. Heine-Geldern, "Urheimat und früheste Wanderungen der Austronesier," *Anthropos*, XXVII (1932), 561-566.

[55] Yawata's view is found in UNESCO, *Japan*, p. 120.

[56] Kobayashi Yukio, *Nihon Kōkogaku Gaisetsu* (An Outline of Japanese Archeology) (Tokyo, 1951 and 1961), pp. 158-161.

[57] Some scholars have attempted to relate the eastward movement of the legendary Emperor Jimmu, from Kyushu to the Yamato district, to the migration of the ethnic group which brought Yayoi culture from Korea to Kyushu and then to Yamato. This theory cannot be supported by other evidence, however.

18

tion. "In important respects," says Beardsley rightly, "these people were Japanese, whereas the people of the Jōmon culture merely happened to live in Japan."[58]

3. A culture-complex hypothesis

Notwithstanding all these ambiguities and uncertainties, various theories have been advanced regarding the components, as well as the process of fusion, of the Japanese people. In recent years many scholars have attempted to analyze the archaic elements of Japanese mythology, religion, social organization, and language with the hope of delineating which cultural elements were transmitted by which ethnic group— and at what stage of the prehistoric period and early historic period. Among many such attempts, probably the most elaborate is the culture-complex hypothesis proposed by Oka Masao.[59] Briefly stated, his hypothesis is based on the following five major typological components that constituted the prehistoric and early historic ethnic culture of Japan.[60]

A. First is an ethnic unit, either of Melanesian origin or of a group that had been greatly influenced by Melanesian culture, which brought to Japan hunting as well as cultivation of taro and yam. This group had a matrilineal tradition and "secret society" system. They believed in what might be characterized as a "horizontal cosmology," that is, in a land of the dead beyond the sea. In Oka's opinion, this type of culture was transplanted to Japan during the middle Jōmon period from some parts of the South Pacific.

B. Second is either an Austroasian ethnic group or at least an Austroasian-speaking group from some region south of the Yangtze River in China. This group was engaged in hunting but also in upland rice

[58] "Japan before History," p. 334.

[59] Oka's magnum opus, "Kulturschichten in Alt-Japan" (doctoral dissertation, University of Vienna, 1933), unfortunately has not been published. However, he has written a number of articles on subjects also treated in his works, such as "Nihon Minzoku Bunka no Keisei," *ZSBT, Jōmon Yayoi Kofun Jidai*, pp. 106-116; "Nihon Bunka no Kiso Kōzō," *NMT*, Vol. 2: *Nihon Minzokugaku no Rekishi to Kadai* (Tokyo, 1958), pp. 5-21; and "Ethno-Historical Formation of the Japanese People," UNESCO, *Japan*, pp. 110-116. See also his view expressed in Oka et al., *Nihon Minzoku no Kigen*.

[60] Oka carefully avoids the question of the "origin" of the Japanese people and culture in a chronological sense. He thinks that it is quite conceivable to postulate sporadic migrations of north Eurasian subarctic hunters as well as of southeast Asian food-gatherers in the prepottery period. He does not even try to establish the origin of Jōmon culture except to say that it had affinities both with cultures of northern and southern Asia. In his opinion, "people responsible for the development of the ceramic culture . . . were gatherers and hunters of a fairly high cultural level." Also, the circum-North Pacific fishery culture must have penetrated northeastern Japan during the Jōmon period (cf. UNESCO, *Japan*, p. 111).

cultivation, and maintained a matrilineal social system. Shortly after this group arrived in Japan, probably at the end of the Jōmon or early part of the Yayoi period, it became assimilated to the first group (A). Each village of this group had shamans, and most probably female shamans acted as tribal chiefs. Some important figures in Japanese myths, such as *Amaterasu* (usually translated as the Sun Goddess) and the motif of brother-sister deities, marrying to beget other deities, are traced to this group.

C. Third is a northeast Asian group, possibly of Tungusic origin, that brought in the early Yayoi period the Ural-Altaic language and a "vertical cosmology," that is, the belief in Deities (*kami*) who descend from heaven to mountaintops, trees, or pillars, as well as shamanism of a Siberian type. This group originally was engaged in hunting and millet cultivation, but later shifted to rice cultivation in southern Korea on its way from Siberia or Manchuria to Japan. The social unit of this group was an exogamous patrilineal clan called the *hala-kala* ("*hara-kara*" in Japanese). Oka traces the crescent-shaped knife and the combed pattern, or Yayoi, pottery to this group.

D. Fourth is a southeast Asian group—probably of Austronesian (Micronesian) origin—that brought both fishing and paddy-rice-field cultivation to Japan during the early Yayoi period from the coastal area of south China. In Oka's opinion, this group provided the greatest impetus to Yayoi culture. The village organization of this group, which was patrilineal in character, was based on "age-class" or "age-grade" groups with elaborate systems of initiation rites. Crescent-shaped stone knives for cutting crops, rituals for harvest, and many important myths are attributed to them.

E. Fifth is an Altaic-speaking, pastoral tribe that subjugated other tribes in southern Manchuria and Korea around the beginning of the Christian era and arrived at the western part of Japan in the third or fourth century. The social unit of this group was a patriarchal clan called the *uji*, and the most powerful *uji* of this group developed into the "Tennō" (imperial) *uji* in the historic period. In many respects, this group shared the same religious and cultural traits as the third group (C), such as shamanism of a Siberian type and a "vertical cosmology." The chief deity of the fifth group, however, was not Amaterasu but Takamimusubi, and it was the order of Takamimusubi that resulted in the "descent" of Amaterasu's grandson, Ninigi, upon the mountaintop of Hiuga, according to Oka's interpretation of Japanese myth. Oka also traces the myth of the founding of the Yamato kingdom (the name of early Japan) by the legendary first Emperor Jimmu to this group's cultural tradition.

20

To recapitulate: according to Oka's hypothesis, there was probably a sporadic infiltration of northern and southern Asiatic peoples into Japan during the early stage of the Jōmon period, if not before. But the main structure of Japanese culture, society, and people developed out of the above five components.[61] To put it simply, various groups which migrated to Japan from south China and southeast Asia with Melanesian, Austroasian, and Austronesian cultural traditions provided the foundation for the agricultural society and civilization of the Yayoi period. Meanwhile, a Tungusic group originally from Siberia or Manchuria also made its contribution to the already pluralistic culture. It must be noted, however, that the process of assimilation of all these groups was a slow one, and that different kinds and degrees of racial and cultural fusion resulted in the development of a number of distinct small local cultures in various parts of Japan toward the later Yayoi period. The unification of all these local groups and cultures was attempted by the Altaic group which migrated to Japan in the third or fourth century A.D. This group had a superb military organization which enabled it to subjugate the agricultural population of Japan. In this situation the Altaic group established itself as the ruling class over earlier settlers, although it was quickly converted to the culture of the conquered peoples. This, in short, is how Oka analyzes the nature of the culture complex, as well as the development of the prehistoric and early historic Japanese society and people. Although such an all-embracing hypothesis is bound to receive many criticisms, as indeed it has, Oka's contribution will be appreciated by many future scholars who will concern themselves with the subject of the culture complex in Japan.[62]

In recent years Egami Namio has proposed a very imaginative hypothesis regarding the Altaic group, which corresponds to the fifth component (E) in Oka's scheme mentioned above. Egami seems to share Oka's analysis of the social and cultural traits of this group but differs slightly in the chronology of its coming to Japan. According to Egami, the Altaic group, which he prefers to call the "Kiba-zoku" or "the tribe of mounted warriors," pushed down to Korea around the

[61] In all fairness to Oka Masao, it must be noted that the above summary translation of his hypothesis, based on his articles mentioned earlier, was the work of the present author, who alone is responsible for any error or misunderstanding of Oka's position.

[62] Oka modestly states that his hypothesis will have to be corrected and articulated by specialists in the various disciplines involved (cf. Oka et al., *Nihon Minzoku no Kigen*, p. 328). In fact, Oka himself has added two or three minor cultural components to the above five, although they do not change the above view substantially (cf. Inouye Mitsusada, *Nihon Kokka no Kigen* [Origin of the Japanese Nation] [Tokyo, 1960], pp. 195-196).

turn of the fourth century A.D. and established its hegemony in the southern tip of the Korean peninsula. Early in the fourth century this "Kiba-zoku" under the leadership of its chief, presumably the Emperor Sujin, invaded Japan, first going to Kyushu but later to the central area, where it established itself as the ruling clan of the Yamato kingdom toward the end of the fourth or early in the fifth century, corresponding to the middle Kofun (Tumulus) period. Being no mean archeologist as well as a specialist in Inner Asian history, Egami can cite various data to support his hypothesis.[63] However, his theory, based on the swift movement of Altaic mounted warriors subjugating many other tribes both in Korea and Japan within a matter of one century— a hypothesis which is not impossible considering the speedy movement of Genghis Khan in the later period—has been questioned by many specialists in philology, history, and archeology.[64] Nevertheless, most scholars recognize that the Altaic cultural influence, if not an offshoot of the Altaic tribe, penetrated Japan either toward the end of the prehistoric or early historic period. The exact identity of the culture-bearing group, however, has yet to be settled.

LANGUAGE, MYTHS, AND RELIGION

Despite numerous difficulties involved, study of the prehistoric and early historic period of Japan has come a long way. This has been especially true since the end of World War II inasmuch as overt and covert governmental restrictions against research concerning the beginnings of the Japanese nation and people have been removed.[65] Of

---

[63] For Egami's hypothesis see "Nihon Minzoku: Bunka no Genryū to Nihon Kokka no Keisei," *Minzokugaku Kenkyu*, Vol. XIII, No. 3 (1949); "Nihon Kodai Kokka no Keisei," *Tōyō Bunka*, No. 6 (September 1951); and his statements and footnotes in Oka et al., *Nihon Minzoku no Kigen*, esp. pp. 104-138, 146-148, and nn. 47, 51, 52-65, 67, 68, 70-72.

[64] Critical comments on Egami's hypothesis concerning "Kiba-zoku" are found, e.g., in Yanagita Kunio and Origuchi Shinobu, "Nihonjin no Kami to Reikon no Kannen sono hoka," *Minzokugaku Kenkyu*, Vol. XIV, No. 2 (September 1949); Higo Kazuo, "Nihon Kodai-shi e no Kanken," ibid., Vol. XIV, No. 2 (December 1949); Kindaichi Kyōsuke et al., "Nihongo no Keitō ni tsuite," *Kokugogaku*, No. 5 (February 1951); Mikami Tsugio, "Nihon Kokka Bunka no Kigen ni kansuru Futatsu no Tachiba—Tennozoku wa Kiba-zoku ka," *Rekishi Hyōron*, Vol. IV, No. 6 (June 1950); Kobayashi Yukio, "Jodai Nihon ni okeru Jōba no Fūshū," *Shirin*, Vol. XXXIV, No. 3 (July 1951); and Inouye, *Nihon Kokka no Kigen*, pp. 183-221.

[65] Two famous cases in recent decades are those of Minobe Tatsukichi and Tsuda Sōkichi. In 1935, Minobe, then a member of the House of Peers, was indicted for his legal theory that while the "office" of the emperor of Japan has the legal basis of administrator of, and spokesman for, the nation and people, it has no divinely sanctioned authority as implied by Japanese mythologies. Although Minobe was given a suspended sentence in 1937, he had to resign from all public offices. In 1940, Tsuda was indicted

the almost feverish research activities by Japanese archeologists in the postwar period, we have made note earlier. Archeological theories, be it noted, even with erroneous conclusions, are based on the tangible evidence unearthed. This is not the case with students of such cultural aspects as dance, drama, and music.

Dance, for instance, has been an important facet of Japanese culture since time immemorial. Even in the mythologies, it is reported that when Amaterasu hid herself in a cave to escape the violent acts of her brother, the *kami* (deities) in heaven made merry in order to lure her out of her cave. On that occasion, a female *kami* called Ame-no-Uzume is said to have danced in a somewhat suggestive manner and was cheered wildly by other *kami*.[66] Dance has been believed to have a magical power in pacifying the *kami*. In the middle of the fifth century, the Emperor Inkyo is said to have played a musical instrument while his empress danced to celebrate the completion of their new palace. But what kind of dance was performed in the early days is not clear. The term *kagura* (or *kami no kura*, meaning the "seat of *kami*") indicates that this type of religious dance, performed by female shamanic-diviners, has always been an important element in religious rituals from early days onward.[67] There is another form of old dance known as *dengaku*, a pastoral dance originally known as *ta-asobi* ("Play in the Paddy Field") performed at the time of rice-transplanting as a form of appeasement of the *kami*. On this occasion, *sa-otome* ("maidens who plant") plant the rice seedlings to the accompaniment of music.[68] Unfortunately, it is an almost impossible task to reconstruct various forms of dance performed in the early historic or prehistoric periods.

Music, too, has been known in Japan from very early days—long before the fifth century when Korean music is said to have been introduced from Silla, Paikche, and Kogryu. We know something of the

---

for nineteen "errors" scattered in his four books: *Jindai-shi no Kenkyu* (A Study of the Age of *Kami* or Gods) (Tokyo, 1924); *Kojiki oyobi Nihonshoki no Kenkyu* (A Study of *The Ancient Matters* and *The Chronicle of Japan*) (Tokyo, 1924); *Nihon Jōdai-shi Kenkyu* (A Study of the Early History of Japan) (Tokyo, 1930); and *Jōdai Nihon no Shakai oyobi Shisō* (Society and Thought of Early Japan) (Tokyo, 1933). In the end, Tsuda was found guilty on only one "error," namely, his theory that the so-called imperial lineage prior to the tenth legendary Emperor Sujin has no historical evidence to support it. On the problem of academic freedom, or the lack of it, before World War II, see Mikasa no Miya Takahito (H.I.H., Prince Takahito Mikasa) (ed.), *Nihon no Akebono* (The Dawn of Japan) (Tokyo, 1959), pp. 263-289.

[66] Cf. Obayashi Taryo, "Die Amaterasu-Mythe in alten Japan und die Sonnenfinsternismythe in Südostasien," *Ethnos*, XXV (1960), 20-43.

[67] Later, however, male priests of Shinto shrines performed the *kagura*. Cf. Yanagita Kunio (ed.), *Minzokugaku Jiten* (A Dictionary of Folklore Studies) (1951), pp. 96-98.

[68] Ibid., pp. 334-335. Cf. also Haga Hideo, *Ta no Kami* (The Rituals of Rice Production in Japan) (Tokyo, 1959).

ancient musical instruments as well as some forms of music, such as *rōyei* ("chanted poems") and *kume-uta* ("war songs"). Music and singing were also used for the purpose of fortune-telling, and often shamans played music (*koto-uranai*) or sang songs (*uta-uranai*) in order to become possessed by the spirits of the *kami*.[69] But as far as the scale structure of ancient Japanese music is concerned, we know amazingly little. Of the two traditional types of scale structure, the so-called Sino-Japanese type, that is, the . . . C D E G A C' . . . series with each note serving as a starting point, thus forming a different five-note mode, such as D E G A C' D', seems to have affinities with the scale structure of Mongolia, China, and Indonesia. The second type, represented by . . . B C E F A B' . . . also allows each note as a starting point, thus again creating a different five-note mode. The most frequently used among them are the three modes, for example, those on A, B, and E. We are told that the second type of scale structure is also known in Indonesia and parts of India.[70] But because of the very nature of music which is so sensitive to external influences and also the changing mood of culture, we are not at all certain about what part of these two types of scale structure can be traced to the early historic or prehistoric periods.[71]

1. Language

Scholars are more sanguine about tracing the development of the Japanese language, at least more so than in the cases of drama and music.[72] Here again a number of problems are involved, since a particular language is not the monopoly of a certain group of people; moreover, there are accidental similarities among languages of different traditions in sounds, system of accentuation, use of vowels, grammatical structure, and vocabulary. Some of the similarities between any two languages may be the result of accidental resemblances or borrow-

---

[69] Yanagita, *Minzokugaku Jiten*, p. 526.

[70] Cf. "Japanese Music," *Encyclopaedia Britannica*, Vol. XII (1962 ed.), p. 962.

[71] On the influence of Buddhist music on Japanese music, see Iba Takashi, "Bukkyo Ongaku," in Tsuji Soichi et al., *Shūkyō Ongaku* (Religious Music) (Tokyo, 1933), pp. 169-211.

[72] There are a number of good introductory works on Japanese language. Among them are Kindaichi Kyōsuke, *Kokugo-shi Keito-hen* (Historical Lineage of the Japanese Language) (Tokyo, 1938); Ōno Susumu, *Nihongo no Kigen* (Origin of the Japanese Language) (Tokyo, 1957 and 1960); Kindaichi Haruhiko, *Nihongo* (The Japanese Language) (Tokyo, 1957 and 1961); and Doi Chūsei et al., *Nihongo no Rekishi* (A History of the Japanese Language) (Tokyo, 1957 and 1961). Probably the most important recent work on the subject is Hattori Shiro, *Nihongo no Keito* (Lineage of the Japanese Language) (Tokyo, 1959).

ing of certain words or forms by one language from the other; or perhaps both languages may have been influenced by a third language.

Undaunted by these problems, an amazing array of theories and hypotheses has been advanced regarding the kinship, plausible or far-fetched, between Japanese and other languages. As early as the last century, Chamberlain was engaged in the comparative study of Japanese with the Ainu and Ryūkyū languages, while Aston compared Japanese with Korean.[73] In our century, Ramstedt compared Japanese with the Altaic languages.[74] Labberton and Whymant traced Japanese to the Oceanic language family.[75] And Parker held that Japanese and the Tibeto-Burmese language belonged to the same linguistic structure.[76] Among Japanese scholars, Kanazawa advocated the common origin of the Japanese and Korean languages,[77] while Matsumoto and others discovered many Japanese words which had been borrowed from the Austroasian languages.[78] Oka is intrigued by a characteristic of the Japanese language, namely, that every syllable ends with a vowel, which seems to be akin to the characteristics of the languages spoken in the northern part of Halmahera Island in Indonesia as well as to the Papuan language of New Guinea. He also points out that many Japanese words denoting parts of the body might have come from Austroasian or Austronesian origin.[79]

More recently, two eminent scholars have undertaken to study the early development of the Japanese language. Johannes Rahder views Japanese as a complex fusion of many linguistic strands. For example, much of the Japanese vocabulary has South Asian, Austronesian, and Altaic origins. In his opinion, however, one structure of the Japanese language was modeled upon an Altaic prototype and is not related to the Chinese or Austric languages. While Rahder's theories are a little too technical for nonspecialists, as far as we can figure out he seems to be optimistic about the possibility of establishing kinship between

[73] B. H. Chamberlain, "Nomenclature of Japan" and "Essay in Aid of a Grammar and Dictionary of the Luchuan Language," *TASJ* (Supplement), Vol. XXIII (1895); W. G. Aston, "A Comparative Study of the Japanese and Korean Languages," *Journal of the Royal Asiatic Society of Great Britain and Ireland*, Vol. III, Part XI (1897).

[74] C. J. Ramstedt, "A Comparison of the Altaic Languages with Japanese," *TASJ*, Vol. I, 2d Ser. (1924).

[75] D. van Hinloopen Labberton, "The Oceanic Languages and the Nipponese as Branches of the Nippon-Malay-Polynesian Family of Speech," *TASJ*, Vol. II, 2d Ser. (1925); A. Neville J. Whymant, "The Oceanic Theory of the Japanese Language and People," *TASJ*, Vol. III, 2d Ser. (1926).

[76] C. K. Parker, *A Dictionary of Japanese Compound Verbs* (Tokyo, 1937).

[77] Kanazawa Shōzaburo, *The Common Origin of the Japanese and Korean Languages* (Tokyo, 1910).

[78] Matsumoto Nobuhiro, *Le Japonais et les langues austroasiatiques* (Paris, 1928).

[79] Cf. UNESCO, *Japan*, pp. 111-112.

the Japanese and Korean languages. If it were possible for him to reconstruct the original language from which both Korean and Japanese developed, only then would he be willing to proceed to reconstruct a still earlier language from which the Korean, Japanese, and Tungusic languages derived.[80] Charles Haguenauer, whose work deals with the geographical environment, the problems of the origin of Japanese culture, and ethnological and other aspects, devotes nearly three-fourths of his book to linguistic considerations.[81] He has given up all hope of relating Japanese to the language of the Taiwan aborigines, the Philippine natives, the Indonesians, and Polynesians. Rather, he concentrates his effort on the relation of Japanese to Korean, East Altaic languages, such as Mongolian and Tungusic, and to Ainu. His conclusion is extremely sober and modest. That is, while he acknowledges much truth in the view that Japanese is closer to the Altaic languages than to any other neighboring language groups, he finds it impossible to establish a definite relationship between Japanese and the Altaic languages at the present time.[82]

Hattori shares the cautious conclusion of Haguenauer and states that in the strict linguistic sense the only language which has kinship with Japanese is the Ryūkyū language, although he also recognizes the possibility that Japanese had some relation to the Korean and Altaic languages. He rejects Ōno's hypothesis that during the Jōmon period the people in Japan spoke a south Asian language which was akin to the Polynesian languages in structure; he asserts rather that during the Yayoi period a south Korean language, which had an Altaic grammar and vowel system, penetrated north Kyushu and gradually spread through other parts of Japan. But in Ōno's view, the early Japanese language thus developed nearly 2,300 years ago had retained a quantity of vocabulary of southern origin.[83] On the other hand, Hattori is inclined to trace the origin of the Japanese language to *ur*-Japanese (*Nihon-sogo*) which was most likely spoken in northern Kyushu about 2,000 years ago, in the Yayoi period. However, he does not think that

---

[80] For Rahder's views, see the series of articles entitled "The Comparative Treatment of the Japanese Language," in *Monumenta Nipponica*, VII (1951), 198-208; VIII (1952), 239-288; IX (1953), 199-257; and X (1954), 127-168. See also his *Etymological Vocabulary of Japanese, Korean and Ainu* ("Monumenta Nipponica Monographs," No. 16) (Tokyo, 1956), and "A Linguistic Study of the Root 'kon,'" in *Buddhism and Culture: Dedicated to Dr. D. T. Suzuki in Commemoration of His Ninetieth Birthday* (Kyoto, 1960), pp. 226-246.

[81] Charles M. Haguenauer, *Origines de la civilisation japonaise: Introduction à l'étude de la préhistoire du Japon*, Part I (Paris, 1956).

[82] Ibid., p. 636.

[83] Cf. Ōno, *Nihongo no Kigen*, pp. 198-200. See Hattori, *Nihongo*, pp. 233-239, for his criticism of Ōno's hypothesis.

ur-Japanese was transplanted by a non-Japanese ethnic group to Kyushu in the Yayoi period as many scholars think. That much he is certain of, but beyond that point he feels that he has to resort to speculation, based however on Glottochronology or Lexicostatistics. Hattori postulates that the *ur*-Japanese and Korean languages separated about 5,000 or 6,000 years ago, whereupon one was spoken in Korea and the other spoken in Kyushu. The latter was destined to absorb vocabulary and certain features of other languages, although it retained the core of its original linguistic structure.[84] He further speculates that a series of migrations of the north Kyushu people who spoke *ur*-Japanese to the Yamato district took place during the second and third centuries. Also, about this time or shortly after, another series of migrations of the same group took place to the Ryūkyū islands.[85] Whether these hypotheses by philologists can be verified or not, we are at least learning today more than ever before something about the characteristics and features of the language of the Yayoi period and its development in the early historic period.[86]

2. *Mythology*

Anyone interested in the religion and culture of the prehistoric and early historic periods of Japan can ill-afford to neglect the study of Japanese myths. The two main sources of Japanese myths are the *Kojiki* (Records of Ancient Matters) and the *Nihonshoki* or *Nihongi* (Chronicles of Japan).[87] Both were compiled in the eighth century, written in Chinese characters, and both betray some Chinese influences although they retain substantially the structure of the early Japanese myths. Other valuable sources—also products of the same cultural milieu—

[84] Hattori, *Nihongo*, pp. 229-232.

[85] Ibid., pp. 83-86. It is interesting to note that Hattori in his recent article, "Nihongo no Keitō," *ZSBT*, Vol. 1: *Jōmon Yayoi Kofun Jidai*, pp. 127-136, suggests that even if Japanese had had some kinship with the Manchurian and Ainu languages, their separation is estimated to have taken place, again based on Glottochronology, about 9,000 and 7,000-10,000 years ago, respectively.

[86] Cf. Izui Hisanosuke, "Jōdai Nihongo ni okeru Boin-soshiki to Boin-kōtai" (The Vocal System and Vocal Interchanges of Eighth Century Japanese), *Miscellanea Kiotiensia* (Kyoto University, 1956), pp. 989-1020.

[87] For translations of these documents, see Basil Hall Chamberlain (trans.), "*Ko-ji-ki*: 'Records of Ancient Matters,'" *TASJ* (Supplement), Vol. X (1882); W. G. Aston (trans.), *Nihongi*: Chronicles of Japan from the Earliest Times to A.D. 697 (2 vols.; London, 1896 and 1956); Karl Florenz, *Japanische Mythologie, Nihongi, Zeitalter der Götter* (Tokyo, 1901). Cf. also Anesaki Masaharu, *Japanese Mythology*, in *The Mythology of All Races*, Vol. VIII, ed. by C.J.A. MacCulloch (Boston, 1928); Tsunoda Ryusaku et al. (comps.), *Sources of Japanese Tradition* (New York, 1958), pp. 26-35; and E. Dale Saunders, "Japanese Mythology," in *Mythologies of the Ancient World*, ed. Samuel Noah Kramer (Garden City, New York, 1961), pp. 409-442.

are the *Kogoshūi* (Gleanings from Ancient Stories), the *Fūdoki* (Records of Local Surveys), the *Shoku-Nihongi* (Chronicles of Japan, Continued), the *Manyōshū* (Anthology of Myriad Leaves), and the *Norito* (Ritual Prayers).[88]

There are a number of hermeneutical problems involved in the study of Japanese myths such as, for example, who compiled them and for what purpose, how to classify them, and how to correlate the analysis of the myths with archeological, linguistic, ethnological, historical, and other types of evidence.[89] Various attempts at reconstructing a coherent story of the origin of the cosmos in the early historic period of Japan out of various myths have not been successful.[90] Usually, Japanese myths are classified in several categories.[91]

A. Cosmogonic myths appear in three versions with three different *kami* as central figures. According to the first version, Umashiashika-

[88] Kato Genchi and Hoshino Hikoshiro (trans.), *Kogoshūi: Gleanings from Ancient Stories* (2d ed.; Tokyo, 1925); Kokusai Bunka Shinkokai (ed.), *Introduction to Classic Japanese Literature* (Tokyo, 1948), pp. 8-13; J. S. Snellen (trans.), "Shoku-Nihongi: Chronicles of Japan, Continued, from 697-791 A.D.," *TASJ*, XI, 2d Ser. (1934), 151-239 and XIV (1937), 207-279; Japanese Classics Translation Committee, *The Manyōshu: One Thousand Poems* (Tokyo, 1940; Chicago, 1941); Donald L. Philippi (trans.), *Norito* (Tokyo, 1959).

[89] Many Japanese scholars of mythology, history, Shinto, Japanese literature, and ethnology have published a number of books and articles on the subject. Among them are Matsumura Takeo, *Nihon Shinwa no Kenkyu* (A Study of Japanese Mythology) (4 vols.; Tokyo, 1955-1958); Higo Kazuo, *Nihon Shinwa no Rekishi-teki Keisei* (Historical Development of Japanese Myths) (Tokyo, 1958); Tsuda Sōkichi, *Jōdai Nihon*, esp. pp. 1-238; Kanda Hideo, *Kojiki no Kōsō* (Structure of the *Kojiki*) (Tokyo, 1959); Takeda Yūkichi, *Kojiki Setsuwa-gun no Kenkyu* (A Study of Classification of the Kojiki Myths) (Tokyo, 1954); Nihon Minzokugaku Zenshu, I, *Shinwa Densetsu-hen* (Myths and Legends) by Fujisawa Morhikio (Tokyo, 1961); Matsumoto Nobuhiro, *Essai sur la mythologie japonaise, Austro-Asiatica*, Vol. II (Paris, 1928); Matsumoto, *Nihon Shinwa no Kenkyu* (A Study of Japanese Mythology) (Tokyo, 1931 and 1946); Matsumoto, *Nihon no Shinwa* (Myths of Japan) (Tokyo, 1956); Matsumoto, "Shinwa no Seikaku" (The Nature of Japanese Myths), *ZSBT*, Vol. I: *Jōmon Yayoi Kofun Jidai*, pp. 304-310; Numazawa Kiichi (Franz K. Numazawa), "Die Weltanfang in der japanischen Mythologie," *Internationale Schriftenreihe für soziale und politische Wissenschaften* (Ethnologische Reihe, Vol. II [Paris-Lucerne, 1946]), and "Tenchi wakaruru Shinwa no Bunkashi-teki haikei" (Cultural Background of the Myth concerning the Separation of Heaven and Earth), *Academia*, I (1952), 4-20; Mishina Shōei, *Kenkoku Shinwa Ronko* (Essays on the Myth of the Founding of the Nation) (Tokyo, 1937); Matsumaye Takeshi, *Nihon Shinwa no Shinkenkyu* (A New Study of Japanese Mythology) (Tokyo, 1960); and Ōbayashi Taryo, *Nihon Shinwa no Kigen* (Origins of Japanese Myths) (Tokyo, 1961). The present author is greatly indebted to the writings of Matsumoto Nobuhiro, Tsuda Sōkichi, Oka Masao, and Ōbayashi Taryo.

[90] See, e.g., the attempt of Post Wheeler, *The Sacred Scriptures of the Japanese* (New York, 1952).

[91] For a traditional classification of Japanese mythology see Robert Karl Reischauer, *Early Japanese History* (ca. 40 B.C.-A.D. 1167), Part A (Princeton, 1937), pp. 4-8. The present writer follows the general outline of Ōbayashi Taryo.

bihikoji ("the kami of the *ashi* or reed") grew out of a reed at the time when chaos existed, before the cosmos came into being; then two other *kami* came into existence, followed by many others. According to the second version, Kuninotokotachi ("the *kami* who founded the nation") is the first *kami* who came into existence, although the motif of this account is similar to the first version. According to the third version, a trio of *kami*—Amenominakanushi, Takamimusubi, and Kamimusubi—appeared in Takamanohara or the "domain of heaven" at the beginning of the cosmos. Since Takamimusubi and Kamimusubi are in effect male and female functions of the first member of the trio, Amenominakanushi ("the central *kami* of heaven") is the creator-ruler of the heavenly domain. The first two versions probably had a southeast Asian origin, while the third was transmitted to Japan from central Asia by the Tennō (imperial) clan.[92]

B. The second component of the Japanese myths is an account of Izanagi ("He-who-invites") and Izanami's ("She-who-is-invited") begetting the islands of Japan and various *kami*. The birth of the *kami* of fire causes the death of Izanami, who then descends to Yomi-no-kuni or the nether world. Izanagi chases her there but runs away when he finds the transformed figure of his spouse. As he returns to heaven, Amaterasu is born from his left eye, Tsuki-yomi ("the Moon deity") from his right eye, and Susanoo ("the Storm deity") from his nose. There follows the struggle between Amaterasu and her brother Susanoo, and she hides herself in a cave to escape her brother's wild acts. Some of these motifs are akin to those of southeast Asian, central Asian, and south Chinese myths, but there is no definitive theory as to how the fusion of these elements took place.

C. The so-called "Izumo Myths" start with the account of Susanoo, the impetuous brother of Amaterasu, going to the Izumo area where he rescues a maiden from the eight-headed snake and marries her. From the tail of the snake appears a sword. The mention of a sword betrays the influence of an iron culture, but the motif of a hero rescuing a maiden from a sacrifice-demanding monster is found in many other cultures.[93] The real central figure of the Izumo myths, however,

[92] According to Mizuno Tasuku, Amenominakanushi is the central figure in the *Kojiki*, which reflected the prestige of the imperial authority under the Emperor Temmu in the seventh century, whereas Kuninotokotachi is preferred in the *Nihonshoki*, which reflected the concerns of the Fujiwara and other bureaucratic-aristocratic clans that wanted to justify their understanding of the nature of Japanese political structure. This view is cited in Ōbayashi, *Nihon Shinwa no Kigen*, pp. 51-52. Also, according to *Ise no Fūdoki*, Amenominakanushi was connected to Ise which later became the dwelling place of Amaterasu.

[93] For such examples see Ōbayashi, *Nihon shinwa no Kigen*, pp. 172-190.

is Ōkuninushi ("The Master of the Great Land"), presumably the sixth descendant of Susanoo. It was he who ruled the land of Izumo with the help of Sukunahikona, a *kami* of midget size from *Tokoyo* ("the Land of Eternity"). Sukunahikona has been variously interpreted as an alter ego of Ōkuninushi or the prototype of the *marebito*, the *kami* who visits human society at harvest season.[94] In the end, the ruler of Izumo offers his jurisdiction of the land to the *kami* in the heavenly domain. This implies, in Matsumoto's opinion, that the so-called Izumo myths were put together for the political intention of the Ya-mato group, which was a community based on the worship of the sun, to subjugate the Izumo group, which worshiped the *kami* of water and storm.[95]

D. With the offering of earthly jurisdiction by the ruler of Izumo, the compilers of Japanese myths take us back to the heavenly domain. To make a long story short, Amaterasu, by the order of Takamimu-subi, sends her grandson, Ninigi, to rule Japan. In this connection, Oka points out that there must have been two sets of myths regarding the Takamanohara ("the Heavenly Domain")—one with Takamimu-subi as the central figure and the other with Amaterasu as the central figure. Although the myth compilers skillfully connected these two *kami* by marrying off Takamimusubi's daughter to Amaterasu's son, thus begetting Ninigi, these two sets of myths were originally unre-lated. The motif of the descent of *kami* to rule the country belongs to the Takamimusubi side of the myth, which is Altaic in origin, while the myth of Amaterasu, who was a goddess in charge of farming and food, was Austroasian in origin. Oka further believes that the original *kami* of the imperial clan was not Amaterasu but Takamimusubi (or Takakimusubi, meaning the "Kami who descends upon a tall tree").[96]

E. The so-called "Hiuga myth" begins with the descent of Ninigi, accompanied by five *kami*, to the mountaintop of Hiuga, which may or may not be the place with the same name located in Kyushu, for the term "Hiuga" simply means "turning toward the sun." At any rate, Ninigi marries Konosakuya ("Princess Blossoming-brilliantly-like-the-flower-of-the-tree") and begets two sons. We are told that the frailty of Ninigi's descendants, that is, the human race, is due to the fact that

[94] Oka holds that this notion of *marebito* is Melanesian in origin, brought by the first group in his scheme (A). Cf. *NMT*, Vol. II: *Nihon Minzokugaku no Rekishi to Kadai*, pp. 7-9. Matsumoto also thinks that the idea of the *kami* coming from the land lying beyond the sea, as exemplified by the story of Sukunahikona, is older than the belief in the *kami* descending from heaven (cf. his *Nihon no Shinwa*, pp. 90-96).

[95] Oka, *Nihon no Shinwa*, pp. 171-177.

[96] Oka et al., *Nihon Minzoku no Kigen*, pp. 45-48 and 330; also UNESCO, *Japan*, pp. 112, 114.

he refused to marry the homely sister of Konosakuya. Be that as it may, Ninigi's great-grandson is said to have led the chosen people from Kyushu to Yamato where he became the first legendary emperor, Jimmu.

Casual readers who are not familiar with the strange names of the Japanese *kami* can hardly be blamed for bewilderment in examining Japanese myths. But myths in early Japan, like their counterparts in archaic societies in other parts of the world, are not childish imagination or superstition.[97] In spite of the compilers' intention to fit myths into the political ideology of the seventh- and eighth-century Japanese regime, these myths preserve the early Japanese understanding of the meaning of the world and of life, and more especially the mode of existence of *kami*. To them, all the events mentioned in myths—the marriage between two *kami* or their method of planting seeds and weaving—took place in mythical time. As Mircea Eliade reminds us: "Everything had taken place and had been revealed at that moment, *in illo tempore*: the creation of the world, and that of man, and man's establishment in the situation provided for him in the cosmos, down to the least details of that situation."[98] As such, myths provided a heavenly model for earthly life, and in this sense "religion" embraced all aspects of existence of the people in Japan during the prehistoric and early historic period.

3. Religion

Any attempt to reconstruct an archaic or primitive people's religion involves many difficulties. This is particularly true in Japan where several different ethnic and cultural streams had already merged in the prehistoric period, leaving very few clues as to their distinct patterns of kinship and marriage, their social organizations, and the modes of their religious beliefs and practices. The only exception is the Ainu, who, because of their historic isolation from the rest of the populace, managed to preserve certain features of their archaic religious and cultural tradition. Unfortunately, the Ainu legacy throws little light on the religion of non-Ainu people in prehistoric Japan.

Regarding the religious outlook of the Jōmon people, we can only speculate that they must have shared the general features of the way of life of hunting and fishing peoples of Eurasia during the neolithic period. There is not enough evidence to warrant the theory that can-

[97] Saunders, "Japanese Mythology," p. 413: "Japanese myths present a somewhat disorganized pattern, episodic rather than epic in nature. They form a miscellaneous body of superstition rather than a co-ordinated system of legends."
[98] *The Myth of the Eternal Return*, trans. W. R. Trask (New York, 1954), p. 105.

31

nibalism was a widespread custom, a theory postulated at one time by some scholars. Fortunately, from the shell mounds we learn something about the burial customs of the Jōmon people. For instance, skeletons found in burials near dwellings frequently have folded limbs. Such a custom may have been based on the belief that a dead person with folded limbs would not haunt the living, or it may have been motivated by an entirely different belief to the effect that those buried in embryonic posture would be assured of rebirth. Skeletal remains of the Jōmon period also indicate that tooth extractions were performed. This operation probably had something to do with the initiation of youths.[99] As many of the latter Jōmon figurines portray women, some scholars think that there was a belief in female deities, and the discovery of large finished stone pieces has led others to conclude that there must have been belief in phallicism.[100] The concentrically radiating circles of flat stones unearthed on northern Honshu and Hokkaido resemble those found in Europe in those places identified as burial sites of the neolithic period.[101] In the main, communities were small in size and mobile, although in the middle and later Jōmon period semipermanent settlements began to be formed. But beyond that we know practically nothing about the social organization or religious practices of the people during this period.

The transition from the fishing-hunting culture of the Jōmon period to the agricultural culture of the Yayoi period must have resulted in changes in religious beliefs and practices, but here again much of our theorizing on the Yayoi culture is conjecture, based, to be sure, on archeological discoveries. It is safe to imagine however, that an agricultural society requires stable settlements, a certain amount of division of labor, a use of a variety of tools, and some kind of community organization. Common cemeteries for villages have been unearthed, and the use of jars—some are of the twin type while others are of the single type with lids—is evident. The customs of tooth extraction and tattooing seem to have been widely observed. Various kinds of ornaments and tools are found in coffins too. In some instances, a set of pottery is placed in front of the coffin as though food and drink were offered to the spirits of the deceased. At Bishamon in Kanagawa Prefecture deer bones that were burnt, presumably for the purpose of

[99] Cf. Miyamoto Hiroto, "Tsugumo Kaizuka-jin no Basshi Fūshū ni tsuite," *JGZ*, Vol. XL, No. 5 (1925).

[100] Torii Ryūzo, "Nihon Sekki Jidai Minshū no Joshin Shinko," *JGZ*, Vol. XXXVII, No. 11 (1922), and "Gojin Sosen Yūshi-izen no Dankon Sonhai," *JGZ*, Vol. XXXVIII, No. 3 (1923).

[101] *ZSBT, Nihon*, Part I, 88-90.

32

fortune-telling, were discovered, whereas on a small island called Tanegashima, south of Kyushu, many ornaments made of shells, believed to be the special marks of female shamans and mediums, have been unearthed.[102] Although there is no conclusive evidence that special religious functionaries existed, some scholars think that the use of bronze bells (*dōshaku*) and sacred jewels (*magatama*) was connected with shamanism. Also the swords and spears made of bronze during this period were not meant for practical purposes, in comparison with their Korean counterparts which had sharper blades, and thus are believed to have been sacred objects of some sort.[103]

In this connection, we are inclined to agree substantially with Oka's previously mentioned hypothesis and view the Yayoi culture as a culture complex, blending (A) the Melanesian elements of a secret society system, matrilineal tradition, horizontal cosmology, and veneration of spirits, especially those of ancestors, (B) the Austroasian elements of village shamans, female tribal chiefs, and the myth of a sun-goddess in charge of agriculture, (C) the Tungusic elements of exogamous patrilineal clans, a Siberian form of shamanism, and vertical cosmology, and (D) the Austronesian elements of age-class and age-group social organization, paddy-rice cultivation, and the custom of initiation rites. We are, however, not certain how these elements came to be blended and at what stages of the prehistoric period. At any rate, the existence of a clearly graded village system in the Ihama section of Mihama village, Shizuoka Prefecture, of a house for a society of young men in Sukumo, Kochi Prefecture, of a *taya* or a house for women during the period of menstruation at Taguchi, Aichi Prefecture, and of the practice of healing and mediumship by shamanic diviners in a state of spirit possession in various parts of Japan even in our own time, can hardly be explained simply in terms of accidental similarities with magico-religious traditions of Japan's neighboring countries.[104]

We also recognize Altaic elements—the fifth component (E) in Oka's scheme—such as a social system based on a patriarchal clan (*uji*); social stratification of occupational groups; the deification of heroes; the worship of celestial deities who are believed to descend upon mountaintops, tall trees, or pillars; and the custom of horseback riding. But we feel that the migration of the Altaic group began around the third century A.D., if not earlier, and continued sporadically, instead of manifesting itself as one great military invasion in the fourth century, as Egami postulates. Admittedly there were some marked

[102] Ibid., pp. 156-161.
[103] Cf. Kobayashi, *Nihon Kōkogaku Gaisetsu*, pp. 118, 146, and 158.
[104] For these examples see Oka, "Nihon Minzoku Bunka no Keisei," pp. 107-112.

changes in the middle Kofun (Tumulus) period, notably a sudden popularity of the horse, and it may be that there was even a dynastic change in Japan about this time as some scholars suggest. But we certainly cannot attribute all changes during the Kofun period to Altaic influence alone.

Fortunately for us, this period left many tangible remains besides great tombs—remains such as stone *magatama* (imitations of sacred jewels), stone knives, and mirrors, which are believed to have been offerings.[105] Stone boats unearthed in several tombs indicate that people of this period may have believed that the souls of the dead were transported to another land. At the sacred compound of the Munakata shrine outside of Fukuoka, Kyushu, many stone horses and boats were discovered.[106] Probably, *kami* were believed to come by horse or by boat.[107] One of the curious items of this period is the *komochi-magatama*, made of stone, that is, a *magatama* (sacred jewel) with several smaller *magatama* tied around it. Since the term *tama* means both soul and round figure, *komochi-magatama* must have had some religious meaning that unfortunately is not clear to us today.[108] Incidentally, the discovery of *magatama*, swords, and mirrors, all made of stone or pottery, as items to be buried with the deceased, anticipates the use of these articles as the three symbols of imperial authority. Also, the female figurine among the *haniwa* earthenware with a piece of cloth hanging down from her right shoulder to the side of the waist is believed to portray *Miko*, the shamanic diviner.[109]

If we assume that the Altaic group, powerful in military affairs but with a relatively undeveloped nomadic culture, penetrated the Japanese islands around the third century and established itself as the ruling class of the early Japanese kingdom in the fourth or fifth century, we can at least arrive at a plausible theory for explaining many of the social, cultural, and religious features and phenomena of Japan during the early historic period. Accepting this view, even on a tentative basis, however, still leaves many problems unsolved and also raises further questions. For example, we are far from certain about the nature of the culture complex developed during the Yayoi period, especially regarding the fusion of different religious outlooks, myths, symbols, and practices. To be sure, we can differentiate typologically the northern

[105] Ōba Iwao, "Jodai Saigishi to sono Iseki ni tsuite," *JGZ*, Vol. XX, No. 8 (1930).

[106] Tanaka Yukio, "Chikuzen Okitsugu no Sekisei Mozōhin," *JGZ*, Vol. XXV, No. 2 (1935). See also Munakata Jinja Fukko Kisei Kai (ed.), *Munakata Jinja-shi* (History of Munakata Shrine), Vol. I (Tokyo, 1961).

[107] Cf. Matsumoto, *Nihon no Shinwa*, chaps. i and ii.

[108] Cf. Kobayashi, *Nihon Kōkogaku Gaisetsu*, pp. 221-222.

[109] Ibid., p. 179.

Asian and southeast Asian elements, so that we can tell that the shamanistic tradition in Japan, for instance, is a mixture of Siberian and southeast Asian or Oceanian types. But outside such a general typological distinction, we have a long way to go before we can pinpoint which specific area of Austroasian cultural tradition or which specific stream of Siberian tradition provided the shamanistic techniques and ideologies of Japan. We are equally at a loss as to the predecessors of many of the Japanese myths, even though we have no difficulty in assigning the myth of Izanagi ("He-who-invites") and Izanami ("She-who-is-invited"), for instance, to the south Pacific region in general without specifying which area thereof.[110] The future articulation of the problem of the culture complex of prehistoric Japan requires, among other things, as Beardsley rightly reminds us, similar studies in prehistoric cultures of "the vast territory of boreal Eurasia and North America, a coniferous and mixed-hardwood forest zone stretching from Finland across Siberia and the Bering Strait into Canada and New York."[111]

Within the Japanese context, too, there is a series of unsolved problems—ethnological, linguistic, archeological, historical, cultural, and religious. In this connection, Hattori makes it very clear that while a philologist can and must take seriously the contribution of scholars of other disciplines, it is his duty to make the final judgment primarily on linguistic grounds.[112] In the study of early Japanese chronicles, Tsuda likewise proposes to study them most assiduously, first and foremost as written documents, even though he recognizes the importance of investigating the historical setting and cultural milieu in which these documents were written.[113] Similarly, in dealing with religion in the prehistoric and early historic periods, historians of religions should view it not simply as an interesting by-product of the process of culture-complex formation but as a genuine religious phenomenon with its own inner logic and structure, expressed in myths, symbols, rituals, and interhuman relations, however mixed they may have been in their origin.

[110] Oka tentatively attributed the Izanagi-Izanami myth to the Austroasian cultural component (B); however, he suggests that it might belong to the Austronesian component (D) (cf. Oka, "Nihon Bunka no Kios Kōzō," pp. 10-13).

[111] Beardsley, "Japan before History," p. 327. Similar views have been expressed by some Japanese scholars. Cf. Oka et al., *Nihon Minzoku no Kigen*; see also Aleksei P. Okladnikov, "The Role of the Ancient Baikal Region in the Cultural Relations between East and West," in Japanese National Commission for UNESCO, *International Symposium on History of Eastern and Western Cultural Contacts*, pp. 141-143.

[112] Hattori, *Nihongo*, p. 240.

[113] Tsuda, *Jōdai Nihon no Shakai oyobi Shisō*, p. 238.

This does not mean, of course, that historians of religions must neglect a critical analysis of the historic processes involved in the development of Japanese religion. Far from it. The ambiguous meaning of the term *kami* alone demands rigorous and multidimensional analysis and research. Its usual translation as "spirit" or "god" is quite unsatisfactory and misleading. Leaving aside the etymological origin of the term *kami*, we must bear in mind that it is used both to designate an impersonal quality, that is, the *kami* nature, somewhat analogous to the *numinous* or sacred, and as the other designation for specific beings endowed with the *kami* nature, be they human, divine, or other animate or inanimate beings.

As such, the pantheon of early Japan included, almost indiscriminately, numerous *kami* of diverse backgrounds.[114] Some of them show every indication of being mixtures of several different *kami*. Amaterasu, for example, came to be regarded as the ancestor and patron *kami* of the imperial clan in the historic period.[115] But she seems to have combined both the status of Takamimusubi, identified by Oka and others as the original chief celestial deity of the Altaic group, and the character of the sun-goddess in charge of agricultural food production, a popular deity of Austroasian origin. In the same vein, the names and characters of other *kami*, as well as those of rituals, festivals, and symbols, might have undergone transformation in the course of time.[116]

Corresponding to the enlargement of the pantheon was the development of Japanese society as the result of gradual fusion of various ethnic and cultural streams. The complexity of the early Japanese social order was due largely to the precarious mixture of different kinds of family, kinship, and social systems, for example matrilineal or patrilineal traditions and age-class or profession as the basis for social stratification. Oka postulates that the predominant pattern of society during the Yayoi period was that of *hara*, derived from the Tungusic term *hala* or *hala-kala* which is a designation of the exogamous patrilineal clans. When the Altaic group entered the scene as the ruling class, its

---

[114] Cf. D. C. Holtom, "The Meaning of Kami," *Monumenta Nipponica*, III, No. 1 (1940), 1-27. (See also Tsuda, *Jōdai Nihon no Shakai oyobi Shisō*, chap. ii, "Kami to Mikoto," pp. 147-238.)

[115] For a traditional account of this *kami* see A. Eustace Haydon, *Biography of the Gods* (New York, 1945), chap. viii, "Amaterasu-Omikami," pp. 199-217.

[116] Nominal Christianization of pagan deities in Europe has been pointed out by many scholars. For a similar transformation of local festivals and deities in India see McKim Marriott, "Little Communities in an Indigenous Civilization," in *Village India*, edited by him (Chicago, 1955), pp. 171-222. It must be kept in mind, however, that a dominant culture or civilization analogous to Christianity in Europe and Aryan civilization in India was lacking in Japan until the penetration of Sino-Korean civilization and of Buddhism in the later period.

uji, the designation of patriarchal clans, was superimposed on the earlier social structure based on *hara-kara*.[117] Oka further suggests that the early Japanese word *kabane*, a designation of occupational clans or groups, derives from the Altaic cultural tradition.[118] At any rate, most scholars agree that Japanese society during the early historic period (or the Kofun period) consisted of many independent *uji* (clans). Each *uji* had *uji-bito* (clansmen), *be* (various hereditary professional groups of persons who were not necessarily blood relations of the *uji-bito* but had permanent relations with the *uji*), and *nuhi* (slaves), all of which were ruled by *uji-no-kami* (the clan chieftain) who later received such honorary appelations as Ōmi, Muraji, Ōbito, Sukuri, or Kimi.[119]

Each *uji* was not only a social, economic, and political unit but also a unit of religious solidarity centering around the *uji-gami* or *uji-kami* (the *kami* of the clan). The *kami* of the clan and his or her shrine were attended to by the *uji-no-kami* (clan chieftain) with the assistance of his wife or sister. While the *kami* of the clan was considered the founder or ancestor of the clan, such a *kami* was venerated not only by the *uji-bito* (clansmen) but also by the members of the *be* who had no blood ties with the clansmen. When a certain clan expanded in size, and some parts of the clan—either clansmen or members of the *be*—had to migrate to a new area, they would establish a branch shrine dedicated to the same *uji-gami*; for the basis of group solidarity in early Japan was sharing the same clan *kami* and not necessarily blood relationship as such.[120] Should one powerful clan subjugate another, members of the latter were incorporated into the former by adopting the clan name of their new master. In such a case, the *kami* of the subjugated clan was propitiated and more often than not transformed into a kinsman of the *kami* of the conquering clan.

[117] Cf. Oka et al., *Nihon Minzoku no Kigen*, pp. 244-246. Today, the Japanese term *hara-kara* is used interchangeably with *kyōdai* ("brethren or kinfolk"), but this term was used as a synonym of *u-kara* and *ya-kara* in ancient Japanese. Ōno traces the origin of *hara-kara* to Manchu *hala*, Korean *kara*, Tungusic *kala*, and Mongolian *xala*, all of which have the meaning of nation, tribe, or kinfolk. He also traces the origin of the Japanese term *uji* (or *udi*) to the Korean term *ul* (tribe), to the Mongolian term *uru-q* (paternal kins), to the Turkish expression *uru* (relatives), and to the Buryat word *uri* (sons or descendants) (cf. Ōno, *Nihongo no Kigen*, pp. 135-136).

[118] UNESCO, *Japan*, pp. 114-115. Ancient Korean vocational groups were also given a general title expressed by a Chinese ideograph meaning "bone." Oka thinks that there was a definite relationship between the Japanese or Korean vocational group structure and the Mongolian patriarchal clan which was also known as "bone."

[119] Cf. Reischauer, *Early Japanese History*, pp. 8-13. Evidently, only those who had blood relations within the *uji* were known as *ukara*, whereas the term *yakara* included both *ukara* and *be*. See Aruga Kizaemon, "Nihon no Iye," in Nihon Jinruigaku-kai, *Nihon Minzoku*, p. 176.

[120] Ibid., pp. 178-179.

The life of the early Japanese was controlled not only by the *kami* of the clan to which they belonged but also by numerous other beings and things which had the *kami* nature. They are usually classified into four types—according to the geographical names, human names, names of things, and functions related to them—or two types—those which are related to social groups, such as clans or villages, and those which control health, fortune, and longevity of individuals.[121] Oka, on the other hand, attempts to classify spiritual beings into the following five types based on the different attitudes toward them on the part of the people. First is the *mono* or spiritual entity attached to human bodies or natural things. Second is the *tama* which may be translated as "soul," although it is not confined always to human bodies or other physical things. Third is the *marebito*, referring to spirits of the ancestors or ghosts who come from distant places to visit human communities. This belief is based on what Oka calls the horizontal cosmology and is related to the development of shrines. Fourth is the real *kami*, typologically speaking, although this term came to be used to designate all beings with the *kami* nature. This belief is based on a vertical cosmology, for *kami* were believed to descend from above to mountaintops, tall trees, forests, or pillars, and originally did not require shrines. Fifth is the celestial bodies, such as the sun, moon, stars, wind, and storms.[122]

However these spiritual beings are classified, it is understandable that the *uji-no-kami* (clan chieftains) were not equipped to deal with them, with the exception of the *kami* of their own clans. No doubt, they depended on many kinds of divination and fortune-telling. A Chinese account mentions the existence in the land of Wa (Japan) of the fortune-keeper who is selected when a group of people go on a voyage. This man "does not arrange his hair, does not rid himself of fleas, lets his clothing [get as] dirty as it will, does not eat meat, and does not approach women." When the voyage was successful, he was rewarded. If it was not, he was killed on the ground that "he was not scrupulous in his duties."[123] The same Chinese record describes a queen, Pimiko, who "occupied herself with magic and sorcery, bewitching the people." According to the writer of this document, Pimiko was not married and had a brother who assisted her in running

---

[121] Yanagita, *Minzokugaku Jiten*, pp. 119-120.

[122] Cf. Oka et al., *Nihon Minzoku no Kigen*, pp. 59-62 (see also Eliade, *Myth of the Eternal Return*, p. 71).

[123] Quoted from "History of the Kingdom of Wei" (*Wei Chih*) in *Japan in the Chinese Dynastic Histories*, trans. Tsumoda Ryusaku, ed. L. Carrington Goodrich (South Pasadena, Calif., 1951), p. 11.

the affairs of the state. She was secluded from people, and only one man "served her food and drink and acted as a medium of communication."[124] But not all the shamanic diviners were in high places. According to Oka, they can be classified into four main types. First is the *Miko*-A, a *Miko* (female shamanic diviner) who is usually a member of that family or clan. Her virginity is a necessary prerequisite. The medium's office is often handed down from aunt to niece. Second is the *Miko*-B who must be either a hereditary *Miko* attached to a shrine, serving as a medium between the *kami* of the shrine and the people who belong to that shrine, or a non-hereditary *Miko* of the countryside who is believed to be chosen by the *kami*. Third is the *Ichiko*, who is a professional traveling shamanic diviner, engaged in fortune-telling, transmission of spirit messages, and healing. It is believed that a special training period is required before an *Ichiko* can establish rapport with her patron *kami* or *tama*. Fourth is the *Monomochi*, either a male or female member of a certain family, believed to be permanently possessed by the *mono* (spirits) of specific animals, such as the fox, snake, or badger. The quality of *Monomochi* is usually handed down from one generation to the next through the female line.[125] While this typology of shamanic diviners is admittedly tentative, there is no doubt that various kinds of *Miko* and the like played important roles in the religious life of the early Japanese.

Of the rituals, ethical and other injunctions, and doctrinal development of this period, we know little. It is probably a mistake to think of early Japanese religion as a unified system with a highly developed theology, metaphysics, liturgics, ecclesiology, and ethics. It is even questionable whether it is appropriate to use such an expression as early Shinto for this phase of Japanese religion. The need of some designation for Japanese religion arose only when Buddhism was introduced later, and two Chinese characters—*shin*, for "*kami*," and *to*, for "the way"—were combined for this purpose. Thus, as Florenz pointed out, the term Shinto was really a translation of a Chinese expression into Japanese, and not the other way around.[126] Be that as it may, adoption of a name does not imply that the religion so designated was in effect a coherent system of beliefs and practices. On the contrary, there is every reason to suppose that early Japanese religion had within it several different traditions, and that it took many centuries before what may be rightly called Shinto took its shape. On the

[124] Ibid., p. 13.
[125] Oka et al., *Nihon Minzoku no Kigen*, pp. 62-84.
[126] Karl Florenz, "Die Japaner," *Lehrbuch der Religionsgeschichte*, ed. Alfred Bertholet and Eduard Lehmann (Tübingen, 1925), p. 267.

other hand, it is also a mistake to think that early Japanese religion is simply a name enveloping a mass of contradictory local religious practices scattered throughout the Japanese islands. Long before the compilation of the *Kojiki* and the *Nihonshoki*, people in Japan knew that they were not left alone, helpless, in this mysterious universe; for they possessed divine models for all human, social, and communal needs and activities. We try to trace the components of the culture complex and reconstruct the process of transmission and development of certain myths, beliefs, and symbols, as well as of cultural features. But people in Japan during the prehistoric and early historic periods, like their counterparts in other parts of the world, took it for granted that they or their ancestors had learned all the necessary knowledge and technique regarding social behavior and practical affairs from the world of the *kami* which was far away from, and yet closely related to, their world, such that the success or failure of their daily work, to say nothing of the meaning of the whole of life, was interpreted religiously.

PART II

Historic Development of Japanese Religion

2. "A Past of Things Present": Notes on Major Motifs of Early Japanese Religions

ALL RELIGIONS define the nature of reality as well as the meaning of space, time, and history by means of myths, doctrines, symbols, cults, and ecclesiastical structures. In this sense, historians of religions share the observation of William Ernest Hocking that religion is "by definition universal in extent as in norms of will: it speaks not primarily to the man-within-the-nation but to the man-within-the-world."[1] This view is most readily applicable to the cross-cultural, cross-national universalistic religions which tend to absorb certain characteristic religious emphases of particular groups and universalize them into a larger religious framework. But how, then, are historians of religions to understand the nature of those religions with a narrower base, such as an ethnic, cultural, or national group, which perceive the world in terms of the experiences of the particular groups involved? Obviously, different approaches are required in order to understand the characteristic ways in which these ethnically, culturally, or nationally based religions have harnessed the soteriological yearning of men and women to their particularistic perceptions of the world. In this study I intend to approach this problem by exploring several major motifs of early Japanese religion and the characteristic Japanese mode of integrating them. My goal is "a descriptive understanding"[2] of the religious ethos that underlies the configuration of these major motifs of the Japanese religious tradition as one example of the category of the nationally based religions.

---

[1] William Ernest Hocking, *The Coming World Civilization* (New York: Harper & Bros., 1956), p. 47.

[2] Joachim Wach (*Religionswissenschaft: Prolegomena zu ihrer wissenschafts-theoretischen Grundlegung* [Leipzig: J. C. Hinrichs, 1924], p. 68): "Die Aufgabe der Religionswissenschaft ist die Erforschung und Darstellung der empirischen Religionen. Sie ist eine beschreibend-verstehende, keine normative Wissenschaft. Mit der historischen und systematischen Bearbeitung der konkreten Religionsbildungen ist ihre Aufgabe erfüllt."

THE MONISTIC WORLD OF MEANING

As far as we can ascertain, the early Japanese took it for granted that the "world" was the world they knew and experienced in the Japanese archipelago.[3] No doubt they were vaguely aware of the existence of other lands, but these other lands were essentially beyond their horizon, consciousness, and concern. They also took it for granted that the natural world was the original world; that is, they did not look for another order of meaning behind the phenomenal, natural world—at least until they came under the influence of Sino-Korean civilization and Buddhism. The one-dimensional meaning structure of the early Japanese is implicit in the term *kami*—the root *mi* plus the prefix *ka*. According to Tsuda,

> *Mi* may be interpreted as a material thing or an embodied spirit possessing some kind of divine potency, or as a non-corporeal spirit, in either case believed to possess an intrinsic magic power, or established as an object of worship. Among corporeal objects of this nature may be numbered such physical elements as fire, water, wood and stone; certain animals; celestial bodies such as the sun and the moon; man-made objects such as swords and mirrors; agricultural products such as grain; and other objects of a similar nature. As for non-corporeal spirits, these include any non-visible elements or attributes having the power to exert some form of strong or violent influence on Nature or to affect man's existence.[4]

Usually the term *kami* refers to all beings that are awesome and worthy of reverence, including both good and evil beings. It would be misleading to consider the religion of the ancient Japanese, which came to be known later as Shinto—the way of the *kami*—as nature worship. While it accepted the plurality of the *kami* as separate beings and objects, its basic affirmation was the sacrality of the total world (cosmos) permeated as it was by the *kami* (sacred) nature.

The unitary world of meaning of the early Japanese is also evident in the ancient myths concerning a three-dimensional universe—the plain of high heaven (*Takama-no-hara*), the manifest world (*Utsu-shiyo*), and the nether world (*Yomotsu-kuni*). These three realms are portrayed as almost interchangeable, in that certain *kami* and heroes move back and forth freely among them. The gulf between the realm of the living and the realm of the dead also was blurred by the frequent

[3] For a fuller account of this motif, see J. M. Kitagawa, "Some Reflections on the Japanese World of Meaning," *Journal of the Oriental Society of Australia* 11 (1976): 3-18.

[4] Tsuda Sōkichi, "The Idea of Kami in Ancient Japanese Classics," *T'oung Pao* 52 (1966), chaps. 4-5, 294.

movements of spirits and ghosts and by other channels of communication, such as oracles, fortune telling, and divination.

With the penetration of Chinese civilization and Buddhism, the simplistic, unitary meaning structure of the early Japanese was greatly enriched. For example, Buddhism introduced the belief in the various realms of existence, whereas the Yin-Yang school offered cosmological theories based on the concepts of two principles (yin and yang), the five elements (metal, wood, water, fire, and earth), and the orderly rotation of these principles and elements in the formation of nature, seasons, and humankind. Nevertheless, these and other theories and concepts from outside never completely obliterated the early Japanese unitary meaning structure. It has, in fact, persisted to an amazing degree to our own time, as evidenced by the doctrines and practices of many of the so-called new religions.

NONSYMBOLIC UNDERSTANDING OF SYMBOLS

"Since man is a *homo symbolicus*, and all his activities involve symbolism," says Eliade, "it follows that all religious facts have a symbolic character. . . . When a tree becomes a cult object, it is not as a *tree* that it is venerated, but as a *hierophany*, that is, a manifestation of the sacred."[5] However, in early Japan, which held to a monistic world of meaning, symbols were not understood symbolically. The epistemological basis of the nonsymbolic understanding of the early Japanese was their aesthetic, magico-religious apprehension of the primeval totality as well as everything within it not as representations of *kami* but as *kami*. To be sure, their world was full of what we now refer to as symbols, but they did not realize that "symbols are a part of the process whereby the experienced world, the world of perception and concept, is created out of the world of physical reality. . . ."[6] Rather, they understood symbols in terms of direct paticipation. The closest analogy to this notion is found in ancient Egypt. According to John Wilson, when the ancient Egyptian said "that the king was Horus, he did not mean that the king was playing the part of Horus, he meant that

[5] Mircea Eliade, "Methodological Remarks on the Study of Religious Symbolism," in *The History of Religions: Essays in Methodology*, ed. M. Eliade and J. M. Kitagawa (Chicago: University of Chicago Press, 1959), p. 95.

[6] Dorothy D. Lee, "Symbolization and Value," in *Symbols and Values: An Initial Study*, ed. L. Bryson, L. Finkelstein, R. M. MacIver, and R. McKeon (New York: Conference on Science, Philosophy, and Religion in Their Relation to the Democratic Way of Life, Inc., 1954), p. 74.

the king *was* Horus, that the god was effectively present in the king's body during the particular activity in question."[7]

Such a motif of "participation," or nonsymbolic understanding of symbols, is clearly evident in the *Manyōshū* [Collection of myriad leaves], the oldest anthology of Japanese poems. In the introduction to one of its English translations, we read: "Japanese appreciation of nature, deep-rooted in religious sentiment, had long been cultivated through an intimate contact between nature and man. In the *Manyō* age nature was animated by such of its phenomena as were still looked upon with religious deference and were identified with personal emotions. . . . Even in such cases, where natural objects are dealt with purely as poetical material, they seem to retain each their individuality and life—a spiritual entity permeated by a mysterious atmosphere. Never are they allowed to lapse into cold lifeless rhetorical ornament or metaphor without some fringe of emotion."[8] To many *Manyō* poets, therefore, mountains were not only the *kami*'s dwelling places; mountains were the *kami* themselves. For example:

> Mount Futagami, round which flow
>   The waters of Imizu,
> When I come out and gaze upon it
> In the rich and blossomed spring,
> Or in the glorious leaf of autumn—
> How sublime it soars
> Because of its divinity,
> And how beautiful it stands,
> With its shapely peaks![9]

Another poet paid homage to the snow-covered Mount Tachi:

> Lofty beyond the mountains,
>   Bright in the rising sun
> Mount Tachi, a [*kami*] standing,
> As tells its sacred name,
> Soars in majesty to heaven
> Through thousandfold white clouds.
> . . . .
> The snow on Mount Tachi lies
> Unmelted all through summer,
> Thanks, indeed, to its divinity.[10]

[7] John A. Wilson, "Egypt," in *The Intellectual Adventure of Ancient Man*, by H. Frankfort, H. A. Frankfort, J. A. Wilson, T. Jacobsen, and W. A. Irwin (Chicago: University of Chicago Press, 1946), pp. 64-65.

[8] *The Manyōshū*, trans. *Nippon Gakujutsu Shinkōkai* (Tokyo: Iwanami Shoten, 1940; New York: Columbia University Press, 1969), p. lix.

[9] Ibid., pp. 144-145.

[10] Ibid., p. 183.

By far the most prominent was Fuji, the sacred mountain *par excellence.*

> Lo! There towers the lofty peak of Fuji
>> From between Kai and wave-washed Suruga.
> The clouds of heaven dare not cross it,
> Nor the birds of the air soar above it.
> The snows quench the burning fires,
> The fires consume the falling snow.
> It baffles the tongue, it cannot be named,
> It is a [*kami*] mysterious.
>
> . . . .
>
> In the Land of Yamato, the Land of the Rising Sun,
> It is our treasure, our tutelary [*kami*].
> It never tires our eyes to look up
> To the lofty peak of Fuji![11]

Similarly, *Manyō* poets sang to and about rivers, oceans, celestial and atmospheric phenomena, animals, birds, insects, and flowers as living beings possessing intimate relations with men and women. Indeed, to them "nature is man's friend and companion and there still exists a sense of mutual sympathy"[12] based on the appreciative awareness of the mutual participation that evokes reverence and affection on both sides. It is not surprising, therefore, that a poet, mourning the death of his beloved wife, wrote:

> Now I know not what to do or say,
> Vainly I seek soothing words
> From trees and stones.
>
> . . . .
>
> Over Mount Onu the fog is rising;
> Driven by my sighs of grief,
> The fog is rising.[13]

What we find throughout the *Manyō* poems is the poets' nonsymbolic understanding of symbols in terms of "participation" in a dual sense. On the one hand was the acceptance of the participation of the *kami* in the being of, say, a mountain, whereby the poet had the immediate sense of standing before the mountain which was the *kami*. That is to say, the mountain was the divine reality in itself and did not point to another reality, that is, the *kami*. At the same time, the poets had a keen sense of nature's participation in their lives as well as their participation in the life of nature. Thus, it was more than a literary embellishment when the poet wrote: "Driven by my signs of grief, the

[11] Ibid., p. 215.
[12] Ibid., p. lix.
[13] Ibid., pp. 198-199.

fog is rising." With such a vivid sense of mutual participation, the early Japanese took it for granted that there existed a continuity and correspondence between the capriciousness of human life and the swift change of the four seasons. Thus, a poet wrote on the uncertainty of life:

> When we look up to the plains of heaven
> The bright moon waxes and wanes;
> On the tree-tops of the mountains,
> Flowers bloom with spring,
> In autumn, with dew and frost,
> The coloured leaves are scattered in the blast.
> So it is with the life of a man:
> The rosy colour fades from the cheek,
> The black hair turns white,
> The morning smile is nowhere found at eve.[14]

In this poem, the poet did not engage in profound speculation about the uncertainty and transitoriness of life; he simply expressed his perception of intimate correlation between the rhythm of nature and that of human life. In so doing, he is not saying that a human being is simply an insignificant element of the natural world and that the meaning of human life is to be understood in terms of the rhythm of nature. He acknowledges that each human being is a reality and should be understood as such, just as each mountain, each river, and each tree exists by its own right. Nevertheless, the meaning of each being was sought not in itself but in its mutual participation, continuity, and correspondence to and with others within the total framework of the monistic world of meaning.

It should be stressed that the above is not meant to portray the historic condition of life in early Japan. Rather, our concern is to depict the characteristic attitude of the early Japanese toward life and the world as well as to what we now refer to as symbols. The actual life of the early Japanese, like that of their counterparts in other parts of the world, no doubt had its share of joy and sorrow, tragedy and happiness. And yet, as Muraoka succinctly points out, the early Japanese outlook "on life and the world was essentially one of unsophisticated optimism. . . . [To them], there could be no better world than this world. . . ."[15] There is every indication that the early Japanese affirmed life in this world, in spite of or even because of its transito-

---

[14] Ibid., p. 163.
[15] Tsunetsugu Muraoka, *Studies in Shinto Thought*, trans. Delmer M. Brown and James T. Araki (Tokyo: Ministry of Education, 1964), p. 59.

riness, as essentially good (*yoshi*) and beautiful (*uruwashi*). Significantly, "good" and "beautiful" were almost synonymous terms, so that the Chinese term *shan* (good or virtuous) was translated into the Japanese expression *uruwashi* (beautiful).[16] This may account for the easy fusion and homology of the aesthetic and religious experiences that have given a distinctive character to the Japanese religious tradition.

THE NATION AS THE MEASURE OF ALL THINGS

As stated earlier, the world—to the early Japanese—was the world they knew and experienced in the Japanese archipelago. It was a special world, hallowed as it was by the participation and the presence of the *kami*. Remarkably, this simple ethnocentric view of the world, very common among pre- and early historic peoples, became the foundation for a full-scale religio-political belief in the sacrality of Japanese national community in the historic period.[17] This does not mean that the nation dictated all dimensions of human activity in Japan, but it implies that the nation became—to paraphrase the Sophists' maxim—the "measure of all things."

Scholars generally hold that the appearance of certain pottery marks from around the fourth millennium B.C. might be considered our earliest evidence of Japan's prehistory, a period lasting until around the second or third century A.D. While we know very little for certain about religious development during the prehistoric period, it is safe to assume that the Japanese had no unified system of beliefs and practices.[18] Most religious functions, except for those in the homes, probably took place around a sacred tree (*himorogi*), sacred rock (*iwasaka*), or in the paddy field and the seashore. It is worth noting in this connection that Chinese records mention the existence in Japan around the third century A.D. of a number of what amount to tribal states of varying size which recognized the religious and political authority of the chief ruler above them. We can only speculate as to where in Japan such a loosely organized kingdom existed and whether or not it was the only kingdom of this sort. According to Chinese sources, some of these Japanese rulers paid tribute to the Chinese courts at various times and received monarchical titles in turn. Based primarily on these

[16] Ibid., p. 58.

[17] For a fuller discussion of this topic, see J. M. Kitagawa, "The Japanese *Kokutai* (National Community): History and Myth," *History of Religions* 13, no. 3 (February 1974): 209-226.

[18] It should be stated that several important works that have relevance to this subject have appeared since I published "Prehistoric Background of Japanese Religion," *History of Religions* 2, no. 2 (Winter 1963): 292-328. [Chapter 1 of this book.]

Chinese accounts, Wheatley and See suggest that the court of the Japanese ruler during that period had some of the characteristic features of a "ceremonial center" which served as the focus of cosmic, social, political, and moral order.[19]

The early historic period, from roughly A.D. 250-300 to 600, corresponds to what archaeologists refer to as the *Kofun* (tomb or tumulus) period, so called because of gigantic mausoleums constructed for aristocrats during this period. Judging from the geographical distribution of these grand-scale tombs, it is evident that the center of political gravity was then situated in the central region (*uchitsu-kuni*) covering the Yamato plain in the present Nara prefecture and its neighboring districts. Unfortunately, we cannot determine conclusively who founded the so-called Yamato kingdom, whether or not there were dynastic changes, and whether the noticeable cultural change in the middle of the *Kofun* period was due to the invasion of a new tribe from Northeast Asia which became the new ruling house of Japan.[20] But we do know that this period witnessed the gradual structural transformation of the Japanese nation from a tribal confederation to a centralized national community under a sacred kingship.

Most scholars agree that the early Yamato kingdom was little more than a confederation of powerful and autonomous *uji* (lineage group usually translated as "clan"). Each *uji* had its blood-related nucleus members (*uji-bito*), various hereditary groups not related by blood but serving the *uji* as a professional work force (*be* or *tomo*), as well as servants and slaves (*nuhi*), all of whom were ruled by the chieftain of the *uji* (*uji-no-kami*). Each *uji* was not only a social, economic, political, and often military unit but also a unit of religious solidarity centering around its progenitor/tutelary *kami* (*uji-gami*), who was usually attended by the chieftain of the *uji*. In a sense, sharing the same *kami* was more important than blood relations. In the event that a certain *uji* should be subjugated by another, the *uji-bito* of the former group were incorporated into the structure of the latter, whereas the *kami* of the former was sometimes venerated as an auxiliary *kami* of the latter *uji*. Among all the *uji* groups that constituted the Yamato confederation the most powerful was the *uji* which claimed solar ancestry; it also excelled in military affairs. In the course of time the chieftains of this *uji* gradually solidified their influence over other *uji* chieftains and received the kingly title from China by paying tribute to the Chinese

[19] Paul Wheatley and Thomas See, *From Court to Capital: A Tentative Interpretation of the Origins of the Japanese Urban Tradition* (Chicago: University of Chicago Press, 1978), p. 75.

[20] See Kitagawa, "Prehistoric Background of Japanese Religion," pp. 309-311.

50

imperial court. They began to assume royal prerogatives within the Yamato confederation, conferring court titles (*kabane*) on other prominent *uji* chieftains, granting sacred seed at spring festivals, and establishing sacred sites for various *kami* as well as regulating rituals for them. But, as Waida points out, the chieftain of the imperial *uji* "was not the absolute monarch ruling over a centralized state but a *primus inter pares* who ran the politics, controlling and being controlled by [other *uji* chieftains in the court]."[21] In fact, the history of the Yamato kingdom was one of a constant power struggle between the imperial and other *uji* chieftains as well as rivalry among several scheming *uji* chieftains. It is also a matter of interest to learn from Korean sources that in the mid-fourth century A.D. the Yamato court, or at least the imperial and some other *uji* chieftains, gained a foothold in the southern tip of the Korean peninsula.

With the penetration of Sino-Korean civilization and Buddhism from the fifth century onward, Japan was destined to undergo a series of social, political, and cultural changes. In addition to the cosmological theories of the Yin-Yang school which have been mentioned earlier, two universal principles, Tao and Dharma, were introduced by Confucianism and Buddhism, respectively. Under the impact of Confucianism and Buddhism, the Japanese were compelled to create a designation for their hitherto unsystematized religious tradition. For this purpose they borrowed two Chinese characters—*shin* for *kami*, and *tō* or *dō* for the "way." The adoption of the nomenclature Shinto only magnified the inevitable tension between the indigenous Japanese understanding of the meaning of life and the world—authenticated solely by their "particular" historic experience—and the claims of Confucianism and Buddhism that their teachings were grounded in "universal" laws and principles. The first serious attempt to deal with this tension was made, if we follow the official chronicles, by Prince-Regent Shōtoku (573-621). He tried to affirm Shinto, Confucianism, and Buddhism simultaneously by holding them in balance, as it were, in the so-called *Seventeen-Article Constitution*. In spite of his devotion to Buddhism and advocacy of Confucian virtues, however, the official chronicles indicate above all his dedication to the cause of solidifying the Japanese nation by appropriating Buddhism and Confucianism in order to uphold the divine prerogative of the throne.[22]

[21] Manabu Waida, "Sacred Kingship in Early Japan: A Historical Introduction," *History of Religions* 15, no. 4 (May 1976): 323.

[22] See "Religions of Japan," in *The Great Asian Religions: An Anthology*, compiled by Wing-tsit Chan, Isma'īl Rāgī al Fārūqī, Joseph M. Kitagawa, and P. T. Raju (New York: Macmillan Publishing Co., 1969), pp. 241, 252-254.

51

During the Taika reform era, which lasted fifty years from A.D. 645, a serious effort was made in the name of the sovereign to replace the *uji*-based court system with a centralized national government structure staffed by the sinified bureaucracy. This attempt was only partially successful, largely because of the residual power of the former *uji*-chieftains and provincial magnates. The reform measures, however, resolved the tension between the particular and the universal decidedly in favor of the former. Shinto was given a preferred status over Confucianism and Buddhism in that the new government structure placed the Council of *Kami* Affairs side by side with the Council of State, both of which were directly accountable to the throne. Confucianism and Buddhism failed to dislodge the institutional supremacy of Shinto because, as Miller points out: "It had for long been inextricably fused with some of the basic considerations that determined the social rank, status and position of the sovereign and the imperial house, and of the many lineage [*uji*] groups that comprised the top strata of Japan's aristocratic society. The pantheon of the native cult [Shinto] provided the majority of such groups with their *kami* progenitors whose alleged relative ranking in mythological times was a direct reflection of the relative ranking and status of their descendants in the seventh century."[23] The underlying rationale of the government reform was two-fold. On the one hand, it was thought that the head of the imperial house had the right and obligation to rule Japan by virtue of being the direct descendant of the Sun Line. On the other hand, the sovereign was the "Manifest *kami*," whose divine will was now promulgated in the form of the "imperial rescript."

The so-called Ritsuryō (imperial rescript) state, referring to the religio-political structure envisaged in the seventh century, was a form of "immanental theocracy."[24] This state was the extension, refinement, and institutional expression of the early Japanese ethnocentric view of the world. And, although the all-comprehensive government structure envisioned by the seventh-century reformers was never fully implemented, the Ritsuryō ideal remained a paradigm in the corporate psyche of the Japanese, authenticating their particular understanding and experience of Japan as the world.

The subsequent development of the Japanese religious tradition confirms that this paradigm was shared by Buddhists, Confucianists, and many Christians in recent history as well. For example, the phrase

[23] Richard J. Miller, *Ancient Japanese Nobility: The Kabane Ranking System* (Berkeley and Los Angeles: University of California Press, 1974), pp. 10-11.
[24] See Kitagawa, "The Japanese *Kokutai* (National Community): History and Myth," p. 219.

Dai Nippon (Great Japan) was first used by Dengyō (767-822), the founder of the Tendai school of Buddhism in Japan, who himself had studied in China.[25] Later, Nichiren (1222-1282), the founder of the Buddhist school bearing his name, in commenting on the passage, "the Buddha appeared in the world," in the *Lotus Sūtra*, stated: "By 'world' Japan is meant." He thereby implied a radical reinterpretation of the Indian Buddhists' notion of the "world" (*lokadhātu*) as "the area on which the light of the sun and moon shines, i.e., the four Continents around Mt. Sumeru."[26] Similarly, many of the Japanese Confucianists, from Kumazawa Banzan (1665-1691) to Fujita Tōko (1805-1855), reinterpreted Confucian ethical universalism so as to uphold Japan's claim to be a unique divine nation. In this connection, Nakamura astutely observes that although nationalism has been advocated by many thinkers in India, China, and the West, "their nationalism was theoretically concerned with the state in general, not with their particular states," whereas in Japan "the particular state of Japan came to be the sole standard upon which all judgments were based."[27] In short, Japanese religious tradition has rarely questioned the ancient Japanese principle that Japan was the world and that the nation, that is, the Japanese nation, was "the measure of all things."

"A PAST OF THINGS PRESENT"

One of the prominent features of the Japanese religious tradition is its unique perception of the meaning of history. It had been nurtured by the monistic world of meaning even before the Japanese learned the art of writing and the importance of historiography from China after coming under the influence of Sino-Korean civilization in the fifth and sixth centuries. We do not intend to deal here with the intricate problem of how the Chinese script, derived from a very different world view and featuring highly developed pictographs, ideographs, and phonetic compounds, was appropriated to a simple, spoken Japanese language with no structural similarities to the Chinese. Nor can we analyze the genre, sources, and contents of such mythohistorical works as the *Kojiki* [Records of ancient matters] and the *Nihongi* or *Nihon-shoki* [Chronicles of Japan], which utilized Chinese scripts.

We must bear in mind, however, that before the Japanese learned the art of writing, they had rich memories of their past, which had

---

[25] Hajime Nakamura, *Ways of Thinking of Eastern Peoples: India-China-Tibet-Japan*, ed. Philip P. Wiener (Honolulu: East-West Center Press, 1964), p. 434.

[26] Ibid., p. 443.

[27] Ibid., pp. 447-448.

been transmitted orally from generation to generation. We read in the preface to the *Kojiki* that there was one Hieda no Are, a young court attendant, who "possessed such great native intelligence that he could repeat orally whatever met his eye, and whatever struck his ears was indelibly impressed in his heart."[28] Presumably, there were others like him who were expert in remembering the lore of the past and/or the knowledge of local legends. It must also be mentioned in this connection that those who were engaged in writing and editing official chronicles in the seventh and eighth centuries were members of the cultural elite. Otherwise they would have lacked the time, opportunity, and motivation to study the native lore as well as to acquire the ability to read and write Chinese. Moreover, unlike the critical historians of our own time, the early Japanese chroniclers were court officials, and as such they shared the outlooks and policies of the government. Thus, they viewed the past history of Japan—reversing the Augustinian formula—as "a past of things present."[29] As the preface of the *Kojiki* explicitly states, it was the task of the chroniclers to correct the mistakes and corruptions of available court documents and provincial records as seen from their "present" perspective. Such a project had its own agenda, rectifying the "mistaken" facts and "corrupt" documents and rearranging if need be the sequence of events in order to recreate or create the past as an integral constituent element of the present.

In the unitary meaning structure of the ancient Japanese various levels of reality coalesced, and the past, present, and future were not seen as mutually exclusive. To be sure they were conscious of time and seasons, but time and season were part of the rhythm of nature. Thus, time was not perceived as an independent reality apart from nature. Moreover, while the early Japanese no doubt recognized that each event had both precedents and consequences, they were not particularly concerned with ordering chronologically the sequence of different events in any strict sense. To them what mattered were only those events which appeared on their horizon, and they viewed those events simultaneously, as many of us today look at distant stars simultaneously, regardless of the difference in distance of these stars. We have already hinted that such a poetic, immediate, and simultaneous awareness was a prominent feature of *Manyō* poems. But those *Manyō* poets, who had a keen sense of the intimate relations between themselves and things as well as events, had no historical interest in our sense of the

[28] *Kojiki*, trans. with intro. and notes by Donald L. Philippi (Princeton, N.J.: Princeton University Press, 1969), pp. 41-42.

[29] Augustine, *The Confessions* (Great Books of the Western World, vol. 18) (Chicago: Encyclopaedia Britannica, 1952), bk. 11, p. 95.

term. Thus, "on the occasion of the transfer of the court from Fujiwara to Nara," which was a major event in the eighth century, the poet only expressed his own psychical reaction to this event.

> Obedient to our mighty Sovereign's word,
> I left my long-loved home,
> And paddled my boat down the Hatsuse,
> Many times looking back toward my home,
> At each of the eighty windings of the river;
> And benighted on the stream I reached
> The River Saho flowing through Nara;
> There from my couch I could see,
> Clearly in the bright moonlight of dawn,
> The night-frost lying like a sheet of linen
> And the river bound with ice as if with rocks.
> Often on such a freezing night, loyal to my duties,
> I paddled down to build the mansion,
> Where I hope my lord will live
> For a thousand ages,
> And that I too may journey here for as long.[30]

Obviously, the old court at Fujiwara and the new capital at Nara, his old home and new residence, the rivers, and the moon were important features of this poet's horizon, but the poet was concerned with neither the sequence of events which had led to the transfer of the court, nor the economic and social factors involved in it.

Similar indifference to historical sequence characterized the provincial historical and geographical records entitled *fudoki* (literally, "records of wind and earth"). These records were compiled by provincial officials in the eighth century in response to the court edict to "make a catalogue of silver, copper, grasses, trees, birds, fish, insects, etc. . . . explain the origin of the names of the mountains, rivers, and plains; report interesting events and traditions. . . ."[31] But the histories of various localities were given in terms of an interesting fusion of myths, legends, and stories. For example, the *Hitachi Fudoki* begins as follows: "When asked about the traditions of the province and counties, the elders answered by saying, 'in ancient times . . .' "[32] In the *Izumo Fudoki*, the historical background of Izumo was explained in terms of myth: "Izumo was named after the words of the God Yatsu-kamizu Omizunu. The august Omizunu . . . spoke majestically,

---

[30] *The Manyōshū*, p. 259.
[31] *Hitachi Fudoki*, with intro. and trans. by Akashi Mariko et al., in *Traditions* 1, no. 2 (1976): 23.
[32] Ibid., p. 27.

'Clouds-rising Izumo is a narrow strip of young land. When the creator gods established the land of Izumo . . .' "[33] The provincial officials who compiled those documents selected those folk stories and myths that were particularly relevant to the expanding imperial government rather than preserving the objectivity and integrity of the historical data as such.

The tendency to view the present and past simultaneously from the perspective of the present is more explicit in the *Kojiki* [Records of ancient matters] and the *Nihongi* [Chronicles of Japan]. The compilation of these mythohistorical works was ordered by the Emperor Temmu after he usurped the throne by defeating a coalition of *uji* groups which had sided with the heir of the Emperor Tenchi. The new emperor established the eight-graded court-rank (*kabane*) system ostensibly to solidify his regime. According to Miller, Temmu's new court-rank system not only gave precedence to imperial relatives as might be expected, but "it also recognized the contributions and influence of other lineage [*uji*] groups not related by blood to the Sun Line, groups which were believed to have been of *kami* or deity lineage. . . . [Also] the lower ranking *kabane* of the new system were intended for *uji* that represented an uneven amalgam of descent types, degrees of power and influence, and service to the Sun Line and the state in both remote antiquity and more recent times."[34] In this situation, the new "present" called for the new "past," rectifying the "mistaken" facts and "corrupt" documents, as stated in the preface to the *Kojiki*. Significantly, the chroniclers perceived two or three factors simultaneously on their horizon: (1) the cosmogonic and other "heavenly" myths that authenticated the genealogical backgrounds of the imperial *uji* (the Sun Line) and of other prominent *uji* which claimed the *kami* lineage; (2) mythohistorical accounts of activities and events connected with the forebears of the imperial and other prominent *uji* who, in accordance with the alleged mandate of the Sun deity, pacified the world, that is, Japan, and established the national community under the sacred king; and, in the case of the *Nihongi* (3) contemporary events that proved the legitimacy of Temmu's regime both in terms of the Shinto mythohistorical tradition and of the *Sūtra of the Sovereign Kings of the Golden Radiance* (*Konkō myō saishō ō gyō*). The latter explicated a Buddhist doctrine that a monarch is "a son of divine being"

[33] *Izumo Fudoki*, trans. with intro. by Michiko Yamaguchi Aoki (Tokyo: Sophia University, 1971), p. 82.
[34] Miller, *Japanese Nobility*, p. 16.

(*Tenshi, devaputra*) "to whom has been given a mandate of Heaven, and whom Heaven will protect."[35]

It was also symptomatic of the ethos of the seventh and eighth century that the chroniclers appropriated the model of Chinese dynastic histories in creating Japan's past history. But in order to do so they had to translate the above-mentioned three factors of their circular horizon into a horizontal, spatial, chronological format by superimposing the Chinese calendrical system on their newly conceived past history,[36] which was now supposed to have commenced in 660 B.C. Moreover, they had placed the so-called age of *kami* as though it chronologically had preceded the historic beginning of the Japanese nation. In spite of such an arbitrary chronological format in the *Kojiki* and *Nihongi*, it is easy to detect the chroniclers' simultaneous apprehension of the present and the past. For example, the prominent activity of the progenitor/deity of the Fujiwara *uji*, Ame no Koyane, in the plain of high heaven and the contemporary activity of the rising Fujiwara *uji* were simultaneous events on the circular horizon of the chroniclers. Or, the *Nihongi*'s account of the legendary first emperor, Jimmu—"In Kashiha-bara in Unebi, he mightily established his palace-pillars on the foundation of the bottom-rock, and reared aloft the cross roof-timbers to the Plain of High Heaven"[37]—was probably the chroniclers' contemporary perception of the monarchs under whom they served.

Significantly, later historians and biographers considered the mytho-historical accounts of the *Kojiki* and *Nihongi* as "a past of things present" as well. In another study I would like to pursue this inquiry by examining the horizon of medieval Japanese historians, especially that of Jien (1145-1225), son of the Regent Fujiwara Tadamichi and prelate of the Tendai monastery at Mount Hi'ei, who authored the *Gukanshō* [Miscellany of personal views of an ignorant fool], and Kitabatake Chikafusa (1293-1354), a royalist general and a devout Shintoist, who authored the *Jinnō-shōtō-ki* [Records of the legitimate succession of the divine sovereigns]. Both Jien and Chikafusa used the imperial chronicles as the basic source for their respective historical studies. Both of them assumed that the previous history of Japan was

[35] Nakamura, *Eastern Peoples*, p. 437.

[36] On this problem, see J. H. Kamstra, *Encounter or Syncretism: The Initial Growth of Japanese Buddhism* (Leiden: E. J. Brill, 1967), pp. 59-65.

[37] *Nihongi: Chronicles of Japan from the Earliest Times to A.D. 697*, trans. W. G. Aston (the first printing by the Japan Society in 1896; Rutland, Vt.: Charles E. Tuttle Co., 1978), p. 132.

"a past of things present." But each of them tried to recast the past history so as to unfold the meaning of the present as the focus of the historical existence of humankind. It was Jien who postulated the reason (*dōri*) as the "permanent universal cyclical law of life and from the end to the beginning which encompasses all history." Thus, he asserts that "to keep in mind 'reason' is then to know the past and the future."[38] Chikafusa, on the other hand, starting from the mythological affirmation of the "eternity" of the imperial line, tries to elicit the "true' reasons" of history. What is new in the medieval historical works is that not only the past history is "a past of things present" but the future is also "a future of things present." Nevertheless, medieval Japanese historians inherited the affirmation of their earlier predecessors concerning the centrality and eternality of the present, as succinctly expressed in Chikafusa's famous statement, "The beginning of Heaven and Earth is today."[39]

[38] Kuroda Toshio, "Gukanshō and Jinnō Shōtōki: Observations on Medieval Historiography," in *New Light on Early and Medieval Japanese Historiography*, trans. John A. Harrison, (University of Flordia Monographs, Social Sciences, no. 4) (Gainesville: University of Florida, 1959), p. 29.

[39] Ibid., p. 38.

3. Some Remarks on the Study of Sacred Texts

A S A HISTORIAN of religions I have been concerned with the relationship between oral tradition and written texts, especially in the context of those religions that do not recognize "canons." Obviously, those religions that have accepted a set of canonical scriptures as normative have developed rules and principles for interpreting their sacred texts by a group of specialists. In fact, Jewish, Christian and Islamic theologies have been decisively influenced by the hermeneutical developments of their canons in their respective religious communities. It is to be noted in this connection that the discipline of history of religions is greatly indebted to theological and/or biblical hermeneutics in developing its own principles and methods for dealing with written texts of various religions, despite the fact that many historians of religions have not appropriated the so-called "pneumatic exegesis" which is based on the claim that there exists a certain affinity between the experiential background of the biblical interpreter and that which is interpreted.[1] Significantly, historians of religions encounter a different set of problems in dealing with religious traditions that do not recognize canonical scriptures. In many of those "non-book religions," oral traditions, or written records of oral traditions, play important roles (although the degree of normativity of those oral traditions or written records varies greatly from one religious context to another). I would like now to turn to two concrete examples, the oral tradition of the Ainu epics called the *yukar* and the ancient Japanese classics, with the hope of delineating the hermeneutical problems involved with each.

THE AINU EPICS (*Yukar*)

I have already discussed elsewhere the bewildering question regarding the relationship between the Ainu and the Japanese: two peoples with different ethnic, linguistic, cultural and religious backgrounds living side by side for at least two thousand years with a minimum of

[1] See Joachim Wach, "The Interpretation of Sacred Books," *Journal of Biblical Literature*, Vol. LV, Part 1 (1936), 61.

interpenetration between them.[2] The present-day Ainus are the descendants of an archaic ethnic group that originated somewhere in central or northern Siberia, from whence they migrated to Sakhalin, Hokkaido, and the Kurile Islands shortly before the Christian era. During the course of slow migration the Ainu came into contact with a number of other ethnic groups including the Samoyed, the Ostyak, the Vogul, the Tungusic, and the Turkic. Importantly, while some Ainu words, symbols, and rituals have some similarities with those of other Paleo-Siberian groups, the Ainu have preserved to the present century their own distinct language as well as a persistent cultural and religious structure conforming to their ancient past. It is interesting to note that the Ainu verb "to speak (*ru-cha-no-ye* or *ru-pa-no-ye*) means to "utter words with rhythm." On formal or ceremonial occasions, when for example they offer prayers or when they engage in negotiation, they are expected to "chant" or "sing" (*sa-ko-ye*: "speak with rhythm") because they believe that without proper rhythm the real potency of words cannot be fully actualized.

One of the amazing facts about the Ainu is that without the aid of written notes they have orally transmitted the rich variety of *yukar* (sacred epics), many of which contain 2,000 to 3,000 lines while the longest ones extend to 10,000 lines. Evidently, the numinous quality of the rhythmic words is such that the *yukar* could only be handed down orally from generation to generation. Only in our own time have a series of *yukar* (memorized by Kannari Matsu) been edited, translated into Japanese and published by Dr. Kyosuke Kindaichi under the title, *Yukara-shu* (Collection of *yukar*); thus far eight volumes have been published.[3] Usually the *yukar* is divided into five categories:

(1) the shamanistic chants or witch songs (*tusu-sinotcha*), believed to be the utterances of the *kamuy* (divine spirits) given through the mouth of the shamaness (*tusu-kur*) during the state of ecstatic possession;

(2) the songs of the *kamuy* (*kamuy-yukar*), which are tales about the *kamuy* narrated by themselves;

(3) the sacred legends (*oina*, also called *oina-yukar* or *kamuy-yukar*), which contain the teachings of the central character of the Ainu pantheon, Oina-kamuy, who is the prototype of the Ainu;

(4) the epics of the hero (*ainu yukar*), which are autobiographical

[2] J. M. Kitagawa, "Ainu Bear Festival (Iyomante)," *History of Religions*, Vol. I, No. 1 (Summer 1961), 95-151.

[3] For further discussion on the *Yukar*, see J. M. Kitagawa, "Ainu Myths," in *Myths and Symbols: Studies in Honor of Mircea Eliade*, ed. by J. M. Kitagawa and C. H. Long (Chicago: University of Chicago Press, 1969), pp. 309-323.

accounts of the adventures of the Ainu hero *par excellence*, Poi-yaumbe; and

(5) the romantic poems or the epics of women (*menoko yukar*).

The study of the *yukar*, like the study of any oral tradition trans-mitted through generations without the aid of written language and records in other parts of the world, presents a number of difficulties that are linguistic, historical, and cultural in nature. The most funda-mental question is whether one should begin with the study of *yukar* or with the study of the Ainu religion and culture as a whole. (Par-enthetically, I might mention that one of my colleagues at Chicago who is working on the Assyrian Dictionary project tells me how im-portant it is for Assyriologists to try to understand the total context of the Assyrian culture, society, and religion in order to comprehend the meaning of particular symbols, myths or rituals.)

In dealing with the *yukar* of the Ainu, I also adhere to a holistic approach. One must acquire sufficient linguistic competence in order to see how the contents of the oral tradition can be construed in the linguistic system of the Ainu as a whole. For example, ancient Ainus regarded rivers as living beings that sleep at night and lose weight in the summer. Rivers were regarded in female terms, so that the mouth of the river was called "o" (the term for the female sexual organ), through which fish enter the body of the river. Even today, the Ainu talk about the river climbing the mountain. From the study of the Ainu language, we learn that the Ainu universe is based on the inter-penetration of numerous kinds of worlds (*moshiri*: "floating earth"), and that the pattern of life in all the *moshiri* is not too different from life in the Ainu village (*kotan*). By far the most frequently used word in the Ainu language is *kamuy*, which is usually translated as "god," "gods," or "spirits." According to the Ainu, the entire universe is per-meated by numerous *kamuy*. Thus, when two persons greet each other, it signifies an encounter between one's *kamuy* and another per-son's *kamuy*.

In my study of the *yukar* of the Ainu, I have come to appreciate the importance of Joachim Wach's notion of "re-cognition," which, ac-cording to him, was the hermeneutical task of "re-cognizing" the meaning of what had been "cognized,"[4] in this case, by the Ainu com-munity. Such a task is far from being a mechanical enterprise; it re-quires creative imagination and reflection in order to construe the meaning-structure of the *yukar*. It is worth noting that the term *yukar*

---

[4] J. M. Kitagawa, "Verstehen and Erlösung: Some Remarks on Joachim Wach's Work," *History of Religions*, Vol. 11, No. 1 (August 1971), 37-38.

means "to imitate" (*i-ukar*) in the sense that the reciter imitates either the manner of the animals or birds which are to be hunted or the personal adventures told by the *kamuy* whom Ainu men and women imitate and follow. By "imitating," the Ainus mean more than impersonating or copying the voice and movements of another being, be it *kamuy*, hero, animal, or bird. Rather, they mean that when one imitates some other being, one can, by magical potency of the rhythmic language, fully participate in the person or being whose words he is reciting or chanting.

There was a time when I considered oral tradition primarily as an archaic legacy of people living in the precivilized stage of civilization. My study of the *yukar*, superficial though it is, has convinced me that oral tradition represents a different mode of religious perception and meaning. I have come to realize that by chanting or listening to the rhythmic words of the *kamuy*, hero, animal, and bird, all of whom are endowed with the *kamuy* nature, the indivisibility of man and *kamuy* becomes renewed and reinforced for Ainu men and women. In this sense, the recitation of the *yukar* is a sacramental act. Admittedly, the Ainu never developed great religious and cultural traditions as did the other peoples of Asia. But they have preserved a very creative way of committing their sacred traditions of myths, history, law, art, science and religion to the *yukar*, which have been "imitated," respected, enjoyed, and followed as the foundation of the community of shared experience.

Professor E. D. Hirsch, Jr., cautions us against three interpretive theories when dealing with written texts. They are: (1) radical historicism, which claims that the meaning of a text is "what it means to us today"; (2) psychologism, which asserts that the meaning of a text is "what it means to me"; (3) autonomism, which views the meaning of a text as independent of that which it was intended to mean.[5] One has to be far more vigilant about these three temptations when we try to "re-cognize" what has been "cognized" by the bearers of oral traditions.

THE ANCIENT JAPANESE CLASSICS

If the study of the Ainu epics (*yukar*) presents difficulties because they are represented in an oral tradition, the study of the ancient Japanese classics presents a different set of problems because (1) they were originally based on oral traditions, (2) they were compiled in order to

[5] E. D. Hirsch, Jr., *Validity of Interpretation* (New Haven: Yale University Press, 1967), pp. viii-ix and 39.

uphold certain religio-political principles, (3) they depended on Chinese historical writings as their model, and (4) they appropriated Chinese scripts and concepts in varying degrees. Moreover, none of these classics was ever recognized as "canon" by Shinto, even though they acquired semi-canonical status in the loose sense of the term.

I have cited important Japanese classics in my paper, "Oral and Written Documentation of Religious Tradition: Early Shinto—a Case Study."[6] As I mentioned in that paper, the compilation of the *Kojiki* (The Records of Ancient Matters) and *Nihongi* (The Chronicles of Japan) was ordered in A.D. 673 by Emperor Temmu in part to justify his accession to the throne after he usurped it from another emperor. By the time these two documents were completed in the eighth century (the *Kojiki* in 712; the *Nihongi* in 720) Japanese intelligentsia were well acquainted with the literary, legal, and philosophical traditions of China. Nevertheless, the compilers of the *Kojiki* and *Nihongi* managed to incorporate vast amounts of indigenous materials, e.g., myths, legends, and folklore which had been handed down through "oral tradition" until their time. Between the two, there is no question that the *Kojiki* preserved more features of oral traditions. Motoori Norinaga (1730-1801), a well-known Shinto scholar and philologist, went so far as to say that "the *Kojiki* accurately records what was orally transmitted from antiquity, without any artificial addition."[7] Nevertheless, the compilers of the *Kojiki* edited and interpreted orally transmitted myths, for example, into literary forms so that the materials in that volume are, at best, hybrid oral tradition. Ironically, these ancient Japanese classics were studied until the last century almost exclusively by scholars of Shinto and the National Learning (*kokugaku*) to support their ideologies. Only in our century, thanks to the influence of Western historical scholarship, especially the school of von Ranke, did Japanese scholars such as Kume Kunitake (1839-1931) and Tsuda Sōkichi (1873-1961) begin to engage in textual criticism of the Japanese classics. Since the end of World War II, with the assurance of academic freedom, scholars of mythology, folklore, ethnology, history of religions, literature, and history (both Marxist and non-Marxist) have been engaged in the critical study of the genre and contents of the Japanese classics.[8]

[6] Presented at the European Study Conference of the International Association for the History of Religions (IAHR) held at Turku, Finland, Summer 1974.

[7] Cited in Shigeru Matsumoto, *Motoori Norinaga 1730-1801* (Cambridge: Harvard University Press, 1970), p. 77.

[8] Ken Matsumaye, *Nihon Shinwa no Keisei* (Formation of Japanese Myths) (Tokyo: Hanawa Shobo, 1970), pp. 489-509.

The compilers of the eighth-century classics were government officials, who viewed the meaning of Japanese history, religion and culture from the perspective of the "immanental theocracy," which was established in the mid-seventh century. By that time, the government administration was no longer dictated by the precarious will of the *kami* transmitted to the emperor through dreams and divination; it was, instead, determined by legal principles and precedents based on the universal principle of Tao that had been introduced from China. Yet, as it turned out in practice, the universal principle of Tao was subordinated to the authority of the emperor who, by virtue of being the descendent of the Sun deity, was destined to rule and reign over the nation. Moreover, the sovereign, now being considered as the Manifest Kami, was expected to communicate his divine will through a series of "imperial rescripts." The religio-political structure thus developed in the seventh and eighth centuries is referred to as the "Ritsuryō (imperial rescript) state." Understandably, the meaning of the Japanese classics was given by the immanental theocratic principle of the government.[9]

Undoubtedly the eighth-century chroniclers in Japan were greatly indebted to Chinese historical writings. Indeed, it was the influence of Chinese thought that initially aroused the historical consciousness of the Japanese, whereby the Japanese began to review their racial memories of the past by using Chinese chronicles as their guide. Thus the meaning (or overarching idea) as well as the significance (the relationship between the meaning of the text and something outside the text) of the *Kojiki* and *Nihongi* will not become intelligible unless we compare them with Chinese historical writings and delineate the differences between the *Kojiki* and the *Nihongi* on the one hand and Japanese and Chinese historiography on the other.

The *Nihongi* is divided into thirty scrolls, and, apart from the first two which deal with the heavenly myths, it provides chronological accounts of the Japanese monarchs from the first legendary emperor Jimmu to Empress Jitō (A.D. 697). The chronology of the *Nihongi* is based on the Chinese calendar system called *kanshi*. According to Professor Kamstra:

Kan is an indication of the Five Elements, after these had been divided by *yin* and *yang* into two groups of five, the older named *e* and the younger "brother" named *to*. Thus there were in total ten "kan," or rather, five pairs of older and younger brothers. *Shi* has two meanings, namely "nucleus" and "something

---

[9] J. M. Kitagawa, "The Japanese *Kokutai* (National Community): History and Myth," *History of Religions*, Vol. 13, No. 3 (February 1974), 209-226.

which is divided within itself." This original meaning was later extended to that of the two verbs for division and addition. Therefore *shi* is a means by which the above-mentioned ten *kan* may be subdivided further. Of these *shi* there were twelve altogether: the twelve signs of the zodiac. . . . In this system the years are indicated by combining one of the ten *kan* with one of the twelve *shi*. Thus 120 combinations can be brought about. They are not all used, as in the *kanshi* system only the odd numbers of both sides are allowed to combine with the even numbers of both. The odd numbers of the one series, however, are not allowed to coincide with the even numbers of the other. Thus only sixty combinations are possible. These sixty combinations provide a sequence of sixty years. Each series starts with the year *kinoe-ne* and ends with *mizunoto-i*.[10]

Kamstra is persuaded that the *kanshi* system was not known in Japan before the final edition of the *Kojiki* was virtually completed in A.D. 681, but was introduced before the final recension of the *Nihongi* was undertaken and provided a calendrical framework for the *Nihongi*. By analyzing the *kanshi* system, we can conjecture as to how the eighth-century Japanese chroniclers fabricated the dates of historical events of early Japan. They accomplished that fabrication by pushing back its antiquity in order to portray Japan as an old (and hence, respectable) nation. To do this, they "historicized" mythological figures into emperors, added legendary emperors, turned local chieftains into monarchs, and stretched the longevity of early monarchs. One of the fantastic byproducts of this fabrication of history was that a legendary cultural hero, Takeuchi, was supposed to have lived several hundred years because of the longevity of the emperor under whom he was supposed to have served. Despite these fabrications, the *Nihongi* is a far richer resource than the *Kojiki* for our understanding of important events in this historical period of Japan.

The *Kojiki* is divided into three scrolls (*maki*). The First Scroll deals with six main themes of heavenly myths: (1) cosmogonic myths; (2) myths concerning the two *kami*—Izanagi ("He Who Invites") and Izanami ("She Who is Invited"); (3) myths concerning the Plain of High Heaven in which Amaterasu (the Sun Goddess) is the central figure; (4) myths of the Izumo region; (5) myths regarding the offering of the Izumo region of Japan to the heavenly *kami*; and (6) myths concerning the descent of Ninigi, the grandson of Amaterasu, from heaven with the divine mission to rule Japan. The Second Scroll deals with earthly myths, probably better characterized as the Yamato myths, consisting of accounts of the first fifteen legendary emperors,

---

[10] J. H. Kamstra, *Encounter or Syncretism: The Initial Growth of Japanese Buddhism* (Leiden: E.J. Brill, 1967), pp. 60-61.

beginning with Jimmu, who is portrayed as the great-grandson of Ni-nigi. The Third Scroll gives genealogical and anecdotal accounts of the Yamato monarchs from the sixteenth emperor, Nintoku, to the Empress Suiko (reigned A.D. 592-628), the thirty-third sovereign. While the *Kojiki* is less "historical" than the *Nihongi*, it preserves more of the indigenous religious ethos than the *Nihongi*.

It is noteworthy that both the *Kojiki* and the *Nihongi* share with Chinese historical writings a common bias that "the only history worthy of name is the history of institutions." It is equally noteworthy that their respective approaches to their own institutional histories are very different. For the most part, as Etienne Balazs points out, traditional historical writing, which cuts history into dynastic slices and was written by official chroniclers of reigning dynasties, was a very stereotyped affair. Most dynastic histories followed the same theme, using the so-called "praise and blame" (*pao-pien*) method in which they tried to demonstrate, for instance, that the last emperor of a dynasty was not worthy, whence the "mandate of heaven had to be taken away from him either by forcing his abdication or by an act of revolt by the founder of the new dynasty, who by virtue of his success was considered worthy to receive the mandate of heaven."[11] The aim of such historical writing was, in essence, "to make judgments and draw moral lessons from the past for application to the present." On the other hand, the significance of both the *Kojiki* and *Nihongi* lies in the central theme that the Japanese imperial family had the divine mission to reign as well as to rule the Japanese nation in perpetuity by virtue of their solar ancestry. That theme is elaborated in the *Nihongi* as the basis for the immanental theocratic state, ideally a "soteriological national community" with the emperor functioning simultaneously as the chief priest, sacred king, and the living *kami*.

Our attempt to understand the meaning of the Japanese classics is further complicated by the fact that all of them depend on Chinese scripts, since at that time there was no written Japanese language. We can readily understand that the task of adopting the Chinese script (with its highly developed pictographs, ideographs and phonetic compounds) to Japanese words was very difficult and complex. In the course of time, some of the Japanese intelligentsia learned the use of the literary Chinese (*kambun*) that was used for the compilation of the *Nihongi* and other official records. Another system used Chinese characters (*kanji*), but they were meant to be read in Japanese. Still another

[11] On the *pao-pien* method of writing history, see Etienne Balazs, *Chinese Civilization and Bureaucracy: Variations on a Theme*, tr. by H. M. Wright, ed. by Arthur F. Wright (New Haven: Yale University Press, 1964), pp. 129-134.

system (*Mannyō-gana*) utilized Chinese characters only for their sound value while disregarding their lexical meaning in order to express Japanese sounds. Notwithstanding such differences in the use of Chinese scripts by the Japanese, the knowledge of written Chinese provided an important channel for the Japanese elite to have access to the immensely rich civilization of China which served as the resource and model for Japan. This also implied that consciously or unconsciously, the Japanese were influenced by Chinese civilization and by Buddhism, which was also introduced from China. The Japanese learned that there were meanings beyond the realm of their immediate experience and that there were different levels of reality. The Japanese learned much from Taoism and Confucianism: that there is a cosmic significance to the natural order and to the sociopolitical order, and that Confucian ethics, political theory, legal and educational institutions were based on the universal principle of *tao* (*michi* in Japanese). Meanwhile, Buddhism taught the Japanese to become aware of the existence of an ultimate reality explicated in terms of *dharma* (*hō* in Japanese), behind and beneath the transitoriness of the phenomenal existence. Inevitably, the Japanese world of meaning that had been a one-dimensional, undifferentiated monistic universe earlier, was destined to become multi-dimensional by the eighth century when classics such as the *Kojiki* and *Nihongi* were produced. The recognition of this historic fact makes it very difficult to reconstruct, as it were, the meanings of ancient Japanese myths, for example, before Japan came under the impact of Chinese civilization and Buddhism.

Finally, it is important to remind ourselves that Shinto never recognized any of the ancient classics as "canon." Among the Japanese classics, probably the *Norito* (ritual prayers) has attained a status closest to being "canonical," because the cultus has historically provided the unifying foundation for Shinto. *Norito* is a general term, referring to a series of stylized prayers addressed to various *kami*. The *Engi-shiki*, compiled in 927, preserves twenty-seven representative forms of *Norito*. As Mrs. Bock rightly points out, "The language of the *norito* differs from the Chinese style (*kambun*) of the other books of the *Engi-shiki*, showing that *norito* had entirely different sources—some of which are earlier than the time of the Taika Reforms (mid-seventh century) and some of which are later."[12] Usually the *Norito* begins with words praising *kami*, followed by lists of offerings and the identity of the petitioner and the reciter, closing with the subject of the prayer.

[12] *Engi-Shiki: Procedures of the Engi Era, Books VI-X*, tr. with intro. and notes by Felicia Gressitt Bock (Tokyo: Sophia University, 1972), p. 57.

In earlier days, before the *Norito* became stylized, there must have been simpler forms of petitions and supplications. Implicit in the *Norito* is the ancient Japanese notion of *koto-dama* (the spiritual power residing in words), according to which beautiful words, correctly pronounced, were believed to bring about good whereas ugly words or beautiful words incorrectly pronounced were believed to cause evil.[13] There is good reason to assume that the ritualized format of the *Norito*, as contained in the *Engi-shiki*, must have been influenced by the Buddhist *sūtra* reciting, which became popular from the sixth century A.D. onward.

[13] *Basic Terms of Shinto* (Tokyo: Jinja Honcho et al., 1958), p. 44.

4. Stages of the Japanese "Religious Universe"

IN HIS presidential address at the Ninth Congress of the International Association for the History of Religions, held in Tokyo in 1959, Raffaele Pettazzoni included the following personal remark:

> I have always felt a particular interest for (the Japanese) religious world; and this induced me . . . almost thirty years ago to publish for the first time in Italian . . . the first two books of the *Kojiki*, in order to extend in my own country a knowledge of the national religion and mythology of Japan. That was in 1929; but my sympathy for Japanese religion is even older. . . . in 1904 . . . I was twenty-one years old and a student at the University of Bologna. It was the time of the Russo-Japanese war, and I was curious to know something of Japanese religion. From this interest emerged an article, which was . . . published by a daily paper of my city ("Il Resto del Carlino," 29 Feb. 1904).[1]

At the same Congress, Pettazzoni also contributed a paper entitled "Sur Prétendu Monothéism Japonais."[2] Pettazzoni was intrigued by the coexistence of a variety of religious experience in Japan. In his own words: "this vitality of archaic forms and of innovating aspirations, this millenary process of action and reaction between the indigenous national religion and the imported supernatural religion . . . gives to the religious history of Japan its characteristic imprint."[3] Thus, in appreciation of his lifelong interest in the subject, it is appropriate for us, as we celebrate the centenary of Pettazzoni's birth, to delineate the meaning of the Japanese "religious universe" in terms of its various historic stages.

"THERE WERE TREES AND HERBS WHICH COULD SPEAK . . ."

Very little can be reconstructed with certainty regarding the character of the religious universe or the nature of the sociopolitical order in the prehistoric or very early historic periods of Japan.[4] To be sure,

---

[1] *Proceedings of the Ninth International Congress for the History of Religions, Tokyo and Kyoto, 1958* (Tokyo: Maruzen, 1960), 831.

[2] Ibid., 393-397.

[3] Ibid., 830.

[4] See J. M. Kitagawa, "The Prehistoric Background of Japanese Religion," *History of Religions* 2 (1963), 292-328. [Chapter 1 of this book.]

archaeological remains and scattered references to Japan in Chinese records provide us with some glimpses of the religious, social, and political features of early Japanese life. What we learn from these sources, however, does not add very much to our conjecture in reference to the religious universe of archaic and early Japanese societies.[5] Thus, for our purpose, we are still compelled to turn to the two mythohistorical writings, the *Kojiki* (the Ancient Matters) and the *Nihongi* (the Chronicles of Japan), to the *Fudoki* (the Records of Local Surveys) and to other works of the eighth century A.D., as well as to the official anthology of poems, the *Man'yōshū* (the Myriad Leaves). All of these works were compiled centuries after the introduction to Japan of Sino-Korean civilization and Buddhism.[6] It must be stated in this connection that while these writings inevitably reflect the religious and political perspectives of the imperial court and aristocracy of the seventh, eighth, and ninth centuries, they also preserve many features of ancient myths, legends, lore, customs and historical records.

As far as we can tell, one of the basic features of the early Japanese religious universe was its unitary meaning-structure, a structure which affirmed the belief that the natural world is the original world, and which revolved around the notion that the total cosmos is permeated by sacred, or *kami*, nature. Undoubtedly, the world to the early Japanese was only that world which they experienced in the Japanese archipelago and which the chroniclers referred to as the "Central Land of Reed-Plains." Everybody and everything in the early Japanese monistic religious universe, including physical elements such as fire, water, wood, and stone, as well as animals and celestial bodies, were believed to be endowed with *kami* nature. It is not surprising, therefore, to read in the *Nihongi* that in the Central Land of Reed-Plains "there were numerous (*kami*) which shone with a lustre like that of fireflies, and evil (*kami*) which buzzed like flies. There were also *trees*

---

[5] Among all the works dealing with the early period of Japan, Paul Wheatley and Thomas See, *From Court to Capital* (Chicago, 1978), takes the records of the Chinese sources most seriously as reliable data regarding the social, economic, and political life of early Japan.

[6] See Donald L. Philippi, trans. with an intro. and notes, *Kojiki* (Tokyo and Princeton, 1969); W. G. Aston, trans., *Nihongi: Chronicles of Japan from the Earliest Times to A.D. 697* (reprint edition, Rutland, Vermont and Tokyo, 1972); The Nippon Gakunjutsu Shinkokai, *The Manyoshu: One Thousand Poems* (reprint edition, New York, 1965); Michiko Yamaguchi Aoki, trans. with an intro., *Izumo Fudoki* (Tokyo, 1971); and Ian H. Levy, *The Ten-Thousand Leaves: A Translation of the Manyoshu* (Princeton, 1981). The introduction to the Nippon Gakujutsu Shinkokai's *Manyoshu* (p. xxxviii) states, with obvious exaggeration: ". . . despite the wide acceptance of Confucianism and Buddhism, almost all the gods to whom (the Manyo man) sang, or who fed the well-spring of his lyric inspiration, were purely Japanese."

70

and herbs all of which could speak."[7] Furthermore, strong intimations that human beings, too, are believed to be *kami*, permeate the ancient myths and legends, although later accounts tend to confer the designation of *kami* primarily to monarchs and royalty—reflecting the ascendency of the imperial house which claimed solar ancestry. To the early Japanese, the natural world (Japan), therefore, was essentially the religious universe, a world in which all facets of daily living were considered religious acts. Such a religious universe was nurtured by myths. These myths taught men and women the meaning of human existence and gave them a sense of identity. This identity, in turn, was kept alive by cults and rituals.

Understandably, the religious universe of the early Japanese people reflected their historical experiences. It is worth noting in this connection that the primary social unit of early Japan was the precursor of what later came to be called the *uji*, or territorially based cluster of lineage groups who share the same tutelary *kami* and which is commonly translated as "clan." Each *uji* was held together by the *uji* chieftain (*uji-no-kami*), whose authority over the land and people within his domain was derived largely from his cultic prerogatives given to him by the *kami* of the *uji* (*uji-gami*). Sometime around the third century A.D., the "imperial" *uji* began to solidify its influence over other *uji*s through its military power and its mythological claim to the genealogical descent from the female solar deity, Amaterasu. As such, the chieftains of the imperial *uji* assumed the prerogative to confer titles on chieftains of other *uji*s, to grant sacred seed at spring festivals, and to establish sacred sites and to regulate rituals for various *kami*.

The early Yamato Kingdom, thus unified by the imperial *uji*, was in effect a loosely knit confederation of semi-autonomous powerful *uji*s. It was the duty of the Yamato monarch to maintain close contact with the Sun deity, Amaterasu—the imperial *uji*'s ancestress and tutelary *kami*—by attending to the rituals (*matsuri*) for her as well as heavenly and earthly *kami*. The monarch was guided in his or her government administration (*matsuri-goto*) by the *kamis*' precarious wills, communicated through oracles, dreams, and divinations. Thus, in principle, there was no line of demarcation between the sacred and profane dimensions of life or between religious rituals (*matsuri*) and government administration (*matsuri-goto*). This principle of the unity of religion and government (*saisei-itchi*) remained the foundation of Japanese religion until the end of World War II.[8] In their political and magico-

[7] Aston, *Nihongi*, Book II, 64. (My italics.)

[8] See J. M. Kitagawa, "Matsuri and Matsuri-goto: Religion and State in Early Japan," *Religious Traditions*, 2 (1979), 30-37. [Chapter 7 of this book.]

religious duties the Yamato monarchs were assisted by administrative and cultic functionaries, including the court poets who not only were prominent priestly figures and ceremonial reciters of ritual verse on important occasions, but also composers of "poems of praise and lament" for the imperial family. Their task was to craft "iconic images which 'prove' the divinity of the imperial family" by appealing to the mythological tradition.[9]

Sometime during the shadowy period of the late third or early fourth century, the Yamato Kingdom gained a foothold on the southern tip of the Korean peninsula, and allied itself with Paekche, one of the Korean states. Through this contact, a number of Korean artisans and scholars came to Japan, introducing to Japan new arts and technologies as well as the Chinese script and Confucian learning. Buddhism, too, was officially introduced to the Japanese court from Paekche in the sixth century, even though it was no doubt known among the Korean settlers before that time.

SACRED MONARCHY, DIVINE NATION, AND RELIGIONS

The penetration of Sino-Korean civilization and Buddhism brought about a series of social, cultural, political, and religious changes. For example, sensing the need to create a designation for their hitherto unsystematized magico-religious-cultural tradition, the Japanese adopted two Chinese characters—*shin* for *kami* and *tō* for "the way"—thus creating the term, *Shintō*, or the "way of *kami*." The adoption of this new name does not mean, however, that Shinto was established as a coherent institutionalized religion overnight. Even its rituals varied greatly according to locality. They centered around numerous local *kami* of heaven and earth as well as tutelary *kami* of *uji* groups. Nevertheless, Shinto represented the indigenous Japanese understanding of the meaning of life and the world. This understanding was authenticated solely by their particular historic experience. On the other hand, the newly introduced Confucian and Buddhist traditions claimed that their "ways" were grounded in universal laws and principles—Tao (the "Way") and Dharma (the "Law"), respectively.

An initial effort to reconcile indigenous and foreign traditions—ostensibly as a way to transform the hitherto loosely knit Japanese society into a unified, centralized nation—was attempted by Prince-Regent Shōtoku and his advisors around the turn of the seventh century. For this task, the Japanese court tried to exalt the throne, as

[9] Levy, *Ten-Thousand Leaves*, 14.

exemplified in its production of the Seventeen-Article Constitution which was, in effect, a guideline for the ministers of the court. The same constitution urged the veneration of Buddhism "as the final resort of all beings," and also invoked the Confucian principle of "propriety" as the basis of government administration.[10] At the same time, the court issued the following edict to promote the veneration of *kami*:

> ... our imperial ancestors, in governing the nation, bent humbly under heaven and walked softly on earth. They venerated the *kami* of heaven and earth, and established shrines on the mountains and by the rivers, whereby they were in constant touch with the power of nature. Hence the winter (*yin*, negative cosmic force) and summer (*yang*, positive cosmic force) elements were kept in harmony. ... May all the ministers from the bottom of their hearts pay homage to the *kami* of heaven and earth.[11]

The court thereby attempted to incorporate certain features of the Confucian and Buddhist traditions on a selective basis, to be sure, into the framework of the indigenous religious universe.

After the death of Prince Shōtoku, the court continued to appropriate Chinese systems of law, administration, land distribution, census, and taxation in order to solidify the central governmental structure. The main objective of the court was to uphold the authority of the sovereign who now was elevated to the status of the living or manifest *kami*, whose divine will was communicated by a series of "imperial rescripts." Accordingly, those penal codes (*ritsu*; *lü* in Chinese) and the civil statutes (*ryō*; *ling* in Chinese), which had been adopted from China, were promulgated in the name of the emperor who, as the genealogical descendent of the solar deity, Amaterasu, claimed the prerogative to reign as well as to rule the nation. The model of the government envisaged by the Japanese rulers in the seventh century is referred to as the *Ritsuryō* (imperial rescript) ideal. Although this ideal was not fully achieved in practice, it nevertheless remained in the minds of many as a theoretical paradigm for the "divine" nation in the subsequent periods of Japanese history.

In order to carry out the Ritsuryō ideal, the imperial government reorganized the court structure by instituting an eight-rank system of hereditary titles of nobility,[12] and ordered the compilation of the two previously mentioned mythohistorical works, the *Kojiki* and the *Nihongi*. The government also compiled records of local surveys or to-

[10] See J. M. Kitagawa, "Religions of Japan," in W-T Chan et al., *The Great Asian Religions: An Anthology* (New York, 1969), 252-254.
[11] Quoted in ibid., 241.
[12] See Richard J. Miller, *Ancient Japanese Nobility: The Kabane Ranking System* (Berkeley and Los Angeles, 1974).

pologies as well as a register of aristocratic families. Within the central government, the Department of Kami-Affairs (*Jingikan*) was placed side-by-side with the Great Council of State (*Dajōkan*), thus according prestige to Shinto while at the same time keeping it under the rigid control of the bureaucracy. The government also controlled the activities of the Buddhist clerics through the Law Governing Monks and Nuns (*Sōniryō*).

The ideal of the Ritsuryō model was not to create a Chinese-style liturgical nation with its sovereign serving as the mediator between Heaven and earth, but rather to make Japan a divine nation—a soteriological national community or a "super church," as it were—with the emperor functioning simultaneously as the chief priest, sacred monarch, and the living *kami*. Accordingly, the imperial court came to be portrayed as the earthly counterpart of the heavenly court of the Sun deity. The stylized court rituals, as prescribed in the "Procedures of the Engi Era" (*Engi-shiki*)[13]—the most elaborate embodiment of the Ritsuryō ideal—were meant to perpetuate the earthly replica of heavenly rituals as told in myths.

Early in the eighth century, the imperial power reached its zenith. The first full-scale capital city, which, by the way, was modelled after the Chinese capital, was established in Nara as the political and religious center of the nation. The court patronized six officially recognized schools of Buddhism, which in turn eagerly served as a religion for the protection of the state. The court also sponsored the building of the national temple, which housed the gigantic bronze statue of Buddha Vairocana. Understandably, the most popular among all the scriptures was the *Sutra of the Sovereign Kings of the Golden Radiance* (*Konkōmyō-kyō*), which explicates a Buddhist doctrine that a monarch is "a son of a divine being" to whom a mandate of heaven is given. Tragically, the state-supported Buddhist institutions and hierarchy ignored the people in the lower strata of society. Rather, it was through the shamanistic folk leaders who came under nominal Buddhist influence that the gospel of the Buddha took roots, however superficially, among the populace.[14] Meanwhile, political corruption, ecclesiastical intrigue, and financial bankruptcy in the second half of the eighth century forced the government to move the capital from Nara to Kyoto.

[13] Books I-X of this work were translated by Felicia Bock, *Engi-Shiki*, 2 vols. (Tokyo, 1970, 1972).

[14] See Ichiro Hori, "On the Concept of Hijiri (Holy-Man)," *Numen* 5 (1958), 128-160, 199-232.

ENLIGHTENMENT AND SALVATION

It is an irony of Japanese history that even before the ideal of divine nation under the sacred monarchy achieved its coherence, it had begun to erode. For example, the ideal that posited the belief that the sovereign held the divinely mandated authority to reign as well as to rule was seriously compromised by the regency of the Fujiwara family. The Fujiwaras effectively ruled the nation from the mid-tenth to the mid-eleventh centuries. The Fujiwaras were followed by the "rule by abdicated monarch" (*insei*) during the eleventh and twelfth centuries, and by the "feudal regimes" (*bakufu*) of Kamakura and Muromachi from the thirteenth to the sixteenth centuries. None of these regimes, however, violated the throne's prerogative to reign over the nation.

While the ninth to the sixteenth centuries thus witnessed the erosion of the Ritsuryō ideal, this period was also marked by unprecedented cultural and religious creativity. It is interesting to note that the unitary structure of the indigenous religious universe was not destroyed by the impact of Chinese civilization and Buddhism. Rather, it was transformed by such syncretistic notions as the equation of the world of nature with *dharmakaya* and native *kami* with Buddhas and Bodhisattvas. This synthesis fostered the Shinto Buddhist amalgam that was advocated both by the newly introduced Tendai (T'ien T'ai) and Shingon (Chên-yen) schools of Buddhism, schools that dominated the Japanese religious scene during the Heian period (ninth to twelfth centuries). Significantly, it was Dengyō Daishi (767-822), the systematizer of the Tendai school, who first used the phrase "Dai Nippon" (Great Japan) after his return from China.[15] Meanwhile, the prevalent fear among the general populace of those spirits of the dead who were not properly propitiated (*onryō* or *goryō*) was such that Taoist, Yin-Yang (Onmyōdō), folk Buddhist and Shugen-dō (an eclectic mountain priesthood) practices of magic, astrology and geomancy were eagerly supported, both by the upper and the lower strata of Japanese society.[16]

New wrinkles were added to the Japanese religious universe during the thirteenth century. While older elite Buddhism and the imperial court-centered aristocratic culture in Kyoto continued to function, the establishment of the feudal regime as the *de facto* ruling power in Kamakura fostered the development of new cultural forms which re-

[15] Hajime Nakamura, *Ways of Thinking of Eastern Peoples: India-China-Tibet-Japan*, ed. Philip P. Wiener (Honolulu, 1964), 434.
[16] See Ichiro Hori, *Folk Religion in Japan: Continuity and Change* (Chicago, 1968), 71-81.

flected warrior ideals such as simplicity, naturalness and directness. The feudal regime also encouraged a heightened religious awakening among the populace, under the influence of a Buddhist apocalyptic notion that the dreadful era of decay and degeneration (*mappō*) had arrived.

The belief in *mappō* provided a strong impetus to a Buddhist pietism which offered a new soteriological option to the Japanese religious universe. For example, the advocates of Pure Land Pietism, such as Hōnen (1133-1212) and Shinran (1173-1262), were persuaded that, in the period of *mappō*, those who believe in the saving power of Buddha Amida (Amitābha) could gain rebirth in Amida's Pure Land, and that faith in Amida superseded all previous Buddhist doctrines, disciplines and practices. On the other hand, Nichiren (1222-1282) advocated Lotus Pietism, in the belief that if people were to adhere to the teaching of the *Lotus Scripture*, the "Three Worlds and the Ten Regions" would be transformed into the Buddha Land and everybody would attain safety of body and peace of mind.[17]

The thirteenth century also witnessed the establishment of two Zen schools, Rinzai Zen, advocated by Eisai (or Yōsai, 1141-1215), and Sōtō Zen, advocated by Dōgen (1200-1253). In sharp contrast to the Pietist movements that stressed salvation by faith in Amida or the *Lotus Scripture*, Zen stressed the path toward enlightenment (*satori*). Zen was favored by the feudal leaders in Kamakura, partly because Zen monks, especially a number of able emigré Ch'an (Zen) monks from China who settled in Japan, were instrumental in introducing contemporary Chinese culture, including Neo-Confucian learning. Significantly, some leaders of the path toward enlightenment shared the conviction with Pietist leaders that the aim of religion is not the protection of the state (*chingo kokka*) but the spiritual welfare of men and women in the realm of the phenomenal world. Their followers learned in turn that religion could provide a basis for group cohesion, transcending kinship, class, and other natural factors that usually divide human society.

The Pietistic and Zen cultural and religious modes, represented by Kyoto and Kamakura, or "the Chrysanthemum and the Sword," to use Ruth Benedict's phrase, were integrated during the fifteenth and sixteenth centuries under the leadership of talented Zen leaders.[18] In

---

[17] These motifs of Nichiren's teachings provide theoretical foundations of the Nichiren Shoshu-Soka Gakkai and other contemporary Japanese new religions of the Nichiren tradition.

[18] See Martin Collcut, *Five Mountains: The Rinzai Zen Monastic Institutions in Medieval Japan* (Cambridge and London, 1981).

the meantime, the decline of the authority of the feudal regime resulted in social and political disintegration during the second half of
the sixteenth century. This was the state of affairs when Ignatius Loy-
ola (1491-1556) and other Jesuits arrived on the Japanese shore to
offer a new gospel of salvation—Roman Catholicism.

TWO MODELS OF "IMMANENTAL THEOCRACY":
TOKUGAWA AND MEIJI

The unification of Japan was achieved firmly in 1600 by Tokugawa
Iyeyasu (1542-1616), who established the third feudal regime in present-day Tokyo. Significantly, the Tokugawa regime accomplished the
ideal which, since the seventh century A.D., the imperial court had only
dreamed about but could not achieve: a tightly knit, hierarchical so-
cial-religious-political organism, a form of "immanental theocracy"
supported by subservient ecclesiastical institutions. The crucial difference was that it was now the shogun and not the emperor who was
at the helm. And, unlike the earlier imperial model which had sought
its legitimation in terms of the mandate of the solar deity, the shogun's
rule in the Tokugawa model was legitimated by the Neo-Confucian
principle that natural laws and natural norms are grounded in the will
of Heaven. The Tokugawa regime looked to the throne, to which it
paid lip service, primarily to add a magico-religious aura to its own
version of immanental theocracy.

The religious policy of the Tokugawa regime was firmly established
by the first shogun, who held that all religious, philosophical and ethical systems were to uphold, and cooperate with, the regime's objective
of establishing a hierarchically controlled social and political organism.
The regime issued stern anti-Catholic policies, and persecuted foreign
missionaries and Japanese adherents on the grounds that Catholicism
was detrimental to the nation's social and political harmony.[19] Moreover, in 1640, the regime took the extreme measure of closing Japan
to all foreign trade, with the exception of limited commerce with the
Dutch at Nagasaki.

In order to eliminate the residual Roman Catholic influence, the
regime required every family to be registered in a Buddhist temple,
thus making Buddhist clerics the arms of the feudal government in
charge of thought control. This measure created a hitherto unprecedented comprehensive Buddhist parochial system in Japan. On the
other hand, Buddhist as well as other religious institutions were tightly

---

[19] See George Elison, *Deus Destroyed: The Image of Christianity in Early Modern Japan*
(Cambridge, Massachusetts, 1973).

controlled by the regime, which tolerated their internal doctrinal disputes but not their deviation from the regime's policy.

As stated earlier, the official guiding ideology of the regime was Neo-Confucianism, which stressed that the will of Heaven was inherent in actual human conditions. And, since Tokugawa society was rigidly divided into warrior, farmer, artisan, and merchant classes (plus special categories, such as imperial and courtier families and ecclesiastics), one's birth was believed to dictate one's status as well as duties to the shogun, to the master of one's fiefdom, to family, and in interpersonal relations. Thus, for example, warriors were expected to live according to the Code of Warriors (*Bushidō*), while farmers, artisans, and merchants were to observe their respective "ways" to fulfill their heavenly given occupations (*tenshoku*).[20]

In the course of time, the policy of national seclusion that enabled the Tokugawa regime to consolidate its feudal system turned out to be the cause of its own downfall; its design to maintain a permanent martial law in order to preserve peace began to erode because of its very success. For instance, warriors—the armed guardians of law and order—turned into civil servants, while the changing economic reality pushed merchants—the lowest professional class—higher on the social scale. Moreover, Confucian scholars, presumably the ideologues for the Tokugawa version of immanental theocracy, began to ally themselves with Shinto leaders, and came to value the principle of the sacred monarchy, a principle which had been barely tolerated through the early Tokugawa period. Meanwhile, some features of Western science and information about the changing world situation began to infiltrate the Japanese intelligentsia through the limited Japanese contract with the Dutch. In this unsettling situation, several messianic and healing cults erupted from the soil of folk religious tradition.

Japanese ports reopened to foreign trade in the mid-nineteenth century under the pressure of Western powers. Nationalistically oriented Confucianists then cooperated actively with the leaders of Shinto and of National Learning (*kokugaku*) for the royalist cause and helped topple the once-powerful Tokugawa regime.

THE LAST Tokugawa shogun surrendered power to the throne in 1867. The young Emperor Meiji pledged in his Charter Oath that "evil customs of the past shall be discarded" and that "knowledge shall

[20] For the Confucian rationale of Tokugawa society, see Yasuzo Horie, *Edo-jidai no Jugaku ni okeru Kokka-ron* (Confucian Theory of State in Tokugawa Japan), in Toho gakkai soritsu jugo-shunen kinen, *Toho-gaku ronso* (Eastern Studies: 15th Anniversary Volume) (Tokyo, 1962), 290-301.

be sought throughout the world in order to strengthen the foundations of imperial rule." The objective of the new imperial rule was not
only a renovation (*ishin*) or innovation, but also a restoration of
(*fukko*) or a reversion to the seventh-century ideal of the emperor-
centered religious-political national polity.[21] Thus, the ethos of Meiji
Japan was a precarious fusion of three elements: (1) Confucian-inspired values and principles that provided the rationale for the Tokugawa society; (2) the ideal of sacred monarchy, divine nation, and the
unity of religious and political administration (*saisei-itchi*), the cornerstone of the Shinto-inspired vision of the ancient imperial polity; and
(3) new knowledge and culture imported from the West. In short, the
goal of the Meiji regime was to establish a modern nation-state with
"economic prosperity and a strong defense" (*fukoku kyōhei*) under the
reign and rule of the living, divine emperor. It was a new form of
immanental theocracy different from, but in part based on, the Tokugawa model.

One of the initial measures taken by the Meiji regime was to dissolve
the age-old pattern of the Shinto-Buddhist amalgam on the grounds
that it was contrary to the pristine indigenous religious tradition. The
regime also created a brand-new, artificial super-religion called "State
Shinto," which all Japanese subjects were to follow, regardless of their
respective religious beliefs and ecclesiastical affiliations. In order to
keep State Shinto from becoming involved in overt sectarian activities,
the regime even concocted the new category of Sect (Kyōha) Shinto,
which included some of the messianic and healing cults that had
emerged in the late Tokugawa period. As might be expected, many of
the Sect Shinto groups show characteristic features of folk religious
traditions: their members venerated sacred mountains, they formed
cults of mental and physical purification, they held utopian beliefs, and
they practiced faith healing.

The Meiji regime was compelled to confront the issue of religious
freedom. Initially, the regime continued the Tokugawas' anti-Christian
policy and arrested a few newly converted Christians as well as three
thousand "hidden Catholics" who had survived the persecution.
Aroused by this event, foreign ministers pressured the Japanese government (which was then trying to revise its unequal treaties with
Western powers) to adopt a policy of religious liberty as a sign of
being a civilized nation. Meanwhile, Buddhist leaders also voiced the
need for religious freedom in order to protect Buddhism from Shinto

[21] See J. M. Kitagawa, "Religious and Cultural Ethos of Modern Japan," *Asian Studies*
2 (1964), 334-352.

domination. Caught in this situation, the Meiji regime stipulated in the new Constitution that "Japanese subjects shall, within the limits not prejudicial to peace and order and not antagonistic to their duties as subjects, enjoy freedom of religious belief" (Article 28). At the same time, the government forbade religious istruction in all schools, public or private, although according to Ordinance 12, "moral teaching, if applicable to all religions, could be given." The intent of the government was clearly to uphold State Shinto above all religions, while ethnocentric patriotism, the emperor cult, and modified Confucian values were taught in all schools as "moral teaching" (*shushin*), applicable to all religions.[22]

Even such a limited religious freedom opened the way for Russian Orthodox, Protestant, and Roman Catholic churches to initiate vigorous evangelistic, educational, and philanthropic activities in Japan. Curious or iconoclastic youth living mainly in urban areas were infatuated with things Western and were lured to Christianity. However, the wind soon shifted. The Christian claim of monotheism came under attack on the grounds that it was incompatible with loyalty to the emperor as the living *kami*.[23]

As might be expected, the ambiguity involved in the Meiji regime's policy of religious freedom was exploited until 1945 by those who opposed it. The situation became especially serious during the 1930s, when all liberal thought and expression was suppressed, and Sect Shinto groups were forced to cooperate with the authoritarian government's aim to extend the imperial rule abroad. The government was also determined to suppress folk religious messianic and healing cults because they tended to venerate *kami* who were not recognized in the Shinto pantheon. Nevertheless, the number of "quasi religions" (*ruiji shūkyō*) increased from ninety-eight in 1920 to over one thousand in 1935, despite severe persecution and harassment by the government. Parenthetically, it was these quasi religions which became the core of the so-called "new religions" which have mushroomed in Japan since the end of World War II.

It is worth recapitulating here that in the period from the seventeenth century to the end of World War II, Japan was governed by two types of regimes, one feudal and one imperial, each one based on its own model of immanental theocracy. Under both regimes, religious and ecclesiastical groups fared similarly, being permitted to function only within narrowly prescribed limits. On the other hand, the gov-

[22] See Robert K. Hall, *Shushin: The Ethics of a Defeated Nation* (New York, 1949).
[23] For a Christian defense, see Hiromichi Kozaki, *Kokka to Shukyo* (State and Religion) (Tokyo, 1913).

ernment could not control much of the unorganized folk religious belief and practice, traceable—through many winding roads, to be sure—to the religious universe of the ancient Japanese.

DESACRALIZED MONARCHY, SECULAR STATE, AND RELIGIONS

Japan's surrender to the Allied Powers had far-reaching effects on the religious foundation of the Japanese nation. The authorities of the Allied occupation forces realized, much as the architects of the Tokugawa and the Meiji regimes realized earlier, that the basic issues involved in the definition of the nature of the nation were religious in character. Thus, each of the measures enforced by the occupation forces was designed to alter religious-and-political principles established by the ancient, the Tokugawa, and the Meiji regimes. First, the newly enforced principle of religious freedom undercut the principle that every Japanese must pledge his or her ultimate (religious) loyalty to the throne, and affirmed the individual's freedom to exercise his or her religious beliefs and practices. Second, the directive that disestablished State Shinto repudiated the special prerogatives accorded to Shinto by the government in the seventh century and reinforced by the Meiji regime. Third, the principle of the separation of religion and state disavowed the age-old dogma of the unity of religion and government (*saisei-itchi*). Equally significant was the imperial rescript issued in 1946, which renounced the divinity of the emperor.[24]

In a sense, those measures taken by the occupation authorities implied the "second opening" of Japan to the family of nations. In the mid-nineteenth century, Western powers persuaded Japan to open her doors, primarily for commercial trade. While the Japanese government reversed its policies of national seclusion and expressed interest to acquire new knowledge from abroad, the government, in fact, welcomed only those Western ideas and technologies that would benefit the material aspects of Japan while preserving, and even solidifying, the *de facto* national seclusion policy as far as political, ethical, and religious structures were concerned. In short, external modernization was designed to consolidate even further the immanental theocracy which was affirmed as the essence and foundation of modern Japan. It was this internal, spiritual, national seclusion that came to an end in 1945.

The twin principles of religious freedom and the separation of religion and state, initially implemented by the Religious Corporations Ordinance in 1945 and by the Religious Juridical Persons Law (*Shū-*

---

[24] William P. Woodard, *The Allied Occupation of Japan, 1945-1952, and Japanese Religions* (Leiden, 1972).

kyō-hōjin-hō) from 1951, greatly altered the religious topography of Japan. For one thing, Shinto has become one religion among many, even though with 80,000 shrines now registered in the Shrine Association and a nationwide network of support structures, it is by far the largest single religious institution. Also, various traditions of Christianity and Buddhism, as well as those religious groups which were formerly classified as Sect Shinto, now practice their religious, educational, and philanthropic activities without fearing interference and harassment by the government.

By far the most conspicuous feature on the postwar religious scene in Japan has been the sudden mushrooming of many "new religions" (*Shinkō Shūkyō*). In the immediate postwar period, many people suffered from uncertainty, poverty, loss of nerve, as well as erosion of national, communal, and family ties. The new religions offered these men and women mundane happiness, tightly knit religio-social organizations, assurances of healing and/or easy salvation, and readily accessible earthly divine agents or self-styled messiahs. While many Western observers characterize these new religions as "crisis religions" comparable to the Ghost Dance and the Cargo Cult,[25] many Japanese scholars point out that the real prosperity of these religions came after the beginning of the Korean War and the heavy trend toward urbanization and economic advancement.[26] Understandably, these new religions—unlike Buddhism and Christianity, which have direct contacts with the global communities of their respective faiths—draw their resources from their own narrow provincial folk traditions. However, they reach a large number of people because of the groups' congeniality.

The contemporary religious situation in Japan shows an amazingly wide range of tendencies which range from nostalgia for the ancient past to seemingly secular options, mingled with touches of national narcissism. The popularity of many new religions—plus the fact that, according to a recent national survey of public opinion, a significant number of young people in their twenties living in urban centers rely on traditional folk beliefs and practices[27]—seems to indicate that since 1945 many people have been suddenly and abruptly cut off from their traditional religious universe and that the spiritual vacuum has not been filled by traditionally established religions.

[25] See H. Neill McFarland, *The Rush Hour of the Gods: A Study of the New Religious Movements in Japan* (New York, 1967).

[26] See Fujio Ikado, "Trend and Problems of New Religions: Religion in Urban Society," in K. Morioka and W. H. Newell, eds., *The Sociology of Japanese Religion* (Leiden, 1968), 101-117.

[27] This phenomenon is analyzed by Noboru Miyata in his unpublished article, *Modern Japanese Society and Folk Belief* (1982).

5. Monarchy and Government: Traditions and Ideologies in Pre-Modern Japan

INTRODUCTION

THIS PAPER attempts to deal with two related religio-political principles of pre-modern Japan, namely, the imperial ideology based on a sacred kingship, and the notion of government as based upon an immanental theocracy. Both developed from the intricate fusion of indigenous and Chinese features. In this connection, as Sansom rightly observes, "one of the difficulties in early Japanese history is to establish the extent to which Japanese ideas about sovereignty [and I might add government] were definitely influenced by Chinese political theory."[1] Our difficulties are compounded by the fact that the two major historical sources, the *Kojiki* (Records of Ancient Matters) and the *Nihongi* or *Nihon-shoki* (Chronicles of Japan) were compiled in the eighth century A.D., centuries after Japan came under the influence of Chinese civilization and Buddhism. Moreover, the compilation of these two documents was ordered by the Emperor Temmu in A.D. 673 in order to justify his accession to the throne after he had usurped it from another emperor.

Clearly, both the *Kojiki* and the *Nihongi* follow the model of Chinese dynastic histories.[2] But the chroniclers utilized—and rearranged—a variety of indigenous myths and legends to support the claim, unprecedented in China, that the Japanese imperial family had the divine mission to reign, as well as to rule the nation, in perpetuity by virtue of their solar ancestry. Here, as I have stated elsewhere,[3] we confront difficult hermeneutical problems of untangling the intertwined processes of "historicization of myths" and "mythologization of history" in order to reconstruct, as it were, the archaic Japanese traditions of kingship and government, and to delineate how Chinese political theories were appropriated to articulate classical ideologies of sacred kingship

---

[1] George Sansom, *A History of Japan to 1334* (Stanford: Stanford University Press, 1958), p. 74.

[2] Ibid. "It cannot be said of any statement in either work (but particularly the *Nihon-shoki*) that it describes native institutions in their purity."

[3] See my article, "The Japanese *Kokutai* (National Community): History and Myth," *History of Religions*, Vol. 13, No. 3 (February 1974), 209-226.

and the immanental theocratic state in the seventh and eighth centuries. Then we may examine how these ideologies came to be modified by the reality of the Japanese situation in subsequent periods.

ARCHAIC BACKGROUND

While this is not the occasion to trace various stages of the prehistory of Japan,[4] it is safe to assume that those who inhabited the Japanese islands—the descendants of different ethnic and cultural groups who had migrated there—attained a degree of self-consciousness as one people by the beginning of the common era. By that time people in Japan knew the art of rice cultivation and they spoke proto-Japanese.[5] Parenthetically, one of the most ambiguous words inherited from proto-Japanese is the term *kami*, which on the one hand refers to an impersonal quality, i.e. the *kami* (sacred, numinous or divine) nature, and also refers to specific beings endowed with the *kami* nature, be they human, divine, or other animate or inanimate beings. It is also worth noting that the social solidarity unit of archaic Japan was the precursor of what came to be called later the *uji* (clan)—a territorially based cluster of families sharing the same tutelary *kami* and, more often than not, kinship ties. Each solidarity unit was held together by its chieftain, whose authority over the land and people within his domain was largely derived from his priestly or cultic prerogatives.

As to the nature of the political organization of archaic Japan, available data in Japan are very fragmentary. But a third-century Chinese record mentions that there were a number of principalities in Japan and that a female shamanic ruler reigned over one of them. We also learn from Korean sources that the Japanese held a military base in the southern tip of the Korean peninsula, while another Chinese record indicates that five Japanese monarchs had official dealings with the Sung Court during the fifth and sixth centuries. Evidently sometime toward the end of the fourth century the chieftain of a powerful "imperial" clan, presumably Ōjin, the fifteenth emperor mentioned in official chronicles, established the so-called Yamato kingdom, which was in effect a confederation of semi-autonomous clans, each of which owned and ruled its respective territory. The Yamato rulers paid tribute to China, and in return received the kingly title from the Chinese

[4] See my article, "Prehistoric Background of Japanese Religion," *History of Religions*, Vol. 2, No. 2 (Winter 1963), 292-328. [Chapter 1 of this book.]

[5] As far as we can ascertain, the phonology of proto-Japanese was somewhat different from that of classical and modern Japanese, but the structure of the language has remained remarkably unchanged througout the ages.

imperial court. Within Japan, however, the Yamato kings solidified their influence over other clans primarily on the basis of their claim to be the genealogical descendants of the Sun deity. As such they assumed the prerogatives of conferring court titles, granting sacred seed at spring festivals, and establishing sacred sites for the *kami* as well as regulating rituals for them. Be that as it may, the Yamato king, as rightly pointed out by Professor Waida, "was not the absolute monarch ruling over a centralized state but merely a *primus inter pares* who ran the politics, controlling and being controlled by [other clan chieftains who held titles in the court]."[6] Significantly, his kingly activities, which were simultaneously political and magico-religious, were often dictated by the precarious will of the *kami* transmitted to him through dreams and divinations.

FOREIGN INFLUENCE

The increasing contacts between Japan and the Asiatic continent resulted in the penetration of Sino-Korean civilization, especially Confucian learning and Buddhism, into Japan during the sixth century A.D. The introduction of the art of reading and writing Chinese script, new technologies, alien forms of art and architecture, sophisticated legal, philosophical and ethical concepts, and complex systems of administering government brought about a series of social, cultural, economic and political changes in Japan. It is to be noted that ideologies of both kingship and government articulated during the seventh and eight centuries, under the combined inspiration of Confucianism and the indigenous Shinto ("Way of the *Kami*") tradition, came to be regarded as paradigmatic in the subsequent periods of Japanese history.

Internally, the Yamato kingdom suffered from dynastic changes during the sixth century—notwithstanding official accounts in the chronicles to the contrary—and rivalries broke out among chieftains of powerful clans who held positions as ministers in the court, especially between those who favoured the introduction of Buddhism and an alliance with the Korean kingdom of Paekche on the one hand, and those who were anti-Paekche on the other. Besides this, there was constant tension between the imperial family and the ministers in the court. In this situation Japan lost its foothold in Korea, not for military reasons, but "because the central government in Yamato could not depend upon the obedience of the great territorial chieftains in western Japan, especially in Kyushu, or upon the loyalty of its repre-

[6] Manabu Waida, "Sacred Kingship in Early Japan: A Historical Introduction," *History of Religions*, Vol. 15, No. 4 (May 1976), 323.

sentatives in Korea, or indeed upon the integrity of its Great Ministers at Court."[7] To make the matter worse, the unification of China in 589 by the Sui dynasty presented a potential threat to the very survival of Japan. Confronted by such internal and external difficulties, the Empress Suiko (reigned 592-628) and her nephew Prince-Regent Shō-toku (573-621), with the help of the chieftain of the powerful Soga clan, tried to unify the nation.

In order to solidify the national fabric, the Imperial Court attempted to articulate its ideologies regarding kingship and the government by relating the particular cultural experience of the Japanese as expressed in Shinto to the two universal principles—*Tao* of Confucianism and *Dharma* of Buddhism—which had been introduced from abroad. In so doing, the Japanes rulers followed the example of the Emperor Wen Ti of Sui China, who authenticated his claim to semidivine authority by depending on Confucian, Buddhist and Taoist symbols. Following Wen Ti's model, the Japanese Court now tried to exalt the throne, as exemplified in the so-called Seventeen-Article Constitution, issued in 604 as a set of guidelines to the ministers and officials of the court. It states: "The Lord is Heaven, the vassal is Earth. Heaven overspreads, and Earth upbears. . . . Consequently when you receive the imperial commands, fail not to carry them out scrupulously."[8] The sinification policy of the Japanese Court was such that a number of talented young officials and Buddhist priests were sent to China to study. Also officials in the Court were given "cap ranks" *à la* Chinese usage. It was not sheer accident that in the message to the Sui Court the Empress Suiko adopted the sinified self-designation of *Tenshi* ("Son of Heaven") and *Tennō* ("Emperor"), which reflected an imperial ideology markedly different from the archaic tribal notion of kingship.

The new ideology of the government, however, was not fully articulated until 645, when the Taika ("Great Change") Reform was commenced. According to the Edict of Reform, the government placed all administrative and fiscal power directly under the throne by, for example, abolishing private titles to land, by instituting registers of population for the purpose of allotment of rice land to cultivators, and by establishing a new system of taxation. The throne also claimed the prerogative of appointing governors of provinces, although in practice great landowners were appointed to the governorships and given court ranks and stipends as well to compensate them for the loss of private ownership of their lands. Thus, among all the reform measures the

---

[7] Sansom, *History of Japan*, p. 47.

[8] Cited in Ryūsaku Tsunoda et al., comps., *Sources of Japanese Tradition* (New York: Columbia University Press, 1958), p. 50.

most problematical was the attempt to apply Chinese systems of land tenure and taxation, both of which were resisted by the hereditary aristocracy and undercut by the practice of granting exceptions and exemptions. Ironically, governmental reform during the latter half of the seventh century was stymied by social disorder, an unsuccessful Korean campaign, and a bloody war of succession.[9] Notwithstanding the practical difficulties involved, the seventh-century rulers of Japan were committed to the principle that the government must have written laws as its foundation. In this respect, the Taihō Penal and Civil Codes (*Taihō-ritsu-ryō*), promulgated in 702 (the second year of the Taihō era), formed the most conspicuous symbol of the reform ideologies regarding monarchy and government, and came to be regarded as paradigmatic in subsequent periods in Japanese history.

RITSURYŌ IDEAL—A CLASSICAL PARADIGM

It goes without saying that written laws were not known in Japan before the introduction of Chinese civilization. It was only in the mid-seventh century that attempts were made to codify civil statutes, but not successfully.[10] Thus, the Taihō Codes may be rightly regarded as the first written law in Japan. They were, however, soon replaced by another law known as the Yōrō Penal and Civil Code (*Yōrō-ritsuryō*), drafted in 718 but not enacted until 757. Understandably, both the Taihō and the Yōrō Codes copied most features of the T'ang codes. While the compilation of written laws was going on, the government established its first full-scale capital city in Nara, which became both the political and religious center of the nation. And, although in the main, government structure was modelled after that of T'ang China, it did possess a peculiarly Japanese feature in the sense that the administrative structure under the throne was divided into civil and religious branches, i.e. the Great Council of State (*Dajōkan*) presided over by the Chancellor (*Dajō-daijin*), and the Department of Kami- or Shinto-Affairs (*Jingikan*) presided over by the Head of Kami-Affairs. Both were directly accountable to the throne, following the principle of the unity of religious and civil affairs (*saisei-itchi*). It is to be noted that the foundation of the government and the law was the sacrality of the sovereign, not only as the genealogical descendant of the Sun deity

---

[9] As mentioned earlier, it was the victorious emperor Temmu who in 673 ordered the compilation of the *Kojiki* and the *Nihongi*, although these works were not completed until the eighth century.

[10] On the legal development of early Japan, see *Engi-Shiki: Procedures of the Engi Era, Books I-V*, trans. with intro. and notes by Felicia G. Bock (Tokyo: Sophia University, 1970), pp. 6-11.

but also as the Manifest Kami (*akitsu-kami*). Incidentally, Sansom also points out another feature of the Japanese system of official grades which differed from the Chinese system, namely that "the hierarchy in Japan was based upon birth and not upon talent."[11]

The adoption of written penal and civil codes implies at least in principle that the government administration was no longer dictated by the precarious will of the *kami* transmitted to the emperor through dreams and divination but by legal principles and precedents based on the principle of Tao. Yet, as it turned out in practice, the universal principle of Tao was homologized with, and was subordinated to, the authority of the emperor who, by virtue of being the descendant of the Sun deity, was destined to rule and reign over the nation. Moreover the sovereign, now being considered the Manifest Kami, was expected to communicate his divine will through a series of "imperial rescripts." The religio-political structure thus developed in the seventh and eighth centuries, primarily based on the homology of Confucian-Shinto principles, is referred to as the "Ritsuryō (Imperial Rescript) State." It was in effect a form of immanental theocracy.

It must be stressed in this connection that the Ritsuryō ideal was not simply to appropriate the classical Chinese idea of the nation as a liturgical community with its sovereign as the supreme mediator between Heaven and Earth as well as between Tao and mankind, but rather to create a soteriological community with the emperor functioning simultaneously as the chief priest, the sacred king, and the living *kami*. With the elevation of the throne to divine status, the imperial court now became the earthly counterpart of the heavenly court of the Sun deity.[12] Thus, just as the court of the Sun deity included various functionaries, the imperial court had similar functionaries who attended to cultic, administrative, military and household duties. The stylized daily court rituals were meant to present the earthly replica of heavenly rituals as told in myths. On special occasions the sovereign

[11] Sansom, *History of Japan*, p. 69. He cites an edict of 682, "which provides that in selecting men for office the considerations are to be first birth, then character, and then capacity."

[12] In this article the term "Sun deity" is used to refer to *Amaterasu-O-kami* (the great Kami that sheds light through all the Heaven), i.e. the Sun as the Kami. "But this Sun Kami may also be interpreted as representing a legendary human character who was supposedly the founder of the Imperial line, from which standpoint this same personality is referred to by the appellation *O-Hirume-no-Mikoto* (the Exalted one who is the Great Light of Day)." Tsuda Sokichi, "The Idea of Kami in Ancient Japanese Classics," *T'oung Pao*, Vol. LII, Book 4-5 (Leiden, 1966), 296. On various theories of the Sun deity, see Fumio Kakubayashi, "Amaterasu-O-kami no kigen" (The Origin of the Sun Deity), *Shoku-Nihongi Kenkyu*, Vol. 180 (August 1975), 1-12.

issued "imperial proclamations" (*semmyō*) which had the connotation of "revealed words issued by the Manifest Kami."[13]

Understandably, it was from this type of immanental theocratic perspective that the two chronicles as well as a series of Records of Local Surveys (*Fudoki*) were compiled. Moreover, in 815 the government issued the New Compilation of the Register of Families (*Shinsen shō-jiroku*) in order to classify the aristocracy into the three arbitrary categories of *shin-betsu* (descendants of *kami*), *kō-betsu* (descendants of royal families), and *ban-betsu* (descendants of naturalized Chinese and Koreans) by fabrication or otherwise. In so doing, the compilers of the Register resorted to the mythologization of historical and genealogical facts for the sake of solidifying the nation around the throne. Side by side with this mythologization of history, the chroniclers indulged in the historicization of myths such as the account of the descent of the Sun deity's grandson from heaven to rule Japan. They also historicized the Yamato myths concerning the legendary first emperor Jimmu, even at the expense of fabricating the year 660 B.C. as the year of the founding of the Japanese nation.[14]

Admittedly, religions, especially Shinto, enjoyed prestige and respect from the government under the Ritsuryō system. At the same time it was the government, or more precisely its Department of Kami-Affairs (*Jingikan*), which controlled all aspects of Shinto. The Department not only supervised all the officially sponsored shrines, but "its duty was [also] to oversee the registers of the entire priesthood (*hafuribe*) and of the religious corporation (*kambe* or *kamutomo*), the personnel of the *Jingikan* itself and the staffing of the principal shrines."[15] Buddhism, too, was successfully incorporated into the Ritsuryō scheme. Thus, while the government patronized Buddhist institutions extravagantly, it enforced the "Law Governing Monks and Nuns" (*Sōniryō*) and rigidly controlled the activities of clerics.[16] Moreover, the government established the Bureau of Yin and Yang (Ommyō-ryō), which was in charge of astrology, calendar-making and chronology. The total character of the Ritsuryō system of government

[13] On this subject, see Zachert Herbert, *Semmyo, die Kaiserlichen Erlasse des Shoku-Nihongi* (Berlin, 1950).

[14] Tsuda points out that the first emperor was also regarded as the Sun Kami. (Tsuda, "The Idea of Kami," 299.)

[15] Bock, *Engi-Shiki*, p. 19.

[16] On *Sōniryō*, see Kenko Futaba, *Kodai Bukkyō-shisō-shi kenkyū* (A Study of Early Japanese Buddhism) (Kyoto: Nagata Bunshōdō, 1962), Part II: "Sōni-ryō no Kenkyu," pp. 131-301; and my article, "Religions of Japan," in Wing-tsit Chan, I. R. al Faruqi, J. M. Kitagawa and P. T. Raju (comps.), *The Great Asian Religions: An Anthology* (New York: Macmillan, 1969), pp. 258-259.

may be succinctly symbolized by the duty of the Chancellor which was defined as "ordering the state and deliberating on the (Confucian) Way" and also as "harmonizing Yin and Yang."[17] In short, what developed during the seventh and eighth centuries in Japan were the two related ideologies of sacred kingship and immanental theocratic government, both of which were authenticated and supported by a "multivalue system"—an intricate homology of Shinto, Confucian, Buddhist and Yin-Yang traditions.

Ironically, while the Ritsuryō system came to be regarded as a classical paradigm in Japan, it never functioned as well as the architects of the system intended. Rather, the reality of Japanese life throughout the pre-modern period compelled the nature of both the monarchy and the government to be modified, without, however, rejecting altogether the Ritsuryō ideal as such.

MODIFICATIONS OF THE RITSURYŌ MODEL

It must be admitted candidly that from the beginning the Ritsuryō system embodied a number of serious contradictions and inconsistencies. For example, the system of land allotments and taxation, which had been borrowed *in toto* from China, could not be applied to the Japanese situation without making a series of compromises, such as granting *de facto* private ownership of land and labour to the landed aristocracy and powerful religious institutions, and/or excluding newly reclaimed land from the allotment system. Such compromises undermined one of the cornerstones of the Ritsuryō system, namely state ownership and control of land and people. Moreover, the failure of the land law coupled with the decline in the efficiency of the administrative machinery resulted in the growth of private manors (*shoen*), which in turn precipitated the rise of the warrior class and feudal institutions in subsequent periods. In a similar vein, all the important government positions, both national and provincial, were occupied by former clan leaders and members of the aristocracy, whose descendants inherited these positions according to the hereditary principle. Moreover, large Buddhist monasteries, exemplified by the national temple, Tōdai-ji, acquired land, wealth and power, competing with the aristocracy.[18] The prestige of Buddhism was greatly enhanced by the piety of Nara monarchs, one of whom declared himself the "servant of the

---

[17] Sansom, *History of Japan*, p. 70.

[18] Yosoburo Takekoshi, *The Economic Aspects of the History of the Civilization of Japan* (New York: Macmillan, 1930), Vol. 1, Chap. VIII, "Monasteries Establish a State within the State," pp. 76-91.

Three Treasures." Taking advantage of the situation, one ambitious Buddhist monk even tried to usurp the throne. Understandably, with the development of private ownership of manors, a hereditary aristocratic officialdom, and powerful religious institutions, the authority of the monarchy and the government was greatly eroded towards the latter half of the eighth century.

The transfer of the capital from Nara to Kyoto in 794 marked a new page in the history of Japan. The leaders of the Kyoto regime were eager to restore the Ritsuryō ideal of imperial rule and the authority of the central government, free from ecclesiastical interference and power struggles among the aristocracy. Their eagerness to perpetuate sacred kingship and an immanental theocratic form of government led them to compile the "Institutes or Procedures of the Engi Era" (*Engi-shiki*), which was a collection of supplementary rules (*kyaku shiki*) to previously promulgated edicts and ceremonial rules.[19] Paradoxically, by the time these procedures were put into effect in 967, the classical Ritsuryō scheme had already been modified by the emergence of the "regency" of the Fujiwara family. Here, the elaborate procedures of the Engi Institutes were applied only to the religious festivals and court ceremonies and had little or no effect on *Realpolitik*. The Ritsuryō system lost further ground by the rise of the "rule by retired monarchs" (*insei*) and finally by the "feudal regimes" of the warrior families. It is significant, however, that the sacrality of the emperor as well as his prerogative to reign over the nation were rarely questioned by the regents, retired monarchs and warrior rulers, at the same time that his power to rule the government was effectively usurped by them.

Regency

Prior to the rise of the Fujiwara oligarchy, regency was exercised only by members of the royal family in order to assist the reigning monarch when such assistance was needed. Historically, the ancestors of the Fujiwaras were hereditary Shinto priests. The family became prominent in the seventh century, and thereafter members of it held important government positions. Meanwhile, they acquired wealth and power from their ever-growing landholdings in the provinces and they also managed to intermarry frequently with the imperial family. It was in the mid-ninth century, when a child emperor was enthroned, that his maternal grandfather, Fujiwara Yoshifusa, then Chancellor, became the regent (*sesshō*), the first of non-royal blood ever to hold

[19] See Bock, *Engi-Shiki*, pp. 11-12.

such an office. When the next child emperor ascended the throne, Yoshifusa's adopted son, Motosune, became both the regent and chief counsellor (*kampaku*).[20] From the mid-tenth to the mid-eleventh centuries the nation was ruled by the Fujiwara regency, called the *sekkan (sesshō-kampaku)* system.[21]

The institutionalization of regency implied a significant redefinition of the Ritsuryō system by the aristocracy. We may recall that the early Yamato kingdom was in effect a confederation of semi-autonomous territorial clans—precursors of the aristocratic families—which was held together by the magico-religious authority of the imperial clan. And, true to their heritage, the aristocratic families never fully accepted at face value the Ritsuryō ideologies of kingship and government. To be sure, they acknowledged the sacrality of the throne, but they expected the emperor to function literally and only as the Manifest Kami, that is to reign but not to interfere with the actual operation of the government, which they took for granted to be the prerogative of the aristocratic officials. This view was based on reading Japanese historical experience through the mental prism of the aristocracy, another form of mythologization of history. Parenthetically, this view of Japanese history was articulated by Jien—the son of a Fujiwara regent and a prelate of Tendai Buddhism—in his famous work, the *Gukanshō* or "Miscellany of the Personal Views of an Ignorant Fool."[22] Because of this view of the nature of kingship and government, the Fujiwaras relentlessly sought political power while venerating the throne. Thus it was no hypocrisy when a regent stated: "Great as are our power and prestige, nevertheless they are those of the Sovereign, for we derive them from the majesty of the Throne."[23]

The regency, however, came to be challenged by ambitious retired monarchs who in turn created another institution which was not anticipated by the architects of the Ritsuryō system.

Rule by retired monarchs (insei)

Throughout Japanese history emperors were known to have abdicated the throne for various reasons, but abdication for the purpose

[20] The combination of *sesshō* (regent) and *kampaku* (chief counsellor) implied that Motosune was to serve as permanent regent, regardless of the age of the reigning emperor.

[21] For other offices unknown in the Ritsuryō system, e.g., the *Kurandōdokoro* (Palace Secretariat) and the *Kebiishi-chō* (Police Commissioners), see Sansom, *History of Japan*, pp. 113-116.

[22] On the *Gukanshō*, see Charles H. Hambrick, *Gukanshō: A Religious View of Japanese History* (Unpublished Ph.D. Thesis, The University of Chicago, 1971).

[23] Quoted in Sansom, *History of Japan*, p. 157.

of ruling the nation behind titular sovereigns did not appear until the eleventh century.[24] In contrast to the Fujiwara regents, who derived their prerogatives from the fact that they were relatives on the maternal side of the nominally reigning emperors, the retired monarchs derived their prerogatives from the patriarchal principle. That is to say, even when an emperor turned over the "charisma of the imperial office" to his son or brother, the abdicated monarch could still control the affairs of the court as the legitimate head of the patriarchal imperial family. Retired monarchs were usually provided with living quarters (*go-in*), staffed with a few servants and attendants, in the rear of the imperial residence. But when retired monarchs became *de facto* rulers, their quarters became the court and administrative offices (*go-in-cho*), well staffed with officials (*in-shi*) and guards. Also, an ordinance issued by the retired monarch (*inzen*) carried the same authority as imperial ordinances, if not more. Probably the most powerful *insei* ruler was Go-Shirakawa (r. 1155-1158 as Emperor; 1158-1192 as *insei*), who dominated the political scene during the reigns of five titular emperors. After his time, *insei* lost much of its influence, although the system as such lasted for another half a century.

The development of *insei* inevitably drove the Fujiwara regents closer to the neglected reigning monarchs, while the retired monarchs attracted those aristocratic families and local magnates who were disgruntled by Fujiwara rule. Also, the fact that some of the retired monarchs took priestly vows resulted in an alliance between *insei* and ecclesiastical institutions. For the most part, the *insei* era was characterized by an ugly power struggle among competing ex-monarchs or between ex-monarchs and titular monarchs and also between *insei* officials and the regency officials, abuse of authority, nepotism, and administrative inefficiency. The result was the general erosion of even the residual structure of the Ritsuryō system, including the monarchy and the civilian form of government. This situation produced the rise of the warrior families who soon supplanted the aristocratic civilian rule centering around the throne and the *insei*.

Feudal regime (bakufu)

Originally, the warriors (*samurai*) were nothing more than armed attendants (*samurau-mono*), subservient to the aristocrats and ecclesiastical authorities who used them as armed guards to protect their manors in the provinces. In the course of time, the warriors developed

[24] On the beginning of the *insei* system, see G. Cameron Hurst, "The Reign of Go-Sanjō and the Revival of Imperial Power," *Monumenta Nipponica*, Vol. XXVII, No. 1 (Spring 1972), 65-83.

their own solidarity groups, based on the feudal relationship of masters and vassals, as well as on regional and kinship ties. Some of the warrior families were charged with maintaining law and order in the capital, where they gained political influence. The two most prominent among these were the Taira and the Minamoto clans, and their rivalry became fierce as they fought on opposite sides in the complex power struggle among emperors, ex-emperors and the Fujiwara family. For a while the chieftain of the Taira dominated the scene and even became Chancellor, which was the highest civilian position in the Ritsuryō scheme. Soon, however, the tables were turned, and the victorious chieftain of the Minamoto clan, Yoritomo, pressured the court to grant him the authority to appoint stewards (*jitō*) and constables (*shugo*) in order to keep order in the provinces and also to collect taxes in certain circumstances. By granting such authority, as Sansom astutely observes, the court "handed to the leader of the military class effective jurisdiction in matters of land tenure and the income derived from agriculture, the vital features of a land revenue economy."[25] Then in 1192 Yoritomo received the coveted title of generalissimo (*Sei-i Tai Shōgun*), and established the feudal regime (*bakufu*) at Kamakura, far from the court in Kyoto. Soon, however, power was assumed by the Hōjō family, which controlled the Kamakura regime as the shogun's regents (*shikken*).

The Kamakura regime was very simple in structure, consisting of three bureaus—military (*samurai-dokoro*), administrative (*kumonjo*, later renamed *mandokoro*), and judiciary (*monchū-jo*). It depended on stewards (*jitō*) and constables (*shugo*) to keep order in the provinces. Also, unlike the elaborate penal and civil codes of the Ritsuryō system, the legislation of the Kamakura regime, called *Jōei shikimoku*, consisted of fifty-one pragmatic principles. By training and by temperament the warriors believed in such simple virtues as frugality, fidelity and justice in the feudal sense. To them, the sacrality of the sovereign was also subordinate to the principle of justice, and thus was neither absolute nor inviolable. Thus in 1221, when the ex-emperor Go-Toba and others undertook an abortive military campaign to eliminate the feudal regime, the Kamakura leaders dared to fight against the imperial authority on the ground of social justice, and afterwards sent three ex-emperors into exile.[26] Even Kitabataka Chikafusa, a high ranking warrior and a chief theoretician of the short-lived imperial rule (1333-1335), wrote in his *Jinnō-shōtō-ki* (Records of the Legitimate Succes-

[25] Sansom, *History of Japan*, p. 318.
[26] See Takekoshi, *Economic Aspects*, pp. 187-188.

sion of the Divine Sovereigns): "Although the Emperor is august, the gods would not allow him to make one person happy and cause many to suffer. According to the right and wrong of ruling there is always to be found a path to righteousness."[27]

The second feudal regime was established by the Ashikaga family, and it lasted until 1573. Unlike the Kamakura regime, which directly controlled the warrior families, the Ashikaga regime controlled only the feudal lords (*shuga daimyō*), who in turn claimed the allegiance of their vassals. Also, unlike the Kamakura regime, the Ashikaga regime was established in Kyoto and absorbed the civilian government of the court into the feudal framework. Thus, the third shogun, Yoshimitsu, became Chancellor and assumed the kingship in his dealings with the Ming court.[28] Following the devastating Ōnin War (1467-1477), however, the authority of the Ashikaga regime declined. During the century of incessant warfare that followed, private manors that had supported the aristocracy and the court were ransacked by self-made *daimyō (sengoku daimyō)*. Inevitably the centuries-old Ritsuryō ideal lost its mystique, and the imperial family and the courtiers barely survived with the help of their magico-religious aura. This situation lasted until the close of the sixteenth century.

The third and last feudal regime, under the Tokugawa family, had the longest career (1603-1867), with its headquarters in Edo (present Tokyo). By design the Tokugawas established permanent martial law, as it were. The nation was divided into 260 fiefs (*han*) of different sizes and importance. The shogun, with the assistance of advisory bodies at various levels, ruled his own territory directly, and other parts of the nation indirectly through the lords of the fiefs (*daimyō*). There were also many administrative posts, e.g., the commissioners of temples and shrines, of finance, and of cities, as well as censors. The populace was permanently divided into four main social classes: warrior, farmer, artisan, and merchant. In addition, ecclesiastics, courtiers and imperial families were recognized as special categories. In spite of lip service paid to the throne, the regime barely supported or tolerated the imperial institution. The Ordinances for the Imperial and Courtier Families (*Kinchū narabini Kegeshū shohatto*), issued in 1615, strictly regulated all the possible activities of the royal family and courtiers, even to the extent that the emperor needed the approval of the regime

[27] Quoted in Toshio Kuroda, "Gukanshō and Jinnō Shōtōki," in *New Light on Early and Medieval Japanese Historiography*, trans. with intro. by John A. Harrison (University of Florida Monographs, Social Sciences, No. 4 [Fall 1959]), p. 37.

[28] It is said that the Court offered the title of ex-emperor (*dajōtennō*) to him upon his death.

to appoint officials in his own court or to grant purple robes to high ranking clerics. Under the constant surveillance of the shogun's deputies (*Shoshi-dai*), the once-powerful sovereign became in effect a glorified prisoner under the Tokugawa rule.

POSTSCRIPT

In retrospect it becomes evident that the Ritsuryō ideologies of monarchy and government, which were developed from the intricate fusion of indigenous and Chinese features during the seventh and eighth centuries, characterized by sacred kingship and an immanental theocratic government, remained a classical paradigm throughout premodern Japanese history. However, the structure of government was transformed by various stresses which saw the rise of the regency, the rule by retired monarchs, and finally the feudal regimes. Furthermore the Ritsuryō ideal of sacred kingship was modified and reinterpreted by the regency, by the retired monarchs and by the warrior rulers, in that the sovereign's authority to reign was recognized, but not his prerogative to rule.

By far the most radical redefinition of the Ritsuryō system was carried out by the Tokugawa feudal regime, which developed its own form of immanental theocracy with its first shogun regarded as the manifestation of the "Sun God of the East" (*Tōshō*) and the guardian of the regime. Space does not allow us to compare in detail the difference between the Ritsuryō ideology of immanental theocracy and that of the Tokugawa regime except for some brief observations. It is probably fair to say that according to the Ritsuryō system the immanental theocratic state had an integral relationship with the sacred kingship, whereby the divine claim of the throne authenticated the soteriological character of the state as the nation of the *kami*. While this ideology was couched in terms taken from Chinese political theories, its theoretical basis was not derived from Chinese sources but rather from the archaic indigenous mythical tradition. In sharp contrast to the Ritsuryō scheme, the Tokugawa regime, which depended on Neo-Confucianism as its guiding "theology," developed its own ideology of immanental theocracy which did not need the sacrality of the sovereign except as a magico-religious embellishment for the continuity of national history. Accordingly, the Tokugawa ideology affirmed that "the order of heaven is not a transcendental substance but is inherent in the conditions of human existence."[29] This form of immanental theocracy

[29] William S. Haas, *The Destiny of the Mind, East and West* (London: Faber and Faber, 1956), p. 140.

looks for its legitimation not in the mythological past, but in the regulative principle which is implicit in the concrete human, social, and political order.

But the fact that even the Tokugawa regime tolerated, and paid lip service to, the imperial institution—itself a vestige of the outdated Ritsuryō system—may be a matter of some significance in our attempt to understand the nature of pre-modern Japan. It may also explain why the modernization of Japan, which commenced with the Meiji Restoration in 1868, owes a significant part of its impetus to the classical Ritsuryō paradigm.

6. The Shadow of the Sun: A Glimpse of the Fujiwara and the Imperial Families in Japan

INTRODUCTION

IN ANY PART of the world a monarchy requires for its survival the support structure and the service of faithful and congenial official-doms. In the case of Japan, the remarkable longevity of the imperial family would not have been possible without the existence of the Fu-jiwara family, which from the seventh century A.D. supported—and utilized—imperial prestige for its own survival. It should be noted that both the imperial and the Fujiwara families, which for centuries had intertwined by marriage and political partnership, justified their re-spective *raisons d'être* in terms of a common mythohistory: the former asserted the right to govern the nation because of its claim of solar ancestry; the latter justified its role as the chief collaborator of the Sun Line by reference to a mythological ancestor who had been an impor-tant figure in the heavenly court of the Sun Goddess. In the course of time the Fujiwara noblemen attained *de facto* dictatorial power to rule, but they never questioned the prerogative of the imperial family to reign over the nation. The Fujiwaras saw themselves to be the "shadow" of the Sun Line and, quite astutely, avoided any temptation to usurp the throne. Even so, during certain periods of Japanese his-tory they literally overshadowed the imperial family.

The intertwining of the Fujiwara and the imperial families—or the "shadow" and the "sun"—is a complex historic phenomenon: as such, no single study can deal adequately with all of its dimensions. This article approaches this phenomenon primarily from the perspective of the history of religions. The imperial family incarnated the native Shinto tradition. The Fujiwara, earlier known as the Nakatomi, was originally a hereditary Shinto priestly family but later became as well a powerful patron of Buddhism. These facts invite an historian of re-ligions to ask how the intertwining of these two families coincided with the development of Japanese religious history.

Let us first take a cursory look at Japan before the time of Fujiwara

(Nakatomi) Kamatari (A.D. 614-669), the first patriarch of the Fujiwara family.

THE EARLY YAMATO KINGDOM

We are not concerned in this article with the prehistoric development of Japanese mythology, religion, language, and social and political organization.[1] Our knowledge of the early phase of the historic period of Japan is scanty. This is true particularly of the beginning of the so-called Yamato Kingdom, which essentially was a confederation of semi-autonomous *uji* (which is a lineage group and is usually translated as "clan").[2] However, there are some references to Japan in three Chinese records. We are led to believe that by the third century A.D. there were a number of tribal principalities in the Japanese archipelago and that there was a female shamanic ruler, Pimiku (Himiko in Japanese, meaning "sun daughter" or "sun princess"), who reigned over one of the principalities, namely Yamatai. Apparently she also had some influence over other principalities as well. Pimiku was reported to be old and unmarried and to have devoted herself to magic. We also learn that she was "assisted in the government of the country by a junior kinsman, classificatorily a 'younger brother'. . . . She herself was . . . totally secluded from the populace while yet being served by a thousand female attendants together with one male, who provided her food and transmitted her pronouncements. . . ."[3]

Evidently, at least eight times between the mid-first and the mid-third centuries A.D. envoys were dispatched to China from some of the principalities in Japan. Similarly, Korean sources tell us, Japanese envoys were dispatched several times during the fourth century to Paekche—one of the Korean kingdoms—and that the Japanese gained a foothold in the southern tip of the Korean peninsula.[4] These foreign sources describe a nation that was growing rapidly in the third, fourth, and fifth centuries. This period of Japanese history is labelled the Tumulus (*Kofun* in Japanese) period: at that time a number of huge mounds were built in the present Nara and Osaka districts. These great tombs of the aristocrats are the archaeological remains of what historians refer to as the Yamato Kingdom. Scholars hold differing opinions

---

[1] See J. M. Kitagawa, "Prehistoric Background of Japanese Religion," *History of Religions* II, no. 2 (Winter 1963), pp. 292-328. [Chapter 1 of this book.]

[2] Among many good studies on early Japan, I would recommend especially Paul Wheatley and Thomas See, *From Court to Capital: A Tentative Interpretation of the Origins of the Japanese Urban Tradition* (University of Chicago Press, 1978).

[3] See ibid., p. 31.

[4] Enoki Kazuo, *Yamatai-koku* (Tokyo, 1960), pp. 164-175.

about various questions: when the imperial family began to claim suzerainty over other autonomous *uji*, whether or not there were dynastic changes, and whether or not a new ethnic group from the Asiatic continent had invaded and established itself as the new ruling power.

At any rate, Japanese chronicles compiled later in the seventh and eighth centuries portray early Japan as a paradigmatic period in which virtuous monarchs reigned over a growing nation. Yet, what comes through the accounts of early monarchs is a picture of tribal chieftains gradually expanding their spheres of influence by combining military force with religious claims that justified their authority. More often than not their actions were dictated by the precarious will of the heavenly and earthly *kami* (semidivine beings), transmitted to them through dreams and divinations. Thus, one of the chief functions of the chieftains of early Japan was to maintain close contact with the *kami*. This was done both through the assistance of shamans, diviners, and other religious functionaries, and through political activities. This unity of religion and political activity was later called *saisei-itchi* (unity of *matsuri* and *matsuri-goto*).[5] According to official chronicles, the tenth legendary emperor, Sujin, became uneasy with living in the palace in which were held religious functions for the imperial ancestress, the Sun Goddess, and the *kami* of the Yamato region (Yamato-no-ō-kuni-tama). As dicated by the message given to him in a dream, Sujin established separate shrines for the *kami*, and appointed imperial princesses to be in charge of their worship. According to the accounts, the eleventh legendary emperor, Suinin, moved the shrine of the Sun Goddess to Ise, as was her wish. The account of the twelfth legendary emperor, Keikō, weaves into the story a tale of a hero, Yamato-takeru, who the story alleges singlehandedly conquered the chieftains of Kyushu Island and the eastern provinces.

The most fascinating account is that of Empress Jingō, or Jingū (literally, the "Shrine of Kami"), the chief consort of the fourteenth legendary emperor Chūai and the shamanic diviner *par excellence*. (Parenthetically, many scholars believe that the model of Jingō's account is the story of Himiko, who was mentioned in the Chinese accounts.) Jingō is portrayed as the real ruler of Japan after the death of her husband and is credited with personally commanding the armada and establishing a military base on the Korean peninsula. Significantly, she was assisted by Takeshi-uchi-no-sukune, probably a male medium who deciphered the messages from the *kami*. It is also to be noted that

<hr />

[5] On this subject, see J. M. Kitagawa, "*Matsuri and Matsuri-goto*: Religion and State in Early Japan," *Religious Traditions* II, no. 1 (April 1979), pp. 30-37. [Chapter 7 of this book.]

some other imperial consorts of early Japan were given the title *na-katsu-sumera-mikoto*, which could mean either "the one who carries on the imperial duty between the death of her husband and the ascension of the next emperor" or "the august medium who transmits the *mikoto* (divine word) of the heavenly *kami*."[6]

As stated earlier, the early Yamato kingdom was a loosely knit confederation of autonomous *uji* (clan), each one a territorially based cluster of families who shared the same tutelary *kami* and kinship ties. Each *uji* was held together by its chieftain whose authority over the land and people within his domain was derived from his priestly or cultic prerogatives and economic control. Evidently, sometime toward the end of the fourth century A.D. the chieftain of the imperial *uji*, presumably Ojin, the fifteenth emperor according to official chronicles, began to exert a measure of dominance over other *uji*. The Yamato (imperial) chieftains paid tribute to China, and in return, received the kingly title from the Chinese imperial court. With their claim of genealogical descendancy from the Sun Goddess, and now equipped with the monarchical title, the Yamato rulers assumed the imperial prerogatives of conferring court titles on the chieftains of powerful *uji*, granting them sacred seeds at spring festivals, and establishing sacred sites and regulating rituals for their *kami*. Nevertheless (as Professor Waida has pointed out), the Yamato king was "not the absolute monarch ruling over a centralized state but merely a *primus inter pares* who ran the politics, controlling and being controlled by [other *uji* chieftains who held titles in the court]."[7] Several *uji* chieftains were influential in the court; among them were the chieftains of the two hereditary Shinto priestly families (the Nakatomi and the Imibe [Imbe]), the hereditary family of the bodyguards of the imperial house (the Otomo), and the family which supplied arms and weapons (the Mononobe). As George Sansom succinctly states, "these grand nobles were in a position to challenge, if they wished, the authority of the Throne, by virtue of their wealth as well as their descent. Of lower rank were the country gentry ('Kunitsuko' or 'Kuni no miyatsuko'), local landholders of various origins, some possessing large estates, others only a modest area of farm land."[8] Invariably, the quarrelsome

[6] See J. M. Kitagawa, *Religion in Japanese History* (Columbia University Press, 1966), pp. 21-22.

[7] Manabu Waida, "Sacred Kingship in Early Japan: A Historical Introduction," *History of Religions* XV, no. 4 (May 1976), p. 323.

[8] George Sansom, *A History of Japan to 1334* (London, The Cresset Press, 1958), p. 38.

uji chieftains were involved in the succession disputes as well as in domestic and foreign policies.

THE PRECURSORS OF THE FUJIWARA: THE RISE OF THE SOGA AND VARIOUS INFLUENCES FROM THE CONTINENT

The political situation in Asia around the turn of the fifth century did not allow Japan to remain isolated from the influence of China and Korea. Among the Chinese immigrants who sought refuge in Japan because of the political turmoil in their homeland were intellectuals and artisans who were quickly welcomed by the imperial court and some of the powerful *uji* leaders as scribes, teachers, accountants, and technicians. Fourth-century Japanese military involvement in the power struggle among Korean kingdoms precipitated close cultural contacts between Korea and Japan. The arrival at about A.D. 400 of Korean scholars who were well versed in Chinese classics marked the official introduction of Sino-Korean civilization into Japan. The infusion of new technologies, of the art of reading and writing Chinese script, of alien forms of art and architecture, of sophisticated legal systems, of Taoist and Yin-Yang philosophies and Confucian ethical concepts, and of complex ways of administering the government brought about a series of social, cultural, economic, and political changes in Japan. Inevitably, tension developed between those members of Japanese society who welcomed and benefited from foreign contact and those who rejected it.

The sixth century A.D. was a turbulent era for Japan both internally and externally. Internally, a series of succession disputes among members of the imperial house involved and encouraged the rivalry among ambitious *uji* chieftains, specifically the Katsuragi, Heguri, Otomo, Mononobe, and Soga. The Katsuragi and Heguri chieftains lost out in the power struggle. Externally, the Japanese enclave on the southern tip of the Korean peninsula was threatened by the rising tide of three competing Korean kingdoms, namely Silla, Paekche, and Koguryŏ. The Otomo chieftain, Kanamura, was accused of taking bribes from Paekche and lost influence in the court. This opened the way for the rise of the Soga chieftain. It was in the midst of such a tense, diplomatic negotiation that the King of Paekche, who desperately wanted military assistance from Japan, presented the Yamato court with an image of the Buddha, some Buddhist scriptures, and various ceremonial ornaments. He urged the Yamato court to adopt Buddhism on the grounds that it would bring immeasurable blessings. This event, which probably took place in A.D. 538 (or in 552 according to other sources), was considered the official beginning of Buddhist expansion into Japan, even though Buddhism undoubtedly had been known earlier among the Chinese and Korean settlers.

The introduction of Buddhism added new fuel to the rivalry between those who favoured Buddhism and an alliance with Paekche (represented by the Soga chieftain) and those who were anti-Buddhist and anti-Paekche (represented by the chieftains of the Mononobe and the Nakatomi). It should be noted in this connection that the chieftain of the Soga *uji*, Soga Iname, consolidated power by adopting new ideas and new methods introduced by Chinese and Korean settlers and by marrying off his daughters to the imperial family. The fact that two emperors, Bidatsu and Yōmei, were his daughters' sons gave Soga Iname a great advantage over the Mononobe chief, who was his primary competitor in the court. In contrast to the "progressive" Soga chief, the *uji* chieftain of the Mononobe, who claimed to control its eighty branch families, stood for the value system of the early Yamato kingdom. This implies a conservative orientation of the Mononobe *uji*. Understandably, the Nakatomi chieftain—a prominent court priest—did not favour the adoption of an alien religion. It is interesting that the introduction of Buddhism resulted in the creation of a designation for the native religious tradition, which was not a unified system of cults and beliefs at the time. At any rate, two Chinese characters—*shin* for "kami" and *tō* for "the way—were combined ("*Shintō*") to refer to the native religious tradition in distinction to *Butsu-dō*, or "the Way of the Buddha."[9]

A colourful drama evolved during the second half of the sixth century as a result of the combination of the pro- and anti-Buddhist controversy, the pro-Paekche versus pro-Silla policy debate, the succession disputes within the imperial family, and the power struggle between the Soga and the Mononobe chieftains. In all of this it was the Soga chieftain who triumphed, precipitating the rise of the Fujiwara (Nakatomi) *uji* in the seventh century.

While the anti-Buddhist Mononobe and Nakatomi chieftains argued that the worship of foreign divinities would offend the native *kami*, the pro-Buddhist Soga chieftain obtained the court's approval to worship the image of the Buddha "as an experiment." But a pestilence broke out when the Soga started their worship of the Buddha. The anti-Buddhist factions then secured the court's approval to throw the image of the Buddha into a canal. With the ascension of the pro-

---

[9] Karl Florenz, "Die Japaner," *Lehrbuch der Religionsgeschichte*, edited by Alfred Bertholet and Eduard Lehmann (Tübingen, 1925), p. 267.

Buddhist Emperor Yōmei, who was the son of a Soga lady, the Soga chieftain Umako (son of Iname) secured in A.D. 584 images of the Buddha and of Maitreya ("the Buddha yet to come"). He built a temple in which to install these images and persuaded three maidens to become nuns. Thus, nourished with royal favour and the patronage of the powerful Soga chieftain, the seeds of Buddhism were planted in Japan.

Meanwhile, the on-again off-again armed conflict in Korea between Paekche and Silla, and between the combined forces of Paekche and Silla against Koguryŏ, accelerated the foreign policy disputes between the pro-Paekche Mononobe and the pro-Silla Soga chieftains in the Yamato court. Although the court sent armed forces to assist Paekche in 554, Paekche was miserably defeated by Silla in the following year. Furthermore, in 562 Silla absorbed the Japanese enclave entirely. There is much truth in Sansom's observation that Japan lost its Korean foothold not for military reasons, but 'because the central government in Yamato could not depend upon the obedience of the great territorial chieftains in western Japan, especially in Kyushu, or upon the loyalty of its representaties in Korea, or indeed upon the integrity of its Great Ministers at Court."[10] To make the matter more complex, the unification of China in 589 by the Sui dynasty presented a potential threat to the very survival of Japan itself.

Following the sudden death of Emperor Yōmei in 587 after a brief reign of two years, the Mononobe chieftain, Moriya, supported Prince Anahobe's candidacy for the throne. However, both the prince and the Mononobe chieftain were attacked and killed by the Soga chieftain and his allies. Emperor Sushun (or Sujun) who then ascended to the throne in this difficult situation was the brother of Prince Anahobe. The new emperor's attempt to undermine the power of the Soga backfired and he was assassinated in cold blood by the Soga's henchmen in 592. With the elimination of his enemies, the Mononobe chieftain and the disgruntled emperor, the Soga chieftain—Umako—could exercise freely his dictatorial power.

EMPRESS SUIKO AND PRINCE SHŌTOKU

In the year 593 Suiko, who was the first Empress in the history of Japan, ascended to the throne. Suiko, the daughter of a Soga lady, was the sister of the late Emperor Yōmei and the widowed ex-empress of Bidatsu. Suiko's appointment of her nephew Prince Shōtoku (573-

---

[10] Sansom, *History of Japan*, p. 47.

621) as the regent echoed the legendary patterns of both the collaboration between Himiko and her brother and the partnership of Empress Jingō and Takeshi-uchi-no-sukune. Nevertheless, it established a new and official precedent for the division of responsibility between the monarch who reigns and the regent who rules. We soon will discuss how this precedent later was followed and fully exploited by the Fujiwara regency. It should be noted that during the tenure of Prince Shōtoku's regency (593-621) the Soga chieftain's dictatorial power, though unrivalled in the court, was somewhat restrained.

Despite numerous pious accounts and idealized legends, not much is known for certain about the life of Prince Shōtoku.[11] There is one account in the chronicle that might give a realistic portrayal of Shōtoku, then called Prince Mumayado (Umayado). In the battle of A.D. 587 between the Soga and Mononobe forces, the prince sided with the Soga:

The army of the Imperial Princes and the troops of the Ministers were timid and afraid, and fell back three times. At this time the Imperial Prince Mumayado, his hair being tied upon the temples . . . followed in the rear of the army. He pondered in his own mind, saying to himself:—"Are we not going to be beaten? Without prayer we cannot succeed." So he cut down a nuride tree, and swiftly fashioned images of the four Heavenly Kings. Placing them on his top-knot, he uttered a vow:—"If we are now made to gain victory over the enemy, I promise faithfully to honour the four Heavenly Kings, guardians of the world, by erecting to them a temple with a pagoda. The Oho-omi Soga no Mumako [Umako] also uttered a vow. . . ."[12]

We are told that when the Mononobe *uji* was annihilated, the prince erected the Temple of Four Heavenly Guardians (Shitennō-ji) in Settsu (present Osaka), while the Soga chieftain built the Temple of the Promotion of the Law (Hōkō-ji) in Asuka, the district where the imperial court was situated. From the above account we learn that Prince Shōtoku's entry into imperial administration as the regent was no doubt approved and supported by the Soga chieftain, who held the position of O-omi ("Great Minister"). We also learn from this account that even though Shōtoku was idealized as the paragon of Buddhist piety, learning, and sainthood, he shared his contemporaries' fascination with the magico-religious aspects of Buddhism. However, this did

---

[11] The idealized accounts of his life recorded in the official chronicles and remembered in popular tales follow what historians of religions call the "law of sacred biography," exemplified by an unusual birth, demonstration of superhuman abilities in childhood and youth, reappearance after death, etc.

[12] W. G. Aston, trans., *Nihongi: Chronicles of Japan from the Earliest Times to A.D. 697* (London, 1896; Rutland, Vermont, and Tokyo, 1972), Volume 2, pp. 113-114.

not diminish his great contribution to the transformation of Buddhism from a *uji*-centred religion to a court-sponsored national religion.[13]

In retrospect it becomes evident that while Prince Shōtoku himself was a pious Buddhist, the policies ascribed to him—as exemplified both by the establishment of the Chinese-style "cap-ranks" of twelve grades for court ministers and officials and by the promulgation of the so-called "Seventeen-Article Constitution"—represented a serious attempt to harmonize Buddhist and Confucian traditions with the native Shinto tradition. Assuming that (even if it was compiled in this form later) this constitution represented some of his basic principles, we gather that Shōtoku exalted the throne and urged the veneration of Buddhism while at the same time he was persuaded that the principle of government administration was "propriety,"[14] as taught in the Confucian tradition. The fourth article of the constitution states:

The ministers and officials should abide by propriety, which is the principle of governing the people. . . . Only when the ministers abide by propriety, the hierarchical ranks will not be disrupted, and when the people abide by propriety, the nation will be governed peacefully by its own accord.[15]

Thus, the constitution is explicit in stating that the Confucian notion of propriety was a new sociopolitical principle for the hierarchically centralized national community that Shōtoku and his advisers were determined to bring about under imperial authority.

Shōtoku's regime had to adapt its foreign policy to the changing balance of power in Korea and the rising power of China under the Sui dynasty. It is interesting to note that after two aborted attempts to send expeditionary forces against Silla, its policy changed to one of conciliation. The regime also reestablished official contact with the Chinese court, a practice which had been absent during the previous 180 years. Undoubtedly, Shōtoku and his advisers were keenly aware of the necessity of securing superior and more up-to-date knowledge and technology from Silla and China in order to elevate the cultural standards and to consolidate the political structure of Japan. Realizing that the projected central government would require formal codes of

---

[13] We share Sir Charles Eliot's observation regarding the introduction of Buddhism to Japan: "though it was judged by the crude standard of its power to stop plague and though it triumphed as part of the principles of [the Soga *uji*], these accidents must not blind us to the fact that it came as the epitome of Indian and Chinese civilization and wrought a moral as well as an intellectual revolution." (Eliot, *Japanese Buddhism* [New York, Barnes & Noble, 1959], p. 202.)

[14] Propriety—*li* in Chinese; pronounced variously as *rei, iya,* or *iyamai* in Japanese.

[15] Cited in W-T. Chan, I. R. al Faruqi, J. M. Kitagawa, and P. T. Raju, *The Great Asian Religions: An Anthology* (New York, Macmillan, 1969), p. 250.

law and trained bureaucrats, the regime sent a number of talented young scholars and Buddhist monks to China for study. Some of them, Minamibuchi-no-Shōan, Takamuko-no-Genri, and Monk Min, for example, remained in China for over thirty years and witnessed the decline of the Sui dynasty and the rise of the T'ang dynasty in A.D. 618. Upon their return they played key roles in the development of law and government reform. Most of the reform measures considered in Shōtoku's regime, however, remained unfulfilled before his untimely death in A.D. 621. In one project Shōtoku asked for the cooperation of the Soga chieftain, Umako, in an attempt to collate in his lifetime "the records of the Sovereigns (*Tennō*), the country, the Imperial Chieftains (*Omi*), the Divine Chieftains (*Muraji*), the Court Chieftains (*Tomo no miyatsuko*), the Local Chieftains (*Kuni no miyatsuko*), the various hereditary corporations (*be*), and the common people."[16] Unfortunately, most of the records compiled for this project were destroyed in the fire of 645.

As might be expected, the death of Prince-Regent Shōtoku prompted the Soga chieftain to strive for more despotic power. For example, he dared to demand a piece of land owned by the imperial house so that it could become the permanent fief of the Soga.[17] While the aged empress diplomatically turned down the presumptuous demand of her maternal uncle, Soga no Umako, this incident indicates the extent to which the Soga took its own prestige for granted. Furthermore, upon the death of Empress Suiko, Umako's son, Emishi, who had become Great Minister, assumed the right to choose her successor. When Emperor Jomei (r. 628-641), whom the Soga party placed on the throne, died, Umako manoeuvred to have Jomei's consort become Empress Kōgyoku (r. 642-645). We are told that Emishi behaved more like a sovereign, conferring high ranks upon his son, Iruka, and others. Moreover, Iruka's forces mercilessly attacked Prince Shōtoku's son, Yamashiro no Oye, whose prestige remained a potential threat to the Soga power. According to the chronicle, Yamashiro no Oye and his family committed suicide at Hōryū-ji, the famous temple built by Prince Shōtoku.

Understandably, the arrogance and tyrannical behaviour of the Soga family solidified the opposition, which then plotted the elimination of the Soga power. The chief architect of the anti-Soga intrigue was Nakatomi, later renamed Fujiwara, Kamatari.

[16] Aston, *Nihongi*, Volume 2, p. 148.
[17] See ibid., p. 138.

THE RISE OF THE FUJIWARA (NAKATOMI)

According to accepted biographies, Kamatari or Kamako (614-669), the grand patriarch of the Fujiwara family, was born in Asuka, where the imperial court was situated. He was the son of Nakatomi Mike, a high-ranking court priest who served under Empress Suiko and Emperor Jomei. His mother was Otomo Kui, or Lady Otomo, whose grandfather Kanamura had lost power in the court because he mishandled the Korean policy. However, there are reasons to believe that Kamatari was born into a less prestigious branch of the Nakatomi *uji*, the hereditary priestly family of the Kashima shrine in the Hitachi district (in the present Ibaraki prefecture).[18] Most likely, Kamatari came as a young boy to Yamato and affiliated with the main branch of the Nakatomi family.[19] This family, known earlier as Urabe ("Diviner"), had adopted the name of Nakatomi (Naka-tori-omi, "the one who mediates between *kami* and the emperor") during the reign of Emperor Kinmei (r. 540-571). This was when Buddhism was just becoming known in Japan. We agree with Professor Tamura's idea that the practice of reciting Shinto prayers (*Norito*) was modelled on Buddhist practices of scripture recitation, and that the Nakatomi priests played an important role in the formulation of Shinto prayers.[20] As we noted earlier, at the time of the Buddhist controversy the Nakatomi chieftain sided with the Mononobe against the pro-Buddhist stance of the Soga. However, after the decline of the Mononobe the Nakatomi became subservient to the all-powerful Soga chieftains. The Nakatomi was given in turn the important office of reciting Shinto prayers before the Sun Goddess's sacred mirror in the court rituals.

It is interesting to note that Kamatari declined the appointment as court priest. His reasons for doing so are not clear: some scholars suspect it was because he was not the real offspring of Nakatomi Mike; others suggest that he had already grown to resent the Soga's dictatorial power in the court. At any rate, he retired to a country estate at Mishima, the present-day Takatsuki in the Osaka prefecture. There he plotted against the Soga power. He discovered that the reigning empress Kōgyoku's son, Prince Naka no Oye, shared the same anti-Soga sentiment. Both Kamatari and the prince studied Confucian classics

[18] See "Hitachi Fudoki," *Traditions*, Volume 1, Number 3 (Tokyo, The East Publications, Inc., 1977), p. 63. The *O-kagami* ("Great Mirror"), a medieval historical work that deals with the prosperity of the Fujiwara family, records that Kamatari was born in Hitachi. It also is interesting to note that Kashima-myōjin is one of the four main *kami* of the Kasuga, the tutelary shrine of the Fujiwara family, in Nara.

[19] Tamura Enchō, *Fujiwara Kamatari* (Tokyo, Hanawa Shobo, 1966), p. 26.

[20] Ibid., pp. 20-21.

under Minamibuchi no Shōan, a scholar who had returned recently from China. Both were determined to eliminate the Soga and to establish a despotic, centralized government structure under the rule of the imperial family. Kamatari, Prince Naka no Oye, and other conspirators staged a *coup d'état* in 645 on the day when the Korean envoys were received by the empress. In the midst of the ceremony Soga no Iruka was assassinated, and the following day Iruka's father, the Great Minister Soga no Emishi, also was killed. Thus ended the Soga family, which had dominated the political scene for half a century.

Following the *coup d'état* Empress Kōgyoku "abdicated" the throne, setting a precedent that was followed many times in subsequent history. Kamatari manoeuvred to get Kōgyoku's brother enthroned as Emperor Kōtoku and Naka no Oye installed as Crown Prince, functioning essentially as a regent. Kamatari himself was made the "consultant" (*naishin* or *uchitsu-mayetsu-gimi*), a position that was lower in rank but in reality far more influential than the Left- and Right-Ministers. The new regime assigned Taika (Great Reform) as the name of the era and promulgated the Edict of Reform. The regime aimed to consolidate the central bureaucratic structure of the government by such sinified measures as land redistribution, revenue collection, and census-taking. It also established the special status of the Kinai ("inner provinces"), or provinces that lay close to the city in which the government was situated.

In spite of the high-sounding rhetoric, the sweeping reform measures were neither adequately understood nor supported. Moreover, the cause of the reform was hindered by rebellion attempts by some members of the imperial family and by the expensive transference of the capital from Yamato to Naniwa then to Kyushu then back again to Yamato and finally to Omi. With the death of the unhappy Kōtoku in 654, the retired empress reascended to the throne as Empress Saimei (r. 655-661). She died in the wake of an ill-fated attempt to rescue Paekche from the combined forces of Silla and T'ang China. At this time a Buddhist rite based on the *Ninnō-gyō* (a *Prajñāpāramitā-sūtra* about a benevolent king who protects his country) was held for the first time within the imperial palace to prevent possible invasion by foreign forces. Thus, the dependency on Buddhist Law for the protection of the nation is a principle that was established by Prince Naka no Oye with the full concurrence of his chief adviser, Kamatari.[21] It should be noted that while the prince became Emperor Tenchi upon the death of his mother, he did not assume the official title until 668.

[21] Ibid., p. 144.

Meanwhile, the Japanese expeditionary forces endeavouring to rescue Paekche were defeated miserably by the Chinese armada, and Korea was destined soon to be united under Silla.

By far the greatest blow to Tenchi's regime was the death of Kamatari, who had guided the troubled nation with a steady hand from behind the throne. It was Kamatari who managed to keep peace between Tenchi's brother and son, the two aspirants to the throne. At his deathbed in 669, Kamatari was given the cap of "Great Woven Stuff" and the rank of O-mi (Minister). He also was given the new surname of Fujiwara.

Two years later, shortly before his own death, Tenchi appointed his 24-year-old son Prince Otomo as Dajō Daijin (Chancellor of the Realm). Presumably, he did so in accordance with the Omi-ryō (Code),[22] which had been compiled under the supervision of Kamatari. Upon the death of Tenchi, Otomo became Emperor Kōbun (r. 671-672). But Tenchi's brother, who had served as the Crown Prince during Tenchi's tenure, usurped the throne after a bloody war of rebellion and became Emperor Tenmu (r. 672-686). Tenmu was succeeded by his consort who ascended to the throne as Empress Jitō (r. 687-697). During the reigns of Tenmu and Jitō the so-called Ritsuryō ("Imperial Rescript") state, a hierarchically centralized national structure, was actualized under Shinto-Confucian inspiration. It is to be noted, however, that the Confucian universal principle of Tao was homologized with, and made subordinate to, the authority of the emperor who, by virtue of having descended from the Sun Goddess, had the prerogative to reign and rule the nation. Thus, the sovereign came to be regarded as the "manifest kami" (akitsu-mikami), whose divine will was communicated by a series of imperial rescripts. It was, in effect, a form of "immanental theocracy."[23]

THE RITSURYŌ STATE AND THE FUJIWARA REGENCY

One of the most important foundations of the Ritsuryō state was laid in 684 by Emperor Tenmu. Tenmu instituted an eight-rank kabane (hereditary titles of nobility) system, which reorganized the traditional court rank system by granting a higher degree of status to those uji that had made useful contributions to the throne. Even

[22] Whether or not this Code was ever enacted cannot be determined. See Felicia Gressitt Bock, Engi-Shiki: Procedures of the Engi Era, Books I-V (Tokyo, Sophia University, 1970), p. 8.

[23] J. M. Kitagawa, "The Japanese Kokutai (National Community): History and Myth," History of Religions XIII, no. 3 (February 1974), p. 219.

though Tenmu could have humiliated those who had fought against his war of rebellion, his regime chose not to abolish the traditional *kabane* system. Thus, it avoided possible social strife. We agree with Professor Miller: "anti-imperial forces were not granted one of the new *kabane*, but they continued to bear their traditional ones,"[24] even though they were superseded by new ones. Miller indicates further that

. . . most important from the point of view of the Sun Line, the new system clearly designated the reigning sovereign's closest collaterally related lineage groups as constituting the top social rank of the new nobility below the level of the sovereign and the other members of the imperial house. As such, the new system, even though traditionally oriented, served to further bolster the claims of imperial surpremacy that lay at the base of so many other reforms carried out in the second half of the seventh century following the Taika coup of 645.[25]

A second important foundation of the Ritsuryō state was provided by the compilation of two mythohistorical writings, namely the *Kojiki* (Records of Ancient Matters) and the *Nihongi* or *Nihon-shoki* (Chronicles of Japan). Their compilation was ordered by Tenmu, in part to authenticate the legitimacy of his imperial prerogative after usurping the throne. We read in the preface to the *Kojiki* that there was a young court attendant who "possessed such great native intelligence that he could repeat orally whatever met his eye, and whatever struck his ears was indelibly impressed in his heart."[26] There probably were others like him who were expert in remembering the lore of the past. Nevertheless, the compilers of these mythohistorical works were court officials who shared the outlooks and policies of the ruling regime. In this connection, the mythology of ancestry, which had been handed down by Shinto tradition, "performed a most practical social role in supporting the emperor and the other Sun Line descendants in their claims to position of social paramountcy within the state, as well as in providing a means of ranking the various aristocratic social strata relative to that supreme position."[27] Therefore, it is not surprising that members of two hereditary Shinto priestly families, the Imibe and Nakatomi (who were blood relations of the Fujiwara), were particularly active on a committee of twelve appointed by Tenmu to compile

[24] Richard J. Miller, *Ancient Japanese Nobility: The Kabane Ranking System* (University of California Press, 1974), p. 141.

[25] Ibid., p. 142.

[26] *Kojiki*, trans. with intro. and notes by Donald L. Philippi (Princeton University Press, 1969), pp. 41-42.

[27] Miller, *Japanese Nobility*, pp. 145-146.

national histories. This may account for the fact that the mythological ancestors' accounts of these two families are so closely related to those of the Sun Line. Furthermore, the preface of the *Kojiki* explicitly states that it was the chroniclers' task to "correct" the mistakes and corruptions, as seen from their "present" perspective, of available court documents and provincial records. Such a project had its own agenda: it rectified the mistaken and corrupt documents and, if needed, rearranged the sequence of events in order to recreate or create the past as an integral constituent of the present.

In accordance with the imperial wish—which was shared by the elders of the Shinto priestly families—the chroniclers took pains to include (1) cosmogonic and other "heavenly" myths that authenticated the genealogical backgrounds of the imperial *uji* (the Sun Line) as well as of other prominent *uji* which claimed *kami* lineage (for example, the Fujiwara [Nakatomi] and the Imibe [Imbe]), and (2) mythohistorical accounts of activities and events that were connected with the ancestors of the imperial and other prominent *uji* who, in accordance with the alleged command of the Sun Goddess, pacified the world (that is, Japan) and established the national community under the sacred king. Significantly, the *Nihongi* included (3) contemporary events that justified the legitimacy of Tenmu's regime both in terms of Shinto mythological tradition and of the teachings of the *Sūtra of the Sovereign Kings of the Golden Radiance*, which explicates a Buddhist doctrine that a monarch is "a son of a divine being" to whom was given a mandate of heaven. Furthermore, the chroniclers imitated the model of Chinese dynastic histories as they arranged their mythohistorical accounts in a chronological format. In so doing, they superimposed the Chinese calendrical system onto their newly conceived past history, which was now supposed to have commenced in 660 B.C. and was viewed to have been preceded by the so-called age of *kami*. Even further, we are told that in the age of *kami* the Sun Goddess once decided to seclude herself behind the rock door of a cave; that the progenitor-*kami* of the Fujiwara, Ame no Koyane, and the Imibe's counterpart, Ame no Futodama (Futotama), in cooperation with other heavenly *kami* persuaded the Sun Goddess to reappear from the cave; and that her reappearance restored light to the world.

Considering the manner in which these mythohistories were compiled, the intertwining of the activities of the progenitors of the imperial with those of the Fujiwara (Nakatomi) families probably reflected the contemporary situation of the seventh century. Nevertheless, the mystique of the mythologies was such that mythical accounts in turn gave a special aura to the Fujiwara family, which before the

112

time of Kamatari was in no position to boast of a close relationship with the Sun Line. Kamatari's son, Fujiwara Fuhito (659-720), following the precedent established earlier by the Soga, married his eldest daughter to Emperor Monmu (r. 697-707); she gave birth to Emperor Shōmu (r. 724-749). Moreover, Fuhito's second daughter, Kōmyōshi, married Shōmu and gave birth to Empress Kōken (r. 749-757). The clever policy of contracting marriage relationships with the imperial family helped establish the Fujiwara as the leading family in the realm.

A third important foundation of the Ritsuryō state was the codification of written laws. We mentioned earlier that Kamatari supervised the compilation of the Omi code. Significantly, Kamatari's son, Fuhito, was credited with the compilation of the Taihō Code of 701 and the Yōrō Code of 718. These two legal documents provided the political, administrative, and juridical framework of the Ritsuryō state. As these written laws were being compiled, the government in 710 established its first full-scale capital city in Nara, which became the political and religious centre of the nation. The government structure was modelled, for the most part, on that of T'ang China; however, it incorporated a peculiar Japanese feature in that the administrative structure under the throne was divided into civil and religious branches. The Great Council of State (*Dajōkan*) was headed by a Chancellor (*Dajō-daijin*) and the Department of Kami- or Shinto-Affairs (*Jingikan*) was directed by the Head of Kami-Affairs. Following the principle of the unity of religious and political affairs (*saisei-itchi*), both were directly accountable to the throne. It is a matter of great interest in this connection that early in the ninth century the head of the Imibe family, Hironari, presented to the throne a history of his *uji* entitled *Kogoshūi* (Gleanings from Ancient Stories).[28] In this history he notes that from the age of *kami* the Imibe and the Nakatomi had served the throne as two hereditary priestly families with equal status. He then laments the fact that during the Tenpyō period (729-749) the Nakatomi took advantage of their powerful position and dominated Shinto affairs at the expense of the Imibe and other hereditary priestly families. In spite of the Imibe's complaints, which had some legitimate grounds, the political reality of the eighth and ninth centuries made it impossible for the Imibe to compete with the powerful Nakatomi-Fujiwara.

There is some irony in the fact that Fujiwara Fuhito's four sons, who founded respectively the Southern, Capital, Northern, and Cere-

---

[28] Translated by Genchi Katō and Hikoshirō Hoshino (Tokyo, 1926).

113

monial lines or houses, died in the epidemic of 737. Moreover, their offspring were split in the succession disputes. In the end it was the Northern House which regained power and prosperity at the expense of the other branches of the Fujiwara, as well as other non-Fujiwara families.[29]

The transfer of the capital from Nara to Kyoto toward the end of the eighth century starts a new page in the history of Japan. The leaders of the Kyoto regime were eager to perpetuate the Ritsuryō ideal of imperial rule, free from the ecclesiastical interference and power struggles among the aristocracy that had characterized the Nara period in the eighth century. Their eagerness led them to compile the above-mentioned *Engi-shiki*, a collection of rules that supplemented previously promulgated edicts and ceremonial directives. Paradoxically, by the time these procedures were put into effect in 967 the classical Ritsuryō scheme as such had already been modified by the emergence of the Fujiwara "regency."

It is important to remember that the Fujiwara power did not depend on military strength, although they utilized the service of the emerging warrior *uji* with a good deal of skill. Rather, they acquired power and wealth from their expanding landholdings in the provinces and from their occupation of key government positions both in civil and religious branches. Moreover, they frequently intermarried with the imperial family and claimed the prerogatives derived from mytho-history to participate in the rule of the nation as the "shadow" of the Sun Line. In the mid-ninth century a child emperor was enthroned: this allowed his maternal grandfather, Fujiwara Yoshifusa (804-872), then Chancellor, to act as the regent (*sesshō*). As such, he was the first leader with non-royal blood ever to be elevated to such a high office. Subsequently, Yoshifusa's adopted son, Mototsune (836-891), became both the *sesshō* and the *kanpaku* (chief counsellor).[30] The combination of these two offices signified that Mototsune was to serve as a permanent regent, regardless of the age or health of the reigning emperor. From the mid-tenth until the mid-eleventh centuries the nation was ruled nominally under imperial rule but effectively by the Fujiwara regency. This was known as the *sekkan* (*sesshō-kanpaku*) system. Under this system the Fujiwara power reached its zenith. In the year 1018,

[29] See Helen Craig McCullough, *Okagami: The Great Mirror, Fujiwara Michinaga (966-1027) and His Times* (Princeton University Press, 1980), Appendix D, "The Fujiwara Role in Japanese Court History from Kamatari to Michinaga," pp. 335-355.

[30] Ibid., p. 340, note 3: "A *kanpaku* was the Regent of a grown male sovereign of sound mind and body, as distinguished from a *sesshō*, the Regent of an Emperor incapacitated by sex, youth, or disability."

for instance, twenty of the twenty-three top administrative and court positions were held by members of the Fujiwara family, headed by Michinaga (966-1027). Only the remaining three positions were held by members of the Minamoto family.[31] True to Fujiwara tradition, a regent stated with or without a sense of hypocrisy: "Great as are our power and prestige, nevertheless they are those of the Sovereign, for we derive them from the majesty of the Throne."[32]

THE RITSURYŌ system, which was modified by the Fujiwara regency, was destined to undergo further changes occasioned by the system of "rule by retired monarchs" (*insei*), which was initiated by ex-Emperor Shirakawa (r., as emperor, 1072-1086; as ex-emperor, 1086-1129) and by the emergence of the so-called feudal regime (*bakufu*) that lasted from 1192 until 1867. It should be noted, however, that the Fujiwara family continued to dominate the imperial court in Kyoto. This court preserved the residual structure of the Ritsuryō system even when the actual political authority rested with warrior-statesmen. In fact, the shogun, or the head of the feudal regime, needed the approval of the imperial court. The Fujiwara family itself was reorganized during the thirteenth century: five branches of the family—Konoye, Takatsukasa, Kujō, Ichijō, and Nijō—came to be designated "*go-sekke*" ("five houses that are entitled to produce the holders of regency").

A most fascinating document reveals the self-understanding of the Fujiwara family: this is the *Gukanshō* (Record of Foolish Random Thoughts), by Fujiwara no Jien (1155-1225).[33] A noted poet and Tendai priest, Jien served four times as the abbot of the Tendai monastery at Mount Hi'ei, near Kyoto. He also was the son, brother, or uncle of the eight Fujiwara regents who held office during his lifetime. He not only had a particularly close relationship with his brother, Kujō Kanezane, but was a trusted friend of three ex-emperors as well as the first shogun of the Kamakura feudal regime, Minamoto no Yoritomo (who ruled, as shogun, 1192-1199). Jien wrote the *Gukanshō* at the time when Kujō (Fujiwara) Yoritsune, even though just a boy, was made titular shogun of the Kamakura regime, and similarly, when the future Emperor Chūkyō, also a young boy, was the Crown Prince. Although Jien's objective was to explicate what he called *dōri* ("meta-

---

[31] Tamura, *Fujiwara Kamatari*, p. 181.

[32] Quoted in Sansom, *History of Japan*, p. 157.

[33] See *The Future and the Past: A Translation and Study of the Gukanshō, An Interpretative History of Japan Written in 1219*, trans. Delmer M. Brown and Ichirō Ishida (University of California Press, 1979). See also Charles H. Hambrick's review of this book in the *Harvard Journal of Asiatic Studies* XL, no. 2 (December 1980), pp. 555-566.

physical principle") which ran through the history of Japan, the perspective from which he viewed Japanese history was unmistakably that of the Fujiwara. Thus, looking to the mythological ancestors of the imperial, the Fujiwara, and the Minamoto families (the Sun Goddess, Ame no Koyane, and Hachiman, respectively), he was persuaded that the destinies of these three families were closely interrelated because their ancestral *kami* were similarly closely related. Because Jien was convinced that the fortunes of the imperial and the Fujiwara families were inseparably intertwined he held the pious hope that when the above-mentioned two boys would attain maturity they would reign and rule Japan as emperor and shogun/regent.

Parenthetically, at the disestablishment of the last feudal regime, the Meiji imperial regime in 1868 appointed Sanjō Sanetomi (1837-1892) as the *Dajō Daijin*. He was the last Fujiwara to hold the top position of the Ritsuryō system; for the position of chancellor was soon replaced by that of the Prime Minister as the head of the cabinet. Nevertheless, the Meiji regime conferred the highest court rank, *kō-shaku* ("Duke" or "Prince"), on the heads of the major branches of the Fujiwara (namely, Konoye, Takatsukasa, Kujō, Ichijō, Nijō, Sanjō, and Tokudaiji), who then were given hereditary seats in the newly created House of Peers. The last of the Fujiwaras to hold a high office was Konoye Ayamaro (Fumimaro; 1891-1945); he was the unhappy Prime Minister during World War II who took his own life after Japan's defeat. The death of Prince Konoye signified the melancholy finale of the Fujiwara family, which had for so long dominated the main stage of Japanese history: they were, indeed, the "shadow" of the Sun Line.

7. *Matsuri* and *Matsuri-goto*: Religion and State in Early Japan

INTRODUCTION

IT HAS OFTEN been asserted that throughout history Japan has maintained the principle of *saisei-itchi* (unity of *matsuri* or religious cult and *matsuri-goto* or government administration). According to Professor Ono Sokyo, a leading Shinto theorist today, the term *saisei-itchi* contains three different but related dimensions:

First, there is the recognition of the significance of Shinto rituals being performed by the State. . . . It is . . . the act of praying, in the name of the State, for peace and prosperity, which are the common desires of the people; it is the performance, on a larger scale, of what communal Shinto worship does centering around the local *uji-gami*. In State Shinto, the State was in a position of synthesizing the local worship of all smaller social units.

Secondly, by placing ultimate responsibility on its celebrants, State worship, which had the Emperor as its highest celebrant, placed restrictions of the purest kind on the conscience of government leaders and rulers. . . .

Thirdly, the concept of *saisei-itchi* has its ultimate basis, not in political considerations, but in the life of each individual. *Matsuri*, or Shinto worship, was not merely religious ritual, but life with the Divine, actively based on the protection and the spirit of the Divine. Government is something derived from it. The word *matsuri-goto*, meaning "government," is derived from the word *matsuri*, which means "worship." In *matsuri-goto* was contained the meaning that each individual should serve the gods [*kami*] and his fellow men through his own individual work in life. . . .[1]

Thus, in interpreting the term *saisei-itchi*, Professor Ono places the accent on the side of *matsuri* (religious cult), while another Shinto scholar, Professor Mitsuma Shingo, gives more emphasis on the side of *matsuri-goto* (political or governmental administration). Professor Mitsuma, like many contemporary orthodox Shintoists, explicates the meaning of primitive Shinto in terms of *kami-nagara-no-michi* (*kan-nagara-no-michi*), which literally means "the way that exactly follows *kami* will." His starting point is the mythological distinction of the

[1] Sokyo Ono, "The Contribution to Japan of Shrine Shinto," *Proceedings of the Ninth International Congress for the History of Religions* (Tokyo: Maruzen, 1960), pp. 390-391.

117

universe into three realms—(1) the domain of heaven (*Takamaga-hara*), which he interprets as the "world of seeds"; (2) the domain of earthly existence, referring to Japan (*Toyoashihara*), which he interprets as the realization of the heavenly domain; and (3) the domain of roots or materials (*Nenokuni*). According to Mitsuma, all *kami* are personi-fications of the supreme *kami* (Ameno-minakanushi), "who is the great life of heaven and earth and of the whole universe." He goes on to say that the central *kami* in the domain of heaven (*Takamagahara*), however, is the Sun Goddess (Amaterasu-ōmikami), who is wor-shipped by other *kami*. "Among these *kami* there is a situational order which derives from the essence of life," and the order thus established in the domain of heaven has been copied or reflected in the traditional "unwritten constitution" of early Japan. In accordance with the "un-written constitution," the emperors have worshipped the Sun Goddess (Amaterasu-ōmikami) as the imperial ancestor, forever keeping and exalting her spirit as their imperial spirit. "This is the basis," says Mi-tsuma, "of the imperial prerogative of Japan and also of [her] national character." In short, the principle of *saisei-itchi* (unity of religion and government), seen from the perspective of Shinto orthodoxy, is insep-arable from two other principles, namely, that of "the reign of the emperor of one dynasty" and that of "the oneness of the emperor and his subjects."[2]

Apparently, Professors Ono, Mitsuma and other Shinto theorists take it for granted that the principle of *saisei-itchi* can be traced back to the pristine religio-political structure of early or prehistoric Japan. Unfortunately, one of the difficulties in dealing with early Japan is the fact that the earliest historical writings, the *Kojiki* (Records of Ancient Matters) and the *Nihongi* (Chronicles of Japan) were not compiled until centuries after Japan came under the influence of Chinese civili-zation and Buddhism. Elsewhere I have already discussed the knotty hermeneutical problems such as mythologization of history and his-toricization of myths in dealing with early Japanese historical writ-ings.[3] Similar problems confront us in our attempt to delineate the meaning of *saisei-itchi*.

It is important to note that *saisei-itchi* was adopted in 1867 as the pseudotheological principle to guide modern Japan. Significantly, in

[2] Shingo Mitsuma, "Treatise on National Character and Government in Relation to the Study of the Constitution," *Proceedings of the Second International Conference for Shinto Studies: Continuity and Change* (Tokyo: Kokugakuin University, 1968), pp. 66-70.

[3] See J. M. Kitagawa, "The Japanese *Kokutai* (National Community): History and Myth," *History of Religions* 13, no. 3 (February 1974).

the same year restoration of imperial rule was proclaimed. In the wording of the proclamation issued by the Council of State (Dajōkan):

Whereas the restoration of Imperial rule is founded upon the achievements initiated by Emperor Jimmu [the legendary first emperor of the ancient Yamato kingdom], and whereas the nation is being restored to a policy of general renewal and *unity of worship and administration*, it is ordered that, first of all, the Department of Shinto Affairs shall be revived, and further that rites and sacrifices shall thereafter be performed.[4]

This proclamation was followed by the government order to separate Shinto from the centuries-old pattern of Shinto-Buddhist amalgamation (*Shin-Butsu Shūgō*). Ironically, while the government was determined to promote Shinto, there were serious disagreements among Shintoists concerning important doctrines and cultic activities of Shinto. Professor Muraoka cites some of the main features of the controversy among Shinto scholars. For example, the opening phrase of the *Kojiki—ametsuchi hajime no toki* (in the beginning of Heaven and earth)—was debated heatedly by those who accepted the creation theory, on the one hand, and those who did not, on the other. Another controversy centred around the interpretation of the "concealed and mysterious" realm of *yomi*, whether or not it meant the afterworld and whether or not souls after death go to *yomi*. Even the question of the number of *kami* to be worshipped in the shrine of the Office of Shinto Affairs—whether the three Creator *Kami* and the Sun Goddess alone should be venerated or whether another prominent *kami* called Ō-kuni-nushi should also be included—had to be resolved by imperial intercession.[5] Furthermore, while many took it for granted that the model for the restoration of imperial rule was the reign of the first legendary emperor Jimmu, there were those who were persuaded that the model was to be found in the reign of the tenth legendary emperor, Sujin, who performed the rites of the *Kami* of Heaven and earth and endeavoured to enlighten his subjects. "In these times, too," stated Kubo Sueshige (1830-1886),

it is the Imperial will to revere the *Kami* of Heaven and earth and to project the radiance of Imperial prestige overseas by adopting the standards of Emperor Sujin's reign. Therefore, as the Emperor establishes relations overseas, foreign people flock to our shores in vast numbers. . . . He accepts the learning

---

[4] Quoted in Tsunetsugu Muraoka, *Studies in Shinto Thought*, trans. Delmer M. Brown and James T. Araki (Tokyo: Ministry of Education, 1964), p. 204. (My italics.)
[5] Ibid., pp. 211-219.

of all countries and disseminates the world's knowledge. . . . All these things are done in accordance with the political structure of Emperor Sujin.[6]

These and other controversies have by no means been resolved even today. Understandably, such a nebulous notion as *saisei-itchi* can be interpreted variously from different perspectives. It is the intention of this paper to delineate different layers of meaning attached to the term *saisei-itchi* with a modest hope of clarifying the nature of the relationship between *matsuri* and *matsuri-goto* in early Japan.

ARCHAIC PATTERN

Our attempt to understand the relationship between early Japanese religion and state might profitably dwell on the discussion of two ambiguous and untranslatable terms, namely, *kami* and *matsuri*.

The term *kami* means (etymologically) "high," "superior," or "sacred." It is usually accepted as an appellation for all beings which possess extraordinary quality, and which are awesome and worthy of reverence, including good as well as evil beings. There is every reason to believe that the early Japanese found *kami* everywhere—in the heavens, in the air, in the forests, in the rocks, in the streams, in animals and in human beings. It would be misleading, however, to consider the religion of the ancient Japanese, which came to be known as Shinto, simply as polytheism or nature worship. While this early religion certainly accepted the plurality of the *kami* as separate beings, its fundamental affirmation tended to stress the sacrality of the total cosmos as such. That is to say, it was taken for granted that within the world of nature all beings, including those which we now call inanimate beings and natural objects, share and participate in the common *kami* (sacred) nature. It is also significant to note that the *kami* in the mythical accounts seem to have human traits, while the princes and heroes (*mikoto*) may be more aptly characterized as *kami* in human form. Moreover, judging from the myths and legends, animals too were regarded as having human-*kami* characteristics. There is no indication, however, that the *kami* were thought to have any supramundane qualities until after the introduction of Chinese civilization and Buddhism.

In the *Kojiki*, *Nihongi* and *Fudoki* (Records of Local Surveys), there are such other terms as *tama* and *mono*, which are frequently used to refer to spirit or soul. For the most part, the term *tama* referred to the spirit of a *kami* or a person, while the term *mono* referred to the spirit

---

[6] Quoted in ibid., p. 220.

of animals.[7] Furthermore, it was widely held that the spirit or soul could leave the body of a person or an animal on certain occasions, so that a special rite called *chinkon* or *tama-shizume* was performed to prevent the soul from leaving the body. There were also various rites to console the spirits of the dead. It is important to note that the spirits of *kami* and animals were believed to be capable of "possessing" men and women.[8] In fact, one of the earliest features of Japanese religion was the existence of the shamanic-diviner, known variously as *miko, ichiko* or *mono-mochi*, who in the state of *kami*-possession performed fortune-telling, transmission of spirit messages and healing.[9] Another important feature of early Japanese religion was the belief in the "spirits residing in words" (*kotodama*). According to this belief, beautiful words, correctly pronounced, were held to bring about good, whereas ugly words, or words incorrectly uttered, were believed to cause evil.[10] This was particularly true when one addressed words or speeches to the *kami*.

It is to be noted in this connection that such documents as the *Kojiki, Nihongi* and *Fudoki* used these terms, *kami, mikoto, tama* and *mono* and *chi (shi)*, almost interchangeably. But, as Professor Anzu points out, some of these terms gradually went out of usage, while the term *kami* began to supersede others as the designation of the divine or sacred beings. In this connection, Anzu cites the edict of the year A.D. 647—*kamu-nagara-mo waga-ko mishirasamu to koto-yose-saki*—and states:

This sentence is believed to mean that *kami* entrusted the rule of the Empire to the children of *kami*. That *kami* in this case refers to the Sun Goddess Amaterasu-ō-mi-kami can naturally be supposed from the evidence in the *Kojiki* and *Nihon Shoki*. The fact that, in this quotation, the actual name of the Sun Goddess does not appear, but that instead the Sun Goddess is referred to simply by the word *kami*—this fact may prove that the word *kami* meant, for certain groups, not an abstract or vague "awesome being" (*kashikoki mono*) but rather an authoritative, sacred being.[11]

---

[7] According to *Basic Terms of Shinto*, compiled by the Shinto Committee for the Ninth International Congress for the History of Religions (Tokyo, 1958), *Ara-mi-tama* is a spirit endowed to rule with authority; *nigi-mi-tama* is a spirit empowered to lead to union and harmony; *kushi-mi-tama* is a spirit which causes mysterious transformations; and *saki-mi-tama* is a spirit which imparts blessings. These are together called *shikon*, or "four spirits" (p. 68).

[8] Kunio Yanagita, gen. ed., *Minzokugaku Jiten* (A Dictionary of Folklore) (Tokyo: Tokyo-do, 1951), pp. 378-389.

[9] Ibid., pp. 550-551.

[10] *Basic Terms of Shinto*, p. 44.

[11] Motohiko Anzu, "The Concept of 'Kami,'" *Proceedings of the Ninth International Congress for the History of Religions*, p. 221.

And by the tenth century A.D. the word *kami* became the exclusive Shinto term for the divine being in contradistinction to various Buddhist terms referring to the Buddhas and Bodhisattvas.

The term *matsuri* refers to a wide variety of religious ceremonies as well as festivities connected with religious ceremonies. (With the honorific added, *o-matsuri* means any kind of festive celebration, religious or otherwise.) Scholars agree that the original meaning of the term *matsuri* is contained in the form *matsurau*, which meant "to be with," "to attend to the needs of," "to entertain," or "to serve," in reference to *kami*, the soul of the deceased, or a person of higher status. It was assumed that the physical act of *matsurau* implied the mental attitude of respect, reverence, and the willingness to listen, serve, and obey.[12] For example, on the occasion of *tama-matsuri* (*matsuri* of the soul) when the ancestral spirits were believed to visit the homes of their living descendants, the head of each household offered meals and drinks and entertained the visiting spirits as though they were alive. A similar motif of *matsurau* was no doubt evident in the *matsuri* for *kami*.

As far as we can ascertain, archaic Shinto did not have fixed liturgies, ecclesiastical organizations, or elaborate rituals. Most religious functions, except for those in the home, took place around a *himorogi* (sacred tree), *iwasaka* (sacred rock), or in the paddy field or seashore. Most scholars hold that religious functions were the prerogatives of the head of the family or clan, or the elder of the community, depending on the case, and that in many instances women served as ritual functionaries. With the gradual emergence of professional priests, the role of women was reduced to that of being a *miko* or shamanic-diviner. Prior to a festival, the participants were usually expected to purify themselves and to abstain from certain foods and sexual intercourse. In order to invite the *kami*, a particular sacred spot was signified by a sacred rope. Inasmuch as *kami* were believed to descend at night, the *matsuri* participants observed a vigil (*yo-miya* or *okomori*). When the *kami* descended, offerings, songs and dances were presented for the enjoyment of the *kami*. One of the essential features of the *matsuri* was the feast (*naorai*), which was enjoyed both by the *kami* and the participants.[13] Another important feature was *norito*, which has long since become stereotyped liturgical prayers, consisting of words of praise, thanksgiving and petition, to be recited by the priest,

[12] Kunio Yanagita, *Nihon no Matsuri* (Japanese Festivals) (Tokyo: Sogen-sha, 1953), p. 42.
[13] Yanagita, *Minzokugaku Jiten*, pp. 539-540.

122

but which originally referred to the human words addressed to the *kami* as well as the *kami*'s words spoken (*noru*) to men.[14]

Fortunately or unfortunately, there is no definitive theory as to when the term *matsuri-goto* came to mean political administration. Nevertheless, if the third century Chinese record of the land of Wa (Japan), ruled by the shamanic-diviner Himiko,[15] can throw any light on the state of archaic Japan, we can readily understand that political administration as such must have been a very simple affair. It is safe to conjecture that one of the important functions of the chieftains of early Japan was to maintain close contact with the *kami*, attending to their needs and being guided by their will communicated through oracles, dreams and divinations. It is also safe to assume that the main task of those lieutenants and functionaries who surrounded the chieftains was to attend to (*matsurau*) the needs of their masters. Certainly the records of the legendary monarchs of the Yamato kingdom support the view that the main activities of the imperial court were the *matsuri-goto* or *matsurau* affairs in the double sense of the term.

Such an archaic religio-political structure, based on the unifying principle of *matsurau*, inevitably had to undergo changes because of the increasing stratification of society and diversification of culture. According to the *Nihongi*, it was the tenth legendary emperor, Sujin, who became uneasy with living in the palace, in which religious functions for the Sun Goddess and the *Kami* of the Yamato region (Yamato-no-ō-kuni-tama) were held. Thus, he established shrines for these *kami* away from the imperial palace (*mi-araka*). He also appointed imperial princesses to be in charge of the worship of these *kami*. This turn of event, and there is no reason to question the historicity of this fact except perhaps its exact dating, signified an important transition, as far as the religious dimension of Japanese life is concerned, from the principle of *matsurau* ("attending to" or "being with" the *kami*) to that of *matsuru* ("to enshrine," "to worship," or "to venerate" the *kami*). Politically speaking, this turn of event implied the change of meaning of *matsurau* from that of being with or attending to the needs of the ruler to that of "faithful obedience" (*kifuku* or *fukujū*) on the part of the subjects, whereas the ruler was expected to reign (*shirasu*, "to listen" or "to govern") over the subordinates.[16]

We might mention in passing that it was toward the end of the

---

[14] Ibid., p. 460.

[15] Ryūsaku Tsunoda, trans., and L. Carrington Goodrich, ed., *Japan in the Chinese Dynastic Histories* (South Pasadena, 1951), pp. 8-16.

[16] Jiro Kamishima, "Nihon no Seiji Bunka" (The Political Culture in Japan), *Nihon-bunka-Kenkyusho-Kiyo*, No. 32 (September 1973), pp. 158-159.

fourth century A.D. that a powerful clan (*uji*), usually referred to as the imperial clan, which had superior military organization, began to dominate other clans. This was the beginning of the so-called Yamato Kingdom. According to the Chinese sources, the chieftains of the imperial clan were given monarchical status by the Chinese court during the fifth century. By that time the Yamato Kingdom had also established a beachhead on the southern tip of the Korean peninsula. And it was through the commercial, diplomatic and military contacts with China and Korea that Chinese civilization and Buddhism were introduced to Japan.

REINTERPRETATION OF SAISEI-ITCHI

Early in the seventh century A.D., the Japanese leaders envisaged a multivalue system that attempted to homologize the seemingly irreconcilable features of Shinto, Confucianism and Buddhism as the religio-political and cultural foundation of the nation. In this situation, the principle of the unity of *matsuri* and *matsuri-goto* took on a new and different meaning. The multivalue system is usually attributed to the innovation of the Prince-Regent Shōtoku (573-621).

Although Prince Shōtoku venerated Shinto and promoted Buddhism, he was persuaded that the fundamental principle of the government was "propriety" (*li* in Chinese; pronounced variously as *rei, iya* or *iyamai* in Japanese), which he had learned from the Confucian tradition. It should be noted, however, that what Shōtoku adopted was not the classical Confucian notion of propriety, but rather the *li* principle as interpreted by Confucianism of the Han period. As Sansom astutely observes, according to Han Confucianism, "the universe is composed of magic elements, different in their nature and function like stars and stones, trees and insects, but all related and combined."[17] Such an understanding of propriety set in a cosmological context provided the theoretical underpinning for reinterpreting political administration (*matsuri-goto*) and religion (*matsuri*) in terms of a hierarchical principle. Thus, in the third article of Prince Shōtoku's Constitution we find a new rationale for political administration: "You should endeavour to obey the imperial commands, realizing that the lord is Heaven while the subject is Earth. . . . [Thus], when the lord speaks, the subject should listen, and when the superior acts, the inferior

[17] George Sansom, *A History of Japan to 1334* (Stanford: Stanford University Press, 1958), p. 71.

124

should obey. . . ."[18] Prince Shōtoku also articulated the new understanding of the principle of *saisei-itchi* as follows:

We are told that our imperial ancestors, in governing the nation, bent humbly under heaven and walked softly on earth. They venerated the *kami* of
heaven and earth, and established shrines on the mountains and by the rivers,
whereby they were in constant touch with the power of nature. . . . May all
the ministers from the bottom of their hearts pay homage to the *kami* of
heaven and earth.[19]

Shortly after Shōtoku's death, the government attempted to insti-
tutionalize the relationship between *matsuri* and *matsuri-goto* by means
of a sinified legal system. Significantly, those penal codes (*ritsu; lü* in
Chinese) and the civil statutes (*ryō; ling* in Chinese) which were modelled after the Chinese legal systems, were issued in the name of the
emperor as the will of the *kami*. The government structure thus developed in the second half of the seventh century is referred to as the
"Ritsuryō" (imperial rescript) state.

Early in the eighth century, the government established the Department of *Kami* Affairs (Jingikan) and placed it side by side with the
Great Council of State (Dajōkan). While such a development testified
to the great prestige accorded to Shinto, it also implied that Shinto
was now under the rigid control of the centralized bureaucracy of the
government. Buddhism, too, prospered by the patronage of pious
monarchs, especially during the eighth century, known as the Nara
period. On the other hand, the activities of Buddhist clerics were
strictly controlled by the Law Governing Monks and Nuns (*Sōniryō*),
which effectively made Buddhism subservient to the authority of the
government.[20]

It was during the tenth century A.D. that the government made the
most elaborate attempt to regulate every detail of *matsuri* and *matsuri-
goto*. This attempt resulted in the compilation of the so-called *Institutes
of the Engi Era* (*Engi-shiki*), which was a collection of supplementary
rules (*kyaku shiki*) to previously promulgated edicts and ceremonial
rules. It consists of fifty books, of which the first ten are devoted to
Shinto matters. Fortunately, we now have a careful two-volume study
and translation of the first ten books of the *Engi-shiki* by Mrs. Felicia
Bock.[21] The contents of these books are as follows:

---

[18] J. M. Kitagawa, "Religions of Japan," in Wing-tsit Chan et al., *The Great Asian
Religions: An Anthology* (New York: Macmillan, 1969), pp. 252-253.
[19] Ibid., p. 241.
[20] See ibid., pp. 258-259.
[21] Felicia Gressitt Bock, trans., *Engi-Shiki: Procedures of the Engi Era* (Tokyo: Sophia
University), Books I-V (1970) and Books VI-X (1972).

I. The Matsuri (festivals) of Four Seasons (i)
II. The Matsuri of Four Seasons (ii)
III. The Extraordinary Matsuri
IV. The Grand Shrine of Ise
V. Bureau of the Consecrated Imperial Princess (*Saigu-ryo*)
VI. The Office of the Princess Consecrated to the Kamo Shrines (*Saiinshi*)
VII. Great New Food Festival for the Enthronement (*Senso-Daijō-sai*)
VIII. Ritual Prayers (*Norito*)
IX. Register of *Kami* (i)
X. Register of *Kami* (ii)

The remaining forty books provide minute regulations concerning the procedures to be followed by government officials. While the *Tale of Genji* and other literary works of the Heian period (A.D. 781-1191) give the impression that courtiers spent all their time chasing butterflies and composing poems, the diaries of noblemen and court records testify that every aspect of the activities of those courtiers was rigidly regulated by official procedures.[22] Clearly, the *Institutes of the Engi Era* (*Engi-shiki*) attempted to carry out to perfection the seventh-century Ritsuryō ideal, which portrayed the life of the imperial court as the earthly replica of the court of the Sun Goddess in the Domain of Heaven as told in myths. Moreover, the implicit assumption of the *Institutes of the Engi Era* was that the interpenetration of *matsuri* and *matsuri-goto* was the *sine qua non* for the kind of "liturgical soteriology" which sanctified the Japanese national community as the holy community.

Historians tell us that shortly after the *Institutes of the Engi Era* was put into effect in the year A.D. 967, its prestige began to erode, due largely to its cumbersomeness, among other defects. Nevertheless, the very fact that such an audacious soteriological model for the whole national community was seriously envisaged between the seventh and the tenth centuries, based on a reinterpretation of the simple, primitive Shinto principle of *saisei-itchi*, is in itself a matter of some significance in our attempt to understand the nature of the relationship between *matsuri* and *matsuri-goto* in Japanese history.

[22] Naoshige Tsuchida, "Heian-jidai no Seimu to Gishiki," *Nihonbunka-Kenkyusho-Kiyo*, No. 33 (March 1974), pp. 206-231.

126

8. Three Types of Pilgrimage in Japan

GERSHOM G. SCHOLEM once stated that "there is no such thing as mysticism in the abstract. . . . there is only the mysticism of a particular religious system."[1] This is an important dictum which students of *Religionswissenschaft* can ill afford to forget. To be sure, it is the task of the historian of religions to delineate universal structures out of the multitude of varied and variable religious data and to telescope long and complex histories of religions by depicting certain significant events and their persistent characteristics. Yet, his conceptions and abstractions must be constantly reexamined in the light of the integrity and the unique cluster of meanings of particular religious systems or phenomena. With this in mind, I would like to depict three types of pilgrimage as expressions of the characteristic pieties of Japanese religious tradition, and hope that it will make a modest contribution to the growing literature on the universal phenomena of religious pilgrimage.

In every religious tradition, the pilgrimage combines, more than other religious acts do, diverse and often contradictory features, which are both spiritual and mundane. Travelling a long distance, visiting holy mountains or shrines, involves physical hardship and endurance, but it also has pleasurable aspects, such as sightseeing and meeting new friends. Usually, pilgrims are motivated by religious objectives, such as adoration of the deities or saints who are enshrined at various sacred places, gaining merit for salvation, paying penance for annulment of sin, or praying for the repose of the spirits of the deceased, but these religious motives are often mixed with the desire to acquire healing, good fortune, easy childbirth, prosperity and other this-worldly benefits. Even the ascetic practices which are usually imposed on the pilgrims, notably sexual abstinence and fasting or dietary restrictions, are interpreted as necessary investments for the expected rewards. Besides, the pilgrimage provides welcome relief from the routine of the dull everyday life of the people. Furthermore, seen from a broader perspective, the pilgrimage, which cements the solidarity of religious groups, also stimulates trade and commerce, dissemination of ideas, and intercultural exchange. Notwithstanding these universal

---

[1] *Major Trends in Jewish Mysticism* (New York, 1941), pp. 5-6.

features, which are shared by the pilgrimages of various traditions, each one tends to show a unique ethos of its own, which can be understood only within its religious and cultural contexts.

Historically in Japan, the development of the pilgrimage was greatly conditioned by the geographical and topographical as much as the religious and cultural factors. According to Shinto, the whole world is permeated by the sacred (*kami*) nature, so that every mountain, river, tree, rock, and human being is potentially an object of veneration. As far as the practice of pilgrimage is concerned, it had little place in early Shinto, because Shinto was closely related to the life of the clan (*uji*), which more often than not was settled in a particular geographical locality. To be sure, in many agricultural communities the *kami* of the mountains were believed to come down and become the *kami* of the rice field during part of the year and then return to the mountains after the harvest. It is conceivable, therefore, that some people might have climbed the mountains in order to experience the mystique of the abode of the *kami*. But such practices were spontaneous and were not regularized as pilgrimages by early Shinto.

The introduction of Chinese civilization and Buddhism during the sixth century A.D. brought about far-reaching religious and cultural changes in the subsequent periods of Japanese history. Eventually, there developed three major types of pilgrimages out of the fusion of indigenous Shinto and folk religious beliefs and practices with Buddhist and Chinese—especially Taoist—elements. They are (1) the pilgrimage to the sacred mountain; (2) the pilgrimage to temples and shrines, based on faith in the divinities enshrined in those sanctuaries; and (3) the pilgrimage to sacred places based on faith in certain charismatic holy men who are believed to have hallowed those places by their visits. It is the purpose of this paper to inquire as to how these types of pilgrimages developed in Japan and also to depict the basic similarities and dissimilarities among them.

PILGRIMAGE TO THE SACRED MOUNTAIN

We have already hinted at the importance of sacred mountains in the religious life of the early Japanese. It is significant to note in this connection that even after the introduction of Chinese civilization and Buddhism people in Japan continued to venerate mountains as the abodes of divinities, and to pay special respect to the "austerity man" (*gyō-ja*), who was believed to have acquired superhuman power by the rigorous ascetic training of the mountain (*sanrin-tosō*). Among the Buddhists, too, there developed in the eighth century a movement called the "Nature Wisdom School," which sought Enlightenment not by the traditional meditation and disciplines within the compound of the monasteries but by being close to Nature in the mountains. Besides, some of the monks and pious laity underwent austerity training in the mountains in order to acquire magical power (*siddhi*). Meanwhile, shamanistic diviners, healers and ascetics, who earlier had no connection with Buddhism, came under Buddhist influence. Their affiliation with Buddhism was very tenuous, but they were called "unordained Buddhist practitioners," (*ubasoku, upāsaka*), and many claimed to have acquired power to work miracles by undergoing austerity training in the mountains. The combined effect of these movements was the emergence of the so-called Order of Mountain Ascetics (Shugen-dō) which, despite its formal affiliation with the Tendai and the Shingon schools of Buddhism, retained many elements of Shinto and folk religious traditions.

The popularity of the mountain ascetics during the eleventh and twelfth centuries was greatly enhanced by the belief prevalent among the aristocrats that pilgrimage to sacred mountains, especially those of Kumano and Yoshino, would enable them to experience while on earth a foretaste of the Pure Land. It was also widely held by that time that the native Shinto *kami* of those mountains were in reality manifestations of Buddhist divinities. Thus, the pilgrimages to these mountains, accompanied and guided by the experienced mountain ascetics, were believed to bring favours from both the Shinto and Buddhist divinities simultaneously. With the decline of the court nobility in the latter part of the twelfth century, the mountain ascetics sought patronage among warriors and other non-aristocratic elements by establishing devotional confraternities (*kō-sha*) in various parts of the country. Most members of these confraternities belonged to local Buddhist and/ or Shinto groups, but they found additional impetus in their devotion to the deities of particular sacred mountains which were often far away from their homes. A number of such confraternities have continued to exist until our own times. Since the main function of these groups was pilgrimage to the sacred mountains, upon many of which women were not allowed, the membership of these confraternities was at first predominantly male. They considered the stiff mountain climbing, conducted by experienced guides, essential for spiritual and physical disciplines, and thus the pilgrimage was often considered an initiatory ceremony for boys who were entering the age of adult life. Eventually miniature models of sacred mountains were established in some parts of the country for the benefit of those who could not make real pilgrimages, and the mountain cult grew in popularity by attracting older people and women as well. It was estimated that in the latter part of the nineteenth century there were 17,000 "senior guides" to sacred mountains, which meant that a considerably greater number of mountain ascetics must have been functioning in various capacities.

The three so-called Sect Shinto denominations of our time—(1) Jikkō-kyō ("practical conduct" religion), (2) Fusō-kyō (religion of Fusō, which is the classical name of Mount Fuji), and (3) Ontake-kyō (religion of Mount Ontake)—are direct heirs of the traditions of the mountain ascetics, while Fuji-kō (devotional confraternity of Mount Fuji), later renamed the Maruyama-kyō, became a subsect of another Sect Shinto denomination called Shinto Taikyō (the great teaching of Shinto).[2] In addition, there are today many formal and informal mountain pilgrimage groups, ranging from those which follow strict disciplines to those whose activities border on the semirecreational.

PILGRIMAGE BASED ON FAITH IN CERTAIN DIVINITIES

In the religious history of Japan, the popularization of pilgrimage was not confined to sacred mountains. Many pious clergy, laymen and laywomen, whose piety was no doubt strengthened by the pilgrimage to the mountains, considered it also meritorious to visit less-hazardous holy places on the plain, usually Buddhist temples or Shinto shrines where certain divinities known for their potencies were enshrined. Such pilgrimages are motivated not by the desire to undergo ascetic practices but by people's devotion to a certain Buddha, Bodhisattva or *kami*, to whom the pilgrims pay homage, offer thanksgiving or ask for special favours. Among the Buddhist divinities, the most sought-after were Kannon (Avalokiteśvara), the Buddhist counterpart of the "goddess of mercy"; Amida (Amitābha), who is believed to have vowed to save all creatures; Jizō (Ksitigarbha), the protector of souls in the realm of hell; Yakushi (Bhaisajyaguru), the "healing Buddha"; and Miroku (Maitreya), the Buddha of the future. The temples which enshrined the statues of these divinities attracted many pilgrims. The most organized of all was the so-called "Pilgrimage to the Thirty-three Sanctuaries in Western Japan" (*Saigoku sanjū-san-sho*), which was based on devotion to Kannon (Avalokiteśvara).

According to a pious legend, the Emperor Kazan (reigned 984-986), upon the death of his consort, abdicated the throne and in priestly attire visited the 33 sanctuaries dedicated to Kannon. Although this legend is not reliable, it is fairly certain that the practice

[2] For these denominations of Sect Shinto, see my *Religion in Japanese History* (New York, 1966), Chap. 5.

of the "Zuda" (*dhūta*) pilgrimage to the 33 sanctuaries of Kannon was undertaken by two Tendai priests, Gyōson and Kakuchū, in the twelfth century.[3] Both of them had previously undergone austere training in the mountains, and they appropriated some features of the pilgrimages to sacred mountains to the pilgrimages to the 33 sanctuaries of Kannon. Evidently, judging from the records of the thirteenth and fourteenth centuries, there were variations in the selection of sanctuaries, even though there was general agreement on the sacred number of 33. It was probably in the fifteenth century that the present arrangement of the pilgrimages to the "Thirty-three Temples in Western Japan" (*Saigoku sanjū-san-sho*) was fixed by common consent. By that time, the pilgrimage was no longer the monopoly of the well-to-do and the clergy. Due largely to the activities of the leaders of new Buddhist movements that arose in the thirteenth century, i.e., the Pure Land, the True Pure Land, and the Nichiren schools, the poor as well as the rich came to accept the belief that they were living in the period of "degeneration of Buddha's law" (*mappō*), whereby they felt the sense of urgent need for the grace and mercy of divinities for their rebirth in the Pure Land after death. Undoubtedly this is why Mount Nachi, believed to be the model of Kannon's Pure Land on earth, was chosen as the starting point of the pilgrimage. Gradually, the attire of the pilgrim—wearing a large sedge-hat, hanging a rosary around the neck, carrying a walking stick, a ladle, a wooden pail and a bell—came to be accepted. On the road the pilgrims sing a rhythmic chant[4] consisting of 33 verses, each referring to Kannon's mercy and miraculous power manifested at one of the 33 sanctuaries. Incidentally, they beg for food and alms which sustain them throughout the pilgrimage.

In the course of time, the pilgrimage to the 33 sanctuaries of Kannon also developed in the eastern and other parts of Japan. Also, many other forms of Buddhist pilgrimages came into existence, such as the pilgrimage to the 25 temples of the Pure Land School, the pilgrimage to the 100 temples of the Nichiren school, and the pilgrimage to the 100 temples in the Higashiyama section of Kyoto. Unlike pilgrimage to sacred mountains, which is taken as a group guided by an experienced mountain ascetic, pilgrimage based on devotion to certain divinities can be undertaken by individuals. Nevertheless, a number of de-

---

[3] It took Gyōson 150 days to complete the pilgrimage, starting from the Hase Temple in the Yamato province and ending at the Senju temple at Mimurodo in the Yamashina province, while it took 75 days for Kakuchū to cover more or less the same course, starting however from Nachi in the present Wakayama prefecture and ending at Mimurodo.

[4] Known as *go-eika* (holy chant) or *junrei-ka* (pilgrim's chant).

votional confraternities arose in connection with such pilgrimages, and their members form small groups of pilgrims for the sake of mutual support and encouragement.

In the Shinto tradition, which also developed the practice of pilgrimage during the last few centuries, the most prominent is the pilgrimage to the Grand Shrine of Ise, the sanctuary of the Shinto deity *par excellence*, Amaterasu-ō-mikami, known as the Sun Goddess. It has been promoted by the Confraternity of Ise (*Ise-kō*), which selects by drawing lots certain members who then represent others in making the pilgrimage to Ise, usually in the spring or autumn. Their departure and return are celebrated by special ceremonies and feasts attended by all the members. Since their expenses are paid by the confraternity, which is supported by membership dues, the pilgrims to Ise—or other Shinto pilgrims for that matter—do not beg for food and alms on the road. Otherwise, the aim of the pilgrimage to Ise is similar to that of Buddhist pilgrimages, except that the object of devotion is the Shinto divinity.

PILGRIMAGE BASED ON FAITH IN CHARISMATIC PERSONS

Next to pilgrimages to sacred mountains and those to sanctuaries of various divinities, there developed in Japan the pilgrimage based on faith in certain charismatic holy men. It is to be recalled in this connection that even before the introduction of Buddhism the Japanese venerated various types of charismatic persons as embodiments of superhuman powers. After the introduction of Buddhism, some of the outstanding Buddhists, such as Prince-Regent Shōtoku, who in the late sixth and early seventh centuries promoted Buddhism as the *de facto* state religion, and Gyōgi, an eighth-century popular Buddhist leader who because of his philanthropic activities and saintly character was called the living Bodhisattva, became the objects of adoration on the part of pious Buddhists. Similarly, many of the founders of Buddhist schools, e.g., Shinran (1173-1262), the founder of the True Pure Land School, and Nichiren (1222-1282), founder of the school bearing his name, came to be regarded as semi-saviours, and their writings became for all intents and purposes sacred scriptures comparable to the *Tripitaka*. It is interesting to note that Japanese Buddhism, unlike its Chinese counterpart, did not produce such men as Fa-hsien, Hsüan-tsang and I-ching, who dared to visit India, crossing the desert or ocean, to set foot on sacred spots which were sanctified by the blessed memories of the historic Buddha. On the other hand, it became the accepted pattern for the Japanese Buddhists to make pilgrim-

132

ages to mausolea of leading Japanese Buddhists, many of whom were known for their charismatic qualities. The most outstanding example in this respect is the cult which developed around the memory of Kūkai or Kōbō Daishi (774-835), systematizer of the esoteric Buddhist school called the Shingon-shū.

Little need be said about Kūkai, whose real life has been buried under layers of pious legends. What is significant is the fact that he is remembered by pious followers as the itinerant holy man who visited many remote areas of Japan, digging wells, healing the sick, and working various kinds of miracles to help the poor and the oppressed. Furthermore, it is widely believed that Kūkai did not die, and that even today he is still walking around under the disguise of a pilgrim helping those who need his assistance.[5] Understandably, the devotees of Kūkai may have visited his birthplace in the island of Shikoku as early as the ninth century, and it is plausible that some sort of formalized pilgrimage in the "four provinces" (Shikoku) might have arisen in the twelfth or thirteenth century. However, the present practice of visiting 88 sanctuaries in Shikoku was not firmly established until about the seventeenth century.

As far as we can ascertain, the "Pilgrimage in Shikoku" is a complex phenomenon. In many ways, it has striking similarities to the "Pilgrimage to the Thirty-three Sanctuaries of Kannon in Western Japan" (*Saigoku sanjū-san-sho*). In both cases, the pilgrims wear similar sedge-hats, carry bells and walking sticks, and their chants are similar in form and sound. In fact, among the "main buddhas" (*hon-zon*) enshrined in the 88 temples, those of Kannon are most numerous with 29, followed by Yakushi with 23 and Amida with 9. Ironically, Dainichi (Mahāvairocana), the supreme Buddha of the Shingon school, which was established by Kūkai, has only 6.[6]

Upon closer examination, however, it becomes evident that the central motif of the "Pilgrimage in Shikoku" is not devotion to the divinities enshrined in the 88 holy sites, which no doubt has become a feature of it, but rather its main emphasis is on the act of "walking with Saint Kūkai." That is to say, the "Pilgrimage in Shikoku" is based on faith in the memory of the charismatic holy man, Kūkai, of whom the walking stick is the living symbol. Thus, even when an individual undertakes the pilgrimage, it is called the pilgrimage of two (*dōgyō ni-*

[5] For a fuller account of legends regarding Kūkai, see my "Master and Saviour," in *Studies of Esoteric Buddhism and Tantrism* (Kōyasan, 1965), pp. 1-26. [Chapter 11 of this book.]

[6] Other Buddhas represented in the 88 holy places in Shikoku are: Buddha Sākyamuni 5, Jizō (Ksitigarbha) 5, Fudō (Acala, the immovable) 4, Kokuzō (Ākāśagarbha) 3, etc.

nin), meaning Saint Kūkai and himself.[7] According to the established tradition, the pilgrimage to Shikoku begins at Mount Kōya, the seat of the Shingon monastic centre established by Kūkai. The pilgrims are expected to pay homage to Kūkai's mausoleum, where he is believed to be sleeping until such time as he returns to this world with the future Buddha, Maitreya. From Mount Kōya, the pilgrims go to one of the ports and cross the strait to Shikoku by boat.

The 88 holy places are scattered unevenly among the four provinces that constitute Shikoku. Historically, the Awa province, which has 23 holy sites, has been called the "exercise arena for the spiritual awakening" (*Hosshin no dōjō*); the Tosa province with 16 holy sites has been called the "exercise arena for ascetic discipline" (*Shugyō no dōjō*); the Iyo province with 26 holy sites has been called the "exercise arena for enlightenment" (*Bodai no dōjō*); and the Sanuki province with 23 holy sites has been called the "exercise arena for the state of Nirvana" (*Nehan no dōjō*). The holy sites are numbered from No. 1 to No. 88. Of them, Nos. 19, 27, 60, and 66 are considered to be "barriers" (*sekisho*), and those who have done misdeeds are said to receive at one of these barriers omens, such as the appearance of a certain bird. Such omens indicate that they have displeased Saint Kūkai, and they must terminate their pilgrimage and start again. Incidentally, the normal course of the pilgrimage is to start from No. 1 and end at No. 88, but, after completing the regular course, one might undertake additional pilgrimage, this time reversing the course from No. 88 to No. 1. It is believed that the chance of encountering Saint Kūkai walking in the disguise of a pilgrim is greater when one follows the reverse course. It is taken for granted that the complete pilgrimage is most meritorious. However, even such partial courses as the "ten holy sites" (*jukka-sho mairi*), the "seven holy sites" (*nanaka-sho mairi*) and the holy sites in "one of the four provinces" only (*ikkoku mairi*) are believed to be quite beneficial.[8]

As in the case of the Pilgrimage to the Thirty-three Sanctuaries of Kannon, the Pilgrimage in Shikoku is often undertaken by individuals or by small family groups.[9] But there are also many kinds of formal

[7] As the pilgrim arrives at an inn or a temple at the end of the day's journey, he cleanses the bottom of the walking stick before he cleanses his own feet. The walking stick, the symbol of Saint Kūkai, is kept in an honored position of the room in which the pilgrim sleeps.

[8] In some communities in Shikoku, girls of marriageable age are expected to undertake the pilgrimage. Usually, young girls are chaperoned by some adults.

[9] It is estimated that approximately 25,000 to 35,000 pilgrims, including those who undertake the complete course and those who undertake partial courses, visit the island of Shikoku annually nowadays.

and informal groups, which sponsor group pilgrimages, such as the Daishi-kō (Confraternity for the Devotion to Kōbō Daishi) and the Kongō-kō (Confraternity of the Shingon Devotees). Equally noteworthy is the development of the confraternities which are dedicated to the task of offering hospitality and assistance to the pilgrims (*settai-kō*). Members of these confraternities believe that by offering hospitality to the pilgrims they are in fact serving Saint Kūkai. Some of these hospitality groups come from distant places, chartering boats to carry food and other items, and set up hospitality centres at various spots along the main course of the pilgrimage.

The popularity of the Pilgrimage in Shikoku was such that from the eighteenth century onward several "miniature eighty-eight sanctuaries of Shikoku" were established in various parts of the country, such as Edo (Tokyo), Chita (near Nagoya), Sōma (in the present Chiba prefecture) and the island of Shōzu in the Inland Sea. These small-scale pilgrimages are of course not so meritorious as the pilgrimage to the real holy sites in Shikoku, but they have provided opportunities to many people who otherwise would not have been able to "walk in faith with Saint Kūkai."

Even such a brief portrayal of the three types of pilgrimages in Japan makes it clear that there are many similarities as well as significant differences among them. The first type, namely, the pilgrimage to the sacred mountains, may be characterized by its corporate activities under the supervision of an expert guide. Its emphasis on ascetic and physical disciplines implies a soteriological path based on self-power (*jiriki*), even though there is in it an element of faith. And the notion that the sacred mountains are the models of Paradise gives strong impetus to the pilgrims to seek the religious meaning of life within the realm of phenomenal existence. The second type, namely, the pilgrimage based on faith in certain divinities, tends to be more individualistic and also lacks rigorous ascetic emphasis because its soteriological path relies on the saving power of the divinities (*tariki*). Even though the pilgrims seek immediate experience of some degree of salvation here on earth, they accept the existence of the future realm as the only real arena of salvation. Finally, the third type, namely, the pilgrimage based on faith in charismatic holy men, has some of the features of the first and the second. But its own unique character is demonstrated in the notion that the saving power has been already actualized in the life of the charismatic holy man, who thus combines the roles of the deity and of the guide. In other words, the pilgrim relies on the other-power (*tariki*), but the other-power is not far away in a transcendental realm, either in space or in time. The saving power, fully actualized in a person, shares every step of the earthly pilgrimage as the real "fellow pilgrim."

It goes without saying that the task of the historian of religions involves many difficulties especially when one deals with a complex phenomenon such as the development of religion in Japan which has homologized diverse features of Buddhist, Taoist, Shinto and folk religious beliefs, symbols, cults, and practices. In such a situation, one meaningful approach may be to study a significant form of religious cult which has developed out of the fusion of various elements. On this score, it is our hope that this preliminary study of the three types of pilgrimage might throw some light on the characteristic pieties of Japanese religious tradition.

PART III

Shinto Tradition

9. Shinto

SHINTO, which is usually translated as the "way of the *kami* (gods)" (*kannagara*), is the indigenous religion of Japan.[1] The term Shinto was coined in the sixth century A.D. by using two Chinese characters—*shin* (in Chinese, *shên*: unfathomable spiritual power, superhuman or god-like nature or being) and *dō* or *tō* (in Chinese, *tao*: way, path, or teaching)—in order to differentiate the loosely organized native religious tradition from Buddhism, which was then being introduced to Japan. The beginnings of Shinto are clouded in the mists of the prehistory of Japan, and it eludes such simple characterizations as polytheism, emperor cult, fertility cult, or nature worship, although these features are embodied in it. Having no founder, no official sacred scriptures, and no fixed system of ethics or doctrines, Shinto has been influenced historically by Chinese civilization, especially Confucianism and Buddhism. Nevertheless, it has preserved its abiding, if nebulous, ethos throughout the ages. Thus, in a real sense, Shinto may be regarded as the *ensemble* of contradictory and yet peculiarly Japanese types of religious beliefs, sentiments, and approaches, which have been shaped and conditioned by the historical experience of the Japanese people from the prehistoric period to the present.[2]

I. BASIC COMPONENTS OF SHINTO

Prehistory of Japan

While no one is absolutely certain, most scholars recognize the appearance of a certain kind of pottery with characteristic rope-like markings somewhere around the fourth millennium B.C. as the first sign of the earliest phase of the prehistory of Japan, known as the Jōmon (literally, "code pattern," which indicates the pottery decoration) period. The Jōmon period, which had a sub-Neolithic level of culture, was followed around 250 B.C. by the Yayoi (so named because of pottery of this period unearthed in the Yayoi district of Tokyo) period,

[1] See J. M. Kitagawa, "Shinto," *Encyclopaedia Britannica*, 1968 ed., 20:517-521.
[2] For a brief sketch of religious history in Japan, see J. M. Kitagawa, "Japan: Religion," *Encyclopaedia Britannica*, 1968 ed., 12:899-904. For fuller accounts, see idem, *Religion in Japanese History* (New York, 1966) and Masaharu Anesaki, *History of Japanese Religion* (London, 1930).

which lasted until about A.D. 250. During this period, hunting and fishing continued, but people also acquired the arts of rice cultivation, spinning, and weaving, as well as the use of iron, and established communities in the lowlands. It is widely held that the culture of this period was a blending of northeast Asian, Korean, Chinese, and other cultural influences with the residual features of the earlier Jōmon tradition. The Yayoi period was succeeded by what archaeologists call the Kofun ("Tumulus") period, which covered the period of A.D. 250-600 or the earliest phase of Japanese history.

Throughout the prehistoric period a number of ethnic groups infiltrated into the Japanese islands from the Asian continent, bringing with them various cultural and religious customs. This migration of people continued until well into the early phase of the historic period. In this respect, most scholars hold that as early as the Yayoi period the inhabitants of the Japanese islands attained a degree of self-consciousness as one people sharing a common (emerging) culture. As to the development of the Japanese language, scholarly opinions are far less unanimous. Even those who are impressed by certain affinities between Japanese and East Altaic languages, such as Mongolian, Tungusic, and Korean, are not ready to accept any definite relationship between them. We are more certain about the gradual fusion of various elements of family, kinship, and social systems which began to take place from the Yayoi period onward and developed into the so-called *uji* (clan) system in the early historic period. According to this system, early Japanese society consisted of many independent clans. Each clan had clansmen and professional groups of persons and slaves, all of whom were controlled by the clan chieftain.[3]

The Kami

As far as we can ascertain, each clan (*uji*) in the early historic period was not only a social, economic, and political unit but also a unit of religious solidarity centering around the *kami* (deity) of the clan (*uji-gami*), who was attended to by the clan chieftain with the assistance of his wife or sister. The *kami* of the clan was considered the founder or ancestor of the clan and was venerated as such by the clansmen as well as by the professional groups of men and slaves who had no blood ties but were permanently affiliated with the clan. When a certain clan expanded in size, requiring some segments of the clan to migrate to a new area, the new group would establish a branch shrine dedicated to

[3] Various theories regarding the prehistory of Japan are cited in J. M. Kitagawa, "The Prehistoric Background of Japanese Religion," *History of Religions* 2, no. 2 (Winter 1963), 292-328. [Chapter 1 of this book.]

140

the same *kami* as the old clan. Apparently the basis of group solidarity in those days was sharing the same clan *kami* but not necessarily blood relationship as such. Should one powerful clan subjugate another, members of the latter were incorporated into the former by adopting the clan name of their new master. In such a case, the *kami* of the subjugated clan was usually transformed into a junior associate of the *kami* of the conquering clan.

The life of the early Japanese was controlled not only by the *kami* of the clan to which they belonged but also by numerous other spiritual powers and beings which had the *kami* (sacred) nature. Some *kami* were connected with geographical regions, such as villages and provinces, while others were believed to reside in mountains, trees, forests, rivers, or in celestial bodies. There were also unseen powers which controlled health, fortune, the longevity of individuals, earthquakes, pestilence, fertility, and other social and natural events. For the most part, the clan chieftain was believed to be able to propitiate and deal with the *kami* of his clan but not with other unseen spiritual powers. Thus, the people depended on divination and fortune-telling in order to find out the will of these other powers. Significantly, the third-century Chinese record, the "History of the Kingdom of Wei" (*Wei Chih*), mentions the existence in the Land of Wa (Japan) of the fortune-keeper who was selected when a group of people went on a voyage. This man did not comb his hair, did not eat meat, and stayed away from women. If the voyage was successful, he was rewarded. If it was not, he was killed for having neglected his duties. The same Chinese record describes Pimiko or Himiko, queen of Yamatai, which was a leading principality in Japan at that time. She is said to have occupied herself with magic and sorcery. Evidently, she was not married and had a brother who assisted her in running the affairs of the state. She was secluded from her people, and only one man attended her, acting as a medium of communication.[4] But not all the shamanic diviners were in high places. There were various other kinds of shamanic diviners—usually women endowed with special sensitivities which enabled them to be "possessed" by unseen spiritual powers and beings—as well as magicians, healers, and sorcerers living close to people in the lower strata of society.

Of the rituals, ethical and other injunctions, and development of religious beliefs of the late prehistoric and early historic periods, we know little. It is probably a mistake to look for a unified religious

[4] See Ryūsaku Tsunoda, trans., *Japan in the Chinese Dynastic Histories* (South Pasadena, 1951), pp. 8-16.

system in Japan during this period. On the other hand, it is also a mistake to dismiss the early Japanese religious beliefs as nothing but vulgar superstitions. Long before their religious beliefs and practices developed identifiable forms and structures, and came to be known as the "way of the *kami*" (*kannagara* or *Shinto*), people in Japan knew that they were not left alone in this mysterious universe; for they possessed in their myths certain divine models for all human, social, and communal activities. That is to say, people in the early period of Japan, like their counterparts in other parts of the world, took it for granted that they or their ancestors had learned all the necessary knowledge and techniques regarding social behavior and practical matters from the world of the *kami*. This world was far away from, and yet closely related to, their world, such that the success or failure of their daily work, to say nothing of the meaning of the whole of life, was interpreted in religious terms.

Early Japanese Myths

Scholarly opinions vary as to how various components of ancient Japanese myths can be traced to different parts of the Asian continent and also how they came to be blended in the course of time. It is safe to speculate, however, that with the ascendancy of the Imperial clan over rival clans starting around the fourth century, its myths provided the prominent motifs of the mythological framework into which myths of lesser clans were incorporated. The central motif of the early Japanese myths which thus developed was the divine origin of the Imperial clan. From this perspective, various myths which had hitherto been transmitted orally were compiled as the foundations for the two eighth-century historical writings entitled the *Records of Ancient Matters* (*Kojiki*)[5] and the *Chronicles of Japan* (*Nihon-shoki* or *Nihongi*).[6] Although these works betray some Chinese and Buddhist influences, which had reached Japan probably from the fifth century onward, we can at least reconstruct some of the important Japanese myths of the earlier period. Between the two works in question, the *Kojiki* shows far less Chinese influence than the *Nihon-shoki*, and for that reason we will follow the former for the discussion of cosmogonic, theogonic, and other myths.[7] It is to be remembered that ancient Japanese myths

[5] See Basil Hall Chamberlain, trans., "*Ko-ji-ki*: 'Records of Ancient Matters,'" Supplement to the *Transactions of the Asiatic Society of Japan*, vol. 10 (1882).

[6] See William G. Aston, trans., *Nihongi: Chronicles of Japan from the Earliest Times to A.D. 697* (2 vols.; London, 1896 and 1956).

[7] On this subject, see Masaharu Anesaki, "Japanese Mythology," in *The Mythology of All Races*, vol. 8, ed. C.J.A. MacCulloch (Boston, 1928); Karl Florenz, *Japanische My-*

presupposed a three-dimensional universe, namely the Plain of High Heaven (*Takama-no-hara*), where male and female *kami* dwell; the Phenomenal or Manifested World (*Utsushi-yo*), where human and other beings reside; and the Nether World (*Yomotsu-kuni*), where unclean spirits dwell. The lines of demarcation between these realms were not sharply drawn, however.[8]

Birth of kami. According to the *Kojiki* account, when the primeval matter had congealed but breath and form had not yet appeared, there emerged in the Plain of High Heaven the three self-created *kami*—Ame-no-minakanushi (heavenly center lord), Takamimusubi (August Producing *kami*) and Kamimusubi (divine generative force *kami*). Next, when the land was not solidified there emerged something like reed shoots, from which came two more self-created *kami*. Next there came into existence the seven generations of *kami*, most of whom are paired as couples, including Izanagi-no-kami (Male *kami* who invites) and his spouse, Izanami-no-kami (Female *kami* who is invited). It was Izanagi and Izanami who were commanded by the heavenly *kami* to solidify land out of the formless, watery chaos in which it was suspended. Thus, the two *kami* stood on the heavenly floating bridge and churned the waters with their jewelled spear. When they lifted the spear, the brine dripping down from the spear became an island.[9] Izanagi and Izanami then came down to the island and were married.

After giving birth to the land, Izanagi and Izanami proceeded to beget other *kami*, such as the *kami* of the wind, of the trees, of the mountain, and of the plains. But Izanami died after giving birth to the *kami* of fire. Izanagi, hoping to meet his spouse, pursued her to the Nether World, but found maggots squirming around her body. Horrified by this sight, Izanagi ran away, and decided to cleanse himself at a river.[10] When he washed his left eye, there came into existence the Sun Goddess (Amaterasu), and when he washed his right eye, there emerged the Moon *kami* (Tsukiyomi). Finally, as he washed his nose, there came into existence Valiant-male-*kami* (Susanoo). Greatly pleased over this, Izanagi gave his necklace to the Sun Goddess and

---

thologie (Tokyo, 1901); and Nobuhiro Matsumoto, "Essai sur la mythologie japonaise," *Austro-Asiatica*, vol. 2 (Paris, 1928).

[8] For the following summaries, I have consulted Chamberlain's translation of the *Kojiki* and that of Donald L. Philippi (Princeton, 1969).

[9] The name of the island is Onogoro. Its identity, however, has not been agreed upon by scholars.

[10] This is the prototype of the purification ceremony. Shinto tends to emphasize defilements rather than moral sins. The source of defilements is traced to the Nether World, based on this myth.

commissioned her to rule the Plain of High Heaven. He entrusted to the Moon *kami* the rule of the realm of the night. Finally, he commissioned Valiant-male-*kami* to rule the ocean.

Amaterasu. At one time, the Sun Goddess, disgusted by the misdeeds of her brother, Susanoo, concealed herself behind the rock-cave. Immediately the Plain of High Heaven became completely dark. The eight hundred myriads of *kami* then gathered together in front of the rock-cave and decided to make merry in order to attract her attention. The Female-*kami*-of-heavenly-headgear became *kami*-possessed, exposed her breasts and genitals, and danced madly, whereupon the other *kami* roared with laughter. Intrigued by all this, Amaterasu opened the rock-cave door slightly, whereat one of the strong *kami*, who was waiting by the door, pulled her out. With the reappearance of Amaterasu, the Plain of High Heaven was illuminated again.

Pacification of the Izumo region. Soon, Susanoo, the impetuous brother of Amaterasu, was driven from the Plain of High Heaven and went to the Izumo district, which is situated in western Honshu. There he rescued a maiden from the eight-headed snake and married her. It was his sixth descendant, Ōkuninushi (Great Land-ruler *kami*), who ruled the Izumo area with the help of a *kami* of midget size from the Land of Eternity. Meanwhile, Amaterasu dispatched two messengers to claim the Izumo region. They persuaded the sons of Ōkuninushi to surrender, whereby Ōkuninushi himself agreed to offer the jurisdiction of Izumo to the heavenly *kami*. However, Ōkuninushi demanded that a palace be built for him, modelled after the heavenly dwelling. This request was accepted, and the Izumo region became the domain of the heavenly *kami*.

Descent of the grandson of Amaterasu to Japan. As the pacification of the Japanese islands was duly reported, Amaterasu decided to send her grandson, Ninigi, to rule the land with the following instruction: "This Land-of-the-plentiful-reed-plains-and-of-the-fresh-rice-ears [Japan] has been entrusted to you as the land to be governed by you. Therefore, you must descend from heaven in accordance with the divine command." As Ninigi was ready to leave the Plain of High Heaven, Amaterasu gave him the myriad curved beads, the mirror, and the "grass-mower" sword, which were to become the sacred regalia of imperial authority. Among the *kami* who accompanied Ninigi were: *Kami*-of-the-little-roof-in-heaven (Ame-no-koyane), the ancestor of the Nakatomi priestly clan; *Kami*-of-grand-bead (Futo-dama), the

144

ancestor of the Imbe abstainers clan; Female-*kami*-of-heavenly-head-gear (Ame-no-uzume), the ancestress of the Sarume performers clan; and *Kami*-of-stonecutter (Ishikori-dome), the ancestor of the mirror-maker clan. Ninigi, leaving the heavenly rock seat, pushed through the myriad layers of clouds and descended to the peak of Mount Taka-chiho, which is assumed to be situated on the island of Kyushu.

Legends

The compilers of the *Kojiki* and the *Nihon-shoki* collected, in addition to ancient myths, many legendary accounts of the *kami* and the heroes. Both works group together myths under the heading of "Divine Age" (*kami-yo*); then comes a section on legendary emperors, which is fol-lowed by accounts of historic monarchs. Because of this emphasis on the undisrupted chronological continuity from myths to legends and from legends to history, it is difficult to determine where one ends and the next begins. At any rate, the accounts of the first ten legendary emperors are clearly not reliable historical records.[11] Probably the ac-counts of the emperors beginning with Ōjin, the fifteenth emperor according to the legendary genealogy, may be trusted as historical rec-ords.[12] It must also be mentioned that the so-called *Records of Customs and Lands* (*Fudoki*) of various provinces, compiled in the eighth cen-tury, also contain many interesting legends which throw light on the religious beliefs and practices of early Japan.[13]

The first legendary emperor, Jimmu. It is to be recalled that the Sun Goddess (Amaterasu) sent her grandson, Ninigi, to Japan. Ninigi mar-ried a daughter of a local *kami* in Kyushu, and they had three children. One of them married a daughter of the *kami* of the ocean, and they had four children, including the Emperor Jimmu and his brother, Itsuse (Lord-of-five-rapids). Jimmu and his brother decided to move eastward from Kyushu, looking for the most strategic place from which to govern the nation. Their journey was not very peaceful, be-cause they had to fight against the unsubmissive local *kami*. In fact, Itsuse died of a wound inflicted during one of the campaigns. Jimmu now commanded his troops alone. In such a manner, he came to Ku-

---

[11] In fact, the first emperor, Jimmu, and the tenth emperor, Sujin, are both called the "Emperor, the August Founder of the Nation" (Hatsukuni-shirasu-sumera-mikoto) in the *Nihon-shoki*.

[12] On the discrepancies between the Chinese and Japanese records in reference to the five Japanese monarchs, see Kitagawa, *Religion in Japanese History*, p. 9.

[13] The legends of Emperor Jimmu, Prince Yamato-takeru, and Empress Jingō that follow are taken from the *Kojiki*; the legend of the snake *kami* is taken from the Records of Customs and Lands of Hitachi Province (*Hitachi Fudoki*). All have been abridged.

mano (in the present Wakayama prefecture) where he saw a large bear lumbering along. Suddenly, Jimmu and his entire army fell asleep. Presently a certain man called Taka-kuraji woke him up and presented him with a mysterious sword. When Jimmu received the sword, all the unruly *kami* in that region were slain instantaneously. Jimmu continued his campaign and eventually settled at Unebi (in the present Nara prefecture) where he established his palace and ruled the kingdom.

Prince Yamato-takeru (Brave man of Yamato). Prince Yamato-takeru was dispatched by his father, the Emperor Keikō, to pacify the unruly *kami* and the unsubmissive people in the western and eastern provinces. On his way to the East, he received from his aunt, who was the priestess serving Amaterasu, the "grass-mower" sword and a bag with instructions to open it in an emergency. When the prince reached the district of Sagamu, the local ruler lured him into the plain and set fire to it in order to kill him. The prince opened the bag and found in it a fire-striking instrument. After mowing away the grass with his sword, he started a counter-fire. Then he killed the evil ruler and destroyed all his clan. In the end, the prince encountered a white boar, which was nothing less than the *kami* of Mount Ibuki. Because the prince dared to speak directly to the *kami*, he became sick. As he came down from the mountain, he could hardly walk. When he died, he was transformed into an eight-foot-long white bird and flew away toward the beach.

Empress Jingō. When the fourteenth legendary emperor, Chūai, was planning to attack the unsubmissive Kumaso tribes in Kyushu, his consort, the Empress Jingō, was *kami*-possessed and uttered words of divine instruction to the effect that the emperor should first attack Silla which was one of the principalities in Korea. Then, she said, the Kumaso, who were aided by Silla, would automatically submit to imperial authority. The emperor, however, did not believe the words of the *kami*, and he died by their curse. Thereupon the Great Minister Takeshi-uchi-no-sukune ordered a great exorcism of the country for the purification of defilements. The empress then became *kami*-possessed again and received the same instructions. The Great Minister inquired through her as to the name of the *kami* who gave the instruction, and the answer was given: "This is the will of the Sun Goddess." The *kami* further instructed that the army be dispatched to Korea. Accordingly, the empress commanded the vessels and crossed the ocean to the shore of Silla. Greatly awed, the King of Silla offered to obey the will of the divine sovereign of Japan. Another Korean principality, Paekche, followed Silla's example. After completing the Korean campaign, the empress returned to Japan. Incidentally, because her child was ready to be born before she completed the mission, she kept a stone around her waist in order to restrain her womb. Only after she reached the Japanese shore was the child born. He later became the Emperor Ōjin.

The Snake kami of the Hitachi Province. Once upon a time there was a certain man named Matachi who cultivated new rice fields in the Hitachi province. His work was greatly hindered by a large number of snakes, which were called the *Yatsu* (snake) *kami* by the local people because they had the bodies of snakes and horns on their heads. Matachi, angered by the interference of the *Yatsu-kami*, chased them toward the mountain. As he came to the foot of the mountain he placed a stick to mark a dividing line and addressed the *Yatsu-kami*, saying: "The territory above this mark is to be the property of the *kami*, but the land below the dividing line is to become man's rice fields. From now on I shall serve as the priest and venerate the *Yatsu-kami*, and I beseech you to bring no curse on us." Then he erected a shrine and offered the first service. His descendants have continued to venerate the snake *kami* to this day.

Poems

In addition to the myths and legends, an important source for the understanding of early Japanese beliefs and attitudes is an anthology of poems called the *Collection of Myriad Leaves* (*Manyōshū*), compiled in the latter half of the eighth century. While some of the poems included in this anthology were composed during the period when the collection was made, others are considerably older and reflect the beliefs and attitudes of the early Japanese people. "And it is noteworthy that despite the wide acceptance of Confucianism and Buddhism, almost all the gods [of] whom [the Manyō man] sang, or who fed the well-spring of his lyric inspiration, were purely Japanese."[14]

Mount Tachi (XVII:4000-4001)
> Many are the mountains and rivers
>> in the land of Etchū [Koshi],
> But only on Mount Tachi above River Nii
>> do imperial *kami* dwell.

[14] Quoted from the "Introduction" of the Japanese Classics Translation Committee's *The Manyōshū: One Thousand Poems* (Tokyo, 1940), p. xxxviii. In translating these poems, I have consulted the renderings of this edition. The citations refer to the original numbering in the *Kokka Taikan*.

147

No wonder it is white with snow
    even on summer days.

. . . .

As I look at Mount Tachi every year
    I am determined to tell others
That one will never tire of viewing
    the snow on Sacred Tachi in the summer.

Prayer (III:379)
    O Noble *Kami*
        who have descended from the Heavenly Plain,
    I pray with the offering of the evergreen branch
        tied with mulberry cloth and perfume
    Together with a wine-jar placed on the earth
        and bamboo rings hanging around my neck;
    I bend my knees with a scarf over me
        and pray from the bottom of my heart;
    And yet, why is it not possible
        for me to meet my beloved?

Nether World (v:905)
    O messenger from the Nether World
        here is some money for you;
    Please carry on your back my son
        who is so young and does not know the way.

Snow (XVII:3923)
    How noble is the reflection of falling snow
        that covers all corners under heaven.

Autumn (II:209)
    As I see the messenger walking on the fallen leaves
        I think of the time when I first met my beloved.

II. DEVELOPMENT OF SHINTO

Early Shinto

The historical development of Japan prior to the sixth century A.D. is largely a matter of conjecture. However, piecing together various sources, we catch a glimpse of a growing Yamato (an old designation of Japan) kingdom, which was in fact a confederation of autonomous and powerful clans centered around the Imperial clan. We are not certain when the Imperial clan established itself in the Yamato region (the present Nara prefecture). Nevertheless, we learn from Korean sources that Japan traded with Korean principalities in the fourth century and established a small colony at the southern tip of the Korean peninsula. We also find in the sixth-century Chinese record that five Japanese monarchs paid tribute to the Chinese court during the fifth and early sixth centuries. Understandably, through these contacts Sino-Korean civilization and religion began to influence Japan. It was through Korea that Buddhism was introduced to the Japanese court during the sixth century. Confucianism followed and provided Japan not only with systematic theories of social and political institutions but also with ethical norms for individuals and society. Other systems, such as Taoism and the Yin-Yang School, also contributed philosophical concepts. By far the most far-reaching religious influence, however, was exerted by Buddhism, as we shall discuss later.

As far as early Shinto is concerned, it did not seem to have fixed liturgies or ecclesiastical organizations. Most religious functions, except for those in the home, took place around a *himorogi* (usually a piece of unpolluted land surrounded by evergreens), an *iwasaka* (a piece of unpolluted land surrounded by holy rocks or stones), or on the paddy field or seashore, where people offered simple worship to the *kami* of their region according to agricultural or fishing seasons. Gradually, these regional *kami* came to be homologized with the *kami* of the clan, which were mentioned earlier. Thus the community festivals, such as those of the harvest and the new year, became important events both for the clan and the regional group.

Among all the clans, the most powerful was the Imperial clan, which claimed both religious and political authority by virtue of its divine and solar ancestry. The emperor delegated political responsibilities to his ministers in the court and shared his priestly office with religious dignitaries, such as the ablutioner, the supplicator, and the liturgist. He also depended on shamanistic diviners in dealing with the *kami* of other clans and of unfamiliar territories. It was taken for granted that the imperial palace was also the shrine of the Sun Goddess Amaterasu, the ancestress of the Imperial clan and the *kami* of the Yamato region. It was the prerogative of the emperor to offer worship to Amaterasu, who in turn communicated to him her divine will through *kami*-possession and dreams. According to the *Nihon-shoki*, it was the tenth legendary emperor, Sujin, who became uneasy about sharing his residence with the *kami*. Thus he entrusted Princess Toyo-suki-iri with the worship of Amaterasu at the village of Kasanui where a *himorogi* was established. He also commissioned another princess to worship the *kami* of the Yamato region away from the palace. During the reign of the eleventh legendary emperor, Suinin, Princess Yamato, who was then in charge of the worship of Amaterasu, visited various places looking for a permanent resting place for the shrine of the imperial ancestress. When the princess arrived in the province of Ise, Amaterasu communicated her desire to dwell there. Thus a shrine was erected at Ise. This is presumably the origin of the Grand Shrine of Ise.

Edicts Concerning Shinto (Jingi-ryō)

Under Chinese influence, Japan during the seventh century became a nation governed by a series of laws, which were promulgated in the form of imperial edicts. One of them was the Edict Concerning Shinto (Jingi-ryō).[15] Among other things, it prescribed a list of national rituals. They are as follows:

Toshigoi festival: to be performed in the second month of every year. Prayers offered for the harvest.

Hanashizume festival: to be performed at the end of the third month. Prayers offered for freedom from sickness.

Kamu-miso festival: to be performed in the middle of the fourth month. Offerings of summer garments made at the Grand Shrine of Ise.

Saigusa festival: the festival of the Isakawa shrine in the Yamato province.

Ōmi festival: to be performed on the fourth day of the fourth month. The festival of the food goddess of Hirose and Tatsuta.

Kaze no kami festival: to be performed on the fourth day of the fourth month to the male and female *kami* of the wind associated with the shrine of Tatsuta. Prayers offered for protection of the crops from storm.

Tsukinami festival: to be performed on the eleventh day of the sixth month. Originally meant to be the monthly service of thanksgiving.

Michiaye festival: to be performed on the last day of the sixth month. Celebrated at the crossroads outside the capital; the *kami* of the crossroads entreated to keep out evil spirits.

Hishizume festival: to directly follow the above. Prayers to keep fire away from the palace.

Kamuniye festival: to be performed in the ninth and tenth months at Ise. (Usually took place on the eleventh day of the tenth month in the palace.) *Kamuniye* (or *kanname*) means "divine tasting" of food and wine made from rice of the new crop.

Aimube festival: to be performed during the eleventh month. *Aimube*

---

[15] For a fuller description of the *Jingi-ryō*, see George B. Sansom, "Early Japanese Law and Administration, Part II," *Transactions of the Asiatic Society of Japan*, 2d ser., vol. 11 (December 1934), 122-127.

means "tasting together," which implies that the emperor partook with the *kami* of wine and food made from rice of the new crop.

Ōniye festival: to be performed during the eleventh month. An extension of the Aimube festival.

The edict specified that, upon the accession of an emperor, all the *kami* should be worshipped and that one month of partial abstinence (*ara-imi*) and three days of complete abstinence (*ma-imi*) were to be observed. Meat-eating and sex were prohibited during these periods. During the partial abstinence, all government offices were still expected to carry on their duties, but they were not allowed to pay visits of condolence upon a death or call upon the sick. During the period of complete abstinence, all government activities were suspended except for ceremonial observances. On the day of a new emperor's accession, the chieftain of the hereditary Shinto priestly family of Nakatomi was to recite the ritual prayers (*Norito*), while the chieftain of the hereditary Shinto priestly family of Imbe was to present the sacred regalia of the mirror and the sword to the emperor.

The edict also specified that the great food festival (*Daijō-e*) should be celebrated once in each reign, but that other festivals were to be celebrated annually. On the occasion of the Great Purification, which was to take place on the last day of the sixth and twelfth months, the Nakatomi chieftain was assigned to offer the *nusa* (expiatory offerings made of hemp or flax) of purification and recite the ritual prayers. Then the chieftain of the hereditary diviners' family of Urabe was to perform the cleansing. Also for the occasion of the Great Purification, all the provinces were expected to furnish from each district one sword, one animal skin, one spade, and other items for offerings.

Shinto Priesthood

The religious situation in Japan during the sixth, seventh, and eighth centuries fostered gradual stratification of the Shinto priesthood. Earlier, it was the common pattern for the clan chieftain to be in charge of religious functions in connection with the *kami* of his clan. Gradually, he delegated the actual performance of rituals to designated members of the clan. In the course of time, some of the religious positions became hereditary. In other cases, men were chosen for religious duties for a certain period of time.[16] Some of them were capable of becoming *kami*-possessed, while others depended on

---

[16] The priests were variously called the *negi* (supplicator), *hafuri* (ablutioner), *kan-nushi* (master of worship), etc. Very common was the so-called *ichinen-kan-nushi*, which literally means a "priest for one year only."

(mostly female) shamanic diviners to speak on behalf of the *kami*. It is important to note that the rapid centralization of the government during the seventh century resulted in the incorporation of the various types of the Shinto priesthood into the jurisdiction of the Department of Shinto Affairs which was established at the turn of the eighth century.

As far as the imperial court was concerned, it had several hereditary Shinto priestly families—the Nakatomi, the Imbe, the Sarume, etc.—who claimed to be descendants of heavenly *kami*. We learn from the *Gleanings from Ancient Stories* (*Kogo-shūi*)[17] that during the reign of the Emperor Kōtoku (middle of the seventh century), the chieftain of the Imbe, named Sakashi, was made the chief official governing Shinto priests. He also was assigned to administer the census registration of imperial princes and princesses and to oversee court rituals, marriages of high government officials, and divinations for the throne and the government. We learn from the same work that the Imbe chieftain was entrusted with the supervision of the construction of the shrine, with such tasks as cutting trees with consecrated axes and excavating with consecrated mattocks. On the other hand, the ceremony for quieting the emperor's spirit (*Mitama-shizume*) was traditionally performed by the chieftain of the Sarume family. In the course of time, however, the Nakatomi family gained prestige and power, overshadowing other hereditary priestly families. Thus, while other priestly families associated with the court were given graded court rank, the Nakatomi family enjoyed the highest rank and dominated the Department of Shinto Affairs, which was considered more important than the great Council of State.

Similarly, in the provincial administration the chief priest, who usually held a lower rank than that of the governor, nevertheless enjoyed greater prestige than the governor in many instances, so that the central government often turned to the Shinto priests in various provinces for their cooperation and assistance in executing government programs. They were in turn well compensated, as evidenced by the account of the *Nihon-shoki* which tells us that the tax collected for the

---

[17] It was compiled in 807 by Imbe-no-Hironari. While this document contains some of the same material as the *Kojiki*, it also records many legends transmitted in the Imbe family but ignored by the *Kojiki*. The author of the *Gleanings* wished to substantiate his claim that the Imbe and the Nakatomi were descendants of Ame-no-futodama-no-mikoto and Ame-no-koyane-no-mikoto, respectively, and that both were equally important priestly families.

shrines was divided into three shares: one for the offerings to the *kami* but two for the priests.[18]

Institutes of the Engi Era (Engi-shiki)

As stated earlier, the ideal of the Japanese government from the seventh century onward was the rule of the nation by means of laws and regulations. Thus, the period between the seventh and ninth centuries produced a large body of minute regulations covering sundry subjects pertaining to government administration. These were compiled in the tenth century as the *Institutes of the Engi Era (Engi-shiki)*.[19] Of the fifty fascicles of the *Engi-shiki*, the first ten are devoted directly to Shinto matters; others make occasional references to various aspects of Shinto.

According to the *Engi-shiki*, festivals are classified into three grades of importance with appropriate provisions for rituals and offerings. All the regular and occasional festivals are minutely described and regulated. For example, on the early spring festival (*Toshigoi-no-matsuri*), which takes place during the second month every year, prayers for harvest are to be offered to 3,132 *kami*, 737 of whom are to be worshipped by the officials of the Ministry of Shinto Affairs and 2,395 of whom are to be attended to by provincial officials. The occasional festivals include such rituals as the ceremony to pacify the *kami* of water, well, or hearth, as well as the ceremony before dispatching an envoy to China or that of seeing off the Chinese envoy from the capital. The *Engi-shiki* also gives fifty-seven general regulations regarding the qualification and duties of the priests as well as rules for complete and partial abstinence.

Especially noteworthy are the regulations pertaining to all aspects of the Grand Shrine of Ise. The shrine buildings should be rebuilt every twenty years. Persons with the rank of Ō (one rank below the imperial prince) or below are not even permitted to present offerings to Amaterasu. The imperial consort and the crown prince, should they wish to make offerings to her, are required to secure the permission of the emperor for it. A diviner, who assists the chief priest of Ise, is to perform divination regarding all the government affairs that take place throughout the year. The *Engi-shiki* also gives detailed regula-

---

[18] This regulation was put into effect in A.D. 677 by the order of the Emperor Temmu.

[19] More strictly, it was called the *Engi-kyaku-shiki*, which meant the "supplementary rules to previously promulgated edicts and ceremonial rules," such as the Kōnin and Jōgan laws, that were revised and systematized during the Engi era.

tions concerning the "Abstinence Palace" (*Itsuki-no-miya*), which is a small palace for the "Abstinence Princess," an imperial princess who serves as the ceremonial high priestess at the Grand Shrine of Ise.

Understandably, the succession of a new emperor and the "great food festival celebrated upon the succession of a new emperor" (*Senso-ōniye-no-matsuri*) are also minutely regulated. For example, as the preparation for the great food festival, crops must be collected from various provinces by government representatives consisting of one priest and three diviners. Other regulations cover the material, style, and shape of the vestments for all the participants, the processes of manufacturing the utensils to be used for the ceremony, and the method of making the rice wine which in itself involves a series of rituals. The *Engi-shiki* also gives a comprehensive list of the 3,132 heavenly and earthly *kami* and the names and locations of their shrines throughout the nation.

Shinto Ritual Prayers (Norito)

Shinto prayers are based on the belief in *koto-dama* (spiritual potency residing in spoken words). The *Norito* usually consist of words praising the *kami*, lists of offerings presented, words identifying the persons on whose behalf the prayer is recited and the persons who are reciting it, and petitions. If the *Norito* were recited correctly and eloquently, it was believed to bring about good results. There are twenty-seven *Norito* for which texts are included in the *Engi-shiki* (Fascicle 8).[20] Among them are the texts of the *Norito* for the annual ritual praying for harvest (*Toshigoi* festival), liturgies for the Kasuga, Hirose, Tatsuta, Hirano, Kudo, and Furuaki shrines, etc.

Probably the most important for the understanding of Shinto is the text for the ritual of the "Great Exorcism celebrated on the last day of the sixth month" (*Minazuki-tsugomori no ō-haraye*). This ritual recounts the myth of Amaterasu sending her grandson to Japan, and how his descendants ruled the nation peacefully, "living in the shadow of heaven and sun." But, the *Norito* goes on to say, with the increase of population, various offences were committed by the people. These offences were divided into two kinds: the "offences to heaven" and the "offences to earth." The former refers to the offences of destroying the divisions of rice fields, covering up irrigation ditches, opening irrigation sluices, sowing seeds over the seeds planted by others, planting pointed rods in the rice fields, flaying living animals or flaying them

[20] See Donald L. Philippi, trans., *Norito* (A New Translation of the Ancient Japanese Ritual Prayers) (Tokyo, 1959).

backwards, and emptying excrement in improper areas. The latter refers to such offences as cutting the skin of the living or the dead, suffering from leprosy or skin excrescences, violating one's mother, daughter, stepdaughter, or mother-in-law, cohabiting with animals, killing the animals of others, invoking evils on others by means of witchcraft, and so on. When these offences are committed, the chieftain of the Nakatomi priestly family is commanded, "in accordance with the ritual performed in the heavenly palace of the Sun Goddess, to cut off the bottom and the ends of a sacred tree and place them in abundance as offerings to the *kami*, and also to cut off the bottom and ends of sacred sedge reeds and slice them into thin pieces, and then to recite the potent words of the *Norito*."

When the *Norito* is recited, the heavenly *kami* will hear the words of petition, and then all the offences and defilements are transferred to "defilements-bearers"—narrow pieces of wood and sedge reeds— which are carried to the ocean. There the offences are swallowed by the *kami* of the currents, and will be blown to the Nether World, where another *kami* will wander off with them and lose them. "And when the offences are thus lost, it is announced that from this day onward there is no offence remaining among the officials of the sovereign's court and in the four quarters of the land under heaven."

III. INFLUENCE OF BUDDHISM AND CONFUCIANISM

Buddhist Influence on Shinto

In the religious history of Japan one of the epoch-making events was the introduction of Buddhism from Korea to the Yamato court sometime during the sixth century A.D. Prior to that time, however, Buddhism was known among the Korean and Chinese immigrants who had settled in various parts of Japan. At any rate, when Buddhism reached Japan it was no longer a simple religion of Indian ascetics. Buddhism by that time had developed lofty systems of philosophy, voluminous scriptures, elaborate rituals, hierarchical ecclesiastical organizations, and its own forms of art and architecture. In his note to the Yamato court, to which he presented an image of Buddha, the King of Paekche stressed two points: firstly, that Buddhist doctrine is difficult to understand, but secondly, that it brings about boundless rewards and blessings in the sense that everything one asks of the Buddha will be fulfilled without fail. Hearing this, according to the *Nihon-shoki*, the Emperor Kimmei could hardly contain his joy. However, the powerful chieftains of the Mononobe and Nakatomi clans were opposed to Buddhism on the ground that, should a foreign *kami* be worshipped, it might incur the wrath of the *kami* of Japan. In the end, it was the reputed worldly benefits of Buddhism which attracted the chieftain of the Soga clan, and he secured the court's sanction to adhere to Buddhism as the religion of his clan. But, inasmuch as the Soga was the most powerful clan in the realm—especially after the Soga displaced the Mononobe from power—Buddhism prospered during the second half of the sixth century.

It was also with the backing of the Soga chieftain that Suiko, the first empress in the history of Japan, ascended the throne. The actual administrative duties, however, were assumed by her nephew, Shō-toku, who was appointed as the Prince-Regent. Shōtoku is credited with having drawn up the so-called Seventeen-Article Constitution. In the second article we read: "You should venerate the Three Treasures, namely, Buddha, Buddha's Law [teaching] and the Buddhist Community, which are the final refuge of all creatures." Shōtoku was also a great admirer of Confucian learning, so he sent many able young Japanese to acquire an up-to-date education in China. On the other hand, he was eager to continue the tradition of his imperial ancestors who had venerated the *kami*. One of his proclamations states: "It would be unthinkable to neglect during Our reign the veneration of the *kami* of Heaven and Earth. May all the ministers from the bottom of their hearts pay homage to the *kami*." In short, what Shōtoku envisaged was the establishment of a multi-religious policy that harmonized Shinto, the Confucian tradition, and Buddhism. This synthesis was to serve as the bulwark of a strongly centralized nation ruled by the throne.

The task of transforming the Japanese nation, which had been little more than a confederation of powerful clans, into a centralized empire was carried out during the second half of the seventh century, known as the Reform Era, by the initiative of sinified bureaucrats, many of whom had been sent to China by Prince Shōtoku. The reformers rejected the notion that the nation was to be ruled by the will of the *kami* which was communicated to the emperor through dreams, divination, and *kami*-possession. Instead, they translated, revised, and appropriated Chinese laws to use them as the guiding principles for the political administration of Japan. As a result of the highly sinified policies adopted during the Reform Era, the eighth century, known as the Nara period, was marked by the strong influence of Buddhism on various aspects of Japanese culture and society. This was epitomized by the construction of the national temple honoring the great statue of Lochana Buddha in the capital city of Nara. Thanks largely to royal patronage, six schools of Buddhism—the Kusha (*Abhidharmakosa*), the Jōjitsu (*Satyasiddhi*), the Sanron (*Mādhyamika*), the Hossō (*Yogācāra*), the Kegon (*Avatamsaka*), and the Ritsu (*Vinaya*) schools—were established as the orthodox systems during the Nara period.[21] In this situation, Shinto inevitably came to feel the strong impact of Buddhism.

Shinto-Buddhist Amalgamation (Shin-Butsu Shūgō)

During the Nara period, the lofty doctrines of Buddhism were appreciated only by the monastics. The laity adhered to Buddhism in order to gain this-worldly benefits and assurances of a life to come. For example, in the famous "Songs on the Buddha's Foot-prints," carved on a stone around the middle of the eighth century, the Buddha is referred to variously as "intrepid hero" (*masurao*), "healer" (*kusuri-shi*), and "sacred visitor" or the "*kami* who visits the world" (*mara-hito*).[22] This had strong pre-Buddhist, Shintoistic connotations. On the other hand, under the influence of Buddhism there developed the notion that the *kami* of Shinto were "protectors of Buddha" (*Gohō-shin*). Amaterasu herself was said to have given her blessing to the construction of the great statue of Lochana Buddha, which was a pious undertaking of the Emperor Shōmu. Thus, a number of Shinto shrines were established within the compound of Buddhist temples, and a number of Buddhist chapels were built on the outskirts of Shinto shrines.

The masses, who received no benefit from the ministry of orthodox Buddhist schools, continued to depend on folk religious leaders, such as shamanic diviners, healers, and magicians. It is to be noted, however, that during the eighth century these folk religious leaders adopted some features of Buddhism and came to be called "unordained Buddhist ascetics" (*ubasoku*).[23] In sharp contrast to the orthodox Buddhist hierarchy supported by the government, these *ubasoku*, who were spiritual heirs of the pre-Buddhist folk religious leaders, advocated simple faith in the *kami* and the Buddha, disregarding the complicated doctrines and disciplines of orthodox Buddhism. Indeed, the tradition of the *ubasoku*, which combined Shinto, Buddhist, and

---

[21] On these schools of Buddhism, see Junjirō Takakusu, *The Essentials of Buddhist Philosophy* (Honolulu, 1947).

[22] All of these songs are carved on a stone in the Yakushi-ji temple near Nara. It was carved in 752, the year in which the statue of the Lochana Buddha was completed. For the texts of these songs and a discussion on this subject, see Donald L. Philippi, "Songs on the Buddha's Foot-Prints," *Nihonbunka-Kenkyujo-kiyō*, No. 2 (March 1958).

[23] The term *ubasoku* is a corrupted form of the Sanskrit *upāsaka* (lay ascetics). On this subject, see Ichirō Hori, "On the Concept of Hijiri (Holy-Man)," *Numen* 5, no. 2 (April 1958), 128-160 and no. 3 (September 1958), 199-232.

folk religious elements, prepared the ground for the development of the Order of Mountain Ascetics (Shugen-dō) as well as the Shinto-Buddhist amalgamation, known as *Ryōbu-Shinto*, in the subsequent period.

The trend toward Shinto-Buddhist amalgamation was greatly enhanced by the establishment of the Tendai and the Shingon schools of Buddhism during the ninth century in the early Heian period. Tendai Buddhism was systematized by Saichō, better known by his posthumous name, Dengyō Daishi (767-822). He studied T'ien T'ai philosophy in China, but attempted to incorporate not only T'ien T'ai doctrines but also Ch'an (Zen in Japanese) philosophy, monastic disciplines (*Kai-ritsu*), and some features of Esoteric Buddhism (*Mik-kyō*) within a doctrinal framework based on the *Lotus Sūtra*. In his attempt to establish as the religious capital of the nation the Tendai monastic center at Mount Hi'ei not far from Kyoto, Saichō took a conciliatory attitude toward the tutelary *kami* of the mountain. Shortly after his death, Saichō's successors stressed the Esoteric elements, whereby the Tendai school came to be known as the "Tai-Mitsu" (Esoteric Buddhism of the Tendai tradition).

Shingon (Chên-yen in Chinese) Buddhism, which was in the tradition of the Esoteric School, was introduced and systematized by Kūkai or Kōbō Daishi (774-835), who was a great synthesizer in both doctrinal and practical matters.[24] In addition to erecting a monastic center at Mount Kōya, fifty miles south of Kyoto, Kūkai served as abbot of Tō-ji, the national temple in Kyoto. His school came to be known as the "Tō-Mitsu" (Esoteric School of the Tō-ji tradition). These two Esoteric schools—Tendai and Shingon—embraced lofty philosophies and magical incantations, and they influenced the courtiers in Kyoto as well as the masses in remote areas. Gradually, the Mountain Ascetics, the spiritual heirs of the *ubasoku* (unordained Buddhist ascetics), allied themselves with the Esoteric schools, and came to be known as the Tendai Shugen-dō and Shingon Shugen-dō, respectively.

With the expansion of eclectic and all-embracing Esoteric schools of Buddhism, the *kami* of Shinto began to lose their status as "protectors of Buddha." Instead, there developed a notion that the *kami*, like other beings, were in need of salvation by Buddha. Soon, however, this notion gave way to a more widespread belief that the original nature of the *kami* was Buddha, and that the *kami* were Buddha's manifestations in Japan. This theoretical formulation made possible the practical

---

[24] On the life of Kūkai, see J. M. Kitagawa, "Master and Saviour," in *Studies of Esoteric Buddhism and Tantrism* (Kōyasan, Japan, 1965), pp. 1-26. [Chapter 11 of this book.]

amalgamation of Shinto and Buddhism,[25] known as the *Ryōbu* ("two-sided") Shinto in the Shingon tradition and the *Sannō-ichijitsu* ("one and true") Shinto in the Tendai tradition. This synthesis lasted until the middle of the nineteenth century.

Shinto Reaction Against Shinto-Buddhist Amalgamation

The medieval period in Japan began, officially at least, in 1192 when the military family of Minamoto established a feudal regime at Kamakura while the imperial court remained in Kyoto. This marked the breakdown of the age-old ideal of the unity of religion (worship) and government (political administration). From that time until the modern period, the imperial court only had nominal, and mostly ceremonial, authority, whereas the feudal regimes held political authority. The appearance of a new political order coincided with internal and external difficulties for Japan, notably a series of natural calamities at home and attempted invasions by Mongol forces from abroad. The thirteenth century was also a period of religious awakening, which resulted in the establishment of indigenous Buddhist schools, e.g., the Pure Land School, the True Pure Land School, the Nichiren School, and the Rinzai and Sōtō Zen schools. The leaders of the new Buddhist schools shared a profound concern for certainty of faith, and while they made no overt attempt to destroy Shinto, they reacted against the easygoing amalgamation of Shinto-Buddhist beliefs and practices that had developed in the previous age.

The spiritual awakening also took place among the Shinto leaders who were attempting to emancipate Shinto from the Buddhist-dominated Shinto-Buddhist amalgamation. The pioneers of this movement were the hereditary priests of the Watarai family who served at the Outer Shrine of Ise; hence the movement was called the Ise Shinto or Watarai Shinto movement. They were instrumental in compiling the *Shinto Gobusho* (Shinto Pentateuch), which stressed purity and honesty as the highest virtues of Shinto. The theoreticians of the Ise Shinto movement, however, were compelled to develop their Shinto apologetics within the framework of the Shinto-Buddhist syncretism because Buddhism was too deeply rooted to be rejected altogether. This movement provided encouragement to loyalists of the imperial cause toward the last years of the Kamakura feudal regime and during the short period of imperial rule (1334-1336). A famous loyalist, Kitabatake Chikafusa (d. 1354), wrote in his work *Jinnō-shōtō-ki* (Records of

[25] Regarding one of the Shinto-Buddhist rituals, see J. M. Kitagawa, "Gohei-Hasami," *Kairos* 8, no. 2 (1966), 114-117.

the Valid Succession of Divine Emperors): "Great Yamato is a divine nation. It is only our land whose foundations were first laid by the divine ancestor." He regarded the three imperial insignias—the mirror, the bead, and the sword—as the symbols of the three Shinto virtues of veracity, mercy, and justice. At the same time, he acknowledged some values of Buddhism and Confucianism on the ground that they contained partial truths of Shinto.

The short-lived imperial rule was followd by the emergence of another feudal regime under the rule of the Ashikaga family. The Ashikaga period (1338-1573), despite continued political and social unrest, witnessed the development of the arts and culture, which was largely inspired by Zen Buddhism. An able nobleman and philosopher of this period, Ichijō Kanera (d. 1481), engaged in theoretical work on Shinto along monotheistic lines, even though he was tolerant of other religions. Following the same motif, Yoshida Kanetomo (d. 1511) advocated "Unique-Shinto" (Yuiitsu-Shinto),[26] which stressed the unity of Shinto, Buddhism, and Confucianism. The Yoshida family belonged to the ancient Urabe (diviner) family and served as hereditary priests at the Yoshida and Hirano shrines; hence his movement is also called Yoshida Shinto or Urabe Shinto. Yoshida Kanetomo was influenced by Taoist metaphysics as much as by Esoteric Buddhism, and he accepted the general framework of Shinto-Buddhist amalgamation. But he reversed the earlier Buddhist argument and suggested that Buddhas and Bodhisattvas were manifestations of the Shinto *kami*.

Influence of Neo-Confucianism on Shinto

The Ashikaga feudal regime, which was in power from the mid-fourteenth to the mid-sixteenth centuries, patronized Zen Buddhists not only as religious leaders but as the elite of that period. In fact, Zen Buddhist priests were engaged in such diverse activities as political administration, foreign service, foreign trade, education, printing, and in all spheres of the arts and culture. Some of the Zen priests who studied in China were also well versed in Neo-Confucianism—more specifically, the school of Chu Hsi (Shushi in Japanese)—and were instrumental in popularizing it in Japan. Not only was Neo-Confucianism taught in Zen temples, which also functioned as schools, but in the fifteenth century, several thousand Zen priests flocked to the Ashikaga Academy, the official school of Neo-Confucian studies,

---

[26] A more exact title of his movement is Yuiitsu-sogen (Unique and Fundamental) Shinto. His works include the *Shintō tai-i* (Outlines of Shinto) and *Yuiitsu Shintō myōbō-yōshū* (Essentials of Unique Shinto).

160

which was staffed by learned Zen priests. Initially, many were Zennists first and Confucian scholars second, but soon they accepted the principle of the unity of Zen and Neo-Confucianism (*Zen-Ju-itchi*). Gradually, some of them began to accept the superiority of Neo-Confucianism to Zen (*shu-Ju kyaku-Zen*); by the seventeenth century, many Confucian scholars in Japan began to reject Zen Buddhism altogether.

In 1603, the Tokugawa family established the last of the feudal regimes. It endured until 1867. The Tokugawa regime utilized Buddhist institutions as arms of the feudal government in order to exterminate the influence of Roman Catholicism. The regime ordered every household to belong to a specific Buddhist temple and to secure a document that certified that no member of the household was an adherent of the "forbidden religion." The Buddhist institutions were in turn rigidly controlled by the Commissioner of Temples. While the Tokugawa regime thus depended heavily on Buddhism as a means of thought-control, as it were, it upheld the Chu Hsi School (*Shushi-gaku*) of Neo-Confucianism as the "official theology" of the regime. This was because "the Confucian concept of a human order established in harmony with immutable natural principles seemed to justify the rigid social cleavages and political absolutism of the Tokugawa system."[27] Accordingly, the founder of the Tokugawa regime appointed a noted Chu Hsi scholar, Hayashi Razan (d. 1657), as the chief adviser to the regime and the head of the official academy for Chinese culture. Also, many of the leading *daimyō* (warrior lords) invited Confucian scholars to advise them regarding administrative policies and educational matters.

Confronted by this task, the Japanese Confucian scholars of the seventeenth century were compelled to interpret "the way of the ancient Chinese sage-kings" so that it fit into the indigenous religious and political tradition of Japan. They were at that time also eagerly trying to be emancipated from the Buddhist framework. These two factors, among others, made them feel emotionally close to the cause of Shinto. For example, Hayashi Razan stressed the importance of the Shinto communal cult as the basis of social cohesion, and wrote a work entitled *A Study of Shinto Shrines in Our Nation* (*Honchō Jinja-kō*).[28] He even equated the *li* (reason or principle) of Chu Hsi with the *dō* (way) of the *kami*.

[27] Edwin O. Reischauer and John K. Fairbank, *East Asia: The Great Tradition* (Boston, 1958), p. 616.
[28] In this work, he attempted to trace the development of Shinto shrines from the time before Shinto came under Buddhist influence in order to repudiate the principle of Shinto-Buddhist amalgamation. This view was refuted by the Tendai abbot, Tenkai

In addition to the Chu Hsi School, there were two other branches of Confucian studies in Japan during the Tokugawa period. One was the Wang Yang-ming School (Ōyōmei-gaku), which was propounded by Nakaye Tōju (d. 1648), Kumazawa Banzan (d. 1691), and others. This school developed into a pseudoreligious system among warriors as well as among upper class farmers and merchants. Although the scholars of this school and those of the Chu Hsi tradition did not agree on metaphysics and epistemology, they shared a pro-Shinto attitude. Another tradition of Confucian studies, known as the School of Ancient Studies (*Ko-gaku* or *Fukko-gaku*), stressed the return to the teachings of Confucius and Mencius. The scholars of this school were split in their attitude toward Shinto. Some of them were preoccupied with Chinese antiquity so they paid little attention to Shinto. But Yamaga Sokō (d. 1685), who was more tolerant toward Shinto, systematized the semireligious Code of Warriors (*Bushidō*), which had strong Shinto elements. On the other hand, Dazai Shundai (d. 1747), a Sinophile *par excellence*, insisted on the superiority of the Way of the Ancient Chinese King to the Way of the *Kami*.

Confucian-Shinto

By far the most extreme pro-Shintoist among all the Confucian scholars during the Tokugawa period was Yamazaki Ansai (d. 1682). Like many other Confucianists of his time, Yamazaki was originally a Buddhist priest. When he was twenty-five years of age, he renounced the Buddhist priesthood and became a scholar of the Chu Hsi School. An able teacher, he attracted nearly six thousand disciples during his lifetime. In later years, however, he attempted to synthesize Confucian ethics and Shinto, and developed a system known as Suiga ("descent of divine blessing") Shinto. The followers of Suiga Shinto venerated Yamazaki as a living *kami* and created various Confucian-Shinto cults, many of which emphasized initiation rites. Yamazaki stressed the virtue of reverence (*tsutusushimi*) as the principle which Shinto and Neo-Confucianism had in common. Considering the *Nihon-shoki* as the highest scripture, Yamazaki equated its cosmogonic myths with Chinese cosmology, and insisted on the basic unity of man and the *kami*. In his view, the Chinese emperor served under the Heavenly Emperor, but the emperor in Japan, being the direct descendant of Amaterasu, was himself the Heavenly Emperor, and thus should be the object of supreme reverence. Understandably, Suiga Shinto, which

---

(d. 1643), one of the advisers to the Tokugawa regime and an eloquent advocate of the *Sannō-ichijitsu Shinto*.

162

combined Neo-Confucianism and Shinto, learning and faith, and justice and devotion, exerted significant influence in all walks of life, promoting emotional nationalism and loyalty to the throne.

There were other forms of *rapprochement* between Confucian tradition and Shinto. Kumazawa Banzan (d. 1691), a noted scholar of the Wang Yang-ming School, spoke for many Confucianists of his time when he asserted that the Way of the *Kami* (Shinto) in Japan and the Way of the True Kingship (*wang-tao* in Chinese; *ō-dō* in Japanese) in China were different in name but the same in substance. That Kumazawa and others overlooked profound differences that existed between Shinto and Confucian tradition is obvious. Nevertheless, many Shintoists who were unhappy over the age-old domination of Shinto by Buddhism happily welcomed the pro-Shinto Confucian scholars. Another important movement within the Confucian circle was the development of the Mito School, supported by the influential Lord of Mito, a member of the Tokugawa family. The Mito School attracted many able Confucian scholars, including Chu Shun-sui (d. 1682), a royalist of Ming China then in exile in Japan. It was the scholars of this school who produced the *History of Great Japan* (*Dai-Nihon-shi*), which aroused historical consciousness among the Japanese intelligentsia and provided a powerful incentive to the royalist movement later on. All in all, Confucian scholarship during the Tokugawa period was characterized by an activist temperament which led Confucianists to concern themselves with politics, economics, jurisprudence, and other practical aspects of human life. This activism was injected, through the Confucian-Shinto alliance, into the veins of Shinto, which became rejuvenated and began to be self-conscious about its own unique heritage.

The effort to synthesize Confucian ethics and Shinto devotion was also evident in the popular ten-volume work entitled the *Japanese Analects* (*Wa-rongo*), which aimed at providing moral teachings for a popular audience.[29] More influential, perhaps, were such semireligious movements as the "Ming Learning" (*Shin-gaku*), founded by Ishida Baigan (d. 1744), which had followers among merchants, and the "Repaying the Indebtedness" (*Ho-toku*), founded by Ninomiya Sontoku (d. 1856), which spread among farmers. To be sure, in these movements both Confucian and Shinto elements were often diluted and mixed with Buddhist and other features. But, precisely because of this ambiguous inclusion of heterogeneous features, these movements

[29] See Genchi Kato, "A Study of the Oracles and Sayings in the Warongo or Japanese Analects," *Transactions of the Asiatic Society of Japan*, 45, part 2 (1917), 1-117.

appealed to strata of society which would not otherwise have been reached by scholarly approaches. And the combination of emphases on such simple virtues as honesty, frugality, filial piety, and the veneration of the *kami* and the throne prepared the ground for the resurgence of ethnocentric Shinto in the nineteenth century.

Resurgence of Shinto

It may be recalled that at the turn of the seventeenth century Shinto was at low ebb. While the Tokugawa regime paid lip service to the Way of the *Kami*, it relied on Neo-Confucianism for its guiding principles and it incorporated Buddhist institutions into the structure of the feudal government. The Buddhist parochial (*danka*) system, concocted by the Tokugawa regime in order to eliminate the influence of the forbidden Roman Catholicism, virtually undercut the traditional Shinto parochial (*ujiko*) system, such that even Shinto priests and their families were expected to belong to Buddhist temples and to be buried by Buddhist priests. It was inevitable, therefore, that many Shinto leaders were motivated to rectify this unhappy situation. Their immediate antagonism was directed against Buddhism. Deguchi Nobuyoshi (d. 1690), a leading priest of the Outer Shrine of Ise, lamented the Tokugawa regime's dependence on Buddhism, which he criticized as being as evil as Roman Catholicism. He attracted many able disciples and also wrote learned treatises against the age-old pattern of Shinto-Buddhist amalgamation. His writings had far-reaching effects and aroused the self-consciousness of later Shintoists. In sharp contrast to their anti-Buddhist attitude, many Shinto apologists consciously and unconsciously depended on Neo-Confucianism. Even Yoshikawa Koretaru (d. 1694), who insisted on the purity of Shinto, interpreted the *kami* as the *li* (metaphysical principle; *ri* in Japanese) à la Neo-Confucianism, and saw the *kami* of Shinto myths as nothing but personalized or deified forms or manifestations of this fundamental metaphysical principle. Likewise, other Shintoists uncritically accepted the emotional alliance of Neo-Confucianism and Shinto, which was initiated mostly from the Confucian side.

The revival of Shinto studies in the eighteenth century was greatly stimulated by the growth of "National Learning" (*Koku-gaku*), which was founded by Keichū (d. 1701), a Buddhist priest, and Kada Azumamaro (d. 1736), a lay priest of the Inari shrine of Kyoto. The first prominent figure of National Learning was Kamo Mabuchi (d. 1769), who undertook careful philological research of the *Manyōshū* and *Norito*. Rejecting both Buddhist- and Confucian-centered interpretations of Shinto, Kamo tried to restore the pre-Buddhist and pre-Confucian meaning of Shinto. Unconsciously espousing the Taoist ideal, he stressed spontaneous simplicity as the basis for morality. Kamo's disciple, Motoori Norinaga (d. 1801), rejected his master's Taoist-inspired interpretation of ancient Shinto, and insisted that Shinto was based on the revelation of Takamimusubi-no-kami ("August Producing *Kami*") transmitted by Amaterasu. Motoori is credited with the most systematic interpretation of the concept of the *kami*: "anything which was outside the ordinary, which possessed superior power or which was awe-inspiring." The *Commentary on the Kojiki* (*Kojiki-den*), which was his lifework, has remained the authoritative interpretation of the theoretical aspects of Shinto. Motoori combined within himself a critical scholarly approach based on the philological method and an absolute faith in the *Kojiki*'s accounts of the *kami*, the solar ancestry of the imperial family, and so on.[30] To him, ancient Shinto (*kannagara*) was a full-fledged Japanese religion with a rich intellectual content as well as liturgical and institutional dimensions. Notwithstanding, he was personally tolerant of Confucianism and Buddhism.

The most passionate spokesman for the purification of Shinto from Buddhist and Confucian influences was Hirata Atsutane (d. 1843). A Confucianist in his youth, he was converted to the cause of Shinto under the influence of Motoori's writings. Originally trained as a physician, Hirata was also well versed in astronomy and military science. In addition, he had more than casual knowledge of Dutch learning and of the Jesuit missionaries' writings in Chinese, parts of which he freely incorporated into his Shinto theological formulation. This may account for his monotheistic interpretation of Shinto myths; he held Ame-no-minakanushi ("Heavenly Center Lord") above Amaterasu. Hirata's Shinto ethics were related to his view of the judgment, presided over by Ōkuninushi-no-kami ("Great Land-ruler *kami*," the original *kami* of the Izumo region in traditional Shinto myths), which would take place in the life to come. Throughout his life, Hirata tried to restore what he termed the Ancient Way (*ko-dō*), which to him was the only true Shinto (*kannagara*). He mercilessly criticized the *Ryōbu-Shinto* (the Buddhist-dominated system of Shinto-Buddhist amalgamation), the *Yuiitsu-Shinto* (the Shinto apologetics based on the principle of the unity of Shinto, Confucianism, and Buddhism), and the *Suiga-Shinto* (the Confucian-Shinto fusion).[31]

[30] While Motoori rejected some of the doctrines of Suiga Shinto, he inherited its principle of absolute faith. His attitude toward the *kami* was strongly influenced by his upbringing as an adherent of Pure Land Buddhism. Parenthetically it might be added that one of his own sisters became a Buddhist nun, and he was very close to her.

[31] However, his emphasis on the veneration of the ancestor-*kami* was strongly influenced by Confucian ethics.

Anesaki once characterized Hirata Atsutane as a "man of great ability but a bigot of a doubtful character."[32] But there is no question that Hirata was dedicated to the cause of Shinto as the guiding principle for the nation. The Tokugawa regime took a dim view of Hirata's excessive emperor-centered nationalism, however, and silenced him a few years prior to his death. But Hirata's disciples carried on their master's mission. Indeed it was the combined influence of the Shinto Restoration School (the name given to the tradition of Motoori and Hirata) and the nationalistic Mito School of Neo-Confucianism which championed the cause of the restoration of monarchical rule and the termination of the Tokugawa feudal regime in the mid-nineteenth century.

IV. SHINTO IN THE MODERN PERIOD

Development of State Shinto

The nineteenth century was a turbulent era in the history of Japan. The power and authority of the Tokugawa feudal regime, which had ruled the nation for over two centuries, declined, but none of the ambitious *daimyō* was strong enough to provide national leadership. It was also the period of the advance of the Western powers in the Far East. Buddhism, with its elaborate institutions, was spiritually bankrupt, and Neo-Confucianism, which had become so thoroughly indigenized, allied itself with Shinto. The combined effects of these and other trends propelled Japan into a new era (in principle at least) under direct monarchical rule. Thus began the regime of the Emperor Meiji in 1868.

The architects of the Meiji regime were determined to transform Japan into a modern nation-state as rich and powerful as the Western nations. The regime was thus pledged to seek knowledge throughout the world in order to strengthen the foundations of imperial rule. Accordingly, able Japanese students were sent to Europe and America to acquire up-to-date knowledge of Western arts, sciences, and technologies. Western teachers were eagerly welcomed at newly established schools in Japan, and even Christianity, the forbidden religion during the Tokugawa period, was tolerated.

On the other hand, the restoration of monarchical rule was considered a return to the ancient polity of Japan with its ideal of the unity of religion and government (*saisei-itchi*), a principle which was advocated by the leaders of the Shinto Restoration School. Based on this

---

[32] Anesaki, *History of Japanese Religion*, p. 308.

principle, the government established in 1868 the Department of Shinto and issued an edict requiring the separation of Shinto from Buddhism (*Shin-Butsu Hanzen-rei*) on the ground that the Shinto-Buddhist amalgamation that had been practiced for nearly ten centuries under various designations was contrary to the ancient Japanese way. Two years later, the government issued the Proclamation of the Great Doctrine (*Daikyō*) that was to restore the "way of the *kami*" (*kannagara*) as the guiding principle of the nation. The Tokugawa policy that required all households to register in Buddhist temples was ended but was replaced with compulsory Shinto registration (*ujiko-shirabe*): every Japanese subject was ordered to belong to the shrine of his residence. Furthermore, the government, under the pressure of the Shinto leaders, actively promoted Shinto funeral rites, thus rejecting the traditional pattern of funeral services conducted according to Buddhist ritual. All Buddhist priests who, according to the practice of the Shinto-Buddhist amalgamation, had been connected with Shinto shrines were either returned to secular life or reinstalled as Shinto priests. All Buddhist ceremonies that had been performed in the imperial household were abolished. Although it was not the explicit intention of the government to eliminate Buddhism, its policy of separating Shinto from Buddhism encouraged many Shinto priests as well as leaders of Confucian and National Learning groups to engage in anti-Buddhist iconoclasm (*haibutsu kishaku*). Many Buddhist temples were thereby either destroyed or forced to consolidate around the country. However, the excessively pro-Shinto policy of the government encountered resistance and criticism from various quarters. As a result, the ill-fated Great Doctrine (*Daikyō*) movement and compulsory Shinto registration were abandoned.

Realizing the impossibility of the immediate Shintoization of Japan, the Meiji regime adopted a far more subtle, and in a sense more far-reaching and devastating, policy. They created an artificial designation—State Shinto—and called it a nonreligious or super-religious cult of national morality and patriotism applicable to adherents of all religions. The Constitution of 1889, which stated that "Japanese subjects shall, within limits not prejudicial to peace and order and not antagonistic to their duties as subjects, enjoy freedom of religious belief," was not interpreted to exclude any Japanese subject from participation in State Shinto and the Emperor Cult. In this situation, Shinto shrines were graded according to their importance and received various forms of government support; Shinto priests were made *de facto* government officials. It is significant to note, however, that it was the government officials and not the Shinto leaders who determined the policies and activities of State Shinto. In the words of a contemporary Shinto scholar: "[From] 1882 to the end of World War II, preaching by Shinto priests during ceremonies was prohibited by law. One view held that the government administrators wished to protect State Shinto from free competition between religions. Another reason was that they were afraid of liberal interpretations and criticisms of priests concerning the established theories of State Shinto."[33]

The Meiji regime, in creating a new religion of ethnocentrism called State Shinto, appropriated Confucian ethics for its moral basis, as is evidenced by the wording of the Imperial Rescript on Education, promulgated in 1890:

Our Imperial Ancestors have founded our Empire on a basis broad and ever-lasting, and have deeply and firmly implanted virtue; Our subjects ever united in loyalty and filial piety have from generation to generation illustrated the beauty thereof. This is the glory of the fundamental character of Our Empire, and herein lies the source of Our Education. Ye, Our Subjects, be filial to your parents, affectionate to your brothers and sisters; as husbands and wives be harmonious, as friends true; bear yourselves in modesty and moderation; extend your benevolence to all; pursue learning and cultivate arts, and thereby develop intellectual faculties and perfect moral powers. . . .[34]

In harmony with this Imperial Rescript, the government also created a compulsory course on "moral teaching" (*shūshin*), which was designed to inculcate "Japanesed" Confucian ethics in order to strengthen faith in the national polity. This was the basis of education for the primary and secondary schools. Beginning with the Sino-Japanese War (1894-1895), the Japanese government followed an expansionist policy, and from that time until the end of World War II, State Shinto was manipulated by the militarists and jingoistic nationalists as a spiritual weapon for mobilizing the nation to guard the prosperity of the throne and the empire.

Sect Shinto Denominations (Kyōha Shinto)

The nineteenth century, that period of social, economic, and political distress, witnessed the birth of spontaneous messianic and healing cults among the lower strata of Japanese society. Some attracted a considerable number of adherents. The Meiji regime, which was compelled to take into account the religious aspirations of the masses as well as the internal disunity of the historic Shinto tradition, decided

[33] Naofusa Hirai, "Fundamental Problems of Present Shinto," *Proceedings of the Ninth International Congress for the History of Religions* (Tokyo, 1960), p. 306.
[34] Official English translation.

to create a category of "Sect Shinto" (Kyōha Shinto) in contradistinction to State Shinto. It was decreed that only State Shinto could apply
the title *jinja* to its shrines and receive direct and indirect support from
the government. Sect Shinto was ordered to use the title *kyōkai*
(church) for its establishments, which of course did not receive any
government support. Between 1882 and 1908, the government recognized thirteen Sect Shinto denominations.[35] Among them, only
three had direct connections with historic Shinto; others had tenuous
connections, if any. Usually, the Sect Shinto groups are classified as
follows:

a. "Shintoistic" groups: Based primarily on certain aspects of Shinto
   beliefs and practices, these emphasize loyalty to the throne and gratitude to ancestors.
   (1) Izumo Taisha-kyō. This group follows the tradition of the
       Izumo Shrine, which agrees with the tradition of the Grand
       Shrine of Ise regarding the three central *kami* to be wor-
       shipped, but adds Okuninushi, the *kami* of the Izumo region,
       as the fourth *kami* to be venerated. Outmaneuvered by the Ise
       group on this question, the Izumo group secured the govern-
       ment's permission to establish itself as a Sect Shinto denomi-
       nation.
   (2) Shinto Tai-kyō or Shinto Honkyoku. This is a loose association
       of diverse subsects that accepted the Great Doctrine (*Daikyō*)
       of the *kami*. An interesting subdivision of this group is Maru-
       yama-kyō, founded by a popular healer.
   (3) Shinri-kyō (literally, "divine truth" religion). It accepts one of
       the mythical heroes, Nigi-hayahi-no-mikoto, as its legendary
       founder, and believes in the limitless miraculous power of the
       heavenly *kami*.
b. "Confucian-inspired" groups: The spiritual heirs of the Confucian-
   Shinto movement.
   (4) Shinto Shūsei-ha (literally, "improving and consolidating" re-
       ligion). It equates the three central Shinto *kami* with the
       Shang-ti of China, and advocates the harmony of Confucian
       ethics and Shinto piety.

[35] For the Sect Shinto denominations, see William K. Bunce, *Religions in Japan: Bud-
dhism, Shinto, Christianity* (Rutland, Vt. and Tokyo, 1955) and Daniel C. Holtom, *The
National Faith of Japan* (New York, 1938). On Kurozumi-kyō, see Helen Hardacre,
Kurozumikyō and the New Religions of Japan (Princeton, 1986). On Konkō-kyō, see
Delwin B. Schneider, *Konkōkyō: A Japanese Religion* (Tokyo, 1962). On Tenri-kyō, see
Henry van Straelen, *The Religion of Divine Wisdom* (Kyoto, 1957).

(5) Taisei-kyō (literally, "great accomplishment" religion). Based on simple Confucian-Shinto motifs, this group offers this-worldly guidance regarding science, the arts, and business.

c. "Mountain-related" groups: The spiritual heirs of the Order of Mountain Ascetics (Shugen-dō), which blended folk religion, Shinto, and Buddhism.

(6) Jikkyō-kyō (literally, "practical conduct" religion).

(7) Fusō-kyō. Religion of "Fusō," which is another name of Mount Fuji.

(8) Ontake-kyō. Religion which venerates the *kami* residing at Mount Ontake, one of the sacred mountains of Shugen-dō.

d. "Purification" groups: Ritualistic and magical groups.

(9) Shinshū-kyō (literally, "divine learning" religion). This sect observes the pre-Buddhist Shinto practices, especially those of purification and *kami*-possession.

(10) Misogi-kyō (literally, "cleansing" religion). It teaches deep breathing for religious and therapeutic purposes.

e. "Utopian or Faith-healing" groups: More monotheistic than the above, these groups were the prototypes of the "new religions" that developed after World War II.

(11) Kurozumi-kyō (so named for its founder, Kurozumi Munetada). This group accepts the eight million *kami* as manifestations of Amaterasu. It advocates breathing exercises for the purpose of infusing cosmic vitality into one's body.

(12) Konkō-kyō (religion of Konkō, which is the name of the *kami* of this sect). This group holds that its founder, Kawate Bunjirō, and his descendants in the male line are the mediators between the *kami* and humanity.

(13) Tenri-kyō (literally, "divine reason" religion). Founded by a charismatic woman, Nakayama Miki, it was originally a Utopian cult, based on oracles, shamanistic practices, and ecstatic dances. In the course of time, its anti-government and anti-foreign features were replaced by ethnocentric patriotism.

It is to be noted that most adherents of the Sect Shinto denominations sought worldly benefits—cure for sickness, protection from disaster and misfortune, and wealth and success in life—which traditional Shinto and Buddhism failed to offer and which the Sect Shinto groups promised. Gradually, however, the new denominations tended to become institutionalized and less concerned with the immediate needs of their adherents. As a result, people began to look for new formulas of incantations and new prophets and shamans, thus creating a large number of small splinter groups inside and outside of the framework of both Sect Shinto and Buddhism. These new splinter groups, which were not recognized by the government, were called pseudo-religions or quasi-religious associations (*ruiji-shūkyō*). It was reported that there were 98 such quasi religions in 1924. The number increased to 414 by 1930, and in 1935 there were over 1,000 quasi-religious groups practicing incantation, divination, fortune-telling, and healing.

Among the numerous quasi religions which prospered before World War II in Japan, mention should be made of the following groups because of their influence in the postwar period. Ōmoto-kyō (literally, the religion of "great fundamentals") was based on the divine oracles given to a *kami*-possessed peasant woman, Deguchi Nao (d. 1918). These oracles were later systematized by her son-in-law, Deguchi Onisaburō (d. 1948). This quasi religion promised the establishment of a new, ideal order on this earth, and attracted many high-ranking officials and prominent persons. Ōmoto-kyō, which started as an antigovernment peasant movement, quickly cooperated with the militarists in the 1930s. But, because the government feared its potential strength, Ōmoto-kyō was suppressed before the war. Meanwhile, one of the former followers of Ōmoto-kyō, Taniguchi Masaharu (1893-), broke away and founded a new cult of faith-healing, which subsequently was called Seichō-no-iye (literally, "the household of growth"). Another follower of Ōmoto-kyō, Okada Mokichi (d. 1955), broke away and established a healing cult, Dainihon-kannon-kai, which adopted the new name of the Church of World Messianity (Sekai Kyūsei-kyō) after World War II. The government looked unfavorably upon the ever-increasing number of quasi religions, and took strong measures to persecute them. Even Hito-no-michi (literally, "the way of man"), which worshipped Amaterasu and built its doctrine based on the Imperial Rescript, was dissolved by government order.

New Religions and Shinto in the Postwar Period

Following the end of World War II, under the directives of the Army of Occupation, the principle of religious liberty was put into effect in Japan. At the same time, another directive disestablished State Shinto and prohibited the sponsorship, support, perpetuation, control, and dissemination of Shinto by national, prefectural, and local governments or by public officials. It also abolished the Shrine Board of the Ministry of Home Affairs. Freed thus from government control, Shinto—now called Shrine Shinto (Jinja Shinto)—began to function as one of many religions in Japan. Of the approximately 100,000 shrines that exist, a little over 80,000 now belong to the Association of Shrine Shinto. The transition from State Shinto to Shrine Shinto has not changed the essential nature of Shinto. Devout Shintoists still perform their daily ablutions, pay homage at the family shrine, and visit their tutelary shrines on special occasions as they have always done. To be sure, the traditional Shinto parochial system has begun to lose its grip on the people, especially in urban areas, but pilgrims and visitors seem to flock to major shrines in greater number than ever before. On the other hand, Shrine Shinto faces such crucial problems as the lack of a coherent theological system and a shortage of clergy.[36] One of the serious questions which confronts Shrine Shinto stems from the legacy of the unity of religion and government (*saisei-itchi*). In principle, Shrine Shinto has accepted the notion of the separation of religion and government which is the basis of religious liberty. Yet there are many Shintoists who are nostalgic for the good old days of State Shinto.

The postwar situation has inevitably affected the Sect Shinto denominations too. Until 1945, the Federation of Sect Shinto (*Kyōha-Shintō-rengō-kai*) included only the thirteen denominations mentioned earlier. Taking advantage of religious liberty, however, many of the subsects of Sect Shinto denominations became independent, so that the number of Sect Shinto groups increased to seventy-five by 1949. Now that they are emancipated from the shadow of traditional Shinto, some are attempting to develop their own, new image. Probably the most successful among them is Tenri-kyō, which is carrying on energetic activities in evangelism, education, and philanthropy. Most other groups also seem to have maintained their prewar numerical strength, and are trying to meet the new social and cultural situations of postwar Japan. However, their prestige and influence have been greatly undercut by the aggressive activities of the "new religions."

The term "new religions" (*Shinkō Shūkyō*) is used to refer loosely to those splinter groups which were once affiliated with Buddhist or Sect Shinto groups but separated from them as well as those new groups which developed in the aftermath of World War II. They are usually classified into five categories: (1) those which stemmed from Buddhism, e.g., Sōka Gakkai ("Society for the Creation of Values") and Risshō Kōseikai ("Society for the Establishment of Righteousness and Friendly Relations"); (2) those which profess a monotheistic or, to be more technical, monolatristic belief, e.g., Tenshō-kōtai-jingū-kyō, commonly referred to as the "dancing religion," and Sekai Kyūsei-kyō

[36] It is estimated that there are roughly 21,000 priests serving more than 80,000 shrines.

("Church of World Messianity"); (3) those which follow a pantheistic belief, even though one *kami* or Buddha among them may be chosen as the center of worship, e.g., Ananai-kyō, which claims to be the synthesis of all the major world religions; (4) those which are utopian and messianic, e.g., Reiyū-kai ("Association of the Friends of the Spirit"); and (5) those which are primarily concerned with practical aspects of life, e.g., PL Kyōdan ("Religion of Perfect Liberty"). There are many other ways to classify them too; it should be noted that many of the new religions fit into more than one category. In addition, most of them are so new that their founders are still living and, because some of them continue to receive new revelations, their doctrinal systems are not clearly defined. Each sect has an independent institutional structure and trains its own teachers, many of whom are volunteers. Members, however, are not always followers of one sect exclusively; more often than not they consider themselves, nominally at least, Buddhists or Shintoists as well.

What gives each of these new religions its distinct character is, to a great extent, the personality of the founder or systematizer. Many of them boast unusual spiritual powers in divination, sorcery, incantation, fortune-telling, and healing. These are the very qualities which have been associated with the leaders of "folk Shinto" and "folk Buddhism" throughout the ages; they still seem to have powerful appeal to the lower strata of Japanese society, in particular to middle-aged and older women. On the other hand, some of the new religions have made inroads among the intelligentsia, the upper middle class, and young people. Significantly, Sōka Gakkai, Risshō Kōseikai, and others have become active in national politics. The spectacular success of Sōka Gakkai in recent elections, for example, seems to indicate that the unity of religion and government retains its popularity. This cardinal principle of traditional Shinto, although abandoned by Shrine Shinto in the postwar era, may yet prove to be an important rallying point for religious groups in Japan.

PART IV

Buddhist Tradition

10. The Saṃgha and the Ecclesia

T HIS PAPER deals with the nature and characteristics of religious communities, with special reference to the Saṃgha of Buddhism and the Ecclesia of Christianity.

Buddhism and Christianity, like other worldwide religions, regard humanity as essentially one community and their religious structures as reflections, albeit imperfect ones, of the ideal human community. All religions have what Mircea Eliade calls "nostalgia for paradise," or the desire of religious man "to transcend, by natural means, the human condition and regain a divine state of affairs."[1] At the same time, all religions have some kind of vision of the beatific end of the world, when all evils will be redressed and the divine order of the cosmos will be restored. Thus, religious rites, symbols, and myths signify simultaneously both the "eternal return"[2] and the celebration of the *telos*. In this connection, van der Leeuw has rightly pointed out that religious man views man's cycle communally: "human life is first of all not the life of the individual, but that of the *community*."[3] Hence the importance of *rites de passage*, such as birth, naming, initiation, death, and burial.[4] Through these communal religious acts, individuals as members of the religious community are related both to the beginning and the end of the world.

Religion is by nature a fellowship and communion. The relationship between religious fellowship and other human fellowships is intricate and complex. It has often been pointed out that primitive man knew only one community, which was both the human and the "holy" community, because "the primitive and precivilized communities [were] held together essentially by common understandings as to the ultimate nature and purpose of life."[5] In such a community the sacred and the secular are interpenetrating, and the individual's biological cycle finds

[1] Mircea Eliade, *Patterns in Comparative Religion*, trans. Rosemary Sheed (Sheed and Ward, 1958), pp. 382-385.

[2] Cf. Mircea Eliade, *The Myth of the Eternal Return*, trans. W. R. Trask (Pantheon, 1954; repr. Princeton University Press, 1971).

[3] G. van der Leeuw, *Religion in Essence and Manifestation*, trans. J. E. Turner (Allen and Unwin, 1938), p. 191.

[4] Ibid., pp. 192-193.

[5] Robert Redfield, *The Primitive World and Its Transformation* (Cornell University Press, 1953), p. 12.

its corresponding social and religious cycles. Furthermore, primitive man considered the earthly community an extension and counterpart of the celestial community.

In civilized societies the social and religious fellowships tend to separate. In this process, some religions—for example, Hinduism, Confucianism, and Shinto—tend to intensify or even transform the human community, while others—for instance, Islam, Christianity, and Buddhism—create their own "holy communities" in the midst of, and yet apart from, other human fellowships.

Historically, Buddhism and Christianity were destined to be rejected in the lands of their origin, basically because they are world religions *par excellence* in the sense that to both of them the fundamental meaning of life and the world cannot be derived solely from the experience of one group of people or one culture. It is but natural that the universalistic tenets of these two religions are reflected in the structures of the Saṃgha of Buddhism and the Ecclesia of Christianity.

The uniqueness of Buddhism, among all religions of salvation, lies in the fact that while accepting Śākyamuni as its founder, it knows no savior in the usual sense of the term. For forty years after his Enlightenment the Buddha preached the gospel of Nirvana. To him, the primary question was not "what is Nirvana?" but "how to attain Nirvana?" From the time of Śākyamuni, his followers were exhorted to take refuge in the Three Jewels, that is, in Buddha, Dharma, and Saṃgha. While the Three Jewels are integrally interrelated, at the same time each is a philosophical and religious focus. Also, behind the Three Jewels lies the beatific vision or "image of Nirvana." Thus, Buddhist ecclesiology cannot be understood without taking into account Buddhology, the doctrine of the nature of reality, and the image of Nirvana. It must also be pointed out that the Saṃgha is more than a sociological entity; what is involved is some sort of dualism, not unlike the Lutheran concept of the invisible church and the visible body, which was rooted in the reformer's paradoxical view of the Deity as *Deus absconditus* and *Deus revelatus*.[6]

Śākyamuni, in creating the Saṃgha, took the name and form of the political *saṃgha* that existed in northwestern India in his time.[7] Originally, the Buddhist Saṃgha was a monastic order, loosely organized and with no specific buildings for its own use. Gradually the *vihara* came into existence for the meditation of the Saṃgha and the lodging

[6] Joachim Wach, *Types of Religious Experience* (University of Chicago Press, 1951), p. 191.

[7] Richard A. Gard, *Buddhist Influence on the Political Thought and Institutions of India and Japan* (Claremont, 1949), pp. 2-9.

of learned men. In the course of time, the Saṃgha took on educational, social, and cultural activities. During the second and third centuries A.D. the pursuit of secular knowledge became an ideal of these monastic institutions, and the doors of the Saṃgha were "thrown open to the students as well, who, if they chose, were at liberty to leave the monastery and embrace once more the life of a house-holder, after their education was over."[8] This changed the character of the Buddhist community from the purely monastic Saṃgha to a mixed community of monks and lay Buddhists. This process of secularization of the Saṃgha also had the effect of narrowing the gulf between the Saṃgha and culture. Increasingly, the Buddhist monasteries developed into important social, educational, and cultural centers wherever Buddhism was established. Inevitably the Saṃgha became highly institutionalized. There is much truth in Przyluski's observation that the development of the Saṃgha had three distinct stages—the egalitarian ideal of primitive Buddhism, the aristocratic ideal of the Theravāda tradition, and the hierarchical structure of the Mahāyāna tradition.[9] While the Saṃgha continues to our day as the normative path for all Buddhists, in the Mahāyāna tradition the philosophical identification of Nirvana with Samsara, coupled with a widening of the "soteriological distance" between the two, has siphoned out the imperative character of the monastic life. In the Theravāda countries, too, the monastic life has lost its imperative character.

In one sense at least, it may be argued that only the monastic orders should be called specifically Buddhist.[10] However, as early as the time of Śākyamuni, the lay disciples were treated as something like associate members of the Saṃgha. Gradually the laity began to play an increasingly active role in ecclesiastical affairs, and today the Saṃgha for all practical purposes embraces all the faithful, monastic or otherwise. Also, various forms of folk piety, which was a mixture of Buddhist and non-Buddhist beliefs, were incorporated into the Buddhist community. Thus, Buddhism developed an uneasy alliance with existing local religions, such as Nat Worship in Burma, Bön religion in Tibet, Taoism and Confucianism in China, and Shinto in Japan. These sociohistoric institutionalized forms of the Saṃgha, however, do not exhaust its religious meaning. Different traditions of Buddhism subscribe to the religious ideal of the Saṃgha universal, of which the empirical Saṃgha is regarded as an incomplete manifestation.

[8] Hasmukh D. Sankalia, *The University of Nalanda* (Madras, 1934), p. 32.
[9] J. Przyluski, *Le Concile de Rājagṛha* (Paris, 1926), pp. 308 ff., 367 ff.
[10] T.R.V. Murti, "Radhakrishnan and Buddhism," in *The Philosophy of Sarvepalli Radhakrishnan* (Tudor, 1952), p. 604.

In the Christian tradition, the inauguration of the church is not attributed to Jesus himself. The Christian Ecclesia was regarded as the new "covenanted" community, built on the structure and history of the old Hebrew covenanted community. The early Christians believed that the hidden potentialities of the Hebrew community were actualized in the Ecclesia. The Ecclesia was viewed as a new kind of community, both visible and invisible, "at once humanly organized and mystically animated, spiritual and cosmic."[11] Hence the affirmation: "credo . . . unam sanctam catholicam ecclesiam."

As the Christian community came to realize that the end of the world was not impending, or perhaps had been partially realized already in the Pentecost, it began to develop its own group consciousness and visible structure, such as the graded offices of ministry, the sacred scriptures, the liturgy, and the creeds. In the course of time, the Christian church developed a special inner community in the form of monastic orders. Eventually monasticism came to be regarded as a higher way of salvation, and it began to exercise a strong influence over the life of the church and society. In this connection, it might be pointed out that the Byzantine church recognized the emperor not merely as the civil ruler but also as the spiritual head of the church, while the Western church was marked by a strong centralization of the polity within the church, which after the fifth century gradually developed into the papacy. The ideal of the medieval papal church was not the spiritual independence of the church. "The full freedom and independence of the Church was only reached when the temporal powers were subordinate to the Church . . . and directed by her in all matters pertaining to salvation."[12] As everything was ultimately related to salvation, the medieval church came to equate soteriology with ecclesiology. To be sure, the historic tension between the earthly Ecclesia and the *ecclesia triumphans* was widened by the insertion of purgatory in between. And yet, the church as the Body of Christ came to be understood almost in a physical sense in that the church was believed to have Christ's power to impart grace on earth.

The Protestant reformers were concerned with reforming and restoring the essential character of the Ecclesia as the covenanted community of the faith. However, in rejecting the papal church's view of the ecclesiastification of the whole social order, the reformers were nevertheless conscious of the fact that the Ecclesia must manifest itself in the social order, which is also ordained by God. Such a view of the

[11] Van der Leeuw, *Religion in Essence*, p. 266.

[12] Ernst Troeltsch, *The Social Teachings of the Christian Churches*, trans. Olive Wyon (The Free Press, 1949), vol. 1, pp. 229-230.

relation of the church to the social order necessarily took seriously the nation-states that were becoming increasingly important, replacing outmoded feudalism in Europe. It is a matter of interest to note that while the expansion of Buddhism was on the whole free from any colonial expansion of Buddhist nations, the Christian missionary movement, which in principle did not accept colonialism, followed the colonial expansion of the modern European nation-states.

It is significant that today both Buddhism and Christianity are keenly aware of the discrepancy between the ideal and the reality of their holy communities. The current interest of Buddhists in the nature of the Samgha, as evidenced by the Sixth Great Council held in Rangoon several years ago, finds its Christian parallel in the so-called ecumenical movement which stimulates discussion about the nature of the Ecclesia.

Recent years have seen the development of two kinds of sociology of religion(s), one as a subdivision of sociology and another as a subdivision of *Religionswissenschaft*. Although both kinds of sociology of religion deal with the nature of various religious and ecclesiastical bodies, one sociology of religion inevitably views the data "sociologically," while the other views the same data "religio-scientifically."[13]

It goes without saying that *Religionswissenschaft* is concerned with a historical and sociological inquiry into the holy communities of various religions. It is also seriously concerned with the religious meaning of these communities, because the development of a holy community cannot be explained solely in terms of historic factors, however important they may be. Just as the concept of the Samgha has changed with the changing image of Nirvana and the corresponding development of the doctrines of Buddha and of Dharma, the Christian concept of the Ecclesia has changed with the historic development of the doctrines of God, Christ, the Holy Spirit and the world. How to relate the sociohistorical and religious dimensions of these holy communities is one of the relevant tasks for students of *Religionswissenschaft* in our time.

[13] Cf. Joseph M. Kitagawa, "The Nature and Program of the History of Religions Field," *Divinity School News* (University of Chicago), November 1957.

11. Master and Saviour

O N THIS memorable occasion, celebrating the 1,150th anniversary of the establishment of the monastic center of Shingon Buddhism at Mount Kōya, it is most appropriate to reflect on the life of its founder Kūkai (774-835), whose blessed memory hallows this sacred mountain. That he transmitted the Esoteric tradition of Buddhism from China and made great contributions to the religious and cultural life of Japan is well known. During his lifetime, Kūkai undoubtedly was a towering figure in scholarship, spiritual perception, and religious leadership.

More significant perhaps, from the standpoint of *Religionswissenschaft* (History of Religions), is the fact that after his death Kūkai, under his posthumous title Kōbō Daishi, has continued to hold a special place in the hearts of Japanese Buddhists. Even today, "his memory lives all over the country, his name is a household word in the remotest places, not only as a saint, but as a preacher, a scholar, a poet, a sculptor, a painter, an inventor, an explorer, and . . . a great calligrapher."[1] It is interesting to note that historically Kūkai was neither the first nor the only patriarch who was given the title of Daishi (or Taishi, "Great Master"), but in the course of time he became the Daishi *par excellence*. Moreover, in the eyes of the faithful, Kūkai was more than a Great Master who had acquired the secret teaching of the Buddha; he himself became a semidivine saviour, a worthy object of adoration and worship. Thus, it is widely believed that Kūkai did not die, and that he is still walking around in various parts of Japan in the disguise of a pilgrim helping those who need his help.

Even such a brief characterization of the life and influence of Kūkai raises a number of important and difficult questions for a historian of religions. Essentially, the figure of Kūkai as we now know him is a composite of many factors—what he actually was, how he was remembered, and the ideal virtues and qualities that were attributed to him by pious tradition. There is little doubt that he was a remarkable individual who reflected the religious and cultural ethos of his time and yet transcended his environment. He was also a learned master and patriarch, having acquired understanding and proficiency in the pro-

---

[1] George B. Sansom, *Japan, A Short Cultural History* (London, 1946), p. 230.

found doctrines and intricate practices of Esoteric Buddhism. Moreover, he might be regarded as what Joachim Wach calls the "classical figure" of Japanese religion, not only in the sense that he was an outstanding representative but also because his personality, activities, and influence illuminate the nature and character of the religious heritage of the Japanese.[2] In dealing with such a multidimensional figure as Kūkai, a historian of religions is naturally intrigued by the cultural situation which nurtured him and the manner in which various kinds of attributes and legends came to be homologized in his person. In so doing, he has to know something about Kūkai's understanding of Buddhism, even though it is not his task to determine whether or not Esoteric (Shingon) Buddhism, transmitted and propagated by Kūkai, actually revealed the secret truth of the Buddha. He would also like to inquire about the characteristics of the soteriological yearning of Japanese Buddhists who have found in Kūkai an image of a saviour.

Our first task is to reconstruct, as concisely and accurately as we can, the life and career of "Kūkai, the Master" and the cultural and religious milieu which nurtured him, and then to discuss the main features of "Kūkai, the Saviour," realizing of course that these two dimensions are inseparably interrelated. Throughout all this, our aim is to depict and understand the significance of such a paradigmatic figure as an important phenomenon in the history of religions.

KŪKAI, THE MASTER

Any effort to reconstruct the life of Kūkai is frustrated by the difficulties in sorting out facts from legends. Although he was a prolific writer throughout his life, he seems to have been more interested in explicating the doctrines of Esoteric Buddhism than recording his autobiography. Even when he made references to himself, Kūkai was more concerned with the development of his thought than with the details of his life. For instance, his first work, the *Sangō-shiiki* (Indications of the Teaching of Three Religions),[3] which compared the doctrinal characteristics of Confucianism, Taoism, and Buddhism, was written to affirm the superiority of Buddhism. The *Sangō-shiiki*, however, may be regarded as the record of Kūkai's conversion to Buddhism, which marked an important turning point in his life. In the

---

[2] "Der Begriff des Klassischen in der Religionsgeschichte," in *Quantulacunque*, in honor of Kirsopp Lake (London, 1937), pp. 87-97. English translation is included in Joachim Wach, *Types of Religious Experience* (Chicago, 1951), pp. 48-57.

[3] See Mori Kanshō, *Sangō-shiiki kōgi* (An Exposition on the *Sangō-shiiki*) (Kōyasan, 1941).

Shōrai-mokuroku (The List of Newly Imported Scriptures),[4] which he presented to the court upon his return from China, Kūkai included an account of his encounter with Hui-kuo at the Chinese capital, describing how he received the secret transmission of the Esoteric Vehicle from this celebrated master. Important though this experience was, and it might be regarded as Kūkai's second conversion, his reference to it was again motivated by his desire to advocate the efficacy of Esoteric Buddhism.

A number of so-called biographies of Kūkai throw very little light on the actual life of Kūkai. There are, however, a few notable exceptions. One is the *Kūkai-sōzu-den* (The Biography of Abbot Kūkai), which was probably written shortly after his death by Shinzei (800-860).[5] Another is the *Zō-daisōjō-Kūkai-wajō-denki* (The Biography of Archbishop Kūkai). Its authorship is ascribed to Kūkai's younger brother and disciple, Shinga (801-879), who, however, was dead before 895, when this work was reputedly completed. Many scholars today are inclined to believe that this biography was actually written by Shōbō (832-909).[6] A more controversial, and yet indispensable, source for the life of Kūkai is the *Go-yuigō* or *Yuigō* (The Last Instructions), consisting of twenty-five injunctions supposedly given by Kūkai to his immediate disciples from his deathbed in 835. Officially the Shingon ecclesiastical authorities have always affirmed Kūkai's authorship of *Yuigō*, but many scholars, including some of the leading Shingon scholars, have come to the conclusion that while it was no doubt based on Kūkai's teachings and instructions, its compilation in the form of the *Yuigō* was done later by one of his disciples. To make the matter more complex, there are at least four different texts of the *Yuigō* with considerable discrepancies and contradictions among them.[7]

[4] English translation of a portion of this document is included in Tsunoda Ryūsaku et al., comps., *Sources of Japanese Tradition* (New York, 1958), pp. 144-147.

[5] According to some scholars, the author was Shinshō. Both Shinzei and Shinshō were Kūkai's immediate disciples. Whether or not this biography was written in 835 as the tradition claims is debatable. It is safe to assume, however, that this biographical account was written before 857 when the title of Dai-sōjō (Archbishop) was conferred upon Kūkai posthumously.

[6] A third work, the *Daisōzu-Kūkai-den* (The Biography of the Great Abbot Kūkai) was compiled in 869. It contains very little relevant material, however.

[7] See Kōyama Taiban, "Kōbō Daishi ni tsuite," *Shūkyō Kenkyū* 3, no. 9 (1918), 71-76. He points out that one of the texts, known as the *Kōyasan-Ezu-no-maki* (The Pictorial Volume of Mount Kōya), includes the description of Mount Kōya which was taken from the diary of Shinzen, dated 875, in spite of the fact that the *Yuigō* was supposed to have been written in 835, immediately following Kūkai's death. Katsuno Ryūshin, *Hiei-zan to Kōya-san* (Mount Hi'ei and Mount Kōya) (Tokyo, 1959), p. 116, tells us that such leading Shingon scholars as Gonda Raifu (1846-1934), Katō Seishin

Nevertheless the *Yuigō* provides important data that are not available anywhere else regarding the early life of Kūkai. For this reason practically all the biographies of Kūkai written in later centuries depend on the *Yuigō* as their basic source.

It is to be noted in this connection that in the cases where the *Yuigō* and other accounts did not agree, the Shingon authorities and biographers invariably accepted the former as authoritative. Thus, for example, it is widely held that Kūkai was born in the year 774. This assumption is based on the account given in the *Yuigō*, and depends on the rejection of the chronology of the *Zō-daisōjō-Kūkai-wajō-denki*. Since pious legends later regarded Kūkai as the reincarnation of Amoghavajra or Pu-k'ung, the celebrated master of Esoteric Buddhism who died in China on the fifteenth day of the sixth month of 774, many biographies of Kūkai take it for granted that he was actually born on that very day.[8] Similarly, the dates usually given for Kūkai's conversion and ordination are based on what might be called a "pneumatic exegesis" of the references given in the *Yuigō*. Notwithstanding these and other difficulties and ambiguities, we must try to piece together available data and reconstruct the portrayal of the human figure of Kūkai.

As far as we can ascertain, Kūkai was born in or around 774 in the Sanuki province (present Kagawa prefecture) of Shikoku. His father was Saegi Ataegimi (Masauji), and his mother was Ato Tamayori.[9] Evidently the Saegi family and the Ato family were related.[10] Although

---

(1872-1956), and Tomita Kōjun (1875-1955) rejected Kūkai's direct authorship of the *Yuigō*.

[8] This theory was first advocated by a famous Shingon prelate, Raiyu (1226-1304), and came to be widely accepted as early as the thirteenth and fourteenth centuries, as evidenced by the reference to it in the *Jinnō-shōtō-ki* (The Records of the Legitimate Succession of the Divine Sovereigns) by Kitabatake Chikafusa (1293-1354).

[9] Kūkai's mother's name, Tamayori, literally means "The one in whom the *tama* (spirit) of the *kami* dwells (yori or yoru)." It was a name often given to a shamanic diviner (*Miko*). See Yanagita Kunio, *Imōto no Chikara* (Power of the Sister) (Tokyo, 1953), p. 66.

[10] There were two divisions of the Saegi family. According to traditional genealogy, one division was traced to the Emperor Keikō and the other to Ōtomo Muroya. The former had settled in Harima (present Hyōgo prefecture), while the latter, to which Kūkai belonged, had settled on Shikoku. Again, according to a legendary account, Kūkai's family is traced to Ame-no-oshihiko-no-mikoto, the son of Takamimusubi-no-mikoto of the mythological pantheon. Ame-no-oshihiko-no-mikoto's descendant, Michi-no-omi-no-mikoto, was closely associated with the legendary first emperor Jimmu in Japanese mythology. Michi-no-omi-no-mikoto's descendant, Takechi-no-mikoto, was supposed to have accompanied the expedition of Prince Yamato-takeru against the northern barbarians and was later given land on Shikoku. Takechi-no-mikoto's son, Muroya, was a minister in the court; and Muroya's son, Mimono, and grandson, Yamatoko, both became governors of Sanuki province in Shikoku. Ōtomo Yamatoko's son was given the family name of Saegi, and his descendants served as governor for four generations. In 646, according to the Taika Reform edict, the position of governor

185

we are not certain exactly how many brothers and sisters Kūkai had, we know that one of his brothers, Shinga, became a disciple of Kūkai, and that two famous Shingon prelates, Shinga and Shinzen, were Kū-kai's own nephews.[11]

When Kūkai was born, he had of course no way of knowing that he was destined to spend his childhood and youth in a very critical period of Japanese history. The impact of Chinese civilization, which began to penetrate Japan in the sixth century, transformed many aspects of Japanese society and culture. The introduction of a written language and of Chinese art and classical literature inevitably created a sharp division between the sinified upper strata and the uneducated masses. Politically, the Yamato kingdom, which earlier had been a *de facto* confederation of autonomous clans, became a centralized empire governed by a series of rescripts and legal codes patterned after the Chinese system. Confucianism provided a coherent system of personal and political ethics hitherto unknown in Japan, while Taoism and the Yin-Yang system contributed lofty cosmological theories as well as magical practices. By far the most far-reaching new influence was Buddhism, which quickly overshadowed the indigenous Shinto religion. Prince-Regent Shōtoku (573–621) adopted a multireligious policy which attempted to preserve a division of labor, so to speak, among Buddhism, Confucianism, and Shinto.[12] However, Shōtoku's pious hope of maintaining a harmonious relationship among the three religions was not to be easily attained. During the second half of the seventh century the imperial court under the influence of Confucian-trained bureaucrats attempted sweeping reforms.[13] One of the important measures of the reform was the establishment of an educational

---

(*kunikko* or *kuni-no-miyatsuko*) was discontinued, and many of the local officials who lost their posts moved to the capital and were given minor government positions.

[11] According to one genealogical account, Kūkai had an older brother, Suzuki-maro. Kūkai's older sister, Chiye, was married to a Shinto priest of Taki-no-miya; their son was Chisen. Kūkai's youngest brother's son was Shinzen. His relation to the Tendai prelate, Enchin (814–891), posthumously called Chishō Daishi, is not certain. According to one theory, Enchin was the son of Wake Iyenari and his wife, who was Kūkai's younger sister. However, according to the Tendai source, Enchin's mother was Kūkai's niece.

[12] Prince Shōtoku was undoubtedly aware of the multireligious policy which was adopted by the first Sui emperor, Wen-ti. On the latter, see Arthur F. Wright, "The Formation of Sui Ideology, 581-604" in John K. Fairbank, ed. *Chinese Thought and Institutions* (Chicago, 1957), pp. 71-104.

[13] On the government Buddhist policies during the second half of the seventh century, see Futaba Kenkō, *Kodai Bukkyō-shisōshi kenkyū* (A Study of Early Japanese Buddhism) (Kyoto, 1962), pp. 23-301.

system based on the teaching of the Confucian classics.[14] Partly as a reaction to the excessive Confucian emphasis of the previous century, eighth-century Japan witnessed an "ecclesiastification" of culture under the influence of Buddhism.

It is worth noting in this connection that the glorious culture of the eighth century (the Nara period) was more than the imitation of Chinese culture to which it has often been reduced by superficial critics. Rather, it would be more correct to say, following the metaphor used by Langdon Warner, that "the T'ang dynasty of China was hanging like a brilliant brocaded background, against which we might look at Japan and its capital city of Nara to watch the eighth century, while *the Japanese were at work weaving their own brocade on patterns similar but not the same.*"[15] What was involved in this process of "weaving" was the integration of diverse threads, great and small, foreign and indigenous, old and new. The establishment of the first permanent capital at Nara, for instance, resulted in dividing sharply the mode of living in the capital, which was greatly influenced by continental customs, from the traditional way of life of the uneducated peasants in the countryside. The exposure to Chinese civilization made the Japanese elite in turn conscious of their own heritage, as evidenced by the compilation of the *Kojiki* (Records of Ancient Matters) and the *Nihongi* (Chronicles of Japan) at the same time as the first collection of Chinese verse by Japanese poets, the *Kaifūsō* (Fond Recollections of Poetry). Officially, the government was still committed to the reform measures of the seventh-century Confucian-trained bureaucrats, but those measures virtually collapsed because of repeated revision made for the benefit of the former clan chieftains and local magnates now emerging as court nobles.

By far the greatest issue of the Nara period was religion. Little need be said about the six schools of Buddhism established during this period, i.e., the Kusha (Abhidharmakośa), the Jōjitsu (Satyasiddhi), the Hossō (Yogācāra), the Sanron (Mādhyamika), the Kegon (Avatamsaka), and the Ritsu (Vinaya). The extravagant support given to Buddhism by the court, plus the religious vitality inherent in Buddhism, gradually transmuted Shinto to the extent that it easily became subservient to Buddhism. It was more difficult for the Buddhist hierarchy to deal with the unorthodox Buddhist holy men called *ubasoku* (*upāsaka*: ascetic, magician, healer, or medium) who were greatly influ-

---

[14] This educational system was more or less kept intact with only minor modifications until the middle of the nineteenth century.

[15] Langdon Warner, *The Enduring Art of Japan* (Cambridge, 1952), p. 6. My italics.

enced by the shamanistic folk piety of the pre-Buddhist period. Their influence was such that the court felt compelled to solicit their support for the construction of the great Buddha statue and appointed Gyōgi (670-749), their leader, to the rank of archbishop.[16] Buddhist leaders were also confronted by the rivalry of learned Confucianists who controlled educational policies and institutions.[17] Some of the orthodox Buddhist priests, dissatisfied with the scholastic emphasis of the established schools in the capital city, sought enlightenment by undergoing austere physical discipline in the mountains and forests in the vicinity of the Hiso Temple at Yoshino.[18] Moreover, certain sutras and practices of Esoteric Buddhism, which enjoyed royal favor in China at that time, infiltrated Japan, and the Hiso Temple came under their influence.

When Kūkai was born in 774, the once-glorious culture of Nara had already begun to disintegrate. Shortly before, an audacious attempt by a Buddhist priest named Dōkyō to usurp the throne then occupied by a superstitious empress had failed, and in 770 a minor prince was suddenly enticed to ascend the throne as the Emperor Kōnin. The new emperor, inheriting a nation suffering from overtaxation, political intrigue and general apathy, attempted to rectify the situation by appointing a number of competent bureaucrats well versed in Confucian learning. Among them were Saegi Imaemishi and Saegi Mamori, both cousins of Kūkai's father, and Ato Ōtari, Kūkai's uncle. It was the Emperor Kōnin's son, the Emperor Kammu (reigned, 781-806), who moved the capital from Nara, first to Nagaoka and again in 794 to the present Kyoto. Understandably, the young Kūkai's outlook was greatly influenced by the political and cultural changes that were taking place during this period.[19]

From all accounts, it appears that Kūkai was initially given a Confucian education at the university in the capital. He was thereby following in the footsteps of his uncle, Ato Ōtari, a Confucian scholar and tutor to the Emperor Kammu's son, Prince Iyo. Kūkai's brilliant academic career, however, was suddenly terminated by his conversion to Buddhism. He thereupon left the university and became a hermit.[20]

[16] See J. M. Kitagawa, "Kaiser und Schamane in Japan," *Antaios* 2, no. 6 (March 1961), 552-566.

[17] See Inouye Kaoru, *Nihon kodai no seiji to shūkyō* (Politics and Religion in Ancient Japan) (Tokyo, 1961), pp. 202-209.

[18] This movement was called the Shizen-chi-shū or the "Nature Wisdom School." Even such leading priests of the Hossō school as Jinyei, Shōgo, and Gomyō were known to have frequented the Hiso Temple.

[19] We have dispensed with Kūkai's secular names to avoid unnecessary complications.

[20] As stated earlier, the *Sangō-shiiki* may be regarded as the record of Kūkai's conver-

There is no doubt that he had a genuine religious experience, even though his conversion was in no small measure the result of intellectual inquiries into the teachings of Confucianism, Taoism, and Buddhism. Probably Kūkai was also disillusioned by the unpredictable nature of government careers, so easily ruined by intrigues at court.[21] Kūkai's activities following his conversion seem to imply that he followed for some time a path of seeking enlightenment by undergoing austere physical disciplines in the mountains near Hiso Temple mentioned earlier. Sometime around 798 Kūkai received the traditional priestly ordination at Tōdai-ji, the national temple during the Nara period and the main sanctuary of the Kegon (Avatamsaka) school. Meanwhile, by chance he came across the Dainichi-kyō (Mahāvairocana Sūtra), and became a seeker after the truth transmitted in the Esoteric tradition of Buddhism.

Shortly after the turn of the ninth century Kūkai aspired to study in China, and sent a petition to the court to this effect. In 804 he was permitted to accompany the Japanese envoy, and after an eventful trip reached Ch'ang-an, the capital of T'ang China. There he received the mysteries of Esoteric Buddhism from Hui-kuo (746-805) of the Ch'ing-lung (Green Dragon) temple. At that time, thanks to the liberal policies of the T'ang monarchs, Manichaeism, Nestorian Christianity, and Zoroastrianism were tolerated alongside Confucianism, Taoism, and Buddhism. Kūkai enjoyed the colorful cosmopolitan atmosphere of Ch'ang-an, where he stayed on, after the death of his master Hui-kuo, and studied Sanskrit and other subjects.[22] After collecting the scriptures and the liturgical ornaments of Esoteric Buddhism, Kūkai returned to Japan in 806. Just before leaving China, he left a poem to his fellow student, Acharya I-ts'ao:

> Studying the same doctrine
> Under one master (Hui-kuo),

---

sion to Buddhism. His conversion took place when he was somewhere between twelve and twenty; the exact date cannot be ascertained because different sources give different accounts on this score.

[21] One of Kūkai's kinsmen, Saegi Imaemishi, was a confidante of Prince Sawara, the younger brother of the Emperor Kammu and his heir-apparent. Because of a certain intrigue, Prince Sawara was banished in 785 to the island of Awaji, and Saegi Imaemishi also lost his position in the court. This turn of events might have influenced the young Kūkai. Subsequently, Kūkai's uncle, Ato Ōtari, also lost his position when Prince Iyo was banished from the court.

[22] It is interesting to note that Kūkai's Sanskrit instructor, Prajna, an Indian monk, is said to have worked with Adam, a Syrian Christian monk, on the translation of the *Shatparamita-sūtra* from a Mongolian text. See I-Tsing, *A Record of the Buddhist Religion as Practiced in India and the Malay Archipelago*, trans. J. Takakusu (Oxford, 1896), p. 224.

You and I are friends.
> See yonder white mists
> Floating in the air
> On the way back to the peaks.

This parting may be our last meeting in this life.
Not just in a dream.
But in our deep thought,
Let us meet again
Hereafter.[23]

By the time Kūkai returned to Japan, his senior contemporary Sai-chō (or Dengyō Daishi, 767-822), who had studied T'ien T'ai Buddhism in China, managed to secure imperial recognition for the Tendai school with its monastic center at Mount Hi'ei. But the Emperor Kammu died in the third month of 806, shortly before Kūkai's return. The Emperor Heizei (reigned, 806-809) succeeded and, distrustful of his own brother, Prince Iyo, forced him to take poison. Kūkai, whose uncle Ato Ōtari was Prince Iyo's tutor, decided to remain in Kyushu, even though he presented to the court the list of scriptures, ornaments, and art objects which he had brought home from China. It was only in the tenth month of 807 that Kūkai was officially permitted to report in person to the court in Kyoto. Even though Kūkai had a reputation as a man of broad and up-to-date Chinese learning, he did not receive encouragement from the Emperor Heizei in his religious activities. During this period a friendship developed between Saichō and Kūkai.

The picture changed considerably under the Emperor Saga (reigned, 809-823), for he patronized Kūkai not only as a man of letters but also as the leading patriarch. In this connection, it might be noted that in sharp contrast to Saichō, who stressed the basic incompatibility between the Tendai system and the old established Buddhist schools of Nara, Kūkai presented the Esoteric Vehicle (Shingon School) as the fulfillment of all other Buddhist schools without rejecting their validity. Thus, in 810 Kūkai secured a key position at the Tōdai-ji of Nara, and began to propagate Esoteric Buddhism from within the framework of the established schools of Buddhism. In the same year, Prince Takaoka, the former heir-apparent who had been deprived of his succession right because he was implicated in a court intrigue, took priestly vows and became Kūkai's disciple. Meanwhile, Kūkai and Saichō were estranged, and the latter left for the Eastern province for an extended evangelistic campaign. In 816 Kūkai was given a charter to establish his monastic center at Mount Kōya. After the death of Saichō

---

[23] Beatrice Lane Suzuki, "Poems by Kōbō-daishi," *The Eastern Buddhist* 5 (1931), 312.

in 822, Kūkai became the unrivaled religious figure in Japan. In the following year, Kūkai was appointed Abbot of the Tō-ji (Eastern Temple) in Kyoto, which came to be known as the temple for the protection of the nation (*Kyō-ō-gokoku-no-tera*).

Kūkai's popularity and influence continued to increase under the reigns of the Emperors Junna (reigned, 823-832) and Nimmyō (reigned, 832-850). He was asked to offer prayers for rain during droughts in 824 and again in 827, and to celebrate the votive service for the protection of the throne in 826. In return, the court showered him with honors and favors. In 828, Kūkai founded a private school, called Shugei-shuchi-in, for the purpose of offering general education. The educational principles of the school were stated by Kūkai as follows: "the rise and decline of any institution depends ultimately on the personnel, and the rise and decline of any person depends basically on the teaching."[24] That is to say, the purpose of this school was training for leadership, both secular and religious, and thus it offered a broad curriculum including the teachings of the Confucian, Taoist, and Buddhist systems. He was convinced that the healthy growth of religion presupposed a cultured society, and vice versa.

Kūkai spent the last few years of his life consolidating the organizational structure of the Shingon school and explicating its doctrines. We are told that in 834 he wandered on Mount Kōya and chose the spot where he would be buried. His affection for Mount Kōya was well expressed by one of his earlier poems:

> Within the quiet forest,
> Alone in the straw-thatched hut,
> So early in the morning
> I hear the sound of a bird.
>> It sings of the Triple Treasure,
>> The Bu-pō-sō [Buddha, Dharma, and Samgha].
> The bird has a voice for singing,
> A man has a mind for thinking,
> The voice and mind,
> The cloud and the stream,
> Express the Buddha-wisdom.[25]

On the twenty-first day of the third month of 835, Kūkai's colorful life came to an end. In 921, the posthumous title of Kōbō Daishi (the Great Master for the Propagation of the Dharma) was conferred upon him by the court.

[24] Quoted in Kaneko Daivei, *Dengyō Kōbō to Nihon Bunka* (Tokyo, 1940), p. 46.
[25] Beatrice Lane Suzuki, "Poems by Kōbō-daishi," p. 312.

KŪKAI, THE SAVIOUR

The transformation of the image of Kūkai from that of a Master to that of a Saviour is a complex problem. A historian of religions, however, is reminded of the fact that deification of saintly figures is a fairly common phenomenon in various religious traditions. In all such cases the personalities and teachings of the men in question may differ greatly, but the "forms" of their biographies as they develop over the years seem to follow an amazingly similar pattern. This is what Martin Dibelius calls the law of sacred biography. According to this law, there is usually a stereotyped notion of a holy man whose life is marked by a series of supernatural events. His birth is accompanied by miraculous elements, and he proclaims his future calling in his youth. He seems to know ahead of time what kind of death is awaiting him, and often such a person is believed to have overcome physical death one way or another.[26] On all these counts, the case of Kūkai follows this general pattern of sacred biography. However, we are here concerned with what particular factors were involved in the deification of Kūkai. In so doing, we will have to deal with the two most important aspects of the problem, namely (1) Kūkai's own claim of what he was and (2) how he came to be remembered by his disciples and followers.

It is well nigh impossible to examine the voluminous writings of Kūkai in the limited space of this essay, nor can we assess Kūkai's self-understanding solely on the basis of his written works. On the other hand, it is not our purpose to evaluate his contributions to many areas of art and culture, even though it is clear that he was endowed with unusual talents and abilities along these lines. Rather, our modest aim is to ascertain his basic approach to religion. This, we realize, is in itself a hazardous undertaking. Kūkai's deeds, teachings, and writings are full of existential contradictions. Nevertheless, it is safe to state that Kūkai throughout his life was concerned with a certain type of religious knowledge and concentrated his attention upon the nature of a reality which can be known only by immediate experience and continued contemplation.[27] This may account for the fact that, brilliant though he was as a student, Kūkai was not satisfied in his youth with the purely academic training of the university and so became a hermit. At least judging from the *Sangō-shiiki*, Kūkai's fundamental question was not primarily an intellectual inquiry into the truth values of Con-

[26] Martin Dibelius, *Die Formgeschichte des Evangeliums* (Tübingen, 1919), trans. Bertram L. Woolf as *From Tradition to Gospel* (New York, 1935), pp. 108-109.

[27] On this problem of knowledge, see F.S.C. Northrop, *The Meeting of East and West* (New York, 1946), pp. 315-317.

fucianism, Taoism, and Buddhism. He was converted to Buddhism precisely because it presented not only metaphysics and ethics but also a concrete path which promised the certainty of enlightenment. This conviction led him to undergo austere physical disciplines in the mountains while at the same time he continued his intellectual endeavor under learned monks. Eventually he found the answer to his soteriological quest in Esoteric (Shingon) Buddhism.

Sir Charles Eliot once stated that it was not easy to determine "how far Shingon as we see it in Japan is the system which Kōbō Daishi learnt in China and how far it is a reconstruction due to himself."[28] While this question can be argued either way, we are inclined to feel that Shingon Buddhism in Japan developed primarily out of Kūkai's own religious search in spite of the fact that he appropriated the philosophical, cultic, and ecclesiastical framework of the traditional Esoteric Buddhism which he studied in China. In this sense, we might rightly regard him as the "founder" of Shingon Buddhism in Japan and not simply its "transmitter." Granting that this observation is an oversimplification, let us now proceed to depict the essential characteristics of Kūkai's religion from this point of view.

Briefly stated, Kūkai's religion was based on three epistemological components: (1) *shōtoku* or *shōgu* (the intuitive function of the mind that enables it to determine moral choices), (2) *shūtoku* (knowledge acquired by learning and experience), and (3) *shinkō* (faith which gives certitude).[29] It was Kūkai's considered opinion that man's intuitive reason is usually hindered by bestial desires. The first step, then, in the religious life is to overcome those desires and to purify one's mind so that one will be able to make moral decisions. Secondly, religious life requires a continuous training of mind and body by following the ethical and religious teachings of sages and saints. However, in the final analysis, one receives the certainty of enlightenment or salvation only by faith. In Kūkai's own case, his ethical and religious pilgrimage culminated in his encounter with the *Dainichi-kyō* (the Great Sun Sutra) which he accepted in faith as the direct teachings of the Great Sun Buddha (Mahāvairocana). Although Kūkai acknowledged the value of Exoteric (public) or relative truths of all the ethical and religious teachings he had received prior to his experience of *metanoia*, he considered them basically to be *prepaeratio* for the Esoteric (secret) truth preached by Mahāvairocana.

The qualitative difference between the Exoteric and Esoteric vehicles

---

[28] Sir Charles Eliot, *Japanese Buddhism* (London, 1935), p. 340.
[29] See Kambayashi Ryūjō, *Kōbō Daishi no shisō to shūkyō* (Tokyo, 1931), pp. 2-11.

was elaborated in Kūkai's major writings, especially in the *Benkem-mitsu-nikyōron* (Treatise on Two Teachings—Public and Secret), the *Jūjūshin-ron* (Treatise on Ten Stages of Spiritual Growth), and the *Hizōhōyaku* (The Jewel Key to the Store of Mysteries). In all these works Kūkai quotes passages from the Indian and Chinese literature of Esoteric Buddhism to prove that the *dharmakāya* (the truth-body of Buddha), which according to Exoteric teachings is formless and colorless, is no other than Mahāvairocana and that he has body and continuously preaches the Law. His main argument is that the Exoteric teachings were given by Śākyamuni, who could not teach the highest truth because he had to adapt himself to the level of his general hearers, whereas Esoteric teaching is the Law understood secretly by Buddha and given to select disciples, like familiar conversation among relatives. These arguments are couched in philosophical language, but they are to be understood as Kūkai's basic affirmation of faith. His "fideist" principle comes through most clearly in his assertion that one who follows the Exoteric teachings must spend hundreds of thousands of years in discipline for the attainment of Nirvana, whereas one who follows the Esoteric Vehicle can attain Buddhahood during his lifetime in his own physical body (*sokushin-jōbutsu*).[30]

The principle of *sokushin-jōbutsu* may be regarded as the final synthesis of the intellectual and practical dimensions of Kūkai's religious pilgrimage. Actually this doctrine is not explicitly taught in the two leading scriptures which Kūkai refers to as his sources—the *Mahāvairocana Sūtra* and the *Vajraśekhara Sūtra*. There is every reason to believe that Kūkai depended on the *Ta-jih Ching Su* (Commentary on the *Mahāvairocana Sūtra*) by I-hsing (683-727) which contains this novel doctrine, even though Kūkai did not acknowledge it.[31] More important probably is the fact that *sokusin-jōbutsu* was a logical goal of Kūkai's practical discipline considered as a search for miraculous power. Kūkai, be it remembered, was a child of an age which took seriously the existence of numerous spirits, both malevolent and benevolent, and even many orthodox Buddhists of his time were awed

---

[30] It must be noted, however, that some scholars, including the late Shimaji Daitō, have questioned the authenticity of Kūkai's authorship of the *Sokushin-jōbutsu-gi* (Principles of Becoming Buddha with One's Physical Body).

[31] See Kambayashi, *Kōbō Daishi*, pp. 264-272. Kambayashi feels that Kūkai's references to two portions of the *Mahāvairocana Sūtra* as the scriptural basis for his soteriology are farfetched. He also examines Kūkai's quotations from the *Vajraśekhara Sūtra* and finds only a suggestion concerning *bodhicitta* but no explicit statement about *sokushin-jōbutsu*. Kambayashi therefore concludes that this doctrine existed in the mind of Śubhākarasinha (637-735), who translated the *Mahāvairocana Sūtra* into Chinese, in rudimentary form but was expounded more fully by his pupil, I-hsing. Kūkai must have known I-hsing's commentary and read its meaning into the *Mahāvairocana Sūtra*.

194

by the example of En-no-Shōkaku, the seventh-century *gyōja* (austerity man) and the reputed pioneer of the shamanistic Buddhists (*ubasoku*). He was believed to have acquired superhuman power by exercise of the magic formulas (*dhāraṇī*) of the *Mahāmāyūrī-vidyārājñī* (*Kujaku-myōō-ju*).[32] Kūkai himself admits, according to the *Yuigō*, that his initial interest in Buddhism was aroused when a certain monk gave him the *Kokuzō-gumonji-hō* (Rules Spoken by the Buddha for Seeking to Hear and Keep the *dhāraṇī* of the Most Excellent Heart, by Means of which the Bodhisattva Ākāśagarbha Is Able to Fulfill All Wishes).[33] It prescribes, among other things, the *goshinshuin* (symbolic gestures for protecting one's body) which give a person who practices them "the protection of all Buddhas and of Ākāśagarbha. They also obliterate all crime, purify the body and heart, increase felicity and wealth, and drive away all demons and *piśācas* (vampires)."[34] Thus, following the examples of the shamanistic Buddhists, many of whom were reputed to be wonder workers, Kūkai underwent many years of austere training in order to acquire supernatural power by practicing the *Kokuzō-gumonji-hō*. It was the *Dainichi-kyō* (*Mahāvairocana Sūtra*) that gave a theoretical basis for Kūkai's practical attempt to acquire miraculous powers (*siddhi*),[35] and it was this magico-soteriological aspect of Esoteric Buddhism that he pursued during his study in China. There he received from Hui-kuo not only the deeper meaning of the scriptures but also the fivefold baptism, instructions on the Three Mysteries, and the Sanskrit formulas both for the Womb and Diamond Maṇḍalas. Upon his return to Japan, Kūkai attempted to synthesize doctrinal and practical approaches to enlightenment on the basis of his experience of religious life; out of this attempt came the principle of *sokushin-jōbutsu*.

The foregoing makes it clear that *sokushin-jōbutsu* was not merely a doctrinal formula for Kūkai. He was convinced that anybody properly trained and initiated into the mystery of the Esoteric Vehicle can ac-

[32] Nanjō Bunyū, *A Catalogue of the Chinese Translation of the Buddhist Tripitaka* (Oxford, 1883), nos. 306-311.

[33] Ibid., no. 501. It is to be noted that Kokuzō (literally, Womb of the Ether or Space), the patron bodhisattva of Kūkai, was believed to be the counterpart of Jizō (Womb of the Earth, Kṣitigarbha), the source of abundant blessings of the earth. The *Kokuzō-gumonji-hō* was based on a section of the *Vajraśekhara Sūtra* called the "Jōju-issaigi-bon" (Chapter on all the meanings of *siddhi*).

[34] M. W. de Visser, *The Bodhisattva Ākāśagarbha (Kokūzō) in China and Japan* (Amsterdam, 1931), p. 41. This Mudra "consists in raising the right hand, and pinching the middle finger with thumb as if pinching incense. The second joint of the middle finger must be bent, its first joint and the point must be straight. After having made this mudra he must place it on the crown of his head and recite the formula once; then place it on his right and left shoulders, heart and throat, each time with one incantation" (p. 40).

[35] On the meaning of *siddhi*, see Mircea Eliade, *Yoga: Immortality and Freedom*, trans. Willard R. Trask (New York, 1958; 2d ed., Princeton, 1969), pp. 85-90.

quire miraculous powers and actualize the Buddhahood which is implicit within him. Kūkai never tired of advocating the benefit of his soteriological path by his lucid writings, eloquent preaching, exquisite art, as well as by practical demonstration of his miraculous powers. Moreover, following in the footsteps of his mentor, the great shamanistic Buddhist Gyōgi, Kūkai traveled widely, initiating charitable activities such as the construction of reservoirs and canals for irrigation, the planting of trees, and the healing of the sick. He also shared with Gyōgi a conciliatory attitude toward Shinto deities, thus strengthening the trend toward the Buddhist-Shinto coexistence which came to be known in later years as *Ryōbu-Shinto*.

As WE TURN to the discussion of how Kūkai came to be remembered by his disciples and followers, we must bear in mind that the tendency to deify religious founders and saintly figures has been unusually strong in Japan. This is due in part to the fact that the Japanese people, not satisfied with the worship of intangible deities believed to reside in another realm, tended to give absolute devotion to certain charismatic persons and outstanding religious leaders who were closer to them.[36] For example, less than a century after the death of Prince Shōtoku in 621, he came to be regarded as an incarnation of Kannon, the Lord of Mercy. According to a legendary account, people revered the seventh-century wonder worker, En-no-Shōkaku, believing that he was able to control even deities and ghosts by his magic spells. Also, the *Shoku-Nihongi* (Chronicles of Japan, Continued) tells us that Gyōgi (670-749) was actually worshipped by the masses and was called a Bosatsu (Bodhisattva) during his lifetime[37] In all these cases, who these men actually were and what they did became less important than what their followers believed they were and did.[38] That is to say, the memories of these men came to be reconstructed by the soteriological yearnings of their pious followers. Furthermore, in their loving adoration of these deified figures these followers tended to demand and keep alive more and more apocryphal and hagiographical accounts of the supposedly historic memories of these men.

[36] See Nakamura Hajime, *Tōyōjin no shii hōhō* (Tokyo, 1948), vol. 2, pp. 114-140; English translation, *The Ways of Thinking of Eastern Peoples* (Tokyo, 1960), pp. 355-377.

[37] See Hori Ichirō, *Waga-kuni minkan-shinkō-shi no kenkyū* (Tokyo, 1955), vol. 1, pp. 299-300.

[38] For a modern example of such a process, see Frank Werfel, *The Song of Bernadette* (New York, 1941), p. 109. Hyacinthe de Lafite, the skeptic, makes a classic remark regarding the authenticity of the vision of Bernadette. He says: "I find that all you gentlemen miss the essential point. The true problem is offered not so much by the little visionary as by the great crowd that follows her. . . ."

It is readily understandable that the memory of Kūkai, one of the most colorful and charismatic figures in the religious history of Japan, underwent the inevitable process of deification after his death. It is important to note that the two biographies mentioned earlier—the *Kūkai-sōzu-den* (The Biography of Abbot Kūkai) and the *Zō-Daisōjō-Kūkai-wajō-denki* (The Biography of Archbishop Kūkai)—portray essentially the human figure of Kūkai, the Master. Of the four editions of the *Yuigō* (The Last Instructions) mentioned earlier, the two earlier editions, presumably written very shortly after Kūkai's death, present him as a human being, albeit an unusually great one. The two later editions of the *Yuigō*, however, give accounts of a markedly deified Kūkai. His death scene is modeled after that of Gautama. Kūkai is said to have proclaimed himself a legitimate object of adoration and worship on the part of his faithful. Furthermore, according to these later accounts, Kūkai declared that after he entered the final state of entrancement—which by implication is different from ordinary death—he would be with Maitreya (Miroku) in Tuṣita Heaven until such time as he would return to this earth with Maitreya. The assurance of his second coming even had a tone of mild warning to the effect that while in Tuṣita Heaven he would be watching closely the behavior of the faithful, and that those lax in their devotion to him would have reason to be sorry.[39]

Once these deified accounts of Kūkai were accepted by pious tradition, his human figure receded into the background. In this connection, we noted earlier that the belief that Kūkai was the reincarnation of Amoghavajra was instrumental in the development of the theory that Kūkai was born on the fifteenth day of the sixth month of 774, which was the day of Amoghavajra's death. In the course of time a large number of highly embroidered biographies of Kūkai have come into existence.[40] Although space does not permit us even to list the important legends about him cited in these works, we might briefly discuss the deified image of Kūkai in terms of three main motifs of the religious heritage of the Japanese.

The first important motif is a preoccupation with the "here and now" of the phenomenal world. This does not imply that the Japanese have not been aware of the existence of other realms of existence. Indeed, the ancient Shinto myths mention the threefold structure of the world (the heavenly, the earthly, and the nether regions) and Buddhism taught the existence of many grades of heaven and hell. Never-

[39] See Kōyama, "Kōbō Daishi," pp. 71-76.
[40] See Katsuno, *Hiei-zan to Kōya-san*, pp. 118-121.

theless, the world of meaning of the Japanese has always been grounded primarily in this world. To put it in religious language, this world is the center of the cosmos and is the very arena of salvation, however this term may be interpreted. It also means that religion is inseparable from the family, community, and sociopolitical order of the nation. It is therefore not without reason that the classical figures of Japanese religious history were not necessarily men of deep spiritual insight but more likely were outstanding men of practical ability who exerted lasting influence on ecclesiastical, philanthropic, cultural, or national affairs. In popular legends, Prince Shōtoku is regarded as a sort of counterpart to King Solomon, endowed with unusual wisdom and compassion.[41] The fame of Gyōgi was greatly enhanced by his reputation as a great philanthropist, and he was also credited with the first census ever taken in Japan.

Admittedly, it is beyond the competence of a historian of religions to determine the authenticity of many of the legendary accounts that have developed around the life of Kūkai. It is worth noting, however, that the popular image of Kūkai is consonant with the tradition of the classical figures of Japanese religious history. For example, his name connotes in the minds of many Japanese a man of great brilliance, an accomplished linguist, a talented painter, sculptor, calligrapher, and a gifted poet and prose writer. We are told that when he accompanied the Japanese ambassador to China, it was Kūkai who impressed the Chinese officials with his mastery of written Chinese. When he called on Hui-kuo, this eminent master of the Esoteric Vehicle welcomed the young Japanese monk by saying "until you came there was no one to whom I could transmit the teachings." After his death, Hui-kuo told Kūkai in a dream: "If I am reborn in Japan, this time I will be your disciple." Kūkai was not only successful in everything he undertook in China, but his achievements after his return to Japan were very impressive. He is credited with having introduced the study of Sanskrit, perfected the two kinds of Japanese alphabet, *Katakana* and *Hiragana*, and originated the *Yamato-e* (Japanese-style painting). His reputed ability to use five brushes simultaneously in painting is reminiscent of the superhuman performance of Prince Shōtoku in another domain. His philanthropic activities matched only those of the celebrated Gyōgi. Kūkai's tender love toward his mother is regarded as a model of filial piety, and his services to the court make him a paragon of loyalty. Needless to say, Kūkai's notion of *sokushin-jōbutsu* (acquiring Buddhahood in this life) had a great appeal to his followers who were nur-

[41] We are told that he was able to listen to ten different law suits simultaneously.

tured in the tradition which regarded this world as the very arena of salvation.

The second motif of the religious heritage of the Japanese, which is closely related to the first, is its apprehension of life as concentric circles, not as a series of separate domains. This motif may be illustrated by the principle of *saisei-itchi* (unity of religion and government) or by the tradition of the inseparability of art and religion. To be sure, historical developments in Japan resulted in the gradual stratification of society and the departmentalization of life, but the Japanese have never lost the insight that various activities of life despite their apparent contradictions share an inherent midpoint.[42] This view of life fostered in religion, as much as in art and philosophy, an emphasis on the harmony of contrasts and a rejection of sharp dichotomies between sacred and profane, good and evil, or phenomenal and noumenal.[43] It also accounts for the traditional Japanese preoccupation with aesthetics at the expense of ethics and metaphysics, and it explains, at least in part, the magico-soteriological accent of Japanese piety.

In a real sense, the image of Kūkai as it has come to be remembered by pious tradition is a personification of the traditional religious apprehension of the Japanese. He himself was nurtured in this tradition, and he had unusual competence in various fields of human activities. Throughout his life he endeavored to harmonize religion and art, philosophy and literature, Buddhism and other religious and semireligious systems, and the spiritual and cultural life of the nation. It was no sheer accident that Kūkai was attracted, among all schools of Buddhism, to the cosmo-theism of the Esoteric Vehicle which regards the whole universe as the body of the Great Sun Buddha (Mahāvairocana). Kūkai was no doubt impressed by the comprehensive nature of the Esoteric doctrinal system which offered a cosmological, physical, and psychological analysis in terms of the six elements (five material elements plus one mental element, i.e., conciousness); but he never attempted to teach the Esoteric Vehicle only as a system of doctrine. Thus, in the *Shōrai-mokuroku* he suggests that the Esoteric doctrines are so profound that they cannot be understood without the help of painting. "The various attitudes and mudras of the holy images all

---

[42] Incidentally, this is exactly the kind of insight which was advocated by G. van der Leeuw. In his *Sacred and Profane Beauty: The Holy in Art*, trans. David E. Green (New York, 1963), p. 34, he says: "We consider the question of religious dance, because after a few decades we have once again recognized the value of the dance as an expression of art and life, and because we recognize that all values must have a connection with the highest and most comprehensive value known to religion."

[43] See my article, "Japanese Philosophy" in *Encyclopaedia Britannica*, 1968 ed., 12:958G-958J.

have their source in Buddha's love, and one may attain Buddhahood at sight of them. Thus the secrets of the sūtras and commentaries can be depicted in art, and the essential truths of the esoteric teaching are all set forth therein. . . . Art is what reveals to us the state of perfection."[44] Kūkai in presenting religion as art represented the central core of Japanese piety, and in this he may be rightly regarded as a paradigmatic figure of Japanese religious history.

The third important motif of the Japanese religious heritage is its tendency to depend on the charismatic qualities of religious leaders as efficacious ingredients for the salvation of man. Indeed, throughout the history of Japan some of the charismatic holy men have been regarded as *de facto* saviours to whom the faithful paid homage and adoration. This motif originated in pre-Buddhist Shinto tradition, as Eliot aptly observes, and it was subsequently amplified by Buddhist piety. "Buddhist and Shintoist ideas thus coalesced and the title of Bodhisattva was conferred on departed Emperors and statesmen—on those, for instance, who are described as Hachiman, the patron of soldiers, and Tenjin, the God of Calligraphy, and even on so recent a personage as Ieyasu."[45] In this respect, the case of Kūkai was one of the most spectacular examples of the homologizing of Shinto and Buddhist saviour motifs.[46]

The deified figure of Kūkai was, as noted earlier, a composite of the many components and stereotypes regarding charismatic persons and saviour images that had been sanctioned and preserved in the communal reservoir of Japanese folk piety. That is to say, the soteriological yearning of the faithful consciously or unconsciously found in the life, teaching and deeds of Kūkai many of the admirable qualities of Prince Shōtoku, En-no-Shōkaku, Gyōgi, and others. While we have no way of ascertaining whether Kūkai believed himself to be more than a Master of the Esoteric Vehicle or not, it is conceivable that his teaching of the attainability of Buddhahood in this life, his beliefs in the potency of *mantra* and *dhāraṇī* as well as in miracles and divine oracles given in dreams, and his claim to the mastery of *siddhi*, contributed to the creation of a spiritual aura around his own personality. It was most

[44] This translation was taken from Tsunoda et al., *Japanese Tradition*, p. 142.

[45] Eliot, *Japanese Buddhism*, p. 183. On the process of deification of Sugawara Michizane, who shortly after his death came to be known as Temma-daijizai-Tenjin, see Watsuji Tetsurō, *Nihon rinri-shisō-shi* (Tokyo, 1927), vol. 1, pp. 232-236.

[46] On the Shinto and folk religious background of this problem, see Hori Ichirō, "On the Concept of Hijiri (Holy-Man)," *Numen* 5, no. 2 (April 1958), 128-160, and no. 3 (September 1958), 199-232. On the saviour motif in Buddhism, see Edward Conze, "Buddhist Saviours," in S.G.F. Brandon, ed., *The Saviour God*, presented to Edwin Oliver James (Manchester, 1963), pp. 67-82.

assuredly Kūkai's intention to dedicate his learning, skills, and miraculous power solely to the purpose of presenting Esoteric Buddhism as the most effective vehicle of salvation for the people. But in the eyes of his followers it was Kūkai himself who became the vehicle of salvation or the saviour, and with this twist his words and deeds took on new soteriological significance.

One of the most attractive forms of adoration paid to the deified Kūkai is a religious ballad called "Namu-Daishi" (Hail to Daishi).[47] It tells the life of Kūkai as remembered in the popular fancy. For example, according to this ballad, when Kūkai was in the palace for a religious discussion, his body suddenly assumed the appearance of Mahāvairocana. "The Divine Light (Kōmyō) streamed out from him, and the whole company, overawed and trembling, fell to the ground and worshipped him" (verse 31). Echoing the pious belief that Kūkai did not really die but only entered a deep meditative trance (nyūjō) and that his body is uncorrupted in his tomb, awaiting the coming of the future Buddha (Maitreya), the ballad goes on to say that "Eighty years after his decease, an Imperial Messenger opened the gate of his sepulchre. His hair, they found, had grown long upon his head; they shaved it off and gave him a change of garments" (verse 57). Later, "when Shinnyu, the Imperial Messenger to the Temple in which our great sage is worshipped, was unable to see the face of the Sage, the Sage himself guided the worshipper's hand to touch his knee" (verse 59). Understandably, the chanting of these verses in corporate worship or during pilgrimages to the holy mountain of Kōya had stirring and cumulative effects on the faithful, and they in turn kept alive the sacred tradition of Kūkai or Kōbō Daishi, who embodied within him the numinous glory of the Great Sun Buddha (Mahāvairocana).

Equally significant was the development of various legends that associate Kūkai with Shinto tradition. According to one legend, the goddess of Mount Kōya, Nifutsu-hime, donated the mountain to Kūkai when he was looking for a place to establish his monastic center. The ballad, "Namu Daishi," put it more dramatically: "In the mountainous districts of the Province of Kii, two dogs, one white and one black, and a hunter, came to show him the way . . ." (verse 35). "Then Nifutsu appeared, the god of that place [Kōya], and offered him that place until the coming of Maitreya, in order that the land might be blessed by him [Kōbō]" (verse 36). According to another account, when Kūkai was appointed as the chief abbot of the Tō-ji, which was

[47] See Arthur Lloyd, *The Creed of Half Japan* (London, 1911), pp. 243-258. I follow Lloyd's translation in this article.

201

called the Temple for the Protection of the Nation, a Shinto *kami* of food and fertility, Inari, appeared at the gate of the temple and told Kūkai: "Together, you and I, we will protect this nation."[48] In many districts, including places where Kūkai could not possibly have visited, there are many legends about what Kūkai did during his lifetime in those places. Popular among them are stories about wells or springs which were believed to have been discovered by Kūkai.[49] These legends provided powerful incentives for the formation of a devotional association based on belief in Kōbō Daishi called the Daishi-kō.[50] It is widely held that Kōbō Daishi walks in disguise with pilgrims or that he visits villages on the night of the winter solstice.[51]

As stated at the outset of this essay, the deification of saintly figures, a common phenomenon in many religious traditions, is an intriguing and fascinating problem to the student of *Religionswissenschaft*. We are inclined to hold that one meaningful way to study this phenomenon is to study some of the "classical figures," in the sense that Joachim Wach used this category. Kūkai or Kōbō Daishi is such a paradigmatic figure in the history of Japanese religion, and a study of his sacred biography will enable us to understand not only the life and teaching of this remarkable Master but also the characteristics of the Saviour motif in the religious heritage of the Japanese.

[48] Regarding the legend of Inari and Kūkai, see Kondō Yoshihiro, *Kodai-shinkō-kenkyu* (Tokyo, 1963), pp. 37-130. It is Kondō's opinion that the legend that associates Inari and Kūkai began to receive wide acceptance during the middle of the Kamakura period.

[49] See Yanagita Kunio, gen. ed., *Minzokugaku-jiten* (Tokyo, 1951), pp. 24-25 and 198-199.

[50] Ibid., pp. 340-341. There are three kinds of *Daishi-kō*. One of them is connected with Shōtoku Taishi (Prince Shōtoku). The second is connected with Kōbō Daishi. The third is strictly an ancient peasant cult which venerated the Taishi (oldest son) of the *kami* who is believed to visit the village between the harvest and the new year. It is to be noted that in the folk tradition these three, especially the latter two, are confused in the minds of people.

[51] Ibid., p. 398.

12. The Buddhist Transformation in Japan

INTRODUCTION

T HIS PAPER deals with some aspects of the problem "Adaptation of Tradition to New Conditions" with reference to Buddhism, more particularly to Buddhism in Japan.* As students of *Religionswissenschaft*, we are all aware of the dialectical relationship that exists between tradition and new conditions in all historical religions. In every situation, the meaning of a new condition is to a greater or lesser degree colored and conditioned by the weight of the given tradition, whereas tradition is inevitably modified and reinterpreted by new conditions. In many cases, the adaptation of a tradition to new conditions is rationalized and authenticated by appeal to certain features of the tradition itself, and thus the new attitudes, new experiences, and new interpretations become incorporated into the body of the tradition. We might add that, generally speaking, the term "tradition" seems to denote the oral transmission of beliefs and customs from one generation to the next without the aid of written material. There are, of course, many scholars who refer to the sacred scriptures as written tradition. However, as Talcott Parsons reminds us, once these sacred books are codified, they "tend to become the focus of specialized intellectual competence and prestige in the religious field and on the cultural level of rationalized systems of religious doctrine."[1] As such, a written sacred tradition is a very special kind of tradition. Therefore, in this paper, we have employed the general meaning for tradition of a nebulous body of beliefs, attitudes, customs, and institutions, with some sort of internal coherence, even though at times it is difficult to draw a sharp line of demarcation between tradition and sacred writings.

Before we go into the main discussion, some preliminary remarks might be made to indicate our general perspectives pertaining to (1) the paradoxical nature of religion, (2) the character of the Buddhist tradition, (3) the cultural pattern of the Orient, and (4) the relevance of the new conditions that confront the Buddhist tradition in our time.

---

* This paper was read to the American Society for the Study of Religion, meeting under the general theme "Adaptation of Tradition to New Conditions," April 24, 1964.

[1] "Introduction" to Max Weber, *The Sociology of Religion*, trans. Ephraim Fischoff (Boston: Beacon Press, 1963), pp. xxxvii-xxxviii.

First, religion, however it is interpreted in different contexts, has both universal and particular dimensions. In the words of Hocking, religion is "by definition universal in extent as in norms of will: it speaks not primarily to the man-within-the-nation but to the man-within-the-world."[2] At the same time, religion must be particular, precisely because the universal elements of religion must be communicated. "And communication is never to human beings in general: it is to specific human beings, having specific difficulties in seeing what is meant, having specific languages and histories with whatever resources of legend and reflection there are to be drawn upon for explanation, also with specific ethical and social questions to meet."[3] In other words, the universal must be particularized and the particular must be universalized, if religion is to be meaningful at all. In this respect, it is our observation that while Buddhism has tended historically to stress particular elements in various parts of Asia, its universal dimension has never been lost completely.

Second, the historic character of the Buddhist tradition has never been too belligerent toward existing local religions and cultures. Both the Theravāda and Mahāyāna schools of Buddhism, despite their apparent disagreements regarding doctrines and practices, share the same spirit of tolerance, as exemplified by the Theravāda Buddhist attitude toward Nat worship in Burma and the Mahāyāna Buddhist attitude toward Confucianism and Taoism in China. Historically, when Buddhism entered a new area, it usually presented itself more as a "supplement" to, than as a "contestant" with, existing religions.[4] "In so doing, Buddhism enriched the local cultures and contributed rich symbols, rituals, and lofty philosophical systems to the religious life of the peoples, but it approximated, rather than challenged, the existing world-views and cultural assumptions in various parts of Asia."[5]

Third, contrary to the oft-repeated affirmation of the unity of Oriental culture, the cultural pattern of Asia might be better understood in terms of "juxtaposition." For example, the two great and self-contained cultures of India and China have developed in relative insularity. In sharp contrast to the cultural development in the Occident,

[2] William Ernest Hocking, *The Coming World Civilization* (New York: Harper & Bros., 1956), p. 47.

[3] William Ernest Hocking, *Living Religions and a World Faith* (New York: Macmillan Co., 1940), p 36.

[4] William Ernest Hocking, "Living Religions and a World Faith," in Arthur E. Christy, ed., *The Asian Legacy and American Life* (New York: John Day, 1942), pp. 206-207.

[5] Joseph M. Kitagawa, "Buddhism and Asian Politics," *Asian Survey* 2, no. 5 (July 1962), p. 3.

where "the interdependence of its relatively autonomous parts depends upon the relationship of those parts to the governing whole," states William S. Haas, "in the East there is neither a natural and continuous interpenetration of the national cultures nor a collaboration in their achievement of common objectives, nor their combination into a single evolutionary process."[6] To be sure, we might argue that Buddhism has provided a common tie among various Oriental cultures, but at no time did Buddhism achieve in Asia the kind of unity—religious, cultural, or political—comparable to medieval Christendom in Europe. Actually, it may be more true to say that Buddhism from the tenth to the nineteenth centuries developed very much as though it were a local religion, each part of it confined to a particular and insular cultural or national region, thus developing a series of culturally oriented Buddhist traditions.

Fourth, confronted by the new conditions in today's world, which will be discussed more fully later, Buddhism is compelled to wrestle with the problem of relating its historic tradition to the living experiences of modern Buddhists. In this process, Buddhism is rediscovering its religious integrity and common heritage, even though there are a number of factors that work against such a trend. At any rate, it is our contention that a brief survey of Japanese Buddhism may serve as a case study of the historical development of the Buddhist tradition and of its adaptation to new conditions in our time.

DEVELOPMENT OF JAPANESE BUDDHISM

As we turn our attention to the Buddhist tradition in Japan, we realize that it is no easy task to make general observations, because what we call Japanese Buddhism is a conglomerate of many sects, schools, divisions, and subdivisions. "Their practices range from the quiet meditation of Zen to the fanatic drum-beating of the Nichirenites and from sophisticated Tendai discussions of reality to the Shingon performances of elaborate rituals. Their tenets are no less diverse than their practices while their adherents comprise philosophical minds of high standing as well as the most superstitious of the populace."[7] Such a bewildering variety of beliefs and practices did not develop overnight. Actually, they are the culminating products of a long series of historical changes and evolutions. In the words of Sir Charles Eliot, "the most salient feature of Japanese Buddhism is its intimate

[6] *The Destiny of the Mind: East and West* (London: Faber & Faber 1956), p. 19.
[7] Masaharu Anesaki, *Religious Life of the Japanese People*, rev. by Hideo Kishimoto (Tokyo: Kokusai Bunka Shinkokai, 1961), p. 45.

205

connection with the general condition of the nation, both political and social. It has vibrated in response to many and abrupt political changes, it has registered them in its sects and expressed in its art the special note of each."[8]

It is important to remind ourselves that by the sixth century A.D., when Buddhism reached Japan, it had already a long history in India, Central Asia, and China. In fact, prior to its penetration of China, Buddhism had developed and articulated its doctrines, scriptures, systems of meditation, monastic orders, and disciplines for the laity. No less important was the adoption of images of Buddhas and Bodhisattvas as objects of worship which, as Zenryū Tsukamoto points out, "contributed to the development of temples for the religious ceremonies built around them and, at the same time, furthered the development of painting, sculpture, music, and crafts."[9] While Buddhist influence was beginning to wane in India around the sixth century, Buddhism in China was then busily establishing itself as an integral part of the life of the people. The voluminous *Tripitaka* was translated into Chinese, indigenous sects and schools arose, monastic and lay disciplines were adjusted to meet the needs of the Chinese nation, and the new faith found eager followers in all walks of life. The genius of Chinese Buddhism was its ability to maintain some basic unifying factors that were Buddhist and Chinese at the same time. The chief characteristic of Chinese Buddhism was its preoccupation with the meaning of human existence in the phenomenal world which, as Wing-tsit Chan has suggested, "contributed to the shift in outlook from otherworldliness to this-worldliness, in objective from individual salvation to universal salvation, in philosophy from extreme doctrines to synthesis, in methods of freedom from religious discipline and philosophical understanding to pietism and practical insight, and in authority from the clergy to the layman himself."[10]

The historical situation in the fifth, sixth, and seventh centuries in Japan brought about a series of social, cultural, political, and religious changes under the influence of Chinese civilization, and of Buddhism. Especially noteworthy was the adoption of a written script from China. This does not imply that the Chinese language as such was accepted or understood by people in Japan. Rather, they managed to develop an ingenious method by which Chinese written characters

[8] *Japanese Buddhism* (New York: Barnes & Noble, Inc., 1959), p. 179.
[9] "Buddhism in China and Korea," in Kenneth W. Morgan, ed., *The Path of the Buddha* (New York: Roald Press Co., 1956), p. 115.
[10] "Transformation of Buddhism in China," *Philosophy East and West* 7, nos. 3-4 (October 1957-January 1958), p. 115.

206

were matched to Japanese words. In this process, the Japanese language was no doubt greatly enriched, but it preserved its basic structure and identity. In a sense, this method of matching Chinese written script to Japanese words is a part of the peculiar Japanese pattern of accepting new ideas, values, beliefs, and institutions from abroad. For example, Japanese leaders depended on certain features of Confucian ethics to define social and interhuman relationships, while the native cult of Shinto eagerly accepted the Chinese notion of ancestor worship. Eventually, even the Buddhas and Bodhisattvas were accepted as foreign counterparts of the native *kami*. This is what was meant by James B. Pratt when he stated that the Japanese people "have done with Buddhism what they have done with everything else that has been brought them from abroad. They have accepted it simply, humbly, in sincere and almost childlike fashion, and then they have laid the stamp of their own transforming genius upon it."[11]

The so-called transforming genius of the Japanese people, however, had some serious drawbacks, too. In the main, it worked better with tangible material things and the external aspects of foreign culture and religion, but it was far more difficult for it to cope with thoughts, ideas, and religious beliefs from abroad. For example, within one century or so after the introduction of Buddhism, the Japanese people learned and mastered the intricacies of Buddhist art, architecture, and rituals. But it is not likely that many understood, or even paid attention to, the profound meaning of the Buddhist doctrines. To be sure, a large number of Buddhist scriptures was introduced, and the government established bureaus for copying these scriptures. The court asked the clergy to recite appropriate scriptures for practical, mundane benefits in the same manner in which the native Shinto liturgical prayers (*Norito*) were recited to bring rain, relief from pestilence, safe childbirth, recovery from illness, and good fortune. And in return for these services, large estates were donated to Buddhist temples, and the clergy were showered with honors and favors by the court. But rarely were questions raised as to the meaning of the Buddha's teaching, except in a very general sense. To most people in Japan, copying the scriptures was in itself a meritorious act, and reciting them effectuated their magical potency. Therefore, it was not only unnecessary but it was better not to translate the scriptures into the Japanese language.[12] There

---

[11] *The Pilgrimage of Buddhism and A Buddhist Pilgrimage* (New York: Macmillan Co., 1928), p. 457.

[12] Hajime Nakamura notes that Kokan Shiren (d. 1346) proudly boasted that "in our country, there is no attempt to translate [Chinese versions of Buddhist scriptures]" (*The Ways of Thinking of Eastern Peoples* [Tokyo, 1960], p. 463).

were, of course, some able Japanese monks who had studied Buddhist doctrines in China, but they constituted a tiny minority, numerically speaking. Also, we are told that Prince Shōtoku (573-621) promoted Buddhist learning by giving erudite lectures on the important Buddhist scriptures, although many scholars tend to feel that the account of Prince Shōtoku's Buddhist activities was greatly embroidered upon in pious legends.

At any rate, the development of Japanese Buddhism between the sixth and eighth centuries exemplified some of the common characteristics of the culturally oriented Buddhist tradition which we mentioned earlier, such as (1) preoccupation with the particular rather than the universal dimensions of religion, (2) accommodation of indigenous religious beliefs and practices, and (3) alliance with local cultural, social, and political structures. In this situation, the historic Buddhist tradition, which had been greatly transformed in China, underwent further transmutation in Japan. Thus, while the Chinese Buddhists had shifted the emphasis in Buddhism from Nirvana to the phenomenal world, the Japanese shifted it again to the more immediate and concrete world of the Japanese people. In China, the goal of Buddhism was directed toward universal salvation rather than individual enlightenment; in Japan, the objective of official Buddhism was primarily the protection of the state. The Chinese Buddhists developed a philosophical synthesis, blending the Buddhist and Chinese philosophical heritages, and stressed the importance of pietism and practical insight. But Japanese Buddhists paid little attention to philosophical understanding and religious discipline; to them, "terms of Indian metaphysics became a kind of fashionable jargon, Buddhist rites a spectacle . . . religion became an art and art a religion."[13] Even religious authority, which shifted from the monastics in India to the laymen in China, came to be sought in the charismatic qualities of special men and women in Japan—diviners, healers, magicians, ascetics, and shamans.

It must be stated, however, that the emergence of the Buddhist tradition in Japan does not imply that the normativeness of the canonical writings and of the historic Buddhist tradition was questioned or ignored by Japanese Buddhism. Rather, the Japanese Buddhists attempted to interpret and appropriate the historic tradition of Buddhism in terms of their particular religious heritage as well as their own concrete experiences, and in this process a new form of Buddhist tradition that is more directly relevant to the Japanese world of mean-

13 This statement, ascribed to George B. Sansom, is quoted in Langdon Warner, *The Enduring Art of Japan* (Cambridge, Mass.: Harvard University Press, 1952), p. 32.

ing came into existence. At the expense of oversimplification, I would like to depict two main threads that run through the colorful tapestry of Japanese Buddhism. The first is that of "national" Buddhism, which tends to depend on, ally with, and accept the control of the ruling regime. This trend is represented by Prince Shōtoku (573-621) who, as the regent under his aunt the Empress Suiko (reigned 592-628), envisaged the establishment of Buddhism as the religion of the throne and the empire. The second is the thread of "folk" Buddhism, which tends to ally itself with the shamanistic folk religion and to present Buddhism as a simple gospel of salvation and a religion of compassion for the oppressed and downtrodden. This trend is represented by the eighth-century saint, Gyōgi (670-749), the shamanistic Buddhist *par excellence*, who was appointed an archbishop at the time when the great Buddha statue was constructed at Nara.

What is significant from our point of view is that both Prince Shō-toku and Gyōgi are not only important historic persons but also par-adigmatic figures. That is to say, in their respective roles both Shōtoku and Gyōgi were "stereotyped," to use Arthur F. Wright's expression, and as such their personalities and careers have been interpreted by the "tradition" as embodiments of attributes and qualities which later Japanese Buddhists admired and idealized.[14] Once these men were "stereotyped," pious legends and popular literature further glorified them, so that the various attributes of Buddhas and Bodhisattvas as well as the virtues of King Aśoka and of an ideal Buddhist layman, Yuima (Vimalakīrti), were incorporated into the sacred memories of Prince Shōtoku and Saint Gyōgi.[15] In the tradition of Japanese Bud-dhism, what Shōtoku and Gyōgi actually did historically matters little. The important thing is that they provided models for Japanese Bud-dhism to the extent that should some historical evidence not agree with the pious legends, it is dismissed as inadequate or irrelevant. Even the most astute contemporary Buddhist scholars in Japan seem to make every effort to place Prince Shōtoku and Gyōgi in the main-stream of Japanese Buddhism by explaining away some apparent in-consistencies between legend and historical evidence.[16] No wonder

[14] "Sui Yang-Ti: Personality and Stereotype," in A. F. Wright, ed., *The Confucian Persuasion* (Stanford, Calif.: Stanford University Press, 1960), p. 47.

[15] Cf. Ichirō Hori, *Waga-kuni Minkan-shinkō-shi no Kenkyū* (Tokyo: Sōgensha, 1955), 1:208-222.

[16] One of the ablest works in this respect is Kenkō Futaba, *Kodai-Bukkyō-Shisō-shi Kenkyū* (Kyoto: Nagata Bunshōdō, 1962). Rejecting the notion of a "national Bud-dhism," Futaba calls the early Buddhism in Japan the "Ritsuryō Buddhism," which implies a Buddhism under the control of laws instituted by the Imperial Rescript (*Ri-tsuryō*). Then he argues that "Prince Shōtoku, standing on the true ground of Buddhism,

various Buddhist leaders after the time of Shōtoku and Gyōgi invoked the examples of either one or both of them in order to authenticate new movements or new interpretations. For example, when Saichō (Dengyō Daishi, 767-822) tried to establish the Tendai (T'ien T'ai) monastic center at Mount Hi'ei, he called it the "chief seat of religion for ensuring the safety of the nation" (*chingo kokka no dōjō*). It is noteworthy that Saichō considered himself the spiritual heir of Prince Shōtoku.[17] On the other hand, Kūkai (Kōbō Daishi, 774-835), the transmitter of the Shingon (Chên-yen) system in Japan, seems to have followed in the footsteps of Gyōgi in promoting social and philanthropic works throughout the country, although he, too, regarded the aim of his religion as the protection of the nation.

Meanwhile, the establishment of the feudal regime (*Bakufu*) in the thirteenth century brought about social, political, and cultural changes in Japan. The new social climate also inspired new types of Buddhist schools, such as the Pure Land School founded by Hōnen (1133-1212), the True Pure Land School founded by Shinran (1173-1262), the Nichiren School founded by Nichiren (1222-1282), the Rinzai Zen School transmitted by Eisai (1141-1215), and the Sōtō Zen School systematized by Dōgen (1200-1253). Some of the leaders of the new Buddhist movements stressed personal experience rather than

---

advocated the realization of selflessness and the subjective universality of human nature, and made efforts for the realization of individual equality. Since these concepts had been understood neither by the Emperor nor by the social strata which controlled the *Ritsuryō* State, the Prince's Buddhism could not have served as the origin of *Ritsuryō* Buddhism, but on the contrary, became the source of *Anti-Ritsuryō* Buddhism" (p. 11, English Summary). Futaba further argues that Gyōgi followed Shōtoku's tradition of *Anti-Ritsuryō* Buddhism, and that "possessing a universal missionary spirit, his movement marked the birth of a free society based on the spirit of Buddhism. . . . The universality of Buddhist teaching can only be realized through individual conversion and the resultant transformation of the personality. The tradition of *Anti-Ritsuryō* Buddhism, which originated with Prince Shōtoku and was formulated by Gyōgi, firmly established itself by the medieval period, and led to the adoption of true Buddhism" (p. 15). In taking this line of thought, Futaba resorts to the view that Gyōgi's "opposition to the *Ritsuryō* State was relentless as long as the latter prevented him from exercising the true Buddhist ideals, but this does not mean that his aim was to start an anti-State movement. It is wrong to assume that, because he was appointed archbishop by the *Ritsuryō* State after his campaign to raise funds for the casting of the bronze statue of the great Buddha, he lost the integrity of the Buddhist faith. . . . Since nothing concerning his Great Buddha campaign appears in any of his chronological biographies . . . it would appear that the campaign was just a temporary duty that Gyōgi rendered the State" (p. 14). This line of exegesis is not altogether convincing, partly because Futaba does not differentiate the historical figures, stereotypes, and popular legends regarding Shōtoku and Gyōgi.

[17] Once Saichō paid a visit to the Shrine of Prince Shōtoku at the Shitennō-ji and offered a poem in which he affirmed his devotion to the Prince and asked the spirit of the Prince to protect him and assist his religious activities. Cf. *Gendai Bukkyō Kōza*, vol. 5: *Seiten Kōsō Hen* (Tokyo: Kadokawa Shoten, 1955), p. 92.

traditional authority; piety and intuition rather than rituals and scriptures; and salvation or enlightenment rather than disciplines and learning. In so doing they instilled new energy and spirit into the old Buddhist tradition in Japan.[18] Ironically, however, these men soon became "stereotyped," much as Prince Shōtoku, Saint Gyōgi, Saichō, and Kūkai had been earlier. Inevitably, the new Buddhist schools developed their own traditions with their own forms of rituals, orders, and ecclesiastical systems. Moreover, these new schools accepted the writings of their founders as *de facto* sacred books, so that Hōnen's *Senjaku Hongan Nembutsu-shū* (Collection of Passages on the Original Vow of Amida in Which the Recitation of Amida's Name is Chosen Above All Ways of Achieving Rebirth), Shinran's *Tanni-shō* (Notes Lamenting Differences) and *Kyōgyō Shinshō* (Testimony for the True Teaching, Practice, and Faith), Nichiren's *Kaimoku-shō* (The Eye-Opener) and Dōgen's *Shōbō-genzō* (Treasury of Knowledge Regarding the True Dharma), for example, have canonical authority for their respective followers. Many of the new Buddhist schools competed with the old schools in offering magical incantations and funeral rites for financial returns, and some of them even developed relic worship. The so-called Nichiren's tooth, preserved at the Daiseki-ji, near Mount Fuji, is a case in point. This relic was one of the sacred objects of the Nichiren Shō sect historically, and it is also venerated by the Sōka Gakkai in our time.

A further change took place in the Buddhist tradition in Japan during the seventeenth century when the Tokugawa shogunate incorporated Buddhist institutions into its political framework. With the prohibition of Catholicism, the Tokugawa regime ordered every Japanese household to affiliate with specific Buddhist temples, thus creating a "parochial system" (*danka seido*) hitherto unknown in the history of Japanese Buddhism. Government patronage, and the financial security that comes with it, enabled Buddhist schools to develop gigantic ecclesiastical superstructures, but they were robbed of nearly all spiritual freedom, influence, and initiative. While Buddhism left conspicuous imprints on poetry, literature, art, and other areas of aesthetics, the intellectual leadership during the Tokugawa period was in the hands of Neo-Confucian and Shinto (or "national learning") scholars who were, for the most part, critical of Buddhism both on philosophical and practical grounds. There were some able Buddhist thinkers who

---

[18] Cf. Masaharu Anesaki, *History of Japanese Religion* (London: Kegan Paul, Trench, Trubner & Co., 1930), p. 168.

tried to reform and rejuvenate Buddhism from within intellectually and spiritually, but their impact was almost negligible.[19]

The significance of Buddhism during the Tokugawa period, that is, from the beginning of the seventeenth century to the mid-nineteenth century, was that it was not only an important arm of the feudal regime; it was also an effective framework for family and social cohesion. Every family and every community as well as numerous professional and devotional associations throughout the country depended on Buddhist temples, which took care of registrations regarding birth, marriage, and divorce, and also conducted funerals, memorial services, and various communal festivities and celebrations. To put it another way, Tokugawa society was based on two parallel systems of hierarchy—one sociopolitical and the other ecclesiastical. This meant that every family was ultimately related to the shogunate through the neighborhood group, village or town, and the *daimyō* or the feudal lord on the one hand, and through the local temple, the main temple, and the Temple and Shrine Commissioner on the other. Among all the schools of Japanese Buddhism, the most effective hierarchy was developed by the True Pure Land School (Jōdo-Shin-shū), commonly known as the Shin-shū. This is the school which owes its origin to the thirteenth-century saint, Shinran, who rejected sacerdotalism, institutionalization of religion, and temporal power. Ironically, it was Shinran's own descendants who established a hierarchical system based on hereditary principles. During the sixteenth century the Shin School developed into a semifeudal power, stronger than many of the *daimyō*. The Tokugawa shogunate maneuvered to divide the Shin School into two main divisions, namely, the Jōdo-Shin-Shū Honganji-ha and Shin-shū Ōtani-ha, commonly referred to as the Western and Eastern Honganji sects, respectively.[20] In both, the hereditary principle was applied not only to the patriarchs but also to the clergy of all local temples, because the Shin School from the beginning had adopted the system of married clergy. In the hierarchical structure of the Shin School, the status of every clergyman from the patriarch to the humble priest in the countryside was clearly defined, and the relationship between the clergy and the parishioners (*danka* or "constituent households") was minutely regulated by ecclesiastical disciplines and customs.[21]

[19] For material about a very interesting but little-known Buddhist thinker, see Hajime Nakamura, "Suzuki Shōsan no Shūkyō-kaikakuteki Seishin" in *Gendai Bukkyō Meicho Zenshū*, ed. H. Nakamura, F. Masutani, and J. M. Kitagawa (Tokyo: Ryūbun-kan, 1960), 8:245-345. It is important to note that Suzuki Shōsan (1579-1655), a warrior turned Buddhist priest, emphasized the religious bases of various secular professions.

[20] There are also some minor subdivisions of the Shin School, such as the Takada-ha, Kōsei-ha, and Bukkōji-ha, etc.

[21] Cf. Kiyomi Morioka, *Shin-shū Kyōdan to Iye-seido* (Tokyo: Sogen-sha, 1962).

212

As far as the majority of the people was concerned (here we must bear in mind that every family was considered Buddhist, at least nominally, during the Tokugawa period), they had little understanding of the profound doctrines of Buddhism. For example, to them the *dharma* as the cosmic law that sustains the universe meant nothing. They had only vague notions about the Buddha. Actually, the term *hotoke* (Buddha) was used commonly to refer to every deceased person.[22] While they accepted the existence of the Pure Land and of hell, the realms beyond this world did not deeply concern them. The only world which was really real to them was this world and the society in which they lived. Probably, they believed in some kind of law of retribution to the effect that good deeds will bring good results and evil deeds lead to evil results. One thing they were absolutely certain of was the gentle tyranny of "tradition" (*dentō*), an amorphous monster that enslaved them. They could not rebel against it, and they knew that it would remain intact long after they had disappeared from this earth. They learned taboos and social duties from religion so that they would not alienate "tradition." When their passions led them against it, the result was bound to be tragic. Even such a rationalist as Tominaga Nakamoto (1715-1746), who was critical of Buddhism, Confucianism, and Shinto, and who had a more independent spirit than many thinkers of his day, nevertheless taught the wisdom of respecting tradition as the "Way of Truth" (*makoto no michi*). Thus he stated: "Try to do your best in ordinary things which you are expected to do, consider today's work as the work of primary importance, keep your mind upright, take proper care of your behavior, be careful in speech, be respectful in manner and bearing, care for and honor parents if you have them, serve your master if you have one, educate your children if you have them."[23] After all, life in this floating world (*ukiyo*) was destined to be full of suffering and misery, but one could find beauty and serenity in the world of nature—in the cherry blossoms in the spring and in the autumn leaves—precisely because nature accepts the reality of transitoriness. Likewise, "those who have heard the voice of Buddha Amitabha" (*myōkō-nin*) accepted this life-as-it-is (*sono-mama*) as the Pure Land.[24]

[22] Hiroshi Takamine, *Kokugo ga sesshu-shitaru Bukkyo-bunka* (Osaka: Nihon Shuppansha, 1944), pp. 28-36.

[23] Cited in Kyōson Tsuchida, *Kokubangaku no Tetsugaku-teki kenkyū* (Tokyo: Daiichi-shobō, 1927), p. 149.

[24] D. T. Suzuki quotes the following utterances of a simple Amida devotee, Saiichi (1851-1933), in his *Mysticism: Christian and Buddhist* (New York: Harper & Bros., 1957):

This world (*sahaloka*) and the Pure Land—they are one; / Worlds as numberless as

In retrospect, it becomes evident that Buddhism during the Tokugawa period paid a high price for the favor and support given by the regime. Toward the end of the eighteenth century the spiritual bankruptcy of Buddhism became as apparent as the decline of the Tokugawa regime. By that time, the leaders of the Shinto revival joined the Neo-Confucian leaders in a campaign against the shogunate and against Buddhism. And when the Tokugawa regime finally collapsed and the imperial rule was restored shortly after the visit of Commodore Matthew Perry, Japanese Buddhism was confronted by a new situation for which it had been totally unprepared.

TRADITION VERSUS NEW CONDITIONS

The year 1868 marked the beginning of modern Japan under the nominal rule of the emperor, although in reality the destiny of the nation was in the hands of a small group of royalists who formulated government policies. The architects of modern Japan faced many problems. In the words of George B. Sansom: "Japan before 1868 was a loose federation of autonomous units, particularist in outlook, suspicious of their neighbors, and jealous of central authority. It was the task of the Meiji leaders to weld them into one nation."[25] In this situation, the architects of the Meiji regime, being superb realists, recognized that none of the traditional religions—Shinto, Confucianism, and Buddhism—could serve as the spiritual axis that would unite the nation. Thus, they decided on a new "non-religious" form of religion based on *kokutai* (literally, "national entity") with the throne as the sacred object.[26] This form of "non-religious" or "super-religious" religion was called State Shinto, and it lasted until the end of World War II. In order to create State Shinto, the government had to transform traditional Shinto, and this meant the rejection of the historic amalgamation of Shinto and Buddhism, known as the *Ryōbu-Shinto* (literally, "Two-sided Shinto"). It so happened that the government's measures to separate Buddhism from Shinto precipitated a popular anti-Buddhist movement (*haibutsu kishaku*) in various parts of Japan.

Understandably, the reaction of Buddhist leaders to the new conditions was marked by bewilderment and anxiety. Many Buddhists, who had taken for granted the power, prestige, and support given by

---

atoms, too, are mine. / "Namu-amida-butsu, Namu-amida-butsu!" [p. 191].

How dreadful! / This world known as *shaba* (*samsara*) / Is where we endlessly commit all kinds of karma. / How thankful! / All this is turned into [the work of] the Pure Land, / Unintermittently! [p. 196].

[25] *The Western World and Japan* (New York: Alfred A. Knopf, 1962), p. 364.

[26] Masao Maruyama, *Nihon no Shisō* (Tokyo, 1961), pp. 28-31.

the Tokugawa regime, were shocked by the policy of the Meiji government to eliminate Buddhism from the position of leadership, and they were deeply hurt by the popular anti-Buddhist movement. Besides, they were alarmed by many features of Western civilization, especially Christian evangelism, that began to infiltrate Japan with the tacit approval of the government. On the other hand, there were some enlightened Buddhist leaders who were determined to accept the challenge of the new situation. For example, Fukuda Gyōkai (1806-1888) publicly stated that he lamented the anti-Buddhist movement, "but not because temples have been destroyed. . . . It is not because we have lost our government stipend. We grieve before heaven and man that we have lost the Way of the greatest Good. In order to regain the lost Way, and for this reason only, priests should pray for the extension of *dharma*."[27] To Fukuda and others like him the anti-Buddhist movement was a blessing in disguise, for it would enable Japanese Buddhism to emancipate itself from entanglement with the particular social, cultural, and political features of Japan, so that the true *dharma* taught by Gautama Buddha could be presented to the people in Japan.

The enlightened Buddhist leaders were not afraid of the onslaught of Western civilization either. Rather, they sensed the need of appropriating Western philological and philosophical scholarship in order to broaden and enrich the Buddhist tradition in Japan. Realizing that Japanese Buddhists had depended solely on the Chinese translation of the Buddhist scriptures, some able Japanese Buddhist scholars were sent abroad to learn Sanskrit, Pali, and Tibetan. For example, as early as 1876, Nanjō Bunyū (d. 1927) of the East Honganji Sect was sent to Oxford to study under Max Müller.[28] Philological scholarship greatly stimulated modern Japanese Buddhist scholars' understanding of the Theravāda and Mahāyāna branches of Buddhism, as well as their reexamination of Japanese Buddhism itself. Equally significant were the efforts of Buddhist thinkers in coming to terms with Western philosophical systems. One of the pioneers of this endeavor was Kiyozawa Manshi (d. 1903) who synthesized Hegelianism and Amidaism. Many able thinkers followed Kiyozawa's footsteps. Probably the most influential among the modern Japanese philosophers is Nishida Kitarō (1870-1945), whose philosophy owed much to William James, Henri Bergson, German idealism, and Zen Buddhism. Inevitably, however, the assimilation of Western scholarship into Buddhological studies cre-

---

[27] Quoted in Hideo Kishimoto, comp., *Japanese Religion in the Meiji Era*, trans. John F. Howes (Tokyo: Obunsha, 1956), p. 126.

[28] It was Nanjō who published in 1883 *A Catalogue of the Chinese Translation of the Buddhist Tripitaka.*

ated an almost insurmountable chasm between the Buddhist intelligentsia and traditional, conservative Buddhists.

In a real sense, the enlightened Buddhists who evisaged a complete overhauling of Japanese Buddhism grossly underestimated the tenacity of the tradition. The idealists and reformers soon realized that they were outmaneuvered by the traditionalists who were determined to regain power and influence for Japanese Buddhism. Meanwhile, the Meiji government began to woo the conservative Buddhist leaders, whose influence could not be discounted, especially in the rural areas, to support various policies of the government. Many Buddhist leaders, on their part, allied themselves with Shinto and Confucian leaders in an all-out campaign against Christianity.[29] From the latter part of the 1880s, a strong nationalist reaction developed in Japan with the enthusiastic cooperation of Buddhist ecclesiastics. Japan's victory in the Sino-Japanese War (1894-1895) and in the Russo-Japanese War (1904-1905) and her annexation of Korea (1910) and participation in World War I resulted in an unholy alliance of the military, financial, and political cliques which eventually led Japan toward aggressive wars in Manchuria and China, and finally to World War II. During the fifty years between the Sino-Japanese War and World War II all religions in Japan were gradually emasculated by the government, which tolerated no criticism or interference from any religion. For example, in 1937, the Chinese Buddhist Association appealed to Japanese Buddhists, calling on them in the name of Buddhism to urge the Japanese government to use diplomatic instead of military methods in Sino-Japanese relations.[30] But the Japanese government would have considered such an act, if taken, one of political interference quite unbecoming for Buddhists. On the other hand, the Japanese government expected the representatives of all religious bodies to visit the front and pray for the victory of Japan.

This does not mean, however, that all religions in Japan succumbed completely to the cause of nationalism, militarism, and imperialism during the war period. There were some individuals who tried to be true to their religious convictions despite persecutions and imprisonment. But for the most part, religious bodies in Japan failed to resist the pressure to conform to the whims of the entrenched powers. As for Buddhism, despite the effort of modern reformers, it carried over many of the negative qualities of the historic Japanese Buddhist tra-

[29] Buddhists called the anti-Christian campaign *haja kensei* (literally, "refutation of evil religion and the exaltation of righteous teaching").

[30] Clarence H. Hamilton, "Buddhism," in *China*, ed. H. F. MacNair (Berkeley: University of California Press, 1946), p. 299.

dition. According to Watanabe Shōkō, a leading contemporary Buddhist thinker, these qualities were: (1) subservience to the political authority and the spirit of nationalism; (2) prevalence of magical incantations and other superstitious beliefs and practices; (3) preoccupation with funeral rites and memorial services for the dead at the expense of providing spiritual guidance for the living; (4) lack of doctrinal integrity that leads to easy compromise with other religions and ideologies; and (5) stress on formalism without equal stress on inner spiritual discipline.[31] To be sure, scholars and the Buddhist intelligentsia disdained these features of Buddhism, but they were removed from practical ecclesiastical affairs, so that they made amazingly little impact on the total life of Buddhists. Generally speaking, a modern Japanese Buddhist had to choose either to become intellectual or pious. He found it difficult to be both simultaneously.

To make matters more complex, Buddhism in Japan was destined to encounter another new condition after the end of World War II. Although it is as yet too early to discern the ethos and characteristics of contemporary Buddhism in Japan, we might indicate in a brief manner some of the more obvious factors and trends. Needless to say, the experience of a prolonged war, Japan's defeat, and the occupation by the Allied Forces have left their marks on Japanese Buddhism. Many temples were destroyed and thousands of potential leaders, both clerical and lay, died during the war. The principle of religious liberty put into effect during the occupation was a mixed blessing to Japanese Buddhism, for the paternalistic hierarchical systems of various Buddhist schools were discarded and the residual rights and privileges of historic temples were lost. Also, the land reform program instituted under the occupation took away from many temples the revenues which had been important sources of their income. Furthermore, industrialization and urbanization broke down the traditional parish system. Moreover, many impatient youths left the Buddhist fold and joined the camps of socialism, communism, or one of the so-called new religions.

The postwar condition, on the other hand, has released some energy hitherto buried and forgotten in the Buddhist tradition in Japan. Never in the history of Japanese Buddhism have laymen and lay women taken such an active part in Buddhist affairs as they do today. Not only have many groups of the laity been organized for retreats for study and for fellowship, but also cooperation between the clergy and laity has been achieved through various activities of a denomina-

[31] Shōkō Watanabe, *Nihon no Bukkyo* (Tokyo: Iwanami Shoten, 1958), pp. 69-139.

tional and interdenominational nature. Even the chasm between the Buddhist intelligentsia and conservative devoteees has been overcome to some extent. Besides, a number of responsible Buddhist leaders have become deeply concerned over the relevance of Buddhism in social, economic, political, and cultural issues. Undoubtedly, the spiritual vitality of Buddhism has been greatly aided by the dedicated efforts of scholars in the fields of philological, historical, philosophical, and comparative studies, combining modern Western and traditional Japanese methodologies. Some of the Japanese Buddhologists have made important contributions to international scholarship too. By far the most significant characteristic of contemporary Japanese Buddhism is, however, its self-conscious awareness of being an integral part of worldwide Buddhism. In sharp contrast to the traditional Japanese Buddhists' indifference and ignorance regarding the Buddhist situation in the Theravāda and other Mahāyāna countries, Japanese Buddhists today have developed a genuine kinship and respect for Buddhists in other lands.

The growing realization of the universal character of Buddhism has, of course, serious implications for the future of Buddhism not only in Japan but in other Buddhist countries as well. Searching questions have already been raised as to what is the norm of Buddhism and where its normativeness is to be located. Fortunately or unfortunately, the sacred scriptures have never provided the basis for standard beliefs in Buddhism as they have in Judaism, Christianity, and Islam. It seems to be just as difficult for Buddhists to reconstruct the life and teaching of Gautama Buddha as it is for Christians to reconstruct the historical Jesus. Besides, the historic division of the Theravāda and Mahāyāna branches cuts deep into the history of Buddhism. Nevertheless, it is the pious hope of Buddhists to attain or regain the unity of Buddhism. Accepting the universal character of Buddhism, however, Buddhists have yet to cope with the meaning of the particular tradition in various parts of the world. For example, how should Japanese Buddhists square the discrepancy between the "universal Buddhist tradition," however it may be understood, and the historic experience of Japanese Buddhism? There are some who are persuaded that the peculiarities and deviations of Japanese Buddhism should be sacrificed in favor of achieving a greater unity of the universal brotherhood of Buddhists. There are others who are more concerned with the responsibility of Buddhism toward the particular needs of people in Japan. They cite the phenomenal growth of the new religions as a sign of the spiritual vacuum that has not been filled by the gospel of Buddha. Basically, the question for worldwide Buddhism today is how to harmonize the various facets of Buddhism—the memory of Gautama Buddha, the authority of the canonical writings, the nebulous but real power of tradition, and the living experience of men and women in their particular cultural and historic situations.

As for the Buddhists in Japan, they are facing today the problem of their own identity in a way they have never faced before. Historically, Japanese Buddhists never raised questions about the meaning of Japanese Buddhism as such. But today, they realize that they are both Japanese and Buddhists simultaneously. They are also aware that being Japanese and being Buddhist are two different components in their own world of meaning. It reminds us of the South Slav peasant in Joseph Conrad's story. The peasant intends to go to America, but is cast away in a Kentish village as the only survivor of the wreck of his ship. The villagers fear and mistrust the strangeness of the man, and ill-treat him, except for a plain girl who takes pity on him, feeds him, and finally marries him. "But, she, too, when, in fever, he reverts to his native language, is seized with a fear of his strangeness, snatches up their child and abandons him."[32] This man, be it noted, at least knew his original identity. Unlike this South Slav peasant, the Japanese Buddhist today is not altogether certain whether he is a Japanese who happens to be a Buddhist, or whether he is a Buddhist who happens to be living in Japan. He has an uncomfortable feeling that "in fever" he might revert to his own real identity. And yet, he is also a bit afraid of finding out who he really is!

[32] Bertrand Russell, "Joseph Conrad," *The Listener* (London), 17 September 1953, p. 463.

13. Buddhist Translation in Japan

The Development of Buddhist Thought as Reflected in Translations of Buddhist Writings in Japanese

ONE OF THE significant characteristics of Japanese historical writings is the smooth transition from myth to history. Actually, very little is known about the religious and cultural situation in Japan prior to the third century A.D. We do know, however, that the Japanese islands were inhabited by different ethnic groups from various parts of the Asian continent. There is no conclusive theory as to how these different groups became assimilated or how the Japanese language became the common tongue for peoples of different backgrounds. Suffice it to say that the early Japanese had no written script, and their language must have undergone considerable change over a period of time. For example, as late as the eighth century A.D., Japanese seems to have used eight vowels instead of the present five (*a, i, u, e, o*).[1]

Sometime around the third century A.D., Japan developed a loosely organized confederation of autonomous clans, chief among them being the so-called "Tennō" (imperial) clan. By the end of the third century, the imperial clan asserted political and religious authority over other clans. The imperial authority was based in part on the claim of solar ancestry for the imperial clan, and the increasing prestige of the throne helped to unify the religious cults and practices of the nation. Later, the religious form thus developed came to be called Shinto or "the way of *kami* [gods]."[2] Meanwhile, the historical situation in the fourth and fifth centuries brought Japan close to the principalities on the Korean peninsula, and Korean as well as Chinese immigrants who settled in Japan brought with them many aspects of Sino-Korean culture, including the Chinese literary tradition.

The introduction of a written script marked a revolutionary change in the cultural history of Japan, for Japanese and Chinese were two entirely different languages. Japanese is a polysyllabic language, composed of simple sounds, such as *a, ka, sa, ta, na*, with three parts of speech—nouns, verbs, and particles. Usually, modifying expressions

[1] Izui Hisanosuke, "The Vocal System and Vocal Interchanges of Eighth-Century Japanese," in *Miscellanea Kiotiensia* (Kyoto, 1956), pp. 989-1020.

[2] Cf. Joseph M. Kitagawa, "Shinto," *Encyclopaedia Britannica*, 1968 ed., 20:517-521.

precede the expressions modified, with the verb at the end of a speech unit. The unique characteristics of Japanese include its use of certain speech styles and status forms as evidenced by the existence of numerous honorific expressions. On the other hand, Chinese usually consists of monosyllabic meaning units (the *tzu*, which is usually translated as "word") having a complicated system of tones. Although not grammatical in the Western sense, Chinese follows the word order of adjective-noun, verb-object, and subject-predicate. The use of compounding enables Chinese to express a wide range of ideas and meanings. When the Japanese first confronted the task of coping with Chinese, they developed a method by which Chinese written characters were matched to Japanese words, and through this hybrid linguistic device they attempted to learn lofty Chinese ideas, e.g., Confucian ethics, Taoist mysticism and Ying-Yang astrology. Confucianism helped to define social and interhuman relationships while the Chinese notion of ancestor worship strengthened the native Japanese religious cults. These and other Chinese and Korean ideas have become important threads in the fabric of Japanese culture.

Through Korea and China, Buddhism was also introduced to Japan. No doubt Buddhism had been known among Korean and Chinese immigrants, but the official introduction of Buddhism did not take place until A.D. 552 (or 538 according to some scholars) when the King of Paekche in Korea presented to the Japanese court an image of Buddha, copies of scriptures, and ceremonial vessels. In his letter, the King stated: "This teaching is the most excellent among all doctrines, but it is difficult to explain and hard to comprehend." The subsequent development of Buddhism in Japan amply demonstrated the difficulties involved in the task of understanding the teaching of Buddha. At any rate, after a period of initial resistance, the new religion became firmly established on Japanese soil.

Ethos of Japanese Buddhism

The rapid growth of Buddhism in Japan owed much to the initiative of Prince Shōtoku (573-621) who was the regent under his aunt, the Empress Suiko (592-628). In the Seventeen-Article Constitution promulgated by Shōtoku, we read: "Sincerely revere the Three Treasures (Buddhism). The Three Treasurers, namely Buddha, the Law, and the Buddhist Community, are the final refuge of the four generated beings, and are the supreme objects of faith in all countries" (Article II). Not only did Shōtoku build temples and monasteries, but he actively promoted Buddhist learning by giving lectures on important Buddhist *sūtras* (scriptures).

In retrospect, it becomes evident that the ethos of Japanese Buddhism was greatly shaped by the example of Prince Shōtoku. Shōtoku, by way of illustration, in elevating Buddhism to the status of a *de facto* national religion, did in no way belittle the importance of other systems, especially Shinto. What he had in mind was a sort of division of labor among various systems—Shinto, Buddhism, and Confucianism—which together were to serve as the spiritual and moral foundations of a centralized government under the imperial authority. Secondly, from the time of Shōtoku, Japanese Buddhism took it for granted that its task was to serve the political interests of the imperial and aristocratic families. Understandbly, one of the most venerated scriptures was *Konkō-myō-saishō-ō-gyō* or the "Sutra of the Sovereign Kings of the Golden Light Ray," which stressed the Buddhist doctrine of the divine kingship. Thirdly, because of the preoccupation on the part of Buddhist leaders with the upper strata of society, the masses in Japan had to depend on pre-Buddhist, shamanistic religious leaders. Fourthly, the emphasis in the religious life of the laymen of the period is suggested by Shōtoku's preferences for the *Lotus Sutra* that had the motif of universal salvation; the *Yuima-Gyō*, the discourses of Yuima (Vimalakīrti), a Buddhist layman; and the *Shōman-Gyō*, portraying the ideal of Buddhist womanhood. (Indeed, it was Shōtoku's intention to realize Buddhist ideals in secular life.) Fifthly, Shōtoku's approach to Buddhist scriptures, namely reading the Chinese texts without translating them into Japanese and giving commentaries on them, established the pattern of Japanese scholarship on Buddhism. "Although Buddhism was so widely propagated among the people," says Professor Nakamura, "its scriptures *were never translated* into the Japanese language." In fact, Kokan Shiren (d. 1346) proudly boasted that "in our country, there is no attempt to translate [Chinese versions of Buddhist scriptures]."[3] In this situation, we may rightly ask whether Japanese Buddhists really understood Buddhism or not. With this question in mind, let us see how Buddhism developed historically in Japan.

Buddhism in Japanese History

Shortly after the time of Prince Shōtoku, the capital was established in Nara, which quickly became the cultural, religious, and political center of the nation. During the eighth century, known as the Nara period, six Chinese Buddhist schools were introduced to Japan. They were: the Kusha (Chü-she or Abhidharmakosa), Jōjitsu (Ch'eng-shih or Satyasiddhi), Hossō (Fa-shing or Yogācāra), Sanron (San-lun or Mādhyamika), Kegon (Hua-yen or Avatamsaka), and Ritsu (Lu or

[3] Nakamura Hajime, *The Ways of Thinking of Eastern Peoples* (Tokyo, 1960), p. 463.

Vinaya) schools.[4] These schools were not sects in the strict sense but were different traditions based on certain scriptures and practices, and some Buddhists felt free to study more than one system. During the Nara period, an increasing number of Buddhist institutions were established, and these temples and monasteries acquired lands and properties in various parts of Japan. Inevitably, Buddhist ecclesiastics became deeply involved in the political affairs of the nation.

The impressive growth of Buddhism during the eighth century, however, was confined to the upper strata of society. While courtiers and high ecclesiastics rode by making a splash in their elegant robes, the masses had neither enough to eat nor the means to clothe themselves. To them, the lofty teachings of the Indian and Chinese sages had little meaning. Far more real to them were the traditional spirits and gods (*kami*) of field and fen and crossroad and of hearth and mattock.[5] It is no wonder shamanic-diviners, healers, and sorcerers continued to exert strong influence in the countryside. In the course of time, these shamanic-diviners came to adopt certain features of Buddhism. The so-called *ubasoku* (*upasaka*,, ascetics), who were unauthorized and unordained "Buddhist" leaders, in this way came into existence. Most of them had no knowledge of Buddhist scriptures nor did they follow Buddhist precepts. Being the spiritual descendants of the pre-Buddhist shamanic-diviners, these *ubasoku* had no use for the orthodox schools of Buddhism. Instead, they advocated the path of the *hijiri* (holy man) outside the framework of Buddhist orthodoxy.[6] The government and the ecclesiastical leaders made serious efforts to control the activities of these *ubasoku*, but with little success. Indeed, it is a matter of great significance that some of the prominent Buddhist leaders in Japan, such as Gyōgi, Kōbō Daishi, and the masters of the Pure Land schools, came out of the tradition of the *ubasoku*. Even today, the Shugen-dō, or the order of the mountain priesthood, still maintains this tradition.

Literary Developments in the Nara Period

In a real sense, the Nara period was also a landmark in the literary history of Japan. The official histories, the *Kojiki* (The Ancient Matters), *Nihongi* (The Chronicle of Japan), *Shoku-Nihongi* (The Further

---

[4] On these schools, see Takakusu Junjirō, *The Essentials of Buddhist Philosophy* (Honolulu, 1947).

[5] Cf. Langdon Warner, *The Enduring Art of Japan* (Cambridge, 1952), chap. 1, "Early Buddhism."

[6] Cf. Hori Ichirō, "On the Concept of Hijiri (Holy-Man)," *Numen* 5, nos. 2-3 (April-September 1958), p. 131.

Chronicle of Japan), as well as the *Manyōshū*, an anthology of over 4,500 poems, were compiled during this period by utilizing Chinese script. The court also encouraged the introduction of an increasing number of Buddhist scriptures from China and Korea, for it was widely held that reciting and copying Buddhist scriptures would bring about temporal benefits such as health, wealth, and longevity. Thus, as early as 651, the Emperor Kōtoku invited over 2,100 monks and nuns to recite sutras, and in 673 the Emporer Temmu sponsored a project for copying the *Tripitaka* (Buddhist scriptures). We are told that during the Nara period special bureaus of copyists were established; one office was dedicated to the copying of the Lotus Sutra and the Sutra of the Golden Light exclusively. Five thousand and forty eight fascicles of Buddhist scriptures were kept by one temple known as Tōshōdaiji in 758.[7] The abundance of scriptures, however, did not imply that those who copied or recited them understood Buddhism. There is much truth in Professor Nakamura's observation that they were, "so hard pressed merely in learning to use Chinese ideographs that they did not get to the point of understanding the thought and assimilating the thought expressed therein."[8]

The Heian Period

Toward the end of the eighth century, the capital was moved from Nara to the present Kyoto, where the Fujiwara family dominated the political scene between the ninth and twelfth centuries although the throne maintained nominal authority. This is known as the Heian period. Early in the ninth century, two new schools of Buddhism were introduced from China. The first was Tendai (T'ien T'ai in Chinese) transmitted by Saichō, also known as Dengyō Daishi (d. 822), while the second was Shingon (Chên-yen in Chinese) transmitted by Kūkai, also known as Kōbō Daishi (d. 835). Both of them taught lofty philosophy as well as the magical incantations of the Esoteric (Tantric) tradition of Buddhism, and both were credited with the theoretical formulation of Ryōbu ("Two-sided") Shinto, a pattern of coexistence or amalgamation between Shinto and Buddhism. It is to be noted that the scheme of Ryōbu Shinto lasted until the nineteenth century. Kūkai is also known as the inventor of the *hirakana* (*i, ro, ha, ni, ho, he, to* . . .) alphabet poem which is a translation of a Chinese poem that can be traced back to a Sanskrit original.[9]

[7] Ui Hakujū, *Bukkyō Keiten-shi* (A Historical Study of Buddhist Scriptures) (Tokyo, 1957), p. 195.

[8] Nakamura, *Eastern Peoples*, p. 471.

[9] Ibid., p. 417.

The impact of Buddhism during the Heian period was such that Buddhist ideas penetrated into literary works, e.g., the *Ise-monogatari*, *Taketori-monogatari*, *Tosa Nikki*, and *Genji-monogatari* (The Tale of Genji). It was also a time when religion became an art and art a religion, at least among the aristocrats. "Certainly," says Warner, "what most occupied the thoughts of those courtiers were ceremonies, costumes, elegant pastimes like verse-making, and even love-making conducted according to rules."[10] In such an atmosphere Indian metaphysics and Buddhist doctrines gave way to a simple, human desire, as far as the aristocrats were concerned, for a happy rebirth in the Land of Bliss, the Pure Land of the Buddha Amida (*Amitābha*, "Infinite Light," or *Amitāyus*, "Infinite Life"). On the other hand, the masses, destined to go through a life of hardship and suffering, had no such optimistic outlook toward the hereafter. They only hoped that their sufferings in hell would be lessened by the mercy of the Jizō (Bodhisattva Kṣitigarbha).

The Kamakura Period

The establishment of the feudal regime (*Bakufu*) in Kamakura in the thirteenth century coincided with these new Buddhist movements. The Rinzai school of Zen (Ch'an) was established by Eisai (d. 1215), and the Sōtō school of Zen was introduced by Dōgen (d. 1253). Hōnen (d. 1212) and Shinran (d. 1262) propagated the Pure Land doctrine, which was a synthesis of belief in Amida and in Jizō. Nichiren (d. 1282), a patriotic prophet, advocated a pietistic movement based on the Lotus Sutra. It is commonly held that indigenous "Japanese Buddhism" developed during the Kamakura period (1192-1333). For example, unlike previous Buddhists who wrote books in Chinese, Buddhist leaders of this period started writing their thoughts in the Japanese language. In doing so, however, Dōgen, Shinran, and others, who were supposedly able to read Chinese texts, willfully "misinterpreted" or "deviated" from the original meaning of the Chinese.[11] It

---

(The Japanese version)
Although fragrant in hue, (blossoms) are scattered. / For everyone, life is impermanent. / This morning I crossed the uttermost limit. / A shallow dream I will not dream, and I am not intoxicated.

(The Chinese poem)
Whatever is phenomenal is impermanent; / Their essential quality is appearance and disappearance; / When these appearances and disappearances come to repose, the tranquility is comfort.

[10] Warner, *Enduring Art*, p. 32.

[11] Nakamura, *Eastern Peoples*, p. 303, n. 9. Nakamura states: "Shinran's wilful misinterpretations were made in response to his own personal philosophical point of view."

is also to be noted that a peculiarly Japanese understanding of Buddhism is conspicuous in the literature of this period, e.g., in such works as the *Hōjōki*, *Tsurezure-gusa*, and *Heike-monogatari*.

The Kamakura period was followed by a warring-state period under the nominal rule of the Ashikaga feudal regime (1338-1573). The Ashikaga rulers depended heavily on Zen priests who then were engaged in all kinds of activities, from teaching the tea ceremony, painting and garden designing, to handling the intricacies of foreign trade. Cultural contacts with China were resumed, and Japan came under the fresh influence of Neo-Confucian philosophy and of ink painting of the South Sung style. The Ashikaga rulers were also instrumental in securing several editions of the *Tripitaka* (Buddhist Scriptures) from China and Korea. Ironically, it was during this period plagued by a succession of wars that such an elegant art form as the *Nō* drama was perfected. The tragic ethos of the time was reflected in the religious sphere as well, for powerful monasteries that were once sanctuaries of sacred training and learning then kept mercenaries and fought among themselves.

The Tokugawa Period

During the Tokugawa period (1600 to mid-nineteenth century) Buddhism was at a low ebb. The intellectual leadership passed on to Japanese Neo-Confucianists, and renewed interest in *Kokugaku* (national learning), the study of pre-Buddhist Japanese culture and religion, did not help the cause of Buddhism. To be sure, Buddhist institutions were well supported by the officials and the masses, but the Tokugawa regime considered itself as the *Religionspolizei* rather than the *Schützpatronat*, to use Max Weber's famous terms.[12] It is significant, however, that there were some outstanding Buddhist leaders during the Tokugawa period. For example, Tenkai (d. 1643) undertook the printing of the entire *Tripitaka* of 6,323 fascicles for the first time in the history of Japanese Buddhism. Although this project was not completed until 1648, it is commonly called the Tenkai edition of the *Tripitaka*. In 1669, Tetsugen (d. 1682) edited and printed the *Tripitaka*, with 6,956 fascicles; this is called the Tetsugen edition or Ōbaku edition. Also, Ninchō (d. 1711) and his disciples engaged in the first comparative textual research of Buddhist texts using the Korean (Kōrai) and the Chinese (Ming) editions of the *Tripitaka*.[13]

[12] *Gesammelte Aufsätze zur Religionssoziologie*, vol. 2: *Hinduismus und Buddhismus* (Tübingen, 1921), p. 288.
[13] Ui, *Bukkyō Keiten-shi*, pp. 199-200.

Japanese Buddhism in the Modern Period

In the summer of 1853, Commodore Matthew Perry, commander in chief of the East India Squadron, was sent by the United States government to negotiate a treaty of commerce with Japan. This date marked the beginning of the influence of the modern West on Japan and it was destined to change the course of Japanese history. With the decline of the Tokugawa feudal regime, imperial rule was restored. The new regime under the leadership of the Emperor Meiji attempted a precarious synthesis of the old and the new, the East and the West. The architects of new Japan tried to restore Shinto as the spiritual foundation of the nation, and for this reason they decreed a separation between Shinto and Buddhism, thus in effect destroying the age-old patterns of Shinto-Buddhist coexistence. In this situation, there arose a movement called *haibutsu kishaku* ("extermination of Buddhism"), that constituted a serious threat to established Buddhist institutions. At the same time, this movement reawakened thoughtful Buddhists.

Japanese Buddhism in the modern period received new insights from Western civilization directly and indirectly. Shimaji Mokurai (d. 1911), a priest of the West Honganji Sect, was sent to the West and India in 1873. Nanjō Bunyū (d. 1927) of the East Honganji Sect was sent to Oxford in 1873. There he studied Sanskrit under Friedrich Max Müller, and eventually published *A Catalogue of the Chinese Translation of the Buddhist Tripitaka* (1883), commonly referred to as "Nanjiō's Catalogue." Stimulated by the new interest in Buddhist scholarship, Shimada Bankon published in 1898 the *Shukusatsu Daizōkyō* (An Abridged *Tripitaka*) of 8,534 fascicles; this edition was reprinted in 1911 in Shanghai. In 1905, the *Manji Zōkyō* (the *Manji Tripitaka*) of 6,990 fascicles was published; this edition had the *kaeriten* or reading marks for Japanese readers of Chinese texts. In 1912, the *Dainihon Zoku Zōkyō*, consisting of 7,144 fascicles was published as a supplement to the *Manji Tripitaka*; this edition was also reprinted in 1923 in Shanghai. By far the most ambitious, and significant, from the scholarly point of view, undertaking was the publication of the *Taishō Tripitaka* (the Taishō edition of the Buddhist *Tripitaka* in Chinese), 100 volumes printed in 1932, under the editorship of Junjirō Takakusu. Takakusu also edited the *Nanden Daizōkyō* (Japanese translation of the Pali *Tripitaka* and Commentaries), in 60 volumes, and (with Mochizuki Shinkyō and Ōmura Seigai) the *Dainihon Bukkyō Zensho* (The Complete Works of Japanese Buddhism), in 160 volumes.

Following the pioneering works of Nanjō Bunyū, Inouye Enryō, and Kiyozawa Manshi, a host of other eminent scholars, e.g., Murakami Senshō, Anesaki Masaharu, Mayeda Eun, Kimura Taiken, and Tokiwa Daijō among others, continued scholarly activities in regard to Buddhism.[14] In the last eighty years, for the first time in the long history of Buddhism in Japan, scholars have begun philological, historical, philosophical, and comparative studies, combining modern Western and traditional Japanese methods. Works by Buddhist scholars in our own time, such as those of Suzuki Daisetz (D. T. Suzuki), Ui Hakujū, Miyamoto Shōson, Yamaguchi Susumu, Tsukamoto Zenryū, Kanakura Enshō, Hanayama Shinshō, Tsuji Naoshirō, Nagao Gadjin, Masutani Fumio, Yūki Reimon, Ōchō Keijitsu, Nakamura Hajime, and others have made important contributions to Buddhist scholarship internationally.[15] It is not without reason that today a number of promising younger scholars are being trained and are engaged in serious Buddhological studies.[16]

We must bear in mind, however, that Japanese Buddhism is confronted by many difficult problems. The dichotomy between the Buddhist intelligentsia and traditional rural Buddhists cannot be easily overcome. The Young Men's and Young Women's Buddhist Associations are active, and a nondenominational lay Buddhist movement called *Zaike Bukkyō* as well as other new groups including Zen study circles have been meeting the spiritual needs of people since the Second World War. But the rural populations are inclined to be ultraconservative and are open to superstitious beliefs and practices; moreover, some of them have been attracted by the so-called "New Religions" that have mushroomed since the end of World War II.[17]

Problems of Translation

Even such a brief historical sketch of Japanese Buddhism makes it evident that Buddhists in Japan never faced up to the problem of translating the sacred texts. Only in the twentieth century have they begun to translate the scriptures into the Japanese language. This is an enormous task, and Japanese translators realize that they have a long way to go. Even the *Kokuyaku Daizōkyō*, published in the 1920s, which purports to be a Japanese translation of the *Tripitaka*, has left most of the old Chinese words intact. In it, however, the word order is

[14] Cf. Kishimoto Hideo, comp. and ed., *Japanese Religion in the Meiji Era*, trans. and adapted by John F. Howes (Tokyo, 1956), pt. 3, "Buddhism."

[15] Cf. *Gendai Bukkyō Meicho Zenshū* (Modern Buddhist Classics), ed. H. Nakamura, F. Masutani, and J. M. Kitagawa, 10 vols. (Tokyo, 1961–).

[16] Cf. *Journal of Indian and Buddhist Studies*, published by the Japanese Association of Indian and Buddhist Studies, Tokyo.

[17] Joseph M. Kitagawa, "Japan: Religion," *Encyclopaedia Britannica*, 1968 ed., 12:899-904.

changed from that of Chinese to Japanese and the Japanese alphabet is used instead of the *kaeri-ten*, as was adopted by the *Manji Zōkyō*, mentioned earlier. Here, we may recapitulate some of the problems of translation that have confronted Japanese Buddhists historically.

Firstly, there never was, until the present century, any effort on the part of Japanese Buddhists to go back to the Indian texts directly; instead they depended solely on the Chinese translation of the *Tripi-taka*. In so doing, they created another kind of problem that is not easy to resolve. (Here we cannot go into the complexities involved in the translation of Buddhist texts from Sanskrit into Chinese.) Suffice it to say that by the middle of the seventh century, or the early period of the T'ang dynasty, most of the important *sūtras* had been translated into Chinese. While Chinese editions tried to translate the meaning of Sanskrit passages, for the most part they had to transliterate the sounds of such phrases as *dhā ranī* (mystic formulas). These formulas were not translatable, so the translators appropriated certain Chinese char-acters that approximated the sounds, for example,迦羅囉怛唎㘃for *kā larā tri ye*.[18] Obviously, the meanings of these letters as such have no relevance, inasmuch as they are used only as symbols for Sanskrit sounds. Some Japanese Buddhists, notably Kūkai and his followers, preferred to use Sanskrit letters rather than their Chinese translitera-tions. But, in the main, these Chinese transliterations, as well as Chinese translations, were introduced *in toto* into Japan, with the fur-ther consequence that Japanese Buddhists learned to read them with the Chinese pronunciation of the T'ang period. Ironically, much as Roman Catholics in Asia still use Latin as their liturgical language, Japanese Buddhists have perpetuated to our day the tradition of recit-ing *sūtras* in this dated Chinese pronunciation. In the course of time, the Chinese pronunciation of the Japanese Buddhist priesthood be-came corrupt, so that in modern times this curious type of Chinese pronunciation is totally unintelligible to Chinese speakers. Japanese laymen, of course, cannot understand the meaning of the scriptures that are recited this way; and more often than not, even the Japanese priests in reciting *sūtras* (*dokkyō*) depend on rote memory of the sounds without being able to follow the actual contents. In other words, Jap-anese Buddhists never faced the necessity of matching Japanese pho-nemes to the Chinese written characters of the Buddhist *sūtras* in com-mon use.

Secondly, those who attempted to interpret and give commentaries

[18] Yoshida Takashi, "Chinese Vocal Sounds in Early Years of T'ang," *Journal of the Tōyō University* 12 (1958), pp. 63-74.

on the Buddhist scriptures had to face numerous kinds of difficulties. As mentioned earlier, the Japanese developed the system of *kaeri-ten* (reading marks) to indicate which word was the subject and which was the predicate in a Chinese sentence. This system worked well in most cases, but some Chinese words had several meanings, none of which might be entirely wrong within the context of a given passage. For example, the word 況 (*iwanya*) is usually used as an adverb meaning "how much more," "still more," "much less," "still less," "not to speak of," or "to say nothing of." In the Buddhist texts, however, this word was used in so many different ways that Japanese translations of *sūtras* that contain it have often resulted in misinterpretations and confusion.[19] On the other hand, Japanese translators and commentators often used the same Japanese word to indicate varied meanings, and this fact added further complications to an already difficult situation.[20]

The ambiguity of the Chinese language, combined with the still greater ambiguity of the Japanese language, has led Japanese interpreters of Chinese Buddhist texts to arrive at conclusions and meanings which were probably not intended by the Chinese translators of the texts from Sanskrit. Professors Nakamura and Watsuji have cited an example that is pertinent to our discussion. In the *Nirvana Sutra*, there is the sentence, 一切衆生悉有佛性 , which can be translated as "all sentient beings have the Buddha-nature." The probable intent of this passage is to stress the fact that all sentient beings that are trapped in present existence have, nevertheless, the capacity to become Buddhas in a future existence. However, Dōgen explains it thus: " 'All-existence' is the Buddha-nature. One part of 'all existence,' whether sentient or not, is the Buddha-nature" (*Shōbō Genzō*, Buddha-nature). Here Dōgen takes the phrase "all . . . have" as a noun meaning an "absolute one." That is, "one who exists universally."[21]

A third problem in translation is the loose, ambiguous, and often erroneous understanding of Buddhist concepts on the part of laymen and laywomen in Japan. It is to be noted that the overwhelming majority of Japanese Buddhists, that is, the laity, have never been concerned with philosophical or doctrinal minutiae. To them, the term *hotoke*, for instance, has a wide range of meanings, including "Buddha-

[19] Kobayashi Yoshinori, "A Study on the Old Method of Reading the Letter *Iwanya*," *Journal of the Tōyō University* 12 (1958), pp. 51-62.

[20] Cf. Johannes Rahder, "A Linguistic Study of the Root 根 ," in *Buddhism and Culture*, dedicated to Dr. Daisetz Teitaro Suzuki in commemoration of his ninetieth birthday (Kyoto, 1960), pp. 226-246. See also Rahder's articles on "The Comparative Treatment of the Japanese Language" in *Monumenta Nipponica*, vols. 7-10 (1951-1954).

[21] Watsuji Tetsurō, *Nihon Seishin-shi Kenkyū*, pp. 348-349, cited in Nakamura, *Eastern Peoples*, p. 303.

nature," the names of various historical and mythological Buddhas and Bodhisattvas, and also "deceased persons." Thus, in common usage, the expression *hotoke ni naru* means "to become a *hotoke*" or simply "to die." Actually, the Japanese language is full of such words of Buddhist origin which have lost their original meanings. The expression *kaku-go* came from the Southern edition of the *Nirvana Sutra*, and in its original usage meant "realization of Truth" or "deliverance from this worldly delusion." In the course of time, it took on the meanings "readiness," "preparedness," "resolution," "expectation," "determination," and even "resignation," which was exactly the opposite of its original meaning. Another curious twist took place with the expression *shō-jin*, which originally meant "concentration of mind" on the path of the Buddha. Since spiritual concentration required abstinence from regular food, especially animal food, it acquired the additional connotation of "vegetarian food" in general. An equally curious change took place with respect to the expression *shusse*, which formerly meant "leaving the world." In Japan, this expression was used when a person entered the monastery. In the course of time, this term was applied to monks of noble lineage who entered the monastic community at Mount Hi'ei near Kyoto. Eventually, the religious meaning of this term was lost, and it has since come to mean "success in this life," "greatness," "promotion," or "upward social mobility."[22]

Lastly, the introduction of Western civilization in the modern period has further complicated the problem of translation for Japanese Buddhists. Space does not permit us to go into the question of the impact of Western philosophy on Japanese Buddhist thinking. Even purely on the philological level, the Japanese language had to incorporate new expressions theretofore unknown in Japan. In confronting this task, Japanese philologists came to depend heavily on words of Chinese origin, such as *-ka-suru* (化する) for translating "-ify," as in *jōka-suru* "to purify," or *risōka-suru* "to idealize." They formed abstract nouns by adding the Chinese word *-sei* (性) as exemplified in *ningen-sei* "humanity," *kyakkan-sei* "objectivity," *kanō-sei* "possibility," *hitsuzen-sei* "necessity," and *fuhen-sei* "universality." The word *-teki*, originally a Chinese (的) suffix-forming adjective, also came into vogue, as seen in such words as *kōka-teki* "effective" and *tamen-teki* "many-sided."[23]

These and many other new, coined words have proved to be indis-

---

[22] For more examples, see Takamine Hiroshi, *Kakugo ga Sesshushitaru Bukkyō Bunka* (Buddhist Culture Which Was Adopted into Japanese Language) (Osaka, 1944).

[23] Cf. Ichikawa Sanki, "Foreign Influences in the Japanese Language," in Inazo Nitobe et al., *Western Influences in Modern Japan* (Chicago, 1931), pp. 141-180.

pensable in recent translations of Buddhist texts from Sanskrit and Pali, as well as from Chinese. In addition to these coined words, modern Japanese has also adopted hundreds of words from German, French, and English, as one can readily demonstrate in modern literature and in the spoken language. Some Buddhist leaders and scholars are already using colloquial forms of Japanese in translating scriptures and in writing commentaries. That for the first time Japanese Buddhist laymen can understand the contents of their sacred scriptures and the general tenets of Buddhism itself is indeed a new phase in the history of Buddhist translation in Japan!

14. The Career of Maitreya, with Special Reference to Japan

What matters ... is not the original meaning of the forms, but the forms themselves, as disclosing to the native sensibility and understanding of the observer potential modes of his own creativeness.—*Oswald Spengler*

MAITREYA (*Metteyya* in Pāli; *Byama-pa* in Tibetan; *Mi-lo* in Chinese; and *Miroku* in Japanese), also known as Ajita or "unconquered," is the only Bodhisattva recognized by the Theravāda tradition. Believed to be the future Buddha, whose coming would signify the fulfillment of the Buddha's Law as well as the establishment of universal concord without conflict, Maitreya is a popular divinity venerated by Theravāda, Mahāyāna, and Tibetan Buddhists. When, and how, the idea of the recurrent Buddhas originated is an intriguing issue, but one that cannot be dealt with in this paper. May it be said simply that many scholars postulate Iranian influences in the belief in the future Buddha, a belief that probably developed in Hīnayānist circles in Kashmir.[1] According to Basham, at any rate, "by the time of the 'Questions of Menander,' around the beginning of the Christian era, the cult of the future Buddha, Maitreya, was widespread among all Buddhist sects."[2]

Maitreya is believed to reside in the Tuṣita heaven, the fourth of six heavens in the world of desire, from which he will descend to the earth at the appropriate time in order to save living beings. Metteyya is not given a prominent place in the Pāli canon. An exception is the *Dīgha Nikāya*, which mentions the Buddha's prophecy that Metteyya would have thousands of followers, a contrast to the Buddha who had only hundreds. (In the early Sanskrit work the *Mahāvastu*, Maitreya is mentioned eleven times.) Also the *Anāgata-Vaṁsa* (History of Future

[1] See Erik Zürcher, *The Buddhist Conquest of China* (Leiden: E. J. Brill, 1959), 2:391, n. 74.

[2] A. L. Basham, *The Wonder That Was India* (New York: Grove Press, 1954), p. 274: "Among the doctrines of Zoroastrianism, which has strongly influenced other religions both East and West, is that of the savior (*Šaošyant*), who, at the end of the world, will lead the forces of good and light against those of evil and darkness. Under the invading rulers of N.-W. India Zoroastrianism and Buddhism came in contact, and it was probably through this that the idea of the future Buddha became part of orthodox belief."

Events), a Pāli poem of 142 stanzas, records a prophecy ascribed to the Buddha which presumably was given at Kapilavatthu in response to a question posed by Sāriputta. The main thrust of the poem is given succinctly in the following verses:

> The Buddha now Supreme am I,
> But after me Metteyya comes,
> While still this happy cycle lasts,
> Before its tale of years shall lapse.
> This Buddha, then, Metteyya called,
> Supreme, and of all men the chief . . . .

The poem gives a history of the previous existence of Metteyya, leading up to his birth as son of the prince of Ajita at the time of the Buddha Gautama. Then the future history of Metteyya is given in connection with the disappearance of the Law that would take place during the long period following the demise of the Buddha. Finally, the Buddha assures that those "who give gifts, keep the precepts, keep fast-days, fulfill their religious duties, . . . those who, in their longing for a Blessed One, shall make a gift, . . . those who further the religion of the Buddha" shall see the future Buddha, "and when they have listened to the Doctrine of the Blessed Metteyya, they shall attain to saintship."[3]

We share T. W. Rhys Davids's two observations about the main features of the Metteyya legend. First, "it is simply built up in strict imitation of the early forms of the Buddha legend, only names and numbers differing." For example, like Gautama, Metteyya was believed to have lived many lives before being born as a prince. And, like Gautama, he forsook his comfortable life in the palace. He attained Buddhahood under a dragon flower tree, which is his "bodhi tree." Metteyya, as the Lord of the Tuṣita heaven, then would watch over the expansion of the Law until the time of his descent to the world. Second, there are several analogies between the notion of Metteyya and the Western idea of a messiah: "The time of Metteyya is described as a Golden Age in which kings, ministers, and people will vie one with another in maintaining the reign of righteousness and the victory of the truth."[4]

In sharp contrast to the Pāli canon—which only tacitly acknowl-

---

[3] See "The Buddhist Apocalypse" in Henry Clarke Warren, *Buddhism in Translations*, Harvard Oriental Series, vol. 3, no. 9 (Cambridge, Mass.: Harvard University Press, 1947), pp. 481-486.

[4] See the article by T. W. Rhys Davids, "Anāgata Vaṁsa," in *Encyclopedia of Religion and Ethics* (hereafter *ERE*), ed. James Hastings (New York, Scribner's, 1908-1927), 1:414.

edged the place of Metteyya—various Mahāyāna sūtras give a very prominent role to Maitreya as well as other savior figures. For example, Maitreya, Avalokiteśvara, Amitābha, Vairocana, and other divinities play more significant roles than Śākyamuni in the *Lotus of the True Law*, despite the fact that the *Lotus* was revealed by Buddha Śākyamuni. In the Diamond Sūtra the following statement is ascribed to Śākyamuni himself: "Five hundred years after my death, there will rise another teacher of religion [Maitreya] who will produce faith by the fulfillment of this prophecy. You should know that He will plant the root of His teaching, not in one, two, three, four or five Buddhas, nor in ten thousand Buddhas, but plant it at the root of all the Buddhas; when that One comes, according to this prophecy, then have faith in Him at once, and you will obtain incalculable blessings."[5] In the course of time, a number of Maitreya texts (e.g., the *Sūtra on the Original Vow of the Bodhisattva Maitreya* and the *Sūtra on the Ascent of Maitreya*) came into existence.[6] Understandably, many Buddhists were eager to be reborn in Maitreya's abode, the Tuṣita heaven, and/ or to hear his forthcoming sermons on the Law.

Maitreya was a favorite subject of the Greco-Buddhist artists of Gandhāra. He often was portrayed as a young prince, since he was not yet a Buddha, wearing a top-knot bound with a fillet and holding a water jar. "In paintings he is usually of a golden color: his statues, which are often gigantic, show him standing or sitting in the European fashion and not cross-legged. . . . There was a famous image of him in Udyāna of which Fa-Hsien (A.D. 399-414) speaks as if it were already ancient."[7]

One of the most fascinating features of Maitreya or Metteyya is the fact that, wherever Buddhism was transplanted, his figure evoked "potential modes of . . . creativeness"—to use Spengler's phrase—in the peoples' religious apprehension and expression. Therefore, let me take a cursory look at the reception of this divinity in Southeast Asia, China, and Korea before discussing the beliefs and cults of Maitreya in Japan.

[5] Quoted by Timothy Richard in his article, "Sects (Chinese)," in *ERE*, 11:310.
[6] See Nanjō Bunyū, *A Catalogue of the Chinese Translation of the Buddhist Tripitaka* (Oxford: Clarendon Press, 1883), nos. 204-209.
[7] Sir Charles Eliot, *Hinduism and Buddhism* (New York: Barnes & Noble, 1954), 2:22. See also Richard H. Robinson, *The Buddhist Religion: A Historical Introduction* (Belmont, Calif.: Dickenson Publishing Co., 1970): "In Central Asia, numerous statues, paintings, and texts discovered by archaeologists testify to his immense popularity. He was adopted by the Manicheans, who fused Mithras Invictus, Jesus Christ, and Ajita Maitreya into one composite savior figure."

METTEYYA had a checkered career in the Theravāda countries of South and Southeast Asia. (I will refer to its quite different career in Mahāyāna countries shortly.) Even before the close of the Pāli canon, Metteyya—the future Buddha who will appear at the end of this world cycle to establish the true Dhamma and the just order over the entire world—had become an important element of popular Buddhism. As such, the figure of Metteyya served to stimulate King Aśoka's efforts in articulating Dhamma as the religiously inspired social and political principle of justice and morality. Ironically, however, the figure of Metteyya became *so* closely associated with that of the Cakkavatti (the ideal universal monarch), as well as that of kingship, that its potential power to arouse the conscience of the ordinary faithful for the cause of social, economic, and political justice was rarely realized until the modern period.

It should be noted in this connection that the word "Cakravartin" initially appeared in the Maitrāyaṇa Upaniṣad, where it denoted a famous king of great power. In the Purāṇas the word carries the meaning of a universal monarch who possesses fabulous attributes. Buddhists further elevated the importance of the Cakravartin, even to the point that both the Buddha and Cakravartin were believed to have the thirty-two marks and the eighty minor marks of a great man (*mahāpuruṣa*). One scripture goes so far as to say that "he is victorious at the head of his troops, just [*dhārmiko = dikaios*], a king of *dharma*. . . . He shall conquer the whole wide earth to the limits of the ocean, and then he will remove from it all the causes of tyranny and misery. He will rule without punishing, without using the sword, through Dharma and peacefulness."[8] Over the course of time, it came to be taken for granted that, just as the Buddha was the supreme ruler of the spiritual realm, the Cakravartin (Cakkavatti) was the supreme ruler of the secular realm. "On this assumption," says Dr. Rahula, "even an ordinary king is given a position far above other laymen. . . . The king, as the defender of Buddhism, was so highly respected that even words originally used in reference only to the Buddha and arahants came to be applied to [him]."[9] Furthermore, influenced, most likely, by Mahāyāna thought, the Theravāda Buddhist notion of kingship appropriated the Bodhisattva ideal; the result was the emergence of "the royal

---

[8] Taken from the Divyavadana (548-549), quoted in Edward Conze, *Buddhism: Its Essence and Development* (New York: Philosophical Library, 1951), p. 75.

[9] Walpola Rahula, *History of Buddhism in Ceylon—the Anurādhapura Period* (Colombo: M. D. Gunasena & Co., 1956), pp. 66-67.

ideal of aspiring to become the Bodhisattva [Metteyya]."[10] Inevitably, with the confluence of the ideas of kingship, the Cakkavatti, and the future Buddhahood, the notion of Metteyya as a *corrective* to the empirical political order never developed in Theravāda countries.

The gradual eclipse of the potencies of the Metteyya ideal in the Theravāda tradition also was due to the counteracting influence of indigenous, autochthonous beliefs as well as of Brāhmanism. Both of these systems were incorporated into the Buddhist framework. Historically, the Hinduization of India's neighboring regions was accompanied by the transplantation of Brāhmanism. Following Aśoka's missionary effort, monastic-centered Theravāda Buddhism was established in Ceylon (presently Sri Lanka) and much of Southeast Asia. However, Buddhism had accommodated many features of Brāhmanism. Furthermore, along with the Theravāda monastic orders was another source of religious authority, namely, kingship. This institution, by now, had combined the role of the defender of the Buddhist religion with such features as the representation of local deities and as the *avatāra* of certain Hindu deities. As the latter, the king served as the earthly counterpart of the head of the celestial pantheon. Thus, the authority of the Buddhist king in South and Southeast Asia was legitimized by indigenous cosmologies as well as by Brāhmanic rituals. This is due to the fact that kingship in these regions was regarded as the apex of the structure of the world, a world which embodied Buddhist, Brāhmanic, and native modes of meaning.

This assimilation of indigenous and Brāhmanic systems does not imply that the ultimate hegemony of Buddhism ever was questioned. On the contrary, Theravāda Buddhism's normative stances were firmly established by the acceptance of the Buddhist kingship which had been amplified—at least in the Buddhist sense—by the convergence of the Cakkavatti and/or Metteyya ideals. Indeed, many Buddhist kings aspired not only to ascend to the Tuṣita heaven but also to become Metteyya in their future lives. Similarly, Metteyya acquired the "complete equipment of a king" in Ceylon as early as A.D. 400.[11] There is a certain irony in this situation: the creative impulse which was at the heart of the original figure of Metteyya (Maitreya), whose anticipated advent promised the purification of Dharma and the rectification of world order, was undercut by the lofty notion of the Cakkavatti (Cakravartin) which now embraced, or appropriated, many features of the

[10] E. Sarkisyanz, *Buddhist Backgrounds of the Burmese Revolution* (The Hague: Martinus Nijhoff, 1965), p. 45.
[11] Ibid., pp. 45-46.

Metteyya ideal. Thus, while many pious Buddhist kings constructed or venerated gigantic statues of Metteyya, they also relied heavily on autochthonous deities for the maintenance of the given social and political order, an order which, to them, reflected the cosmic law of the Buddha. In this sense, the checkered career of Metteyya in the Theravāda countries may be seen as a sign of the particularization and domestication of the universal dimension of Buddhism of which he was an embodiment.

It is only in the modern period that the Metteyya ideal was infused with a revolutionary impulse of the political leaders and peoples in South and Southeast Asian nations. For example, after Burma's independence, U Nu, "who was looked upon by many people as a Buddha in the coming,"[12] attempted to establish an earthly Nirvana (Lokka Nibban). In the words of Sarkisyanz:

> This socialist world, in U Nu's formulation, was not to be an ordinary world but an abode of saintly hermits (Rahans) and of the Future Buddha [Metteyya], a world in which the highest stages (of Deliverance) are reached by meditation. Whereas traditionally the perfect society was expected to result from the maximalization of Dhamma observance through the perfection of man at the time of the Future Buddha [Metteyya], in U Nu's vision of Buddhist socialism the establishment of a perfect society was to permit a maximum observance of the Dhamma to the point of human perfection, making possible man's sublimation into future Buddhahood.[13]

Opinions vary as to why the attempts of U Nu and others to lead people to the "collective Metteyya ideal" failed in Southeast Asia. Nevertheless, the fact that such attempts were made is of some significance. And for those Buddhists who now live under regimes hostile to Buddhism in Indochina, the anticipation of the "descent" of Metteyya, a motif that has not been stressed thus far, may become an important existential experience.

IT IS interesting to note that the figure of Maitreya evoked a different range of "potential modes of . . . creativeness" in the religious life of the peoples of China, Korea, and Japan.

In sharp contrast to Theravāda Buddhism, which established itself as an unrivaled religious tradition in Ceylon and Southeast Asia, Mahāyana Buddhism in China had to cope from its earliest days with systems such as Confucianism and Taoism that were already well established. This may account for the fact that for the most part Bud-

[12] Ibid., p. 225.
[13] Ibid., pp. 224-225.

dhism failed to influence the core of the Chinese political structure. To be sure, Chinese history records many pious Buddhist monarchs who were inspired by the Maitreya and Cakravartin ideals, but the tradition of a Buddhist monarchy as such never gained permanent ground. Rather, Buddhism developed elaborate systems of devotional cults that were inspired initially by the devotion to Maitreya. And, while the Maitreya cult was later superseded by the Amitābha cult, the former left lasting marks on the beliefs and the piety of the latter. Moreover, the Maitreya ideal, which never became the mainstream of the Chinese Buddhist tradition, continued to inspire the revolutionary impulse of sectarian movements outside the strict Buddhist folds that have played important roles in the political history of China.

It is worth recalling that many of the early missionaries to China came from Central Asia where the idea of the future Buddha, Maitreya, had been widely accepted. Understandably, the statues of Maitreya, as well as those of Śākyamuni, Amitābha, Avalokiteśvara, and other Mahāyana divinities, found their way into China. According to Z. Tsukamoto's analysis of the statues preserved in the Lung-men caves, the prominent divinities venerated under the Northern Wei dynasty (roughly A.D. 500-530) were Śākyamuni and Maitreya, whereas those under the T'ang dynasty (roughly A.D. 650-710) were Amitābha and Avalokiteśvara.[14]

The early missionaries also transmitted the memory of the Indian King Aśoka of the third century B.C. as the paradigm of a Buddhist ruler who provided the best norm for the relation of Buddhism to the sociopolitical order. Accordingly, from the beginning Chinese Buddhists sought the conversion as well as the patronage of the rulers. Thus, while Hui-yüan (A.D. 334-417) wrote that "a monk does not bow before a king," Chinese Buddhism for the most part paid extravagant homage to the monarchs who favored Buddhism. Conversely, some of the monarchs appropriated pretentious Buddhist honors. For example, Emperor Wu of the Liang dynasty in the sixth century was called variously "Emperor Bodhisattva," "Saviour Bodhisattva," and "Bodhisattva Son of Heaven," while Wen-ti (roughly A.D. 581-604) of the Sui dynasty styled himself a "Cakravartin king."[15] Empress Wu (roughly 684-705) of the T'ang dynasty claimed to be the incarnation

[14] Tsukamoto Zenryu, *Shina Bukkyō-shi kenkyū: Hokugi-hen* [A Study of Chinese Buddhism: Section on the Northern Wei Dynasty] (Tokyo: Kobun-do, 1942), pp. 364-385.
[15] See Arthur F. Wright, *Buddhism in Chinese History* (Stanford, Calif.: Stanford University Press, 1959), pp. 51, 67.

of Maitreya.[16] Indeed, Wen-ti went so far as to say: "The Buddha entrusts the true Dharma to the rulers of the states. We, being honored among men, accept the Buddha's trust."[17]

Such distortion by these Chinese rulers of the meaning of Maitreya and the Cakravartin notwithstanding, there developed genuine devotional cults among the sincere Buddhists—clergy and laity—who were inspired by the figures of Maitreya and/or Amitābha. Tao-an (A.D. 312-385) initiated an organized cult of Maitreya in 370. According to Zürcher, Tao-an's fear of having distorted the meaning of the scripture was dispelled by a vision of the Arhat Piṇḍola, who urged him to turn to Maitreya, the "divine patron of exegetes [of Buddhist scriptures]."[18] Zürcher also points out that "Piṇḍola was regarded as one of the Arhats who had voluntarily remained in the world to protect the Doctrine until the coming of Maitreya."[19] We are told that Tao-an and his disciples assembled before a statue of Maitreya and made a vow to be reborn in the Tuṣita heaven, and that one of his disciples "bowed everyday five hundred times before the Buddha, and never stopped repeating the name Maitreya."[20] In the cult there were two main soteriological motifs, namely, the "ascent" and "descent" of Maitreya. Some devotees of Maitreya took the ascent motif seriously: they aspired to follow Maitreya by being reborn in his Tuṣita heaven in order to meet him face to face. Other devotees aspired to prolong their lives until the descent of Maitreya or to be reborn on this earth at the time of his descent so that they could hear his preaching in person. And, as Ch'en points out, "it was also hoped that this descent would occur during the reign of the Northern Wei Dynasty, so that Maitreya would make use of that dynasty to pacify and unify the world."[21]

The cult of Maitreya in China, however, was destined to be superseded by that of Amitābha, the Buddha of Infinite Light, whose abode is the glamorous Pure Land, Sukhāvatī. The Amitābha cult, first initiated by Tao-an's younger contemporary, Hui-yüan (A.D. 334-417), was very similar in form to the Maitreya cult, the basic difference being that the devotees of Amitābha vowed to be reborn in Amitā-

---

[16] See Kenneth Ch'en, *Buddhism in China: A Historical Survey* (Princeton, N.J.: Princeton University Press, 1964), p. 428.

[17] Quoted in Arthur F. Wright, "The Formation of Sui Ideology, 581-604," in *Chinese Thought and Institutions*, ed. John K. Fairbank (Chicago: University of Chicago Press, 1957), p. 98.

[18] Zürcher, *The Buddhist Conquest*, 1:194.

[19] See ibid., 2:391, n. 73: "This belief . . . seems to foreshadow the development of the Bodhisattva doctrine, and . . . this is one of [its] earliest traces in Chinese Buddhist literature."

[20] Ibid., 1:200.

[21] Ch'en, *Buddhism in China*, p. 178.

bha's Pure Land. In one sense, the Amitābha cult may be regarded as the extension of the ascent motif of the Maitreya cult. But faith in Amitābha (A-mi-t'o-fo), who had vowed to bring all sentient beings to his Pure Land, steadily gained adherents, so that by the seventh century—as graphically shown by Tsukamoto's study of the statues in the Lung-men caves—Amitābha and Avalokiteśvara (Kuan-yin), the two savior figures of the Pure Land School, became the most popular divinities in China. The figure of Maitreya, meanwhile, was badly neglected by the mainstream Buddhist community in China, only to reappear during the eleventh century in the guise of the jovial, potbellied, laughing Buddha, a figure that had totally lost the original meaning of Maitreya.[22]

If the "ascent" motif of the Maitreya cult had been taken over by the Amitābha cult, and if the original meaning of the figure of Maitreya had been forgotten by the established Chinese Buddhism, the "descent" motif of Maitreya had penetrated the consciousness of the Chinese people, especially among those members of the sectarian movements outside the Buddhist fold.[23] For the oppressed and those disgruntled by injustice, the Maitreyan eschatological notion was alluring. As early as A.D. 610, Maitreyan rebels attacked Ch'ang-an, the capital of the Sui dynasty. Three years later two Maitreyan rebel movements were led by Sung Tzu-hsien in Hopei and Hsiang Hai-ming in Shensi. In the early eighth century, Wang Huai-ku led a rebellion in Hopei in the name of the "new Buddha" Maitreya, and from the middle of the T'ang dynasty, the Maitreya sect, whose members could be recognized by their long hair and white robes, spread among the populace. In 1074, Wang Tse of Hopei led his Maitreya sect in a short-lived rebellion. Following a ban against the Maitreya societies imposed by the Sung regime, the Maitreyanists went underground. Soon, however, Maitreya elements were absorbed by the White Lotus Society, a group that gave many headaches to the Mongol rulers of the Yüan dynasty. Two notable rebellions occurred during the Yüan period. One was led by Pang Hu, who claimed to prepare the way for Maitreya. Another rebellion was led by Han Shan-t'ung under the slogan, "The country is in great confusion, and Maitreya is coming down to

[22] On this interesting subject, see ibid., pp. 405-406.
[23] On this subject, see Daniel L. Overmyer, *Folk Buddhist Religion: Dissenting Sects in Late Traditional China* (Cambridge, Mass.: Harvard University Press, 1976), pp. 80-108; Shigematsu Shunsho, "Tō-Sō-jidai no Mirokukyō-hi" [The Maitreyan Sectarian Bandits of the T'ang and Sung Periods], *Shien* 3 (1931): 68-103; and idem, "So-Gen-jidai no Kō-kin-gun to Gen-matsu no Miroku-Byakurenkyō-hi ni tsuite" [Concerning the Red Turbans of the Sung and Yuan Periods and the Maitreya and White Lotus Sectarian Bandits during the Late Yuan Period], *Shien* 24 (1940): 79-90.

earth."[24] One of the followers of Shan-t'ung's group, Chu Yüan-chang, deposed the last Mongol monarch and established himself as the first emperor of the Ming dynasty in 1368. The White Lotus Society remained active during the Ming and its successor, the Manchu dynasty. Some of the rebel movements during the Ming and the Manchu dynasties continued to be inspired by the motif of the descent of Maitreya, who is (was) expected to establish universal peace and concord.

It is evident in retrospect that the historic meaning of Maitreya has undergone radical changes in China. The image was appropriated and distorted, as it was in the Theravāda countries, by the Chinese rulers as they sought to enhance the Buddhist kingship. In doing so, the Maitreyan image lost its prophetic role. On the other hand, the cult of Maitreya, which emerged in Chinese soil in order to meet the genuine spiritual needs of the clergy and laity, was soon superseded by a more popular Amitābha cult. It is tragic that popular minds have associated Maitreya with the jovial laughing Buddha, an image which had lost the historic meaning of the lofty Bodhisattva who was expected to become the future Buddha. A historic irony lies in the fact that the Maitreyan eschatological notion was kept alive for centuries among the oppressed sectarian faithful outside the established Buddhist fold. Unfortunately, the naive romanticism of those Maitreyan sects, coupled with a lack of coherent ideology and rational organization, prevented those oppressed sectarians from leaving a more lasting impact on Chinese society and religion. On the positive side, however, we might point out that the cult of Maitreya not only prepared the ground for the Amitābha cult but, through the latter, left a lasting impact on Chinese Buddhist modes of piety and belief. Moreover, the Maitreya cult, as much as the Amitābha cult, played an important role in shaping the religions of Korea and Japan.

IN KOREA, Maitreya had a short but colorful career. Our attention to its history, accordingly, will be brief: our primary concern is how the Korean cult of Maitreya influenced the Maitreya cult in Japan.

Buddhism was introduced to Korea during the fourth century A.D., an era known in Korea as the period of Three States: Kokuryō in the north, Paekche in the southwest, and Shilla (Silla) in the southeast. All three were in the cultural orbit of China, and each one developed its own style of Buddhism under Chinese influences. In turn, Buddhist

[24] Ch'en, *Buddhism in China*, p. 340.

scholars and clerics exerted considerable influence on Buddhist developments in Japan.

Present evidence shows that the earliest belief in Maitreya can be traced to the early fifth century in Kokuryō.[25] The *Nihongi* (Chronicles of Japan) also tells us that a stone figure of Maitreya was brought to Japan from Paekche in A.D. 584 and that a golden statue of Maitreya was sent to Japan by the king of Shilla in A.D. 623. Professor Tamura points out in this connection that both Siddhārtha—the Śākyan prince who became the Buddha—and Maitreya were represented in half-length meditative statues. In fact, many half-length meditative statues sent during the fifth century from China to Korea or from Korea to Japan were those of the Buddha before his enlightenment, whereas "after the latter half of the sixth century when the faith in the future image of Buddha prevailed in China, the half-length future image of Buddha [Maitreya] appeared in place of the image of Princely Buddha."[26] We can see from the number of half-length Maitreya statues that have been preserved in Korea up to our time that they were produced between the mid-sixth and the early eighth centuries, and that there were adherents of Maitreya in all three Korean kingdoms.[27] The cult of Maitreya evidently eroded in Korea after the unification of the peninsula by Shilla in A.D. 735.

One of the landmarks of the Maitreya cult in Korea was the Mi-rūk (Maitreya) Temple, constructed by King Mu (reigned A.D. 600-640), who, according to the legend, encountered Maitreya coming out of a pond. It is to be noted that the construction of this temple was motivated not by the desire to follow the ascent of Maitreya but by the hope of waiting for his descent, "when he shall hold his three meetings under the dragon-flower tree, explicating the Dharma."[28] This belief in Maitreya's descent and his "three meetings" was transmitted to, and preserved in, Japan.

[25] Tamura Enchō, *Kodai Chōsen-Bukkyo to Nihon-Bukkyo* [Ancient Korean Buddhism and Japanese Buddhism] (Tokyo: Yoshikawa Kōbun-kan, 1980), p. 9.

[26] Tamura Enchō, "Meditative Buddhist Statues and Worship of Prince Shōtoku" (English excerpt), in *Shiragi to Asuka-Hakuō no Bukkyō-bunka* [Shilla and Buddhist Culture during the Asuka-Hakuo Periods (in Japan)], ed. Tamura Enchō and Hong Soon-Chang (Tokyo: Yoshikawa Kobun-kan, 1975), p. 7.

[27] See ibid., pp. 59-60 for the list.

[28] Tamura, *Kodai Chōsen-Bukkyo*, p. 86. Also, Dr. James Huntley Grayson, in his Ph.D. thesis (University of Edinburgh, 1979), "The Emplantation of Religion: The Development of Buddhism and Christianity in Korea," points out that the queen of King Mu was the daughter of King Chin-p'yong of Shilla, thus, "frequent and extensive cultural relations between the two states naturally existed and flourished during this period." According to Tamura, the King of Shilla sent 100 carpenters to assist the construction of the Mi-rūk Temple.

In Shilla the Maitreya cult was closely associated with a unique institution called the *Hwa-rang Do*, a club of aristocratic youths who shared recreational, educational, and military activities. Its members, called *Hwa-rang*, were handsome young men of good upbringing who believed they were protected by Maitreya. The famous monk Wōn-kwang exerted great influence on the *Hwa-rang Do* by instilling in the young men both Buddhism and patriotism. Grayson tells us that a member of this group, Mi-ri-rang—also known as Mi-rūk Sōn-hwa ("Sacred Flower of Maitreya")—was regarded as an incarnation of Maitreya. Another member, Kim Yu-shin, who later served as the commander of Shilla forces at the time of the unification of Korea, gathered around him a number of *Hwa-rang* as the "Perfumed Followers of the Dragon-flower" (*Yong-hwa Hyangdo*). "It would seem possible," says Grayson, that Kim's followers "practised the rite of washing the images and attended lectures at which the sūtras were expounded."[29] It is conceivable that the patriotic Buddhism that was inspired by the Maitreya cult that developed in Shilla provided the model for Japanese Buddhism.

One of the most fascinating Buddhist leaders in Shilla, Wōnhyo (617-686), also had a close association with the *Hwa-rang Do*. A talented evangelist, musician, and writer, he left the priesthood and lived as a nonsectarian missionary. "It is said that he would play a six-stringed instrument . . . in front of local shrines for the entertainment of the farmers, frequented wine shops, practised meditation in the mountains, sang songs with a Buddhist import as he passed through the countryside."[30] He was also a confidant of Kim-Yushin of the *Hwa-rang* and an advocate of the synthesis of Buddhism with a nationalism that was independent of Chinese tutelage.[31]

We can only speculate why Maitreya, whose early career in Korea appeared to be so promising, went into virtual oblivion after the unification of the peninsula in the eighth century. But meanwhile he had already crossed the ocean and found admirers and devotees in Japan, where he was destined to enjoy more longevity.

The manner in which the figure of Maitreya initially entered the Japanese scene was anything but auspicious. The first Buddhist statue recorded in Japanese history, a gift from the king of Paekche to the Japanese court at the official introduction of Buddhism to Japan in the mid-sixth century, was that of Śākyamuni. In that court, heated controversies arose between the pro-Buddhist Soga clan chieftain and anti-

---

[29] Grayson, "Buddhism and Christianity in Korea," pp. 170 and 383, n. 29.
[30] Ibid., p. 165.
[31] See Tamura and Hong, *Shiragi*, pp. 65-68.

Buddhist factions who feared the anger of the *kami* of the indigenous cult (later called Shinto, or the "*Kami* Way"). The statue was given to the Soga, who built a family temple for its veneration. After a pestilence broke out—an event which the anti-Buddhist factions regarded as the revenge of the native *kami*—the anti-Buddhists burned the Soga temple and threw the statue into a canal. As the replacement of the lost statue of Śākyamuni (Prince Siddhārtha of Śakya), as it were, the Soga family in A.D. 584 secured a statue of Maitreya (Prince of Ajita), which was most probably one of the "half-length meditative statues" popular in Korea at the time.[32] "This," says the *Chronicle of Japan*, "marked the establishment of the Buddhist Law in Japan."[33]

The amazing expansion of Buddhism in Japan during the seventh century owed much to the persistent advocacy of the powerful Soga family and the active promotion of this new religion by Prince Shōtoku (573-621), who served as the regent under his aunt, Empress Suiko. Prince Shōtoku, following the Sui and T'ang imperial model, envisioned a hierarchically centralized Japanese national community under the supreme authority of the imperial family which—by virtue of its solar ancestry—was to rule the nation. With this in mind, he established a policy of balancing Shinto, Confucian, and Buddhist traditions under the rule of the throne through the central government.[34]

Many Japanese historians have given credit to Prince Shōtoku for transforming Buddhism from a private religion of a limited number of families and clans to the religion of a nation. Undoubtedly, because his tutors were Korean monks, Shōtoku was acquainted with, and influenced by, the synthetic development of Buddhism and nationalism on the Korean peninsula, especially in Shilla. Therefore, it was not without reason that Shōtoku, although a lay devotee, came to be venerated by subsequent Buddhists as the spiritual head or founder of Japanese Buddhism. Moreover, very shortly after his death Shōtoku became the object of the Taishi (Prince) cult, which was in effect a homology of the veneration of Śākyamuni (Prince Siddhārtha), Maitreya (Prince of Ajita), and Prince Shōtoku. The convergence of the Maitreya cult and the cult of Shōtoku Taishi is demonstrated conspicuously by the fact that six of the seven temples built either by Shōtoku or by his followers in his memory have half-length Maitreya statues as the central object of worship, while the seventh has the statue of Bud-

---

[32] Tamura, *Kodai Chōsen-Bukkyo*, p. 39.

[33] See J. M. Kitagawa, "Religions of Japan," in *The Great Asian Religions: An Anthology*, ed. W.-T. Chan et al. (New York: Macmillan Co., 1969), p. 251.

[34] See J. M. Kitagawa, "The Japanese *Kokutai* (National Community): History and Myth," *History of Religions* 13, no. 3 (February 1974): 209-226, esp. 219.

dha Śākyamuni. That four of the six temples enshrining Maitreya statues are nunneries indicates that nuns were the ardent advocates of the
Maitreya and the Taishi (Shōtoku) cults.[35] While the Maitreya elements gradually receded in the course of history, the Taishi cult—
which was inspired initially by the figure of Maitreya—has survived
into our own time.

The Maitreya cult, as well as the Amitābha cult (which came to
supersede the former in Japan as it did in China), were enhanced by
the popularity of the Lotus Sūtra, which had been promoted initially
by Prince Shōtoku. It was believed that the recitation of, and meditation on, this sūtra (*Hokke Sammai*) had the dual benefits of *metsuzai*
(extinguishing sins which have been committed in the past) and *mei-
fuku* (heavenly bliss and happiness of deceased ancestors, parents, and
relatives). As de Visser states, "the latter idea was based upon the
former. To take away the sins of the dead is to give them felicity.
Moreover, rebirth in the heaven of Amitābha or Maitreya was promised . . . to the faithful readers of this text."[36] In 1070, Emperor Go-
sanjo erected a Tendai temple, Enshū-ji. There six priests practiced the
Lotus Meditation (*Hokke Sammai*)—which included the *hangyō hanza*
(partly moving, partly sitting) *samādhi*—"in distant expectation of the
days of the Dragon-flower," or the descent of Maitreya on earth.[37] De
Visser further notes that "the Enshū-ji Hokke-e . . . was an annual
festival of the twelfth month, lasting five days, and celebrated in the
kōdō (expounding hall) of the sanctuary" before the images of Śākyamuni, Maitreya, and other divinities.[38]

It is interesting to note that of the two motifs—the ascent and the
descent of the figure of Maitreya—the ascent was stressed by the
Hossō (Yogācāra, or the "mere-ideation") School, while the descent
was emphasized by the Shingon (*Mantra*, or "true word") School in
the ninth century, during the Heian period. The Hosso, one of the six
established schools in the eighth century (Nara period), traced its
teachings to the celebrated Indian monk Asaṅga, who was reputed to
have studied under Maitreya.[39] Its chief objective was the investigation
of the nature and qualities of all existence (both material and mental)
by means of the practice of self-contemplation. This practice consisted
of ten ascending stages that led to a state wherein the innermost nature

---

[35] See Tamura and Hong, *Shiragi*, pp. 81-94.
[36] M. W. de Visser, *Ancient Buddhism in Japan* (Leiden: E. J. Brill, 1935), 2:653.
[37] Ibid., 2:672.
[38] Ibid., 2:687.
[39] See Takakusu Junjirō, *The Essentials of Buddhist Philosophy* (Honolulu: University of
Hawaii, 1947), p. 98.

of all existence could be realized. Only those adepts who had attained such a lofty spiritual state could share the bliss of Maitreya's Tuṣita heaven. Ironically, due to the aristocratic tendency of the Hossō School ("the attainment of spiritual heights being the privilege of a select few"[40]), the meaning of Maitreya, which was based on the notion of eventual salvation of all beings, was not transmitted by this school to the people. Not surprisingly, the Hossō School, probably the most influential system in the Nara period, lost its vitality shortly afterward.

The Shingon (Chên-yen in Chinese) School was introduced and systematized in Japan by Kūkai (also known posthumously as Kōbō Daishi, A.D. 774-835), one of the most talented, colorful, and influential figures in Japanese religious history. According to his school, the phenomenal world is the manifestation of the Cosmic Body of the Great Sun-Buddha, Mahāvairocana. And, as a contemporary Shingon spokesman says, "since all beings and all things are of the same essence . . . one should, by thought or other means, by acts of mystical value, by the practice of our symbols, of our incantations, and of our formulas, strive to feel and to understand . . . [that] we *are* the cosmos, and the cosmos *is* ourselves."[41] Kūkai was reputed to have acquired miraculous powers through his earlier practice of austerities on the mountain and because of his training in the Shingon system. Upon Kūkai's death the reigning emperor praised him as "the master of Shingon, the foremost teacher of Esoteric Buddhism, on whose protection the state depended, and to whose prayers animals and plants owed their prosperity."[42] Moreover, legends developed after his death to the effect that "Kūkai had not died but had merely entered into eternal samādhi and was still quite alive on Mt. Kōya as a savior to all suffering people: for Kūkai has specially descended to earth between the appearances of the Buddha Śākyamuni and the future Buddha Maitreya."[43] Here the descent motif of Maitreya inspired and merged with the cult of Kōbō Daishi, who became the Japanese counterpart of Maitreya himself.[44]

[40] Anesaki Masaharu, *History of Japanese Religion* (London: Kegan Paul, Trench, Trubner & Co., 1930), p. 96.

[41] Quoted in E. Steinilber-Oberlin, *The Buddhist Sects of Japan*, trans. Mark Logé (London: George Allen & Unwin, 1938), p. 104.

[42] Cited in Yoshito S. Hakeda, *Kūkai: Major Works* (New York: Columbia University Press, 1972), p. 60.

[43] Ibid.

[44] J. M. Kitagawa, "Kūkai as Master and Savior," in *The Biographical Process*, ed. Frank E. Reynolds and Donald Capps (The Hague: Mouton, 1976), pp. 319-341. [See also chapter 11 of this book.]

Maitreya also exhibited great dexterity very early in his career in Japan by allying himself with the native Shinto tradition as well as with less organized folk religious traditions. For example, Maitreya's association with Hachiman (a Shinto deity of obscure origin) at Usa on Kyushu goes back to the early eighth century, when a Maitreya chapel (Miroku-ji) was established by Emperor Shōmu within the compound of the Usa Hachiman shrine. One notes that Usa Hachiman foreshadowed the pattern of the Shinto-Buddhist amalgam (*Shin-Butsu Shūgō*) that existed until the late nineteenth century.[45] Characteristically, Usa Hachiman, protected by Maitreya, came to the capital city of Nara and blessed Emperor Shōmu's construction of the national temple, Tōdai-ji, which housed the famous great statue of the Buddha.

Maitreya also came to be associated with mountain worship, an old feature of indigenous Japanese religions. For example, Mount Yoshino—known then as Kimbu-sen in Yamato province and considered a sacred mountain from ancient times—came to be regarded as a likely spot for Maitreya's descent. Thus, when Emperor Shōmu, who was in need of gold for the construction of the great Buddha statue, sent a messenger to pray for it, the imperial messenger was told by "an oracle [or in a dream] that the gold of this mountain could be taken and used only when Maitreya had appeared in the world [from the Tuṣita heaven]."[46] This belief is not confined to Mount Yoshino. Mountain-tops—often referred to as *on-take*—of various sacred mountains, Fuji, Kiso, Asama, Hi'ei, and Kōya, for example, also were considered the potential Pure Land of Maitreya (*Miroku-jōdo*). The most conspicuous example of the merging of the Maitreya cult and mountain worship was the development of the devotional confraternity centering on Mount Fuji (*Fuji-kō*), which attracted enough adherents to become an independent religious sect.[47]

The penetration of the simplistic belief that Maitreya's descent will bring about peace and prosperity has brought about a wide variety of religious expressions among the common folk in Japan. One such expression is the Maitreya Dance (*Miroku-odori*) that is performed to facilitate the arrival of Maitreya's boat (*Miroku-bune*)—a Japanese counterpart of the Cargo cult—along the seacoasts. Another is found in the singing of various verses sung in agricultural communities at

[45] Hori Ichirō, *Minkan-shinkō-shi no sho-mondai* [Some Problems in the History of Folk Religion] (Tokyo: Mirai-sha, 1971), p. 93.

[46] De Visser, *Ancient Buddhism*, 2:643.

[47] Miyata Noboru, *Miroku-shinkō no kenkyū* [A Study of the Miroku Belief] (Tokyo: Mirai-sha, 1975), pp. 138-155.

the time of the planting of rice seeds. These songs ask Maitreya to bless the people with a good harvest.[48] For the most part, however, Japanese folk religious traditions appropriated the Maitreya cult solely into their aspirations for this-worldly benefits. Only in the modern period, when the foundation of the Tokugawa feudal regime was shaken prior to the establishment of the Meiji imperial regime, has the "descent" motif of the figure of Maitreya inspired the notion of the rectification of the social order (yo-naoshi). This corrective to the social order precipitated the emergence of many folk-based new religions such as Tenri-kyō, Konkō-kyō, and Ōmoto-kyō. And yet, Japan never saw anything like the belief in Maitreya that was held by the rebellious sectarian groups in China or Burma. The only exception to this might be the messianically colored Ōmoto-kyō; however, the suppression of this sect by the government in 1921 effectively destroyed its messianic features.

Sir Charles Eliot once remarked that "the most salient feature of Japanese Buddhism is its intimate connection with the general condition of the nation, both political and social. It has vibrated in response to many and abrupt changes, it has registered them in its sects and expressed in its art the special note of each."[49] In this respect, the figure of Maitreya (Miroku) in Japan typifies the character of Japanese Buddhism in its many aspects.

[48] Ibid., pp. 74-80; Hori, *Minkan-shinkō-shi*, p. 94.
[49] Sir Charles Eliot, *Japanese Buddhism* (London: Edward & Arnold, 1935), p. 179.

15. Paradigm Change in Japanese Buddhism

PARADIGM CHANGE in Japanese Buddhism has often been discussed in terms of either the Japanization of Buddhism or the Buddhaization of Japanese religion. I have learned much from both approaches. Nevertheless, as an historian of religions, I would like to approach the subject from a slightly different perspective. I would like to attempt to understand this nebulous phenomenon as the convergence of two intertwining processes of paradigm change—one in Japanese religion and the other in the Buddhist tradition. My schema will compel me to give attention as well to two subsidiary factors—first, the impact of China as both the main source of cultural inspiration for Japan and the secondary center of Mahāyāna Buddhism (the tradition of Buddhism that penetrated Japan); and second, the mediating and tutorial role of Korea in the cultural and religious contacts between China and Japan.

It is my modest hope to try to untangle the crisscrossing web which provided both the threads and the pattern of the colorful brocade of Japanese Buddhism, woven by the combination of historical "givens" and religious creativity at several crucial phases of Japanese historical, cultural, and religious experience.

BUDDHIST PARADIGM CHANGE UNDER KING AŚOKA

As is true with other religions, there are three related but different levels of meaning attached to Buddhism: (1) Buddhism as religion, (2) Buddhism as culture, and (3) the Buddhist-related or oriented sociopolitical order. With respect to the first, Buddhism takes for granted the necessity for the human being to see the meaning of all existence in relation to Nirvana, the ultimate meaning. This spiritual insight, derived from the Buddha's own religious experience, has been expressed in doctrines, scriptures, cults, ethics, and the ecclesiastical structures of the Buddhist religion. On the second level, Buddhism nurtures and impregnates its ethos into the domain of values, ideology, the arts, and the imagination, that is, into culture. On the third level, Buddhism is related variously to actual sociopolitical structures and organizations. In Buddhism, paradigm change usually involves not only important changes in each of these three levels of meaning but also alteration in the balance of and the relationship among the three levels.

It is well known that Buddhism had undergone significant paradigm changes before reaching China. The significance of early Buddhism lies in the fact that it began, as E. J. Thomas astutely points out, "not with a body of doctrine, but with the formation of a [community] bound by certain rules" (Thomas 1933, p. 14).* In sharp contrast to the metaphysico-social principle of the Brahmanic-Hindu tradition based on three foci—the eternal cosmic dharma, the divinely ordered social structure, and the sacred kingship—the Buddhist metaphysico-social principle affirmed that the true Dharma, which was discovered and preached by the Buddha, could be realized only in the corporate life of the Buddhist community (Saṃgha). This principle was clearly expressed in the early Buddhist creed of the threefold refuge (*tri-śaraṇa-gamana*): taking refuge in the Buddha, Dharma, and Saṃgha. Even though early Buddhism was an insignificant regional movement of monastics and laity in northeastern India, its concern was the universal and perennial problem of existence in the world (*loka*).

Shortly after the demise of the Buddha, northeastern India was exposed to a strong Brahmanic-Hindu cultural influence. At the same time, Buddhism was gradually consolidated and institutionalized under the leadership of monastics. The oral traditions of the Buddha and his immediate disciples were codified, modified, and interpreted. Philosophical inquiries into the nature of Dharma produced a series of doctrines, written scriptures, and ethical precepts for monastics and laity. The Buddha, who shortly after his death was deified in the minds of the faithful, came to be identified with the popular image of the supreme universal monarch (Cakravartin) who was believed to be "a divinely ordained figure with a special place in the cosmic scheme" (Basham 1954, p. 83).

The most far-reaching paradigm change in Buddhism took place during the third century B.C. under the influence of the newly converted Buddhist king, Aśoka (r. 274-232 B.C.). He proudly stated in the Bairāt Buddhist Texts Edict his "great reverence for and faith in Buddha, the Dharma [and] the Saṃgha" (Sen 1956, pp. 30, 134-135). His strong advocacy of the practice of Dharma notwithstanding, Aśoka's understanding of the term included a whole series of moral

* The reader is directed to the list of references at the end of this chapter for bibliographical information on the works cited in the text.

deeds: mercifulness; charity to Brahmans, ascetics, and all other human beings; truthfulness; purity of thought; honesty; gentleness; gratitude; non-injury of all other beings; relieving the suffering of the aged; tolerance toward other religions; and other deeds, all of which, according to Professor Sen, form "the basic teachings of all Indian religions, with this exception that he lays emphasis on non-killing of life as was taught by Buddhism and to a much greater extent by Jainism" (Sen 1956, p. 34).

The new paradigm of Buddhism which emerged may be characterized as blending two levels and structures of meaning, the classical formula of the Three Jewels (Buddha, Dharma, Saṃgha) and a second triple schema of the kingship, the state, and Buddhist-inspired morality. According to the new paradigm, the king is not only the political head; he is endowed with religious authority, a claim not made by any previous Buddhist monarch. In Aśoka's own words, "Whatever the Lord Buddha has said, Reverend Sirs, is of course well said. But it is proper for me to enumerate the texts which express the true Dharma and which make it everlasting" (Nikam and McKeon 1959, p. 66). Not only did Aśoka thus assume as king the prerogative to evaluate doctrines; he also exercised his authority to require monks and nuns to observe the discipline. As Rahula points out, the notion of establishing

the Śāsana or Buddhism as an institution in a particular country or place was perhaps first conceived by Aśoka himself. He was the first king to adopt Buddhism as a state religion, and to start a great spiritual conquest which was called Dharma-vijaya. . . . Like a conqueror and a ruler who would establish governments in countries politically conquered by him, so Aśoka probably thought of establishing the Śāsana in countries spiritually conquered . . . by him (Rahula 1956, pp. 54-55).

At the same time, Aśoka considered it the king's religious duty to protect and honor all faiths found in his realm. Clearly, Aśoka conducted himself according to the mythological model of the idealized supreme monarch, the Cakravartin. Many scholars have pointed out that Aśoka never mentions Nirvana in his Edicts. Instead, he repeatedly mentions his pious hope to attain "heaven" in the next life (Sen 1956, p. 78).

The link between the two triads of the new paradigm, Buddha-Dharma-Saṃgha and kingship-state-morality, was the notion of sacred kingship modelled after the image of the Cakravartin. Aśoka succinctly expressed the lofty ideal of king as ruler and agent of Dharma:

The king [as a ruler] will forgive those who can be forgiven: and, for that they may be induced by me to practise the Dharma; and, that they may attain (the happiness of) this world and of the next world (Sen 1956, p. 116).

As might be expected, such a new paradigm had immediate and far-reaching effects, both positive and negative, on the Buddhist tradition. (1) The new paradigm enabled Buddhism to locate religious meaning in the sociopolitical order and sociopolitical institutions. (2) The model of the Buddhist path, which had been understood earlier as that of leaving the world to enter the stream in the hope of Nirvana, took on the new meaning of reentering the world "for the benefit of all beings," thus giving a positive missionary impulse to Buddhism. (3) Because the religious base shifted from the "community of faith" to the concrete geographical regions of the Buddhist-inspired state, demarcated by its "boundaries" (*sīmā*), Buddhism had to come to terms with the customs, institutions, legends, and beliefs, as well as with the indigenous gods and spirits, of the localities which it claimed. (4) Such a "spatialization" of Buddhist religion (*Śāsana*) on earth coincided with cosmic "spatial" speculation about multiple Buddha-lands, thus fostering the development of cosmologies as a soteriological framework. (5) The excessive royal favor and support of monastic institutions had some negative results. Says Rahula,

Allured by the high status and comforts granted to the [monastic order] by the emperor, undesirable and corrupting elements entered the order, thereby disturbing its unity and peace (Rahula 1956, p. 12).

(6) Schismatic tendencies had already threatened the Buddhist community. After the time of Aśoka, they became more accentuated because of the combined effect of internal and external forces. As a result, Buddhism split into the Hīnayāna (or Theravāda) and Mahāyāna traditions.

After Aśoka's time, the missionary enterprise of Buddhism established secondary centers of Buddhist expansion: Sri Lanka for the southern expansion of the Hīnayāna (Theravāda) tradition; China for the East Asian expansion of the Mahāyāna tradition; and, later, Tibet for the expansion of the Tantric tradition into the Mongolian steppe. Meanwhile, the political development of northwest India from the third century B.C. to the third century A.D. brought from without non-Indian cultural and religious influences. In the Mahāyāna tradition, these stimulated creativity in Buddhist art and the emergence of new soteriologies based on multiple Buddhas and Bodhisattvas. Just as the southern Buddhist expansion followed the overseas route into south-

253

east Asia, Mahāyāna expansion followed the overland trade route, the "Silk Road," and eventually reached the border of China.

CHINESE BUDDHISM—A NEW PARADIGM

Prior to the penetration of Buddhism into China in the first century A.D., the Han empire (206 B.C.-A.D. 220) had been engaged in active transcontinental trade with Europe and had extended its political influence to some of the oasis kingdoms along the Silk Road. Frederick Teggart, who has examined the relationship between Rome and China in the years 58 B.C. to A.D. 107, points out that "of the forty occasions on which outbreaks [of war] took place in Europe, twenty-seven were traceable to the policy, or change of policy, of the Han government" (Teggart 1939, p. vii). The Silk Road provided an avenue not only for commercial traffic but also for Persian, Greek, Indian, and Chinese cultural and religious contacts. It was from Buddhist communities in the Central Asian oasis kingdoms that Buddhism was introduced into northwest China.

From the beginning, it was apparent that Buddhism in China could not follow the Aśoka paradigm, which was based on (1) a "Buddhist king," the *de facto* earthly political counterpart of the Buddha; (2) a comprehensive "national morality" inspired by Dharma; and (3) a "Buddhist state" as an idealized and expanded image of the Buddhist community. Among the three, the most important for Chinese Buddhists was the notion of kingship. This notion had to be heavily modified in light of the indigenous Chinese understanding of the emperor. The designation "emperor," or Huang-ti, was originally chosen by the first emperor of the dynasty preceding the Han, the Ch'in, in the third century B.C. Combining two terms which referred to divinity and mythical heroes respectively, it was based on the notion of the Mandate of Heaven (*t'ien-ming*). Only by the Mandate of Heaven was the ruler—usually referred to as the "Son of Heaven"—entrusted with governing "all under Heaven," which included responsibility for the "destiny of the state" (*Kuo-yün*). The importance which Chinese Buddhists attached to the protection and patronage of their religion by the ruler is exemplified by the legend they created about the dream of the Emperor Ming (A.D. 58-75). In his dream, Ming saw a radiant figure who was identified as the Buddha. As a result, he dispatched an envoy to India to bring back monks, Buddha statues, and Buddhist scriptures to China. According to Tsukamoto:

This tale of the Emperor's dream appears to have originated about A.D. 200. It was invented and propagated by Buddhists for the purpose of spreading their religion in a cultural atmosphere in which the strength of traditional ideas was very great. By pretending that Buddhism was received at the center of government by command of the Emperor, they sought to invest their religion with an authority that the people of China could not easily deny (Tsukamoto 1956, p. 184).

Throughout Chinese history, Buddhism had easier access to the throne when Confucian or Taoist influence in the court was not strong. One such period was the time when "barbarian" dynasties ruled North China between the fourth and the mid-sixth centuries. Arthur Wright calls our attention to the similarity between Caesaropapism and the relationship that developed between northern Buddhism and the monarchy. The reigning emperor of the Northern Wei dynasty, for example, was regarded as a Buddha incarnate, whereas southern Buddhism "had been content to make of the politically feeble emperors great lay patrons (*mahādānapati*) and wielders of kingly power for the good of the faith in the manner of the Indian Cakravārtin-rāja." We might note, however, that southern Buddhism, too, called Emperor Wu of the Liang dynasty (r. 502-549) Huang-ti p'usa (Emperor Bodhisattva), Chiu-shih p'u-sa (Savior Bodhisattva), and P'u-sa t'ien-tzu (Bodhisattva Son of Heaven) (Wright 1959, p. 51).* After the reunification of northern and southern China by the Sui dynasty in 581, the first Sui emperor, Wen-ti, made this revealing statement:

With the armed might of a Cakravārtin king, We spread the ideals of the ultimately enlightened one. With a hundred victories in a hundred battles, We promote the practice of the ten Buddhist virtues. Therefore We regard the weapons of war as having become like the offerings of incense and flowers presented to Buddha, and the fields of this world as becoming forever identical with the Buddha-land (quoted in Wright 1959, p. 67).

The Dowager Empress Wu (r. 684-705) of the T'ang dynasty claimed equally pretentious honors by allowing herself to be styled Maitreya or Kuan-yin (Eliot 1954, p. 261).

Despite such serious efforts on the part of Chinese Buddhism to

---

* Wright 1959, p. 62. Ch'en 1964, p. 152, cites the legend that in 454, "a stone figure of the Buddha in the likeness of the emperor was set up" in the Northern Wei capital, and that "it was found to have black spots on the face and feet, corresponding exactly to similar marks on the emperor's face and feet. This remarkable coincidence recalled an earlier statement by Fa-kuo that the emperor was the present-day Tathāgata and the populace became even more impressed."

curry the favor of the throne, and despite the willingness of certain monarchs to accept Buddhist honors, in the long run the influence of Buddhism could not alter the traditional Chinese notion of the sovereign as the "Son of Heaven" as that notion was defined and authenticated in Confucian terms.

The Buddhist impact on Chinese moral norms and the Chinese state was equally insignificant. Two centuries prior to the entry of Buddhism, China had made a transition from feudalism to an imperial state supported by a highly developed bureaucracy. Side by side with this development in the political sphere, the Confucian tradition abandoned its ancient ethos, which had reflected the mentality of the feudal age, and developed into an urbane eclectic system referred to as "Han Confucianism," a system "that became the organizing power behind the scholar-officials and gave full expression to their interests, ideas, and ideals" (Balazs 1964, p. 7). With the *de facto* canonization of the Five Classics, which provided the basics for the training of the scholar-officials, moral norms for Chinese society came to be dictated by the Confucian system. To be sure, this system had incorporated certain features from other schools of thought, e.g., Taoism, Legalism, and the Yin-Yang School. Historians remind us that there were times when Confucian influence in the central government waned and the vacuum was filled temporarily by Taoist or Buddhist influences. But through it all, the ruling class remained solidly Confucian in outlook. Neither Buddhism nor Taoism was able to dislodge Confucian dominance in statecraft; they had little to add to Confucian virtues which were exactly suited to a hierarchically organized imperial state: "respect, humility, docility, obedience, submission, and subordination to elders and betters" (Balazs 1964, p. 7). Rather, Buddhists attempted to translate their moral principles into a Confucian moral framework (Nakamura 1957, pp. 156-171; Ch'en 1973, pp. 14-64).

Although Chinese Buddhism was thus excluded from participating meaningfully in political leadership and from contributing positively to the moral norms of society, it exerted significant influence on Chinese cultural life. When Buddhism reached China, it was no longer a simple religion of mendicants and humble lay followers. It brought with it a variety of Indian Buddhist cultural forms, which had been further enriched by Greco-Persian influences in the oasis kingdoms of Central Asia. R. Grousset tells us that:

The Aurel Stein Mission . . . found in Rawak, in the region of Khotan, around various stūpas going back to the first centuries of our era, purely Graeco-Buddhist reliefs, and in Niya, on a site abandoned about the end of the third century A.D., intaglios of Roman workmanship, as well as coins from the Kuchan dynasty that reigned between A.D. 30 and 244 over Afghanistan and Punjab. In Miran, . . . south of Lop-Nor, Aurel Stein has discovered third century Buddhist mural paintings of purely Graeco-Roman workmanship (Grousset 1959, p. 139).

When the Chinese were initially exposed to Buddhism, it is not surprising that they were more impressed by the elegant Buddhist art and architecture, the colorful pageantry of rituals, the elaborate cere-monial vestments and ornaments, than by lofty doctrines which they could not comprehend because of linguistic and cultural barriers. For the evangelizing purposes of the Buddhist missionaries,

the Buddhist imagery, with its expressive representations, whether it had to do with the human life of the Buddha Śākyamuni, with its moving episodes, or with the paradise of the coming Buddhist 'messiahs' and 'saviors,' Maitreya, Avalokitêśvara or Amitābha, was as effective as any preaching. . . . moved by these pious considerations, the Buddhist missionaries borrowed their imagery from every source, especially as some came from the valley of Kabul and Pun-jab, with their Gandharan 'Saint-Sulpice,' while others stemmed from the 'seminaries' of Kashgaria where the most curious amalgam of images from every source was being developed, and in addition these last preachers were simple Chinese neophytes who naturally introduced into Buddhism the whole tradition of the popular religious images of Taoism (Grousset 1959, p. 156).

Buddhist missionaries, eager to communicate the contents of the faith, began translating scriptures and commentaries into Chinese, the language destined to become the religious language of Buddhists in East Asia. The early translators, both foreign missionaries whose un-derstanding of Chinese was limited and their Chinese collaborators who knew little Sanskrit or Pali, appropriated many terms and con-cepts from the Taoist tradition to express Buddhist meanings. Bud-dhists and Taoists also found each other congenial aesthetically. Their influences upon each other in art, literature, and poetry greatly en-riched the Chinese cultural tradition.

EVEN SO brief an overview as I have attempted makes it clear that a new paradigm for Buddhism emerged in China, replacing the Aśokan paradigm of Indian Buddhism. (1) Chinese Buddhism clung to the Aśoka-inspired image of the Buddhist king, but at the same time it had to adjust itself to the Confucian-oriented Chinese notion of the Emperor as "Son of Heaven." Monastic orders sought royal favor and in turn were controlled by the throne. (2) In China, Buddhism as-sumed a humbler role than in South and Southeast Asia in reference to moral norms and the institution of the state. It did not replace but

257

merely supplemented the dominant Confucian moral norm and the Confucian-oriented bureaucracy. (3) Chinese Buddhism accepted the monastic and lay paths as religious options rather than as graded soteriological levels. (4) A unique Chinese tradition of Gentry Buddhism developed following the model of Vimalakīrti. In the words of Arthur Wright, Vimalakīrti

was not a naked ascetic but a rich and powerful aristocrat, a brilliant talker, a respected householder and father, a man who denied himself no luxury or pleasure yet possessed so pure and disciplined a personality that he changed all whom he met for the better (Wright 1959, p. 52).

(5) In the main, Chinese Buddhism was preoccupied with the meaning of human existence in the phenomenal world. This preoccupation, as Wing-tsit Chan succinctly suggests,

contributed to the shift in outlook from otherworldliness to this-worldliness, in objective from individual salvation to universal salvation, in philosophy from extreme doctrines to synthesis, in methods of freedom from religious discipline and philosophical understanding to pietism and practical insight, and in authority from the clergy to the layman himself (Chan 1957, p. 115).

(6) In spite of occasional new input from Indian Buddhism, and in spite of the sincere effort of Chinese pilgrims to secure authentic and up-to-date Buddhist doctrines and practices in the land of their origin, Chinese Buddhism for the most part generated its own dynamics. These dynamics derived from the Chinese experience of trying to find Buddhist meaning in Chinese culture and society and from its give-and-take relationship with Confucian, Taoist, and other traditions. Characteristically, Chinese Buddhism found religious resources not only in Chinese translations of sūtras and commentaries but also in Chinese Buddhists' reflections, commentaries, and doctrinal formulations. (7) Not only did Chinese Buddhism develop its own art and culture; it made a great contribution to the total culturual life of China. (8) China became the secondary center of diffusion for the Mahāyāna tradition, extending its religious and cultural influence beyond its borders.

EARLY JAPANESE RELIGION

Very little of the religious situation in Japan before the introduction of Chinese civilization and Buddhism can be reconstructed with certainty. Our conjectures are based primarily on the scattered references to Japan in Chinese and Korean sources and on carefully scrutinized myths, legends, lore, and customs of the archaic and early Japanese as recorded in such eighth-century documents as the *Kojiki*, the *Nihongi*, the *Fudoki*, and the official anthology of poems called the *Man'yōshū*.

By the phrase "Japanese Religion" I refer to the unnamed, unorganized, and unsystematized cluster of religio-magical views, beliefs, and practices of early Japan. Unlike Buddhism and Confucianism, which claimed universal validity for Dharma and the Tao respectively, early Japanese religion was derived from the particular experience of the Japanese archipelago. Opinions vary greatly as to how far back Japan's prehistory can be traced, but most scholars agree that its earliest phase goes back to 3,000 to 4,500 years before our era. More importantly, Japan's prehistory lasted until around the mid-third century A.D., that is, long after the establishment of a great civilization in China. As far as we can ascertain, various ethnic-cultural groups had drifted into the Japanese islands from northern and southern parts of the Asiatic continent as well as from South Sea areas during the prehistoric period, and they had attained a degree of self-consciousness as one people, developing a common language (proto-Japanese), before the beginning of the historic period.

Although the Japanese islands were isolated from the Asiatic continent, some Koreans sporadically migrated to Japan, crossing the strait shortly before and after the beginning of our era, a trend which continued throughout the early historic period. Evidently there were a number of tribal states in Japan, mostly in the western island of Kyushu, and some of them paid tribute to the Han court in China during the first, second, and third centuries A.D. We learn from Chinese records that there was a female shamanistic ruler, Himiko or Pimiko, whose prerogative as the head of the state of Yamatai was duly acknowledged by the Chinese court.

In talking about early Japanese religion from around the turn of the fourth century A.D. we are on surer ground. At that time, the Yamato court began to consolidate its power in the present Nara prefecture by forming what amounted to a confederation of powerful *uji* (clan) groups. The Yamato rulers paid tribute to China, and in return they received the kingly title from the Chinese court. Within Japan, they claimed to be descendants of the Sun deity (*kami*). They continued to solidify their influence over other *uji* chieftains and assumed the prerogatives of conferring court titles, granting sacred seed at spring festivals, and establishing sacred sites and regulating rituals for the *kami* (deities). Significantly, their kingly activities, which were simultaneously political and magico-religious, were usually dictated by the precarious will of the *kami*, transmitted to them through dreams and divination.

The Yamato court was not idle in extending its influence to Korea. It gained a foothold on the southern tip of the peninsula during the fourth century A.D. Japanese forces fought side-by-side with the army of one of the Korean kingdoms, Paekche, against the armies of the rival kingdoms, Silla and Koguryo. Through such contacts, an increasing number of Korean artisans, artists, scholars, and technicians came to settle in Japan, and it was through Korea that Chinese civilization and Buddhism were introduced into Japan. Sometime during the sixth century the term "Shinto" was coined, to refer to the hitherto unnamed and unsystematized native magico-religious tradition, in contradistinction to Confucian and Buddhist traditions. It was assumed that the myths, symbols, and cults of Yamato's ruling house were to be accepted as the paradigm of Shinto, but actually the court-sponsored Shinto could not incorporate all the features of early Japanese religion. In fact, many such features remained outside the framework of official Shinto. They have usually been placed in the category of "folk religion." At any rate, there is good reason to retain the designation "Japanese religion" to refer to the subsequent development of religion in Japanese history, even though its earlier paradigm was destined to expand by the infusion of Confucian, Taoist, Ying-Yang, and Buddhist influences.

As I have stated repeatedly elsewhere, one of the basic features of the early Japanese religious universe was its unitary meaning-structure, a structure which affirmed the belief that the natural world is the original world. According to this paradigm, the total cosmos—including physical elements such as fire, water, wood, and stone, as well as animals and celestial bodies—is permeated by sacred, or *kami*, nature (see Kitagawa 1980, pp. 27-42). In such a world-view, there were no rigid lines demarcating various activities such as religion, commerce, arts, and recreation. It is not surprising, therefore, that human beings and *kami* of multiple forms were believed to constitute a single community.

The term *kami* refers to all beings and things, both good and evil, which are awesome and worthy of reverence. According to the *Nihongi*, "There were numerous [*kami*] which shone with a lustre like that of fireflies, and evil [*kami*] which buzzed like flies. There were also trees and herbs all of which could speak" (Aston 1972, bk. 2, p. 64). Moreover, when a mountain, for example, was called *kami*, that implied that the mountain was the sacred reality itself, not a symbol of it. Human beings were also regarded as *kami*, although later accounts tend to reserve this status primarily for monarchs and aristocrats. When Buddhism was introduced, the Buddha was understood as a foreign *kami*. In the course of time, the early Japanese recognized many types of *kami*, such as those of geographical regions, of social groups, and those who were believed to control people's health, fortune, and longevity. The early Japanese also took for granted the existence of *tama* and *mono* (souls and spirits), which were often interfused with the notion of *kami*. It was believed that *mono* (usually spirits of the fox, the snake, and the badger) were capable of possessing men and women as the *kami* did. Spoken words were also believed to have souls (*koto-dama*). This became an important motif in the development of ritualized Shinto prayer (*Norito*).

To the early Japanese, what we now refer to as religion was a matter of the ritualization of various aspects of life. Early Japanese religion had no fixed liturgies until it came into contact with Chinese and Buddhist ritual forms, but most rites had three basic features. The first was the practice of demarcating sacred space for the *kami*, usually marked by a sacred rope hung with paper strips. Second was the emphasis on purification. Third was a variety of activities called *matsuri*, often translated as "ceremony" or "festival." These were rites of thanksgiving, petition, paying homage, and presenting offerings of rice wine and food to the *kami*, followed by joyful celebrations. The meaning underlying *matsuri* is "to be with" or "to attend to the needs of" the *kami*, the ancestral soul, or a person of higher status. A related notion is political administration (*matsuri-goto*). The Yamato rulers were expected to attend to the needs of their solar ancestress, who communicated her will to them for practical implementation. This principle of the interrelatedness of *matsuri* and *matsuri-goto* was later articulated in terms of the unity of religion and national administration (Kitagawa 1979, pp. 30-37).

Early Japanese religion was closely related to the structure of the primary social unit, the precursor of what later came to be called the *uji*, a territorially based cluster of families which shared the same tutelary *kami* and kinship ties. The *uji* was the social, economic, political, and religious unit. It was held together by its chieftain, whose authority over the land and the people was derived from his cultic prerogatives and economic control. With the ascendency of the Yamato ruling house as the supreme *uji*, chieftains of other great *uji* groups were given court titles and various ranks. The growing prestige of the ruling house was reflected in the expansion of its pantheon and mythological tradition. Both pantheon and tradition gained acceptance among subordinate *uji* groups, thus fostering both the transition of Japan from the confederation of semi-autonomous *uji* groups to a kingdom and a trend toward unifying the hitherto fragmented cultic, mythological, and religious tradition of early Japan. The actual impetus for the new paradigm of Japanese religion, however, came with the introduction of Chinese civilization and Buddhism during the fifth and sixth centuries A.D.

PARADIGM CHANGE IN JAPANESE RELIGION

As stated earlier, Chinese civilization and Buddhism penetrated Japan not directly from China but through Korea, which since the second century B.C. had been a cultural satellite of China. Although this is not the occasion to trace the relationship between Korea and Japan, we might mention in passing that there were close cultural affinities between southern Korea and Kyushu in the prehistoric period. The same type of dolmens have been unearthed in both places, and the veneration of sacred mountains and sacred rocks was shared by ancient Koreans and Japanese (Ki-young 1975, pp. 3-59). Professor T'aek-kyu Kim, a Korean historian, is persuaded that

the foundation of the Japanese religion prior to the introduction of Buddhism has many such aspects as can be construed as the colonized and developed features of our own [meaning Korea], and the number of [*kami*] revealed in ancient Japanese records, their mythology, attributes of those female priests who appear in their ancient legend, status of women as revealed in their royal lineage, relations between men and women and so forth closely resemble those of Shilla [Silla]. Besides, the ancient immigrants from the Korean Peninsula to the Japanese islands exerted a great influence on the religious lives of the Japanese as exemplified by festivals, funeral services, prayers for rainfalls, etc., and it is easy to surmise that the various features of our religion based on a polytheistic foundation were transplanted into the religion of the Japanese (Kim 1975, p. 35).

During the first and second centuries A.D., there was a prosperous colony of Chinese "gentry in the area around the present North Korean city of P'yong-yang, which was an essential staging-post for the tributary envoys of south Korean and Kyushu tribal states en route to the Chinese capital" (Gardiner 1969, p. 20). "It also seems possible," according to Dr. Gardiner, "that some of the Pyon-han *kuo* [tribal states of Pyon-han, Benkan in Japanese, in southern Korea] acknowledged the overlordship of the Japanese Queen Himiko in the mid-third century A.D." (Gardiner 1969, p. 48). With the decline of Chinese influence over the Korean peninsula in the fourth century, three Korean kingdoms—Koguryo, Silla, and Paekche—established their respective domains and staged a series of fierce conflicts that

262

lasted for three centuries. In this struggle, Paekche sought Japan's military assistance, and the Yamato rulers gave it. Later, Japan established contact with Silla.

From the fourth century onward, Japan's close contact with Korea brought a number of Korean immigrants to Japan. The earlier group of immigrants included prominent Koreans of Chinese descent, who came to be known in Japan as the influential families of Hata, Aya, and Fumi. During the sixth and seventh centuries, immigrants from Koguryo and Silla as well as those from Paekche settled in Japan. They and their descendants, the naturalized citizens, taught Japanese the Chinese script, Confucian literary classics, astronomy, medicine, and various technologies, all of which greatly enriched Japanese cultural life. It was a revolutionary experience for the Japanese, who had no written language of their own, to learn to read and write Chinese script. This achievement was rendered even more impressive by the fact that the medium of instruction was Korean, the language of immigrant teachers. Even through such hazardous procedures, newly imported knowledge quickly had a great impact on Japan. For example, the Japanese intelligentsia learned from the Yin-Yang School not only fascinating cosmological theories but also the underlying principle that the human mind could know the structure and dynamics of the mysterious universe. They also learned that unlike the Japanese worldview, which was derived from their "particular" experience, there was the "universal" law of Tao that underlies Confucian ethics, political theory, and legal and educational institutions.

The paradigm of the earlier Japanese religious universe, the simplistic unitary meaning-structure, inevitably underwent changes.

In addition to Chinese civilization, Buddhism, too, was transmitted to Japan through Korea. I do not need to recount the well-known events of the controversy that followed the official presentation of the Buddhist image to the Yamato court from the king of Paekche in the sixth century A.D. We should note, however, that due to their affirmation that everything is potentially a manifestation of *kami* (sacred power), the early Japanese never developed representations of *kami* in anthropomorphic form. Thus the symbolization of the sacred or Buddhahood in a human-like image was a new revelation, which had far-reaching effects on the Japanese attitude toward sacral reality. Moreover, those court ministers who argued against accepting the statue of the foreign *kami* (the Buddha) presented their case from the perspective of the earlier "particular" Japanese religious universe, while the chieftain of the powerful and pro-Buddhist Soga *uji* was attracted by the Buddhist claim of its "universal" validity. At any rate, Buddhism

263

was initially sponsored by the Soga chieftain as the "religion of *uji*" and not as the religion of the Yamato court.

It was Prince Shōtoku, the regent under his aunt, Empress Suiko, around the turn of the seventh century, who sensed the necessity and desirability of a paradigm change in Japanese religion. He "particularized" the two universal principles, the Tao of Confucianism and the Dharma of Buddhism, so as to strengthen the foundation of the hierarchically centralized national community under the sacred monarchy. Himself a devout Buddhist tutored by eminent Korean Buddhist masters, Shōtoku held a grandiose vision inspired in part by King Aśoka's triple schema on two levels—Buddha, Dharma, and Saṃgha on the spiritual level and sacred kingship, moral norm for society, and religio-political state on the empirical level—and in part by the example of Emperor Wen Ti (r. 581-604) of the Sui dynasty, who united China by domesticating Buddhism, Confucianism, and, to a lesser degree, Taoism, as arms of the semidivine emperor (Kitagawa 1974, pp. 209-226).

Shōtoku's untimely death was followed by a series of bloody power struggles in the court. However, his vision was implemented substantially by Emperor Temmu (r. 672-696), the real architect of the so-called Ritsuryō (Imperial Rescript) state. The Ritsuryō state attempted to reorient Shinto, Confucian, Buddhist, and Taoist traditions to cooperate under the authority of the sovereign, who claimed the prerogative to reign and to rule the nation on the basis of the myth that the imperial house possessed a solar ancestry. Accordingly, the sovereign was now regarded as the "manifest *kami*" whose divine will was communicated by a series of imperial rescripts. This type of "immanental theocracy" became the new paradigm of Japanese religion.

In order to solidify such a new synthesis of religion, society, polity, and culture, the government reorganized the court structure (Miller 1974) and ordered the compilation of two mythohistorical works, the *Kojiki* and the *Nihongi*. The government also kept records of local surveys or topologies (the *Fudoki*) and made the "New Compilation of the Register of Families" (*Shinsen-shōjiroku*). Moreover, the penal codes (*ritsu*) and the civil statutes (*ryō*), modelled after the Chinese legal system, were issued in the name of the throne. The fact that the Department of Kami-Affairs (*Jingikan*) was placed side by side with the Great Council of State (*Dajōkan*) accorded prestige to Shinto while keeping it under the rigid control of the government bureaucracy. The government also controlled the Buddhist clerics through the "Law Governing Monks and Nuns" (*Sōniryō*).

The objective of the Ritsuryō synthesis was not to create a Chinese-style "liturgical community" with its sovereign as the mediator between Heaven, Earth, and Man, but to make the entire Japanese nation a "soteriological community," as it were, with the emperor functioning simultaneously as the chief priest, the sacred king, and the living *kami*. Accordingly, the imperial court now became the earthly counterpart of the heavenly court of the Sun deity. The stylized court rituals, as prescribed in the *Engi-shiki* (Institutes or Proceedings of the Engi Era)—the most elaborate embodiment of the Ritsuryō paradigm—were meant to perpetuate the earthly replica of heavenly rituals as told in myths (Kitagawa 1981, pp. 217-232).

It is an irony of history that even before the Ritsuryō synthesis achieved its coherence, it had begun to erode due to the changes in both the Japanese religious universe and the sociopolitical order. The latter change was exemplified by the Fujiwara regency, the rule by retired monarchs, and feudal regimes (*bakufu*). Nevertheless, the Ritsuryō ideal has remained as the only viable paradigm of Japanese religion throughout Japanese history—at least, until the modern period. And it is of great significance that the Meiji regime, despite its westernized modern trappings, attempted to return to the Ritsuryō paradigm by means of the emperor cult, a national morality, and a sacred national community.

JAPANESE BUDDHISM AND ITS PARADIGM

The foregoing makes clear, I hope, that the development of the Buddhist tradition in Japan was closely intertwined with the development of Japanese religion. Some historical factors can help us understand the characteristics of Japanese Buddhism.

First, Buddhism was initially understood in Japan to be one of the components, along with the Confucian, Taoist, and Yin-Yang schools, of the superior Chinese civilization. All of these modes of belief were accepted without serious resistance by the Japanese simply because, at the time, Japan did not possess any organized intellectual or religious systems which could compete with the Chinese traditions.

Second, following the Korean example, Japan accepted Buddhism solely in its Chinese form and took little interest in its Indian origin. Thus, unlike the Chinese Buddhists, who had translated the Buddhist scriptures into their own language, the Japanese Buddhists made no effort to translate the scriptures into Japanese, at least until our own time (Kitagawa 1963, pp. 53-59). To complicate matters further, the early Buddhist teachers in Japan were mostly Koreans who had only a limited knowledge of Japanese. Thus only a small group of the most gifted Japanese, mostly descendants of Korean emigrés, could comprehend the intellectual content of lofty Buddhist doctrines and philosophies during Buddhism's initial period in Japan.

Third, Buddhism was initially accepted in Japan for cultural and political reasons as much as for magico-religious reasons, first by the influential *uji* groups and later by the imperial court. Lavish temples were built, elegant Buddhist statues were imported or created, a series of scriptures were copied, and colorful rituals were performed mostly to gain mundane benefits, but very few efforts were made to understand the subtleties of doctrine.

Fourth, the sponsorship of Buddhism shifted from the *uji* groups to the imperial court, thanks to the effort of the pious Buddhist prince, Shōtoku, who promoted Buddhism as one foundation, albeit an important one, of the "multivalue" polity explicated in his Seventeen-Article Constitution. Thus, Buddhism became a significant religious, political, and cultural institution for Japanese society. For example, the famous temple, Tennōji, established by Shōtoku in the port city of modern-day Osaka, was an important center of educational and philanthropic as well as religious activities. As Anesaki states: "It was there that the embassies, missionaries, and immigrants were admitted and welcomed to the country, through the gateway of Buddhist communion" (Anesaki 1930, p. 58).

Fifth, with the consolidation of Japanese religion, society, and governmental structure that followed the establishment of the Ritsuryō system, Buddhism received generous support from the central government. But it was also rigidly controlled by the civil authorities, who acted more as a *Religionspolizei* than as a *Schützpatronat*. Since then, Buddhism has been expected to ensure the protection of the sovereign and the nation (Nakamura 1948, p. 221).

Chinese Buddhism had to be satisfied with a subordinate position because of the dominant place occupied by the Confucian and, to a lesser degree, by the Taoist traditions. In comparison, Japanese Buddhism overshadowed indigenous Shinto and established itself as the dominant Japanese religious tradition—or at least as the "half-creed" of Japan, to use Arthur Lloyd's phrase. Japanese Buddhism exerted tremendous influence at various stages of the development of Japanese religion generally, and the indigenous Shinto tradition was not immune to Buddhist influence. Even *Norito*, the stylized Shinto liturgical prayers, were influenced by the format of Buddhist sūtra recitation (Tamura 1966, p. 21). Still, the development of the characteristic ethos of Japanese Buddhism cannot be understood without taking into

266

account the impact of basic features of Japanese religion, such as the mythological legacy which authenticated the sacred monarchy and the national community, the affirmation of the sacrality of the world of nature, and the nebulous notion of the sacred (*kami*). Thus it is important to recognize the parallel processes and the convergence of development and paradigm change in Japanese religion and in Japanese Buddhism.

Space does not permit us to analyze the various stages of the transformation of Japanese Buddhism (Kitagawa 1965, pp. 319-336), but I will depict some of the basic and enduring features of its paradigm.

First, Japanese Buddhism is nationalistic in character. Its nationalism emerged from the combined influence of the mythohistorical legacy of Japanese religion and the nationalistic ethos of Korean Buddhism, especially of the Buddhism of Silla. Throughout its history, Japanese Buddhism has tried to maintain a difficult balance among such motifs as mundane benefits, individual and universal salvation, and *chingo-kokka* (the "protection of the nation") (Nakamura 1948, pp. 91-140; Watanabe 1958, pp. 76-89).

Second, Japanese Buddhism is syncretistic, as epitomized in the Shinto-Buddhist amalgam (*Shin-Butsu Shūgō*), which lasted until the late nineteenth century. Both of the main Buddhist traditions established during the Heian period, the Tendai and the Shingon schools, fostered syncretism through promoting *Sannō-ichijitsu-Shinto* and *Ryōbu-Shinto*, respectively. Both patronized a still more syncretistic cult, the Shugen-dō or Order of Mountain Priesthood. Moreover, Japanese Buddhism appropriated religious features of the Confucian and Japanese ancestor cults.

Third, Japanese Buddhism inclines toward magical beliefs and practices. It reflects a strange homology of the archaic Japanese legacy, Korean shamanism, magico-religious elements of the Indian and Chinese Buddhist tradition (especially its esoteric [*Mikkyō*] elements), and the all-pervasive influence of Onmyōdō, the Japanese appropriation of the Yin-Yang School. (On magical tendencies, see Watanabe 1958, pp. 89-102; on *Onmyōdō*, see Murayama, 1981.) When Buddhism was first introduced into Japan, statues of the Buddha were believed to possess the power to bring about worldly benefits magically. Buddhist clerics were expected to recite sūtras constantly and to offer magical incantations for all conceivable occasions. Hori points out that even the *Nembutsu*, the practice of reciting the holy name of Amida, was used as a form of magic (Hori 1968, pp. 83-139).

Fourth, Japanese Buddhism tends to depend on the charismatic

267

qualities of religious leaders as an efficacious soteriological means of adhering to historical Buddhist disciplines. While the *Vinaya* was preserved in certain officially recognized monastic centers, the history of Japanese Buddhism is full of charismatic figures who had only tenuous connections with the official Buddhist hierarchy, e.g., private monks (*shido-sō*), unordained priests (*ubasoku*), and holy men (*hijiri*). Even in the official Buddhist circles, such saintly persons as Prince Shōtoku, Gyōgi, and Kūkai have been in effect deified. The influence of charismatic leaders originated in the pre-Buddhist Japanese religious tradition, and was incorporated into Buddhist piety. Buddhist and Shinto ideas thus coalesced, says Eliot,

and the title of Bodhisattva was conferred on departed emperors and statesmen—on those, for instance, who are described as Hachiman, the patron of soldiers, and Tenjin, the [*kami*] of calligraphy, and even on so recent a personage as [Tokugawa] Ieyasu (Eliot 1954, p. 183).

The veneration of saintly figures such as Hōnen, Shinran, and Nichiren became an important feature in the schools of Kamakura Buddhism.

Fifth, Japanese Buddhism has a propensity for understanding the meaning of life and the world aesthetically rather than ethically or metaphysically. This understanding was undoubtedly grounded in the pre-Buddhist Japanese emphasis on the artistic and the poetic, but it was furthered by the importance that the cultural expression of Buddhism held from the time of the introduction of Buddhism to Japan. The aesthetic tendency was reiterated by Kūkai and subsequent Buddhist leaders.

Sixth, Japanese Buddhism affirms the sacrality of the world of nature. This feature is probably the most basic to the Japanese Buddhist understanding of reality. It reflects a synthesis of the pre-Japanese notion of a cosmos permeated by *kami* (sacred) nature with the Chinese Buddhist emphasis on the phenomenal world as the locus of soteriology and the Taoist notion of "naturalness" (*tzu-jan*). According to Balazs, Taoist "naturalness" had three related meanings: (1) "nature without human intervention," (2) "the spontaneous liberty of the individual," and (3) "the 'absolute'—another name for Tao" (cited in Wright 1959, p. 29). With the articulation of the sacrality of the world of nature in terms of *Jinen-hōni* (*Tathatā*; things as they are, spontaneity without cause) or *hongaku* (innate Buddha-nature), Japanese Buddhism at last became self-conscious as the heir of both historic Buddhism and Japanese religion.

268

REFERENCES

ANESAKI, Masaharu
 1930 *History of Japanese Religion*. London.
ASTON, W. G., trans.
 1972 *Nihongi*. Rutland, Vermont and Tokyo.
BALAZS, Etienne
 1964 *Chinese Civilization and Bureaucracy*. H. M. Wright, trans. New
  Haven.
BASHAM, A. L.
 1954 *The Wonder That Was India*. New York.
CHAN, Wing-tsit
 1957 "Transformation of Buddhism in China." *Philosophy East and
  West* 7, nos. 3-4, pp. 107-116.
CH'EN, Kenneth
 1964 *Buddhism in China: A Historical Survey*. Princeton.
 1973 *The Chinese Transformation of Buddhism*. Princeton.
ELIOT, Charles
 1954 *Hinduism and Buddhism*, vol. 3. New York.
GARDINER, K.J.H.
 1969 *The Early History of Korea*. Honolulu.
GROUSSET, R.
 1959 *Chinese Art and Culture*. Haakon Chevalier, trans. New York.
HORI, Ichirō
 1968 *Folk Religion in Japan: Continuity and Change*. Chicago.
KI-YOUNG Yi
 1975 "The Buddhist Land Ideologies of Shilla and Japan Prevalent in
  the Seventh and Eighth Centuries as Viewed from the Viewpoint
  of Their Symbolic Expression." In TAMURA and HONG 1975.
KIM, T'aek-kyu
 1975 "On the Phases of Integration of Gods and Buddha as Revealed
  in Shilla and Japan." In TAMURA and HONG 1975.
KITAGAWA, J. M.
 1963 "Buddhist Translation in Japan." *Babel* 9, nos. 1-2, pp. 53-59.
  [Chapter 13 of this book.]
 1965 "The Buddhist Transformation in Japan." *History of Religions* 4,
  no. 2, pp. 319-336. [Chapter 12 of this book.]
 1974 "The Japanese *Kokutai* (National Community): History and
  Myth." *History of Religions* 13, no. 3, pp. 209-226.
 1979 "*Matsuri* and *Matsuri-goto*: Religion and State in Early Japan."
  Religious Traditions 2, no. 1, pp. 30-37. [Chapter 7 of this book.]
 1980 " 'A Past of Things Present': Notes on Major Motifs of Early
  Japanese Religions." *History of Religions* 20, nos. 1-2, pp. 27-42.
  [Chapter 2 of this book.]
 1981 "Monarchy and Government: Traditions and Ideologies in Pre-

Modern Japan." In A. L. Basham, ed., *Kingship in Asia and Early America*. Mexico City. [Chapter 5 of this book.]

MILLER, Richard J.
1974   *Ancient Japanese Nobility: The Kabane Ranking System*. Berkeley.

MURAYAMA Shūichi
1981   *Nihon onmyōdō-shi sōsetsu* [The general view of the history of the Yin-Yang School in Japan]. Tokyo.

NAKAMURA Hajime
1948   *Tōyō-jin no shii-hōhō* [The ways of thinking of eastern peoples], vol. 2. Tokyo. (English trans., Tokyo, 1960.)
1957   "The Influences of Confucian Ethics on the Chinese Translations of Buddhist Sutras." *Liebenthal Festschrift (Sino-Indian Studies 5,* no. 4, pp. 156-171).

NIKAM, N. A., and McKEON, Richard
1959   *The Edicts of Aśoka*. Chicago.

RAHULA, Walpola
1956   *History of Buddhism in Ceylon*. Colombo.

SEN, Amulyachandra
1956   *Aśoka's Edicts*. Calcutta.

TAMURA, Enchō
1966   *Fujiwara no Kamatari* [Kamatari of Fujiwara]. Tokyo.

TAMURA, Enchō, and HONG Soon-Chang, eds.
1975   *Shiragi to asuka-hakuhō no bukkyō-bunka* [The kingdom of Silla and the Buddhist culture of the Asuka and Hakuhō periods]. Tokyo.

TEGGART, Frederick J.
1939   *Rome and China: A Study of Correlations in Historical Events*. Berkeley.

THOMAS, E. J.
1933   *The History of Buddhist Thought*. New York.

TSUKAMOTO Zenryū
1956   "Buddhism in China and Korea." Leon Hurvitz, trans. In Kenneth W. Morgan, ed., *The Path of the Buddha*. New York.

WATANABE Shōkō
1958   *Nihon no bukkyō* [Japanese Buddhism]. Tokyo.

WRIGHT, Arthur F.
1959   *Buddhism in Chinese History*. Stanford.

PART V

The Modern Phase of the Japanese Religious Tradition

16. The Religious Ethos of
Present-Day Japan

I N PREPARING this talk on "The Religious Ethos of Present-Day Japan," I was reminded of a statement made by the former Vice President of Indonesia a few years ago. He said: "He who claims to understand the Indonesian situation today must be badly informed." A similar observation could be made regarding present-day Japan, and especially about its religious ethos.

I have a feeling that many of you, especially those who were born in the sixties, cannot imagine that until quite recently Japan and other parts of Asia were not prominent on the mental map of people in the West. To be sure, since ancient times the Orient has always had a mysterious spell on some Western minds. However, until World War II, Asia symbolized something "far away and long ago."[1] Today, the situation is entirely different. Japan, for example, has come into the immediate experience of many Americans. People are getting used to a variety of things Japanese—art, literature, cuisine, cinema, karate, judo, Zen meditation, as well as transistor radios, television sets, and small cars.

Yet mere exposure to external features of other people's cultures does not automatically bring one an understanding of the spirit, *Geist*, or ethos of other cultures and religions, and let us not underestimate our enormous capacity to misunderstand other cultures and religions.

My reflections on "the religious ethos of present-day Japan" are based on a simple premise: that people everywhere share the same humanity. We are all psycho-physical and spiritual beings, endowed with memory, intelligence, and sexuality, trying to make sense out of our transitory existence in this vast and mysterious universe. On the other hand, each cultural tradition has developed its own characteristic way of comprehending the meaning of life, a comprehension that is nurtured and preserved by the particular culture's language, customs, myths, and religious forms.

As far as we can ascertain, every individual, culture, religion, and people lives not only in a geographical, physical world but also in a

[1] See Christy's own article in Arthur E. Christy, ed., *The Asian Legacy and American Life* (New York: The John Day Co., 1942).

"world of meaning." Some are more self-conscious than others about the mental and psychic processes involved in ordering the diverse experiences and meanings that comprise the mystery of life. Helen Keller's memorable book entitled *Teacher* tells us how Miss Keller's teacher, Annie Sullivan, began to teach the deaf and blind child:

> She began at once spelling into Helen's hand, suiting the word to the action, the action to the word, and the child responded by imitating the finger motions like a bright, inquisitive animal. . . . [One day,] while Annie Sullivan pumped water over her hand it came to the child in a flash that water, wherever it was found, was water, and that the finger motions she had just felt on her palm meant water and nothing else. In that thrilling moment she found the key to her kingdom. Everything had a name and she had a way to learn the names.[2]

Although it may be an extreme example, this event makes clear the process whereby each one of us emerges from that phase of life Helen Keller called "a phantom living in a world that is no-world."[3] To put it another way, to be fully human means to be able to shape one's own structure of meaning, through association and imagination, education and effort, with regard to things we observe and experience. And, like an individual, each society and culture undergoes various phases of growth and development. Our "world of meaning" stems in large measure from what has been handed down to us; our world of meaning consciously or unconsciously reflects our individual and collective historical experiences.

AT THE EXPENSE of oversimplification, let me reflect on the various layers of the Japanese "world of meaning."

At the bottom layer lies the dim memory of the ancient magico-religious tradition that held a strong cosmological outlook. Japan is a small island archipelago, whose total land area is less than that of California. To the ancient Japanese people, however, this small land was the only world they knew and experienced. No doubt, the natural beauty, which is enhanced by seasonal change, nurtured the people's belief that Japan is a sacred land and is permeated by numerous *kami*, or divine spirits.[4] Unlike many Westerners who feel that this world is a fallen world, the early Japanese took it for granted that the natural world *was* the original world, and they did not look for another order

[2] Helen Keller, *Teacher: Anne Sullivan Macy*, intro. by Nella Braddy Henney (Garden City, N.Y.: Doubleday, 1955), pp. 11-12.
[3] Ibid., p. 8.
[4] See J. M. Kitagawa, *Religions of the East*, rev. ed. (Philadelphia: Westminster Press, 1968), pp. 278-309.

of meaning behind or beyond the natural world. They also held the simple belief that human beings are *kami*, or spiritual beings; later, however, the status of *kami* was reserved for monarchs and royalty.

It is important to point out that the most important religious figure in ancient Japan was the poet. Many poets wrote verses that responded to a variety of human situations as well as to the poignant beauty and wonder of the four seasons and the landscape. These poets were not inhibited in expressing the tender passions of love or the gentle throbbing of hearts as they bade farewell to friends or in times of grief. Throughout these poetic verses they depicted the similarity between the capriciousness of human life on the one hand and the swift change of the seasons on the other. Life for the ancient Japanese had elements of sorrow, tragedy, trial, and tribulation; yet they affirmed life in this phenomenal existence as essentially good (*yoshi*) and beautiful (*uruwashi*).[5] Basically, to them the world (Japan) was the religious universe, in which living itself was a religious act in the broadest sense of the term. Such a religious universe was nurtured by myths and poetic verses, which taught men and women the meaning of human existence and gave them a sense of identity.

There is much truth in the art historian Langdon Warner's observation that from its early days Japan's native religion, Shinto, had been the artist's way of life: "Natural forces are the very subject matter for those who produce artifacts from raw materials or who hunt and fish and farm. Shintō taught how such forces are controlled and these formulas have been embedded into Shintō liturgies."[6]

This simple yet all-embracing ancient Japanese world of meaning was destined to undergo changes due to external influences—namely, the various religious and cultural traditions that came to the Japanese shores from outside like a series of waves. It is to be noted that each time a new religion or culture reached Japan, a threefold response followed. At first, the new religion or culture was eagerly welcomed; then there was a second period of integration or assimilation; and finally, in the third stage the new religion or culture was either rejected or transformed as the Japanese reasserted their old spiritual heritage. Let me illustrate this threefold process in connection with the introduction into Japan of Chinese civilization and Buddhism, of Roman Catholicism, and of modern Western civilization.

[5] Tsunetsugu Muraoka, *Studies in Shinto Thought*, trans. D. M. Brown and J. T. Araki (Tokyo: Ministry of Education, 1964), p. 58.
[6] Langdon Warner, *The Enduring Art of Japan* (Cambridge, Mass.: Harvard University Press, 1952), p. 18.

THE INITIAL foreign cultural wave penetrated Japan in about the fifth and sixth centuries of our era from Korea and China; it introduced to Japan the ethical teachings of Confucianism, the magico-mystical teaching of Taoism, and the gospel of Buddhism. During the first period that followed, roughly from the seventh through the eighth centuries, the impact of these continental beliefs overshadowed Shinto to the extent that during the eighth century, called the Nara period, Japan appeared very much like a miniature of China. Under the influence of the humanistically oriented Confucianism, people in Japan learned that human society had its own structure of meaning apart from the world of nature. Side by side with Confucianism and its legacy of social morality and political, legal, and educational institutions, Buddhism stimulated the Japanese people to reflect on the meaning of human nature and human destiny. Such simple Buddhist notions as moral causation (*karma*) and rebirth were added to the Japanese vocabulary. This reinforced the earlier Japanese notion of the interrelatedness of all beings, as exemplified by a popular Buddhist phrase: "Beasts in the present life might have been our parents in a past life." During the second period (the Heian period), from roughly the ninth to the twelfth century, Confucianism and Buddhism were gradually assimilated by the Japanese, so that something like a "division of labor" developed among religious and semireligious systems. While national and communal cults remained the prerogatives of Shinto, public and private morality were delegated to the Confucian system and spiritual and metaphysical problems became the concerns of Buddhism.[7] Finally, during the third period (roughly the thirteenth century), the pendulum swung the other way. As Kublai Khan, the Mongol emperor of China, attempted to invade the little island kingdom, which only a few centuries earlier had looked up to China with dreamy eyes, Japan asserted herself and fought the Chinese armada. Most likely Japan would have been invaded by the Mongol forces had not a windstorm, called the divine wind (*kamikaze*) by the Japanese, driven back the Chinese armada. It was more than a matter of military conflict, however. In the religious domain, we find the emergence during this time of native Japanese schools of Buddhism, such as the nationalist Nichiren sect, Amida Pietism, and Zen Buddhism, as well as the resurgence of Shinto. The threefold cycle was complete.

[7] On this point, see Hideo Kishimoto, "Some Japanese Cultural Traits and Religions," in *The Japanese Mind*, ed. C. A. Moore (Honolulu: East-West Center Press, 1967), pp. 110-121.

A SECOND significant cultural wave, this one from Europe, penetrated Japan in the sixteenth century. The first Europeans to come to Japan were the Portuguese, who were then establishing a great overseas empire in India and other parts of Asia. The Portuguese traders were soon followed by Roman Catholic missionaries: the famous Jesuit, Francis Xavier (d. 1552), and his companions arrived on the Japanese shore in 1549. Roman Catholicism, then known as *Kirishitan*, followed the general pattern of the thirteenth-century Pure Land, Nichiren, and other Buddhist sects. Since at that time the political order and social fabric were disintegrating, many people felt the need for social identity and solidarity as well as the certainty of religious salvation. *Kirishitan* offered both a concrete form of religious society and the sacramental assurance of salvation for souls. On the other hand, Roman Catholicism was also a symbol of the medieval European civilization which had attracted the trade-hungry warlords. Oda Nobunaga, the strongman of Japan, favored Catholicism partly to counterbalance the excessive power of established Buddhist monasteries. But this factor alone does not explain the rapid growth of Catholicism in Japan during the sixteenth and early seventeenth centuries. (According to one report sent to the Vatican, there were about 150,000 Japanese *Kirishitan* near the end of the sixteenth century.) The Japanese also learned from Catholic missionaries about Western medicine (especially surgery), geography, and other scientific subjects.[8] It was difficult, however, to assimilate Catholicism into Japanese religious and cultural life: unlike Confucianism and Buddhism, Catholic Christianity professed a singleness of allegiance, demanding an 'either/or' decision from the people. Feudal rulers issued edicts prohibiting Catholicism time and time again, but the number of *Kirishitan* adherents continued to grow. In the end, a severe blow came to Catholicism when, in 1637, thousands of *Kirishitan* men and women on the western island of Kyushu rebelled against the feudal regime. Although they fought valiantly, they fell when their food and ammunition were exhausted. When the uprising was quelled, Japanese *Kirishitan*s were ordered to renounce their faith; if they did not, they were either tortured or shipped out of the country. This brought an end to the colorful history of medieval Catholicism in Japan.

Following the *Kirishitan* uprising, the feudal regime took the far more drastic measure of national seclusion, cutting off trade and other

[8] See Arimichi Ebisawa, *Kirishitan no shakai katsudō oyobi Namban igaku* [The social works of *Kirishitan* and European medicine] (Tokyo: Fuzanbo, 1944).

277

contacts with all foreign powers except the Dutch. During the two and a half centuries of national seclusion, Japan developed a rigidly controlled, hierarchically organized feudal society. The warriors, who were on top of the social scale, followed the semireligious Code of Warriors (*Bushi-dō*), while the general populace found meaning and consolation in an eclectic religious form which blended Shinto, Buddhism, Taoism, and indigenous folk religion.[9] Because of their policy of seclusion, most Japanese did not know that events were moving quickly in the rest of the world, among them the birth of a new republic across the Pacific. From this nation, "Black Ships" led by Commodore Matthew Perry appeared off the shore of Japan in 1853.

A new cycle of the threefold process began in the mid-nineteenth century and ended with World War II. When modern Western civilization was first introduced to Japan in the nineteenth century, Japan eagerly adopted many Western institutions, such as a postal system, a civil service system, banks, a parliament, a constitution, railroads, electricity, an army, a navy, and an educational system. Many iconoclastic youths, living mostly in urban areas, felt that they had been emancipated from their traditional cultural and religious values by Western science, democracy, Christianity, or atheism. As early as the 1870s, the writings of Mill, Darwin, Huxley, and Spencer were introduced, and soon Voltaire and Rousseau began to attract college students. A little later, Kant, Hegel, and Schopenhauer became the intellectual idols. Japanese Buddhists found great inspiration in Schopenhauer, Spinoza, and Hegel. Among all forms of Western thought the most controversial was Christianity. While it never regained its earlier strength, many young, urban intellectuals became its eager followers.

After a decade of initial enthusiasm for Western civilization, the situation began to change. The hope of Christian missionaries and of iconoclastic young Japanese to see Japan completely Christianized or westernized gave way to serious disappointments. In this connection, I would caution against the simplistic interpretation prevalent in many Western college textbooks that the termination of the feudal regime and the beginning of imperial rule in 1867 meant an abrupt change from premodern to modern Japan. To be sure, in one sense the new imperial Meiji regime eagerly joined the modern world: it welcomed new knowledge from the West. But it soon became evident that the aim of the imperial regime was not only a renovation (*ishin*) that implied forward motion, but also a restoration (*fukko*) or a reversion to

[9] Yasuzō Horiye, "Edo-jidai no Jugaku ni okeru Kokka-ron" [Views on "State" according to Confucian schools during the Edo period], in *Eastern Studies Fifteenth Anniversary Issue* (Tokyo, 1962), pp. 290-301.

the ancient ideal of the emperor-centered religious, political, and national polity. In short, the Meiji regime intended to develop a modern nation-state without losing the traditional Japanese religious and cultural framework. Thus, while the new Constitution guaranteed a limited freedom of religion, the government banned religious instruction of any kind from all schools with the provision that "moral teaching, if applicable to all religions, could be given." At the same time, the government concocted State Shinto and interpreted it not as a religion but as a cult of national morality and patriotism.[10] Henceforth, education became the government's way of inculcating ethnocentric nationalism and strenghtening the emperor cult. Meanwhile, the Sino-Japanese War (1894-1895), the Russo-Japanese War (1904-1905), and the annexation of Korea (1910) strenthened Japan's military clique, and the country's alliance with Britain during World War I fattened the financial community. From 1918 onward, however, much to the consternation of the conservative statesmen, financiers, and militarists, the people's demands for universal suffrage became vocal. Industrial workers began to organize unions, labor strikes became frequent occurrences, and a small Marxist group began to attract students. In fact, Japanese historians call the 1920s the period of Taishō Democracy.[11]

In the 1930s Japan entered the third stage. All liberal thinking and expressions in religion, philosophy, art, and culture were condemned as dangerous. The rights of freedom of the press, of thought, and of assembly were violated. Some elder statesmen and moderate parliamentarians who resisted the militarists' expansionist policies were assassinated. In 1936, Japan joined Germany in an anti-communist pact, and the government began to press all religious bodies to cooperate in extending imperial rule abroad. The threefold process was once again complete.

AFTER Japan's surrender to the Allied powers at the end of World War II, another cultural wave penetrated Japan, this time primarily from the United States. Under the Allied occupation (1945-1952), Japan began to orient herself economically, politically, and culturally almost singularly toward America. In analyzing the present-day religious situation in Japan, opinions are sharply divided. Some people think that

[10] Shigeyoshi Murakami, *Japanese Religion in the Modern Century*, trans. H. Byron Earhart (Tokyo: University of Tokyo Press, 1980), pp. 41-44.

[11] See Shūichi Katō, *"Taishō* Democracy as the Pre-Stage for Japanese Militarism," in *Japan in Crisis: Essays on Taishō Democracy*, ed. B. S. Silberman and H. D. Harootunian (Princeton: Princeton University Press, 1974), pp. 217-236.

American influence, like the cultural waves which have penetrated Japan in the past, is bound to go through the traditional threefold cycle. On the other hand, some claim that the postwar Japanese experience does not follow the previous pattern because of a new element which complicated the picture: the Allied occupation. Holders of both views, however, agree that the year 1945 marked a significant line of demarcation between two worlds of experience for the Japanese. Japan's surrender was undoubtedly the most traumatic event in the historic memory of the Japanese people. In spite of its industrial potential, its huge reservoir of skilled workers, and its technological sophistication, many Japanese then questioned whether their nation would ever again become a world power. Their temporary loss of nerve was coupled with great anxiety about the uncertain future under the military occupation of a foreign nation. In this situation, General MacArthur—nicknamed the "Star-spangled Mikado"—issued a series of directives, much as the emperors and shoguns had done, ordering the captive Japanese government to enact constitutional revisions, undertake educational and land reforms, release political prisoners, dismantle the armed forces and the financial oligarchy (*zaibatsu*), and initiate other novel measures.

Among all the changes brought about by the occupation forces, the most radical and far-reaching steps were those relating to the religious foundation of the Japanese nation. Each of the measures enforced by the occupation authorities was designed to alter religious and political principles which had been held by the ancient, feudal, and Meiji regimes. First, the newly declared principle of religious freedom undercut the notion that every Japanese person must pledge his or her ultimate loyalty and commitment to the throne and the nation. This involved more than the people's freedom to worship and to form religious associations; the principle of religious liberty affirmed the individual's essential freedom, if need be, to obey higher principles than the laws of the government. Second, State Shinto—that gigantic superreligion created by the Meiji regime—was disestablished by a new directive which prohibited the sponsorship, support, perpetuation, control, and dissemination of State Shinto by the Japanese national, prefectural, and local government, or by public officials. Third, the new principle of the separation of religion and state nullified what had been regarded as sacred from the time of early Shinto, namely, the notion of the unity of religion and government (*saisei-itchi*). On the basis of this principle, Buddhism and Confucianism had been made subservient to the Shinto-inspired sacred monarchical system in the seventh century. Similarly, the feudal regime in the seventeenth cen-

tury banned Roman Catholicism on the grounds that it was irreconcilable with the polity of the regime. In the more recent past, this
principle had been invoked as the Meiji regime required every Japanese
subject to adhere to State Shinto, which was placed above all religious
systems. Given this history, one can readily understand the profound
effect that the newly declared principle of separation of religion and
state had on the transformation of Japan.[12]

Equally significant was the imperial rescript issued in 1946 which
denied the divinity of the emperor. This rescript made it clear that the
Japanese people's traditional world of meaning and their understanding of history, which counted the sacred sanctions of the ancient
Shinto myths as historical facts, could no longer be preserved in postwar Japan.[13] This meant that the Japanese people were cut off suddenly and abruptly from their own past and their own historical experience, which could be traced all the way back to the ancient
cosmological world-view.

In addition to the loss of this cosmological orientation, the Japanese
also faced the erosion of the family system, which had always been the
cornerstone of Japanese society. After the war, the new civil code of
1947 effectively abolished the traditional system of interlocked households (*iye-seido*) as a legal institution. The erosion of family cohesion
weakened both the parish system which had supported Buddhist temples and the local communities which had supported Shinto shrines.
Consequently, individuals were no longer bound by the established
religious affiliation of their households. These elements are only part
of the sweeping changes initiated by the occupation forces, changes
which presumably had been approved by Washington. Ironically, the
policies of the United States toward Japan were far from consistent.
For example, in 1945 the occupation authorities announced that they
would create an advanced democracy, such that Japan was to become
a neutral, demilitarized "Switzerland in Asia." Only two years later,
American policy in Asia underwent a radical change. The occupation
policy of democratizing Japan shifted to one of making Japan a strong
anti-communist citadel in the Pacific. Even then, MacArthur was convinced that the seeds of democracy which he had planted would bear
fruit in the years to come, that Christianity was making great strides
in Japan, and that the military occupation was being conducted according to the tenets of the Sermon on the Mount.[14] In 1950, Japanese trade with Western nations was reestablished, and the peace treaty

[12] See Murakami, *Japanese Religion*, chap. 12, especially pp. 118-119.
[13] Ibid., pp. 119-120.
[14] Recollection of author.

was signed in San Francisco in the following year. In 1952, administrative agreements on the terms for American bases in Japan were signed, and, parenthetically, the first anti-American riots took place in Tokyo.

In spite of a number of serious issues and ambiguities involved, the significance of the Allied occupation of Japan should not be overlooked. As I have stated elsewhere, the occupation signified the "second opening" of Japan to the family of nations. In the mid-nineteenth century, Western powers persuaded Japan to open her doors primarily to commercial trade. While the Meiji regime declared its eagerness to welcome new ideas from abroad, the architects of the Meiji regime sensed the danger that the spirit of modernity presented: it might undercut the foundation of the imperial institution which was sustained by ancient myths. Thus, although they officially reversed the policy of national seclusion, the imperial regime welcomed only those Western ideas and technologies that would benefit Japan materially. Domestically, the regime preserved and even solidified this policy of seclusion as far as political, ethical, and religious structures were concerned. It was this internal, spiritual insularity of Japan that was broken in 1945 by the occupation forces. But was it really broken down? That is the crucial question!

SEEN FROM this perspective, it is readily understandable that the issues of religious liberty and the separation of religion and state cut deeper than the usual questions regarding just how free people in present-day Japan are in exercising their religious scruples and idiosyncrasies. These issues are related to a more basic question: How *new* is new Japan? Outsiders already know many of the new features of the science, technology, industry, and commerce of new Japan. But what is the *religious* ethos of present-day Japan? It is not easy to resolve this question adequately.

Unfortunately, the principle of freedom of religion was interpreted mechanically and too literally both by the occupation authorities and by Japanese government officials. Another lamentable occurrence was that many questionable groups claimed to be religions in order to receive tax exemptions and other privileges. In order to rectify this unfortunate situation, a new law—the Religious Persons Law—was adopted in 1951.[15]

Under the new law, Shinto has become one religion among many,

---

[15] William P. Woodard, *The Allied Occupation of Japan 1945-1952 and Japanese Religions*, pt. 4 (Leiden: E. J. Brill, 1972), pp. 76-102.

having lost its government subsidy. Nearly 80,000 shrines now belong to the Shrine Association. Shinto faces many serious problems: for too long it had depended on the government for its survival and had not developed any coherent theological system. On the other hand, Shinto has a nationwide network of shrines and local support structures, and it has remained alive through festivities and communal rituals. The potential danger facing Shinto is that it could provide a ready-made channel for national narcissism, which in turn could be manipulated by vote-hungry politicians. This is something they have been trying to do in recent years.

Christianity faces the exact opposite set of problems from Shinto. During the war, Christian churches were harassed and had to compromise their religious convictions in order to survive under the "divine" emperor. Thus, the initial postwar task for Christianity was as much to undergo a spiritual rehabilitation as to undertake the physical reconstruction of its churches and institutions. Although the immediate postwar period was marked by some curiosity about Christianity on the part of many Japanese people, popular interest in Christianity waned quickly. This was due in part to the occupation leaders' naive identification of Christianity with an anti-communist stance. Also, however salutary the motives of the Western churches in sending material help and missionaries, the sheer presence of so many ill-prepared foreign missionaries who had no understanding of the complex situation in Japan tended to emphasize the foreignness of Christianity, a trademark that the Japanese churches could ill afford. Moreover, churches today seem to lack quality leadership in comparison with the prewar period when small Christian groups produced outstanding thinkers and leaders.

Postwar Japan presented many problems as well as new opportunities to Buddhism. Acute economic problems and the policy of religious freedom impaired the traditional hierarchical relationship between the main temples and subordinate temples and weakened the Buddhist parochial system. Religious freedom resulted in the independence of many subgroups; by 1951, the number of Buddhist groups had grown to 170, roughly three times the number before the war. Fortunately, Japanese Buddhism was greatly stimulated by a worldwide association of different Buddhist groups called the World Fellowship of Buddhists. It also was encouraged by the growing interest in Buddhism both in Europe and America. Nevertheless, Japanese Buddhism is caught between its own past and the demands of the new age. Many enlightened leaders are disquieted over the old Buddhist habits of subservience to political authority, the spirit of eth-

283

nocentric nationalism, the prevalence of magical practices, and the preoccupation with funerary rites for the dead at the expense of providing spiritual guidance to the living. But by far the greatest challenge and threat to established Buddhism comes from the so-called "new religions" (*Shinkō Shūkyō*).

ONE OF THE most conspicuous features on the postwar Japanese religious scene is the sudden mushrooming of many new religions.[16] During the period when many people suffered from uncertainty and poverty as well as the erosion of national, communal, and family ties, the new religions offered mundane happiness, tightly knit organizations, assurance of healing and/or easy salvation, and readily accessible divine agents or self-styled messiahs. This is why many Western scholars have classified them as "crisis religions" and compare them to the Ghost Dance and the Cargo Cult.

It may be surprising to many people, however, that the real growth of the new religions came after the beginning of the Korean War, which marked a heavy trend toward urbanization and industrialization in Japan. Indeed, it has only been since 1955, after life became much more comfortable, that such new religions as the Sōka Gakkai ("Society for the Creation of Values"), Risshō Kōseikai ("Society for the Establishment of Righteousness and Friendly Relations"), and the PL Kyōdan, to name only the most obvious, have gained strength among the new middle class.

Many observers of Japanese new religions are impressed by their skillful use of modern techniques of organization, administration, and propaganda as well as the charismatic qualities of their founders. Many of these new religions, however, lean toward ethnocentrism. Unlike Buddhism and Christianity, the new religions have no direct contact with the global communities of their respective faiths. Apparently, the fact that new religions have inherited their ethos primarily from the folk religious tradition enables them to reach very easily a large number of people who respond to their naive optimism. One great danger the new religions face is that they may serve unwittingly as spiritual tranquilizers, in effect contributing to social, political, and religious inertia. My candid observation is that many of the new religions are now "suffering" from social, political, and organizational success at the expense of adequate inner religious resources.

My overall impression of the religious situation in Japan may be

[16] J. M. Kitagawa, "New Religions in Japan," in *Religion and Change in Contemporary Asia* (Minneapolis: University of Minnesota Press, 1971), pp. 27-43.

succinctly stated as follows. The newly declared principles of religious freedom and the separation of religion and the state make the "second opening" of Japan theoretically possible. There seem to me to be three possible outcomes. They depend largely on (1) whether the people in Japan will resort to some kind of coherence derived from the past (as the so-called new religions seem to advocate); (2) whether they will pursue their future primarily in terms of technology, industry, and commerce (i.e., secular options); or (3) whether they will develop the way to a creative reshaping of their lives, collectively and individually, in the framework of genuine religious freedom.

17. Some Reflections on Foreign Scholars' Understanding of Japanese Culture and Shinto

THE LATE Sir George B. Sansom once stated: "Few countries have been more copiously described than Japan, and perhaps few have been less thoroughly understood."[1] This is particularly true of its religious dimension.

It is apparent that due largely to geographical and historical factors Japan was not accessible to people in other parts of the world until the modern period. To be sure, Japan's immediate neighbors had ample opportunities to deal with the Japanese, as evidenced by frequent references to Japan and the Japanese in the Chinese and Korean records from the early centuries of the Christian era. But people beyond the borders of China were not even cognizant of the existence of Japan until the ninth century when the ambiguous designation of *Wak-wak*, probably a corrupt form of *Wa-kuo* (an old Chinese name for Japan), appeared in some of the Persian geographical writings. Although Marco Polo's account of *Cipangu* aroused curiosity in certain quarters of Europe, this reputed land of gold remained in the memories of Europeans only as a romantic never-never land. "Later Arabic and European writers supposedly refer to the Japanese," according to Professor Lach, "but none of them is clear on the precise location of the insular kingdom. The first definite approximation of the word Japan ("Jampon") in a European document appeared in the *Suma Oriental* of Tomé Pires, perhaps written as early as 1513."[2]

The picture changed greatly with the chance arrival of three shipwrecked Portuguese seamen on Japanese soil in 1543. Soon Portuguese merchants found their way to Japan, followed by Jesuit and other *Kirishitan* (Roman Catholic) missionaries. In 1547, at the request of Francis Xavier who two years later inaugurated Catholic missionary activities in Japan, Captain Jorge Alvarez wrote a narrative description of Japan in which some differences in beliefs and practices

[1] Sansom's "Foreword" in Edwin O. Reischauer, *Japan—Past and Present* (New York, 1953), p. vii.
[2] Donald F. Lach, *Asia in the Making of Europe*, vol. 1, bk. 2 (Chicago, 1965), p. 652.

were observed between Buddhism and Shinto. During the second half of the sixteenth century, with the arrival of a large number of European missionaries in Japan and sporadic visits of the Japanese in Europe, Europeans came to know something about various aspects of Japan, including its religious situation.[3] In this respect, a few general observations may be made for the purpose of our discussion.

Firstly, despite great differences that existed between European and Japanese cultures and societies, there were certain congenialities between them. "In fact," as Professor Reischauer points out, "when the Europeans first arrived in Japan in the sixteenth century, they found political and social conditions which were completely understandable to them in terms of the sixteenth-century Europe they knew."[4]

Secondly, most reporters on Japan in the sixteenth and early seventeenth centuries were motivated by spreading Catholic Christianity and not by the understanding of Japanese culture for its own sake. Some of the missionaries might have been characterized as "keen and intelligent observers of the mundane life that went on around them,"[5] but their knowledge of Japanese history before the sixteenth century was practically nil, and they reported only those matters which had immediate relevance to their missionary activities. Besides, their reports were censored at home, so that matters which might have interested European intellectuals were withheld from them. In the words of Professor Lach:

> It is obvious from what we know now that the Jesuits had a much clearer idea of the doctrines and strength of the Japanese religions than they were willing to admit in print during the sixteenth century. Polanco and other European censors seem to have been determined not to let the European public know too much of Shinto and Buddhism and of their hold upon the Japanese.[6]

Thirdly, the relationship between Europe and Japan was regarded by Europeans as a one-way street, whereby the former was to be the giver and the latter the receiver. Moreover, missionaries as well as many merchants came from the Latin, Catholic segments of Europe, and they tried to present Europe to the Japanese primarily in terms of their religion.[7] Just as they did not want Europeans to learn too much

---

[3] See George Schurhammer, *Shintō: The Way of the Gods of Japan. According to Printed and Unprinted Reports of the Jesuit Missionaries in the XVI and XVII Centuries* (Bonn, 1923).

[4] Edwin O. Reischauer and John K. Fairbank, *East Asia: The Great Tradition* (Boston, 1958), p. 578.

[5] C. R. Boxer, *The Christian Century in Japan* (Berkeley, 1951), p. 50, n. 3.

[6] Lach, *Making of Europe*, vol. 1, bk. 2, p. 728.

[7] Arnold Toynbee, *The World and the West* (New York and London, 1953), p. 54.

about the reality of Japan, they did not want Japanese to learn too much about the arts and cultures of Europe. Even when the emissaries of the *Kirishitan daimyō* (nobility) were dispatched to Europe at the initiative of the Jesuits, "they were not to learn anything of Christian divisions and especially nothing about Protestantism. Their tour was carefully chaperoned and of limited duration so that they would receive only the best possible impression of Catholic Europe."[8] Consequently, during the later sixteenth and early seventeenth centuries, the Europeans and the Japanese were prevented from establishing free and direct cultural and intellectual contacts, which if properly exploited could have developed mutual understanding between them.

It is significant to note that even such one-sided cultural and religious contact between Europe and Japan came to be terminated by the Tokugawa regime's edict of national exclusion which followed the *Kirishitan* uprising at Shimabara of 1637-1638. As a result, between 1640 and 1853, only a limited number of Chinese and Dutchmen were allowed to visit Japan. Thus, during the two centuries of Japan's isolation from the rest of the world, there was virtually no opportunity for Westerners to learn anything about the internal development of Japanese thought and culture. This marked a sharp contrast to the case of Chinese culture, which found enthusiastic admirers among European intellectuals from the time of the Enlightenment. One can of course question whether the European Sinophiles, including such notables as Voltaire, Leibnitz, Christian Wolff, and Eustace Budgell, really understood Confucianism or only projected their own ideals onto their image of Confucius. It is certain that serious Sinology as such did not develop in Europe until early in the nineteenth century. Nevertheless, the fact remains that Chinese culture, unlike that of Japan, was readily accessible to Europeans during the seventeenth and eighteenth centuries.

More important, perhaps, is the fact that, during the period of Japanese isolation, the Europeans and the Japanese were exposed to very different kinds of social, political, economic, and cultural experiences. For example, as Sansom reminds us, by the seventeenth century feudal institutions in Europe had been replaced by nation-states with centralized monarchical governments, whereas feudalism had only just reached maturity in Japan.[9] Also, the intellectual climate of Europe was greatly influenced by the Renaissance, Reformation, Enlightenment, Industrial Revolution, and French Revolution, as well as by the

[8] Lach, *Making of Europe*, vol. 1, bk. 2, p. 691.
[9] George B. Sansom, *Japan: A Short Cultural History*, rev. ed. (New York, 1943), p. 442.

increasing interplay and competition among different nationalities, while Japan on the other hand received practically no new inspiration and stimulation from outside sources.[10] The problem for Japan now was how to conserve and increase her own resources, economically as much as culturally, intellectually and religiously. In short, the experience of the Europeans encouraged them to be more outgoing, extrovert, and to place their faith in the future, while the experience of the Japanese compelled them to be more traditional, introvert, and to put their faith in the past. There were undoubtedly many exceptions to such oversimplified characterizations on both sides. Nevertheless, we cannot overlook the fact that the differences in mental outlook remained, as before, an obstacle to Western understanding of Japanese culture when Japan opened its doors to the rest of the world in the mid-nineteenth century.

The opening of the country and the emergence of modern Japan were brought about by the combination of internal and external forces, about which various interpretations and analyses have been advanced.[11] Most scholars agree, however, in depicting as contradictory the objectives of the Meiji regime, namely, restoration and innovation. Practically, this implied the goal of establishing a modern nation-state with all the technological skills of Western civilization without losing the spiritual foundation of ancient Japan, as evidenced by the last article of the Charter Oath which states: "Knowledge shall be sought throughout the world in order to strengthen the foundation of imperial rule." Thus, during the initial phase of the Meiji era, able Japanese students were sent abroad for the study of various subjects, and a host of foreign scholars, teachers, technicians, and advisers were invited to Japan. Indeed, as Professor Anesaki recalls, "there was never a period in Japanese history when foreign assistance was so welcomed and made use of as in the eighth decade of the nineteenth century," even though, as he adds, "the memory of these foreign advisers has been much obliterated, partly wilfully, due to the conservative reaction in the nineties."[12] The opening of Japan also attracted other kinds of foreigners from various Western countries—missionaries, merchants, art collectors, and travelers. There were even those men such as William Sturgis Bigelow, Percival Lowell, John La Farge, Henry Adams, Ernest Fenollosa, and Lafcadio Hearn who sought "a true spiritual

[10] One must remember, however, that during the period of national exclusion Chinese books were available to Japanese intellectuals. Also, through the meager Dutch trading post at Nagasaki, some aspects of Western knowledge trickled into Japan.

[11] See Joseph M. Kitagawa, *Religion in Japanese History* (New York, 1966), chap. 5.

[12] Masaharu Anesaki, *History of Japanese Religion* (London, 1930), p. 350.

home where the whirlwinds of life are calmed and absolute truth might be found."[13] These men and women who gravitated to Japan for different reasons viewed Japan from their own perspectives and produced a wide variety of learned and less scholarly books and articles, travelogues, reports, and letters, portraying different images of Japan, its people, culture, and religions.

In retrospect, one is impressed by the fact that while many Japanese intellectuals were busily studying various aspects of Western learning during the Meiji era, pioneers of Western Japanology, such as William G. Aston, Ernest M. Satow, Basil Hall Chamberlain, Karl Florenz, Charles Eliot, and George B. Sansom,[14] were engaged in serious attempts at understanding Japanese history, language, art, culture, and religion. The magnitude of their task is well characterized by Sansom's description of Aston's work:

Aston had hardly any aids to study. He started from scratch, so to speak. He had to write his own grammar, to work out his own chronology of Japanese history, to read deeply and widely in Japanese literature without the benefit of translation or commentary. He devoted great analytical power to the study of early Japanese religion and he translated with valuable critical notes the greatest of the Japanese chronicles, the *Nihongi*. Amidst these preoccupations he found time to learn Korean and to look into Korean history. All this was the work of a busy official in not very robust health.[15]

If the pioneers of Japanology had to go through linguistic jungles and philosophic swamps, they also had some favorable conditions under which to work. Not only were they men endowed with strength of character and excellence of mind, but they had the benefit of a good classical education which gave them a sense of broad perspective. The pace of life was more leisurely then, and they had the sense of excitement of working in virgin territory which was not only novel for foreigners but was largely untouched even by native Japanese scholars, at least according to the canons of the Western humanistic disciplines.[16]

[13] Arthur E. Christy, ed., *The Asian Legacy and American Life* (New York, 1942), p. 43. Christy adds that in 1886 when a reporter inquired of Henry Adams and John La Farge as to their purpose in visiting Japan, La Farge replied that they were "in search of Nirvana" (pp. 43-44).

[14] These are only the most obvious of the pioneers, or "Giants" to use Sansom's expression, of Japanology. Another name which might be added is that of John Batchelor, the pioneer of Ainu study, although he cannot be considered a Japanologist in the usual sense of the term.

[15] "Address Delivered by Sir George Sansom" at the Annual Ceremony of the School of Oriental and African Studies (London) in 1956, reprinted in *The Journal of Asian Studies* 24, no. 4 (August 1965), p. 566.

[16] This sense of excitement comes through in Sansom's own account of the writing of his small classic, *Japan: A Short Cultural History*. He says: "I had spent a decade or

This does not mean that they were not aided by Japanese collaborators, but their collaborators were little more than informers and linguistic assistants who left the major task of interpretation in the hands of Western Japanologists.

The first-generation Western Japanologists not only laid the foundation for Japanology in Western countries but also stimulated native Japanese scholars. Soon, however, their dominance in Japanese studies was taken over by native Japanese scholars who appropriated Western scholarly methods and techniques in dealing with Japanese religion, history, and culture. And inevitably, as Dr. Nitobe astutely observed: "To any proud people tutored by a foreigner [there] comes a time when their consciousness awakes and asserts itself in obstinate questionings as to the merits of the model—questionings that proceed from the unsatisfied hunger of the inmost soul."[17] In their own ways, these first-generation modern Japanese scholars of Japanese studies were great pathfinders. They questioned—despite their great appreciation—the adequacy of the Western Japanologists' understanding of Japanese subjects, because the Westerners asked different kinds of questions and from their own perspectives. The task of the native Japanologists was complicated by the fact that the intellectual climate of Japan was undergoing changes due to the impact of the West. In this situation, they appeared to be too Western to the traditionalists because of their methods of inquiry, and yet they appeared to be too traditional to the modernists because of their subject matter. Nevertheless, these Japanese pioneers—e.g., Anesaki Masaharu in the Science of Religion, Takakusu Junjirō in Buddhology, Katō Genchi in Shinto study, and Yanagita Kunio in Folklore study—by their dogged determination and effort established their respective disciplines and trained many younger scholars.

For those of us who are interested in the discipline of *Allgemeine Religionswissenschaft*, it is significant to note that as early as 1896 a group of Japanese scholars organized the Society for the Comparative Study of Religions (*Hikaku Shūkyō Kenkyū-kai*), and that in 1905 the

---

more in the society of Japanese artists, scholars, collectors, archaeologists, monks, museum directors, actors, farmers, and fishermen. There is very little mentioned in the book with which I was not familiar—paintings, sculptures, buildings, landscapes, mountains, and rivers. Every circumstance was favorable. . . . I had much leisure and frequent opportunities to travel in China and Korea as well as in Japan. Much of the MS was written while I was drifting in a sampan on Lake *Chūzenji*. In those years I had a happy life, robust health, and was blessed with memoria capax sed non tenax. . . ." (Quoted in "Sir George Sansom: An Appreciation" by Marius B. Jansen, Donald Keene, and Arthur F. Wright, *The Journal of Asian Studies* 24, no. 4 [August 1965], p. 561.)

[17] Inazō Nitobe et al., *Western Influences in Modern Japan* (Chicago, 1931), p. 13.

first chair of the Science of Religion was established at Tokyo Imperial University. Also, government as well as private institutions of higher learning—Buddhist, Shinto, and Christian—established chairs of different religious studies. In this situation, the role of Western scholars, especially in religious studies, inevitably changed from that of the first-generation Western Japanologists. While they no longer were expected to provide tutelage and leadership, a number of them, e.g., W. Gundert, M. C. Haguenauer, H. Hammitzsch, August Karl Reichauer, M. W. de Visser, J. Witte, Herbert Zacher, and Heinrich Dumoulin, made important contributions in dealing with specific problems or subjects. Although these were perhaps less grandiose in scope than those of their predecessors, they were more thorough because of the utilization of the researches of native scholars. Ironically, it was in the area of Shinto study in which both Japanese and Western scholars' researches were greatly inhibited. This was because, from 1882 until the end of World War II, the Japanese government, which overtly and covertly propagated what is known as State Shinto, did not permit the critical study of Shinto. To be sure, in 1882 the Research Institute for the Imperial Classics was founded; the establishment of the Kokuga-kuin University followed in 1890. But scholarly research in Shinto was permitted only in regard to the external aspects of Shinto, and even that had to conform to the government's party line.[18] Such a climate was not favorable to Shinto research by Westerners, except for those who were willing to work within this narrow framework[19] or those who were in general sympathy with State Shinto.[20]

For better or for worse, World War II brought about marked changes in Japanese studies both in the West and in Japan. Before 1941, Japanology was considered a marginal and esoteric subject in most Western countries. Both in Europe and North America, the relatively few courses on Japan offered in colleges and universities dealt mostly with Japanese language or culture, either as a minor part of general "Oriental" studies or as one aspect of social studies which provided specialized data to historians, geographers, political scientists, and sociologists. Where Comparative Religion was taught, attention was given to Japanese Buddhism with little or no regard for Shinto. For the most part, competent scholars of the Far East, to say nothing

[18] As early as 1892, the learned historian Kume Kunitake was expelled from the Tokyo Imperial University because of his view that Shinto was the survival of a primitive cult.

[19] E.g., a series of monographs on various Shinto shrines by Richard A. B. Ponsonby-Fane.

[20] E.g., books and articles by J.W.T. Mason.

of Japanology per se, were scarce; and, as Dr. Cameron rightly observed, college administrators "did not always apply very exacting standards in choosing faculty members for it [Far Eastern studies chairs]. Mere residence in the Far East was often taken as automatically conferring systematic and communicable knowledge of everything from Burma to Hokkaido."[21] With the outbreak of war, various programs were improvised almost overnight to train experts on Japanese subjects. Also, an amazing array of books and articles, from the very scholarly to the ridiculous, appeared. Western interest in Japan, once aroused during wartime, did not diminish with the end of the war; rather, it grew even more in the postwar period, in part due to the Allied occupation which provided opportunities for many Western scholars and potential scholars to establish firsthand contacts with Japan even under such abnormal circumstances. Certainly in the United States the phenomenal growth of the Association of Asian Studies and other groups testifies to the continuing interest in Japan as well as in other parts of Asia. It is worth noting that, thanks to the availability of fellowships and research opportunities as well as languauge instruction many social scientists who hitherto had no tradition of acquiring language competence are engaged in the study of various aspects of Japan side by side with scholars of the humanities.[22] We are not altogether certain, however, that the increase in technical knowledge regarding specific problems, areas, and historic periods of Japan has improved Western scholars' general understanding of Japanese culture as a whole. Even in the study of Japanese religions, many of the new Western scholars tend to be narrow specialists, dealing with a specific sect or school, or perhaps with religious development in a particular period, at the expense of the total picture.

In Japan, too, specialization has become the vogue in academic circles. Even in the field of religious studies, a number of young scholars have discovered new methodological tools in sociology, psychology, and other social sciences for use in dealing with religious data. On the other hand, the necessary tension between the philosophy of religion and the historical-phenomenological study of religion is not always maintained. In a sense, the general tenor of religious studies in Japan may be characterized, following the usual division of *Religionswissenschaft* into *allgemeine Religionswissenschaft* and *spezielle Religionsge-*

[21] Meribeth E. Cameron, "Far Eastern Studies in the United States," *The Far Eastern Quarterly* 7, no. 2 (February 1948), p. 116.
[22] See Felix M. Keesing, "Problems of Integrating Humanities and Social Science Approaches in Far Eastern Studies," *The Far Eastern Quarterly* 14, no. 2 (February 1955), pp. 161-168.

schichte, by its tendency to lean toward the latter with little appreciation for the former. This is partly due to the fact that many scholars' study of religion(s) is motivated by their religious quest and not by the effort to understand the religious phenomena. Thus, to those who are so inclined, faith is a more important prerequisite than critical method of inquiry in religious studies. While they recognize the value and necessity of exacting methods in dealing with textual, historical, and doctrinal studies, the ultimate aim of understanding is regarded as a matter of one's own religious awakening and growth. This is what Dr. Suzuki was driving at fully three decades ago when he said:

Formerly Buddhists were glad to welcome a scientific approach to their religion. But nowadays a reaction seems to have taken place among them. Instead of relying on scientific arguments for the rationalization of the Buddhist experience they are at present trying to resort to its own dialectics. There is a growing conviction among the Buddhists that their philosophy does not require the support of Western logic, especially modern science.[23]

Parenthetically, those who hold this view consider the Japanese Association for Religious Studies[24] to be a sort of interfaith fellowship as much as a learned society of scholars.

Today, there is the feeling in some quarters in Japan that it is almost impossible for foreign scholars to understand Japanese culture and religions. Here the question lies in what kinds and levels of understanding are involved. It must be readily acknowledged that Japan is more than a field of study in the usual sense of the term. Japanese culture, like other great cultures, has an enduring individuality with its own history, language, art, religious tradition, philosophy, politics, and economics; thus, in a sense, only those who live within Japanese culture and society can fully understand the mystique of Japan, although not every Japanese attains such a lofty goal. On the other hand, a disciplined foreign scholar can experience the structure and integrity of Japanese culture and attain a certain kind and level of understanding. This is what Professor Redfield used to call "thinking about a civilization," which is "something different from getting information and acquaintance, though this third activity requires and is guided by the first two. It is to develop formed and namable thoughts about the civilization. It is to conceive it, to make it a mental artifact, a shaped work of the intellect."[25] In this connection, it might be added that this

[23] Quoted in A. Eustace Haydon, ed., *Modern Trends in World-Religions* (Chicago, 1934), p. 38.
[24] *Nihon Shūkyō Gakkai*, organized in 1930.
[25] Robert Redfield, "Thinking about a Civilization," in Milton Singer, ed., *Introducing India in Liberal Education* (Chicago, 1957), p. 3.

type of "thinking" is required not only of foreign scholars but also of Japanese scholars; otherwise, a meaningful collaboration on the scholarly level is impossible between them.

Inevitably, such an intellectual endeavor as thinking about a culture, civilization, or religion necessitates a certain amount of selectivity. For instance, any scholar, Japanese or foreign, has to do some telescoping of the history of Japan or Shinto, because no one mind can deal with the totality of the past. And this is precisely where the differences in perspectives, sensitivities, and methodologies between the native and foreign scholars are bound to arise, especially when a native scholar of, say, Shinto is himself a committed believer who looks at Shinto tradition through the eyes of faith as much as the eyes of scholarship. In this case, he certainly has every right to reject misguided criticisms of Shinto by non-Shintoists—Japanese and foreign[26]—and offer scholarly criticisms of non-Shinto scholars' works on Shinto. He might also contribute toward the systematic, apologetic, and constructive tasks of Shinto belief and theology.[27] But, pertaining to the study of Shinto on the part of non-Shinto scholars, he cannot question "Man's Right to Knowledge" (to use the terminology of the Columbia bicentennial theme) and should not expect them to share his theological perspective.

Among the Western scholars dealing with Japan today, there are again different perspectives involved: that of the general Japanologist, the social scientist, the "Shintologist," and the Historian of Religions. All of them, however, share some basic problems and difficulties as well as blind spots. For example, one of the common temptations is to view Shinto or Japanese history or culture by means of an oversimplified division, namely, traditional and modern. Indeed, many Western scholars today tend to depict only those significant events, peculiar institutions, and values of the traditional period which are relevant, positively or negatively, to their understanding of modern development. In this respect, Sansom was right when he criticized many "new" Western historians of Japan by saying that they were "too much under the influence of ideologies, too anxious to prove things, too hasty with comparisons, and often ignorant of general historical matters."[28] On the other hand, in their eagerness to enter as deeply as possible into the inner sanctuary of the "world of meaning" of Japanese culture or Shinto, some Western scholars are tempted not only

---

[26] See Kenzō Kobayashi, *Gendai Shintō no Kenkyū* (Tokyo, 1956), pp. 19-47.

[27] E.g., Haruo Ogasawara, "Shinto no Risō to Genjitsu," *Nihon Bunka Kenkyusho-kiyō*, no. 9 (October 1961), pp. 103-131.

[28] Quoted in Jansen, Keene, and Wright, "Sir George Sansom," p. 562.

to try to understand but to adopt the native Japanese world-view or the affirmation of the Shinto's faith. That a certain kind of *metanoia* is involved in one's effort to understand another culture or religion is taken for granted. However, a foreign scholar should also exercise his own critical and comparative insights which are not always open to those who stand within a tradition, and thus he should, if need be, even point out the blind spots of those who work from within.

In the final analysis, Japanese culture, or Shinto for that matter, must be seen both by Japanese and foreign scholars not only as a series of important events, but also as the view a group of people held concerning their vital relations to this mysterious universe and their mode of being human in it. To think about it and to understand it is a hazardous, and yet exciting, intellectual undertaking which requires the highest degree of cooperation and collaboration between Japanese and non-Japanese scholars. In today's world, no one in the scholarly world can evade this responsibility, especially those who are engaged in the discipline of *Religionswissenschaft*.

18. Buddhism and Modern Japanese Thought

BOTH PHILOSOPHY and religion are Western terms derived from the Western attempt to divide human experience meaningfully into different facets and dimensions. In the East, such a division did not come into vogue until the modern period. Still, in retrospect, we can try to analyze the development of the Eastern tradition by means of Western concepts such as philosophy and religion.

Historically, Buddhism developed what might be termed three secondary centers of diffusion: Ceylon for the Hīnayāna tradition, China for the Mahāyāna tradition, and Tibet for the Vajrayāna tradition. Until recently, Japanese Buddhism has always meant Chinese Buddhism and nothing else. Unlike the Chinese Buddhists, who had translated Indian texts into Chinese, the Japanese accepted Chinese Buddhist texts as, so to speak, sacred. They did not bother with Indian texts, nor did they translate Chinese texts into Japanese. During the initial, formative period (the sixth and seventh centuries), Korean Buddhist masters who could read Chinese but could not speak Japanese were the only teachers of Buddhism available in Japan. They taught in Korean, which for the most part only the children of Korean immigrants could understand. Questions have been rightly raised as to how much and how well early Japanese Buddhists understood Buddhism. Most likely they did not understand much. These historic factors may be responsible for the tradition of writing commentaries on Chinese Buddhist texts, a practice which became the most important intellectual activity of Japanese Buddhists.

Early Chinese Buddhists had devoted their intellectual efforts to two tasks: translating Indian texts into Chinese and writing commentaries. The term "commentaries" carried a different connotation in the China of that period than it does for us now. Prior to the introduction of Buddhism, China had already developed sophisticated intellectual traditions: Confucianism, Taoism, Mohism, Legalism, and others. Both of the Buddhist intellectual activities—translating and writing commentaries—attempted, in brief, to reconcile Buddhist *dharma* with Chinese *tao*. As Walter Liebenthal once observed, Chinese Buddhist schools "originated [with] the Chinese and had no relation to Indian controversies. The Chinese asked all the questions and Indian Buddhist revelation supplied the answers."[1] By the time Buddhism was introduced to Japan, the interpenetration of Buddhism and the native Chinese intellectual traditions had proceeded a long way. Buddhism was accepted by the Japanese as one facet of Chinese civilization.

In Japan, Buddhist leaders had to reconcile Dharma, Tao, and the native religious tradition, later called Shinto, which had at that time very little systematic intellectual content. The resolution was attempted along the lines of religion, politics, and society rather than along the lines of philosophy (cf. the Ritsuryō synthesis). From the time of Prince Shōtoku (573-621), Japanese Buddhists adopted the Chinese formula of questions and answers as their simulated intellectual agenda, and they discussed the relations between the two dimensions of the Chinese tradition, inner (Buddhist) and outer (Confucian/ Taoist).

Significantly, Prince Shōtoku is credited with having lectured and written commentaries on three scriptures which had a great impact on the character of Japanese Buddhism: (1) the *Lotus sūtra* with its affirmation of universal salvation; (2) the Discourse of Vimalakīrti (*Yuima-gyō*), a wealthy lay-Buddhist sage and a patron saint of lay Buddhism in China and Japan; and (3) the Discourse between Buddha and Queen Srīmālā (Shōman), the paradigm of Buddhist womanhood.

NARA BUDDHISM

During the eighth century, when the influence of Chinese civilization on Japan reached its zenith, six Chinese Buddhist schools were established in the capital city at Nara: two schools of the Hīnayāna, the Kusha (Abhidharmakośa) and the Jōjitsu (Satyasiddhi), both of which were concerned with analyzing cosmological and psychological problems; the Ritsu (Vinaya), which was primarily concerned with monastic disciplines; the Sanron (Mādhyamika), devoted to a dialectical analysis of concepts and theories of knowledge for the purpose of realizing perfect knowledge; the Kegon (Avataṃsaka), usually characterized as a form of cosmo-theism; and the Hossō (Yogācāra), probably the most philosophical of the six schools, which stressed a physical and psychological analysis of the nature of things.[2] For the most part,

---

[1] Walter Liebenthal, *The Book of Chao* (Peking: Catholic University of Peking, 1948), p. 147.

[2] For more details on the six schools of the Nara period, see Junjirō Takakusu, *The Essentials of Buddhist Philosophy* (Honolulu: University of Hawaii Press, 1947; reprint ed., 1949).

these schools—which were not schools in the sectarian or denominational sense but monastic academies for students supported by government stipends—stressed the importance of learning the Chinese scriptures and commentaries written by Chinese masters. They gave very
little encouragement to philosophical inquiry.

Also by the eighth century, Japanese Buddhists had outgrown their
sole dependence on Korean masters. A number of Japanese monks
visited China and studied directly under Chinese masters. For example,
a Hossō monk, Dōshō (628-700), studied under the celebrated
Hsüan-tsang (596-664), and lived in the same room with K'uei-chi
(632-682). You may recall that Hsüan-tsang, the Chinese pilgrim *par
excellence*, returned to China in 645 after seventeen years of studying
in India and Central Asia. He then commenced the ambitious undertaking of correcting the old translations of the scriptures by Kumāra-
jīva and others. The so-called "era of new translation" initiated by
Hsüan-tsang stimulated creative philosophical inquiry in China.

Opinions vary among scholars as to when the "new translation" was
introduced into Japan and accepted there. But most scholars agree that
Japanese Buddhists, having been oriented to the "old translation," felt
threatened by the "new translation" to the extent that in A.D. 718 the
government had to issue an official letter to the chief priest (*sōgō*) providing guidance for the learning of monks, apparently for the sake of
resolving the conflict between the old and new translations.[3] There is
no evidence, however, that the "new translation" encouraged philosophical discourse in Japan. Nara Buddhism produced learned apologists for the respective schools but no creative thinkers.

HEIAN BUDDHISM

A new era in the history of Japanese Buddhism was ushered in by
the establishment of the Tendai and Shingon schools, which were introduced from China, indigenized, and systematized by Saichō (767-
822) and Kūkai (774-835) respectively. Both schools had a vision of
the grand harmony of all religious truth. Following the formula of the
"Five Periods and Eight Doctrines" that classifies the Buddha's teachings chronologically, Saichō attempted to synthesize moral precepts,
monastic disciplines, esoteric cults, and Zen (Ch'an) meditation within
the framework of the Ekayāna, the one great vehicle that comprises
both Hīnayāna and Mahāyāna, as stressed in the *Lotus sūtra*. Kūkai,
however, graded various religious teachings, including the Hīnayāna

---

[3] Enchō Tamura, "Early Buddhism in Japan," *Bulletin of the Faculty of Literature* 13
(Fukuoka: Kyushu University, 1971), p. 28.

and other Mahāyāna schools, vertically in terms of ten levels, with the Esoteric School at the apex. This system was based on his own philosophical inquiry rather than on the Chinese Chên-yen tradition. Both the Tendai and the Shingon traditions developed a rapprochement with Shinto.

Some of the Tendai monks introduced the belief in the Pure Land and the cult of Amida (Amitābha). The rapid acceptance of the Amida cult was precipitated by the popularity of an eschatological notion of the "Last Period" (*mappō*). It was widely believed that in the dreadful period of *mappō*, which was descending if it had not already descended, the only way to be liberated from the wrath of empirical life was to depend on the saving grace of Amida to gain rebirth in his Pure Land. Although the realization of being caught between individual *karma* and the verity of the dreaded last period (*mappō*) did not produce systematic philosophical reflection, it did influence the art and literature of the Heian period, as exemplified by the *Tale of Genji*.

KAMAKURA, MUROMACHI, AND TOKUGAWA BUDDHISM

The new sociopolitical situation created by the erosion of the aristocracy and the rise of the warrior-regime (shogunate or *bakufu*) brought about a new religious ethos. Not an ethos of philosophical sophistication but one of a direct search for certainty in salvation, it was epitomized by Hōnen (1133-1212) and his disciple Shinran (1173-1262), the two founders of the Japanese form of the Pure Land School, and by Nichiren (1222-1282), the founder of the school bearing his name. The search for enlightenment also led some Buddhist leaders to turn to Zen (Ch'an).

The turbulent Kamakura period, accentuated by tension between the imperial court and the shogunate and the abortive attempts of Mongol forces to invade Japan, made sensitive Buddhists ask about the religious meaning of contemporary events. Fujiwara no Jien (1155-1225), the abbot of the Tendai monastery at Mount Hi'ei, wrote what many consider to be the first Buddhist philosophy of history. Unlike his Shinto counterpart, Kitabatake Chikafusa, who traced the meaning of Japanese history to the ancient Japanese mythohistorical tradition, Jien speculated on *dōri* (the metaphysical principle) as the main thread of history.

Jien's younger contemporary, Dōgen (1200-1253), who established the Japanese school of Sōtō Zen and who had attained *satori* while in China, had an independent philosophical mind. What distinguished Dōgen was his search for a coherent philosophical foundation for Buddhism. For this reason, he often disagreed with the views of Indian and Chinese Buddhist masters. For example, according to H. Nakamura, the Chinese Buddhists translated *dharmatā* as the "real aspects of all things," which refers to all aspects of all kinds of phenomena and which consists of two contradictory elements, i.e., "all things" and "the real aspect." Dōgen, however, sided with the Tendai interpretation that "the real aspect is all things." He felt that the truth for which people search was none other than the world of our daily experience. To him, the fluid aspect of impermanence was in itself the absolute state. "Impermanence is the Buddhahood. . . . The impermanence of grass, trees, and forests is verily the Buddhahood. The impermanence of the person's body and mind is verily the Buddhahood." Similarly, in contrast to a phrase in the *Mahāparinirvāṇa-sūtra*—"He who desires to know the meaning of the Buddhahood should survey the opportunity and conditions and wait for the occasion to come. If the opportunity comes, the Buddhahood will be revealed of itself"—Dōgen was convinced that "Buddhahood is *time*." Thus he asserted that "he who wants to know Buddhahood may know it by knowing *time* as it is revealed to us. And as *time* is something in which we are already immersed, Buddhahood also is not something that is to be sought in the future but is something that is realized where we are."[4]

At the same time, some Japanese Zen monks who had studied in China introduced Neo-Confucianism into Japan, initially as an intellectual and cultural fashion of Sung China. In the course of time, Neo-Confucianism, especially of the Chu Hsi School—which combined metaphysics, physics, psychology, and ethics under the influence of Zen Buddhism—provided Japan (including Japanese Buddhists) with a philosophical language. During the politically unstable Muromachi period (mid-fourteenth to late-sixteenth centuries), Zen monks were the "bearers of culture" (*Kulturträger*). They were Neo-Confucian scholars as well as connoisseurs of Chinese art, poetry, and literature.

During the Tokugawa period (seventeenth to mid-nineteenth centuries), the shogunate ordered every Japanese household to belong to a particular Buddhist temple. Its purpose was to extirpate the influence of the "forbidden religion," Roman Catholicism. Buddhist institutions thus became an arm of the feudal regime. They enjoyed the prestige and support of the shogunate. Yet the shogunate obtained a philosophical rationale for its administrative policies from Confucian schol-

[4] Hajime Nakamura, *Ways of Thinking of Eastern Peoples: India-China-Tibet-Japan* (Honolulu: East-West Center Press, 1964), pp. 351-352.

ars. A number of leading Confucianists were ex-Zen monks, and their hostility toward Buddhism drove them to ally with scholars of hitherto neglected Shinto and National Learning. Confucian scholars initiated critical philological and philosophical inquiries into the Chinese classics, while scholars of National Learning engaged in similar inquiry with respect to the Shinto classics.

Ironically, Buddhist schools which had well-staffed denominational colleges (*Gakurin*) were preoccupied with internal ecclesiastical matters and took little interest in philological or philosophical pursuits. In this situation, a wealthy Osaka merchant and rationalist Confucian philosopher, Tominaga Nakamoto (1715?-1746), as part of an attempt to develop a comprehensive philosophical world-view which synthesized Shinto, Confucianism, and Buddhism, reexamined and rejected the traditional Buddhist sectarian systems of classifying various tenets of Buddhism. Instead, he engaged in critical-historical and philological studies of the Buddhist scriptures.[5] His thesis that Mahāyāna did not represent the Buddha's teaching did not please the Buddhist authorities, but it had an impact on Buddhist scholarship in the late nineteenth and early twentieth centuries.

BUDDHIST PHILOSOPHY AND PHILOSOPHY INFORMED BY BUDDHISM IN MODERN JAPAN

In one sense, the distinction between Buddhist philosophy and philosophy informed by Buddhism is an artificial one, and in some cases it does not hold water today. However, it was crucial in Japan during the mid-nineteenth century.

In 1853, the United States sent Commodore Matthew Perry to open Japan's door to trade with the West. The reluctant Tokugawa shogunate saw no alternative but to yield to American pressure, and soon the other Western powers also wanted to trade with Japan. When the shogunate decided to send able Japanese youths abroad to learn the ways of Western people, the United States could not welcome them because of the Civil War.[6] Thus, in 1863, the shogunate sent two men, Nishi Amane (1829-1897) and Tsuda Masamichi (1829-1903), to Holland, a country which had had limited intercourse with Japan even during the Tokugawa period of national seclusion. These

[5] On Tominaga, see Hajime Nakamura, "Tominaga Nakamoto no jinmonshugi-teki seishin," in *Gendai Bukkyo Meicho-Zenshū*, ed. H. Nakamura, F. Masutani, and J. M. Kitagawa (Tokyo: Ryubunkan, 1960), vol. 3: *Nihon no Bukkyo*, pp. 346-402.

[6] Thomas R. H. Havens, *Nishi Amane and Modern Japanese Thought* (Princeton: Princeton University Press, 1970), p. 42.

two men studied social sciences and philosophy in Leiden, Holland until 1865. Nishi became interested in British Utilitarianism, while Tsuda was attracted to Comte's Positivism. Upon his return to Japan, Nishi coined the new term "*Kitetsugaku*" (the Science of Questioning Wisdom) in order to differentiate his form of thought, which was informed by Western philosophy, from Confucian and Buddhist philosophy. Nishi is credited with coining many philosophical terms which have survived to our day. Even today, the term *tetsugaku* (philosophy) usually refers to Western philosophy: from Plato and Aristotle to contemporary European and American philosophers, with a heavy dose of German thinkers, especially Kant, Hegel, and Heidegger. A person who wishes to study Buddhist philosophy must go to the Department of Indian Philosophy (*Indo-tetsugaku*), which also deals with Hindu philosophy and with the philological and textual study of Hindu and Buddhist texts. In some leading national universities, there is also a Department of the Science of Religion (*Shūkyō-gaku*). Depending upon who occupies the chairs, this department may come very close to being a philosophy department, as it is at Kyoto University thanks to the influence of Nishida Kitarō and others. Or it may come close to being a Department of Indian Philosophy, as it once was at Tokyo University where the Professor of the Science of Religion, Anesaki Masaharu, was at the same time a renowned scholar of Buddhism and Buddhist philosophy.

A number of well-established universities are affiliated with various Buddhist sects and denominations. They are descendents of the denominational academies of the Tokugawa period. Enlightened Buddhist denominational leaders foresaw the need to learn about the Western religious situation and Western religious scholarship. As early as 1873, the West Honganji (one of the True Pure Land sects which began with the thirteenth-century saint, Shinran) sent Shimaji Mokurai to study Western religions and to visit the Middle East and India. Shimaji was accompanied by Akamatsu Renjō and other younger scholars. In 1876, the East Honganji dispatched Nanjō Bunyū and Kasahara Kenju to Oxford to study Sanskrit with Max Müller and A. A. Macdonnell. Nanjō later became famous for the so-called *Nanjio Catalogue of the Chinese Tripitaka*. In 1881, the West Honganji sent Kitabatake Dōryū to France, and in the following year, it also sent to France Fujishima Ryōon, who later published *La Bouddhisme Japonaise*. In 1893, Shaku Sōyen, a follower of Zen, attended the World's Parliament of Religions in Chicago.[7] Meanwhile, Takakusu Junjirō left

[7] On Shaku Sōyen, see J. M. Kitagawa, *The 1893 World's Parliament of Religions and*

Japan in 1890, studied Sanskrit and Indian classics at Oxford, moved to the University of Kiel in order to work with H. Oldenberg and P. Deussen, and then moved again to Berlin to learn Tibetan and Mongolian. He also spent some time in Paris with Sylvain Lévi. In 1900, Anesaki Masaharu and others went to Germany, where they were exposed to Buddhological scholarship as well as to German idealism.

Contact with Western scholarly investigations of Buddhism broadened the vista of Japanese Buddhist leaders. They began to take Buddhist traditions in India, South and Southeast Asia, and Tibet seriously. In 1899, Kawaguchi Ekai visited Tibet and brought out a number of precious scriptures, commentaries, and cult objects, as did Teramoto Enga in the following year. From 1903 to 1914, three archaeological expeditions were conducted by Japanese Buddhist scholars in Central Asia. More important from the religious and philosophical perspective was the increasing contact between Japanese Buddhism and Hīnayāna Buddhist schools in South and Southeast Asia from the late nineteenth century to the present.

Japan Buddhists may have felt threatened by Western thought, but they were also greatly inspired by such Western thinkers as Hegel and Schopenhauer. The Western scholars who exerted the most direct influence on Japanese Buddhological scholarship during the modern period, however, were F. Max Müller, whose entire personal library was bought for Tokyo University by Baron Kunio Iwasaki of Mitsubishi but was destroyed by the great Tokyo earthquake of 1923; T. W. Rhys Davids and his wife, Caroline Rhys Davids; Ernst Leumann; Hermann Oldenberg; Sylvain Lévi; E. J. Thomas; Sir Charles Eliot; Sergi Oldenberg; and Louis de La Vallée Poussin. Their impact helped revolutionize the scholarly foundation and framework of Japanese Buddhists in terms of philological-textual, critical-historical, and philosophical-religious pursuits.

After the end of World War II, an all-inclusive Japanese Association of Indian and Buddhist Studies (*Indo-gaku Bukkyo-gakkai*) was formed. Through this association, it is easy today to have a bird's-eye view of which scholar is doing what in which institution. However, in looking at the prewar situation, one is forced to survey several major institutions and some of the leading scholarly journals.

Major institutions where Buddhist studies were carried on may be divided into (1) former imperial universities, e.g., Tokyo, Kyoto, To-

Its Legacy, Eleventh John Nuveen Lecture (Chicago: University of Chicago Divinity School, 1984), pp. 5-7.

hoku, and Kyushu; (2) institutions affiliated with Buddhist denominations, e.g., Taishō (Jōdo, Shingi-Shingon, etc.), Komazawa (Zen), Risshō (Nichiren), Ōtani (Higashi-Honganji, where D. T. Suzuki taught), Ryūkoku (Nishi-Honganji), and Kōyasan (Shingon); and (3) private universities, e.g., Waseda, Keiō, Nihon, etc.

Some of the leading scholarly journals before the war included *Bukkyo Kenkyū* (Journal of Buddhist Studies), *Bussen-Gakuhō* (Journal of the Buddhist College of Kyoto), *Eizan-Gakuhno* (Journal of the Eizan Senshū-gakuin, a Tendai seminary), *Mikkyō Kenkyū* (Journal for the Study of Esoteric Buddhism, published by Kōyasan Shingon University), *Risshō Daigaku Ronsō* (Journal of Risshō University), *Ryūkoku Gakuhō* (Journal of Ryūkoku University), *Seizan Gakuhō* (Journal of the Seizan Buddhist College), *Taishō Daigaku Gakuhō* (Journal of Taishō University), and *Zengaku Kenkyū* (Journal of Zen Studies, published by the Rinzai-gakuin).[8] There were two other important journals in which learned articles on Buddhism appeared: *Shūkyō Kenkyū* (Journal of the Science of Religion), whose office was located in the Tokyo Imperial University, and *Tetsugaku Kenkyū* (Journal of Philosophical Studies), edited by scholars of Kyoto Imperial University. The Tokyo and Kyoto groups still edit these two journals today.

It might be helpful to compare the different styles, concerns, and approaches represented by the Tokyo and Kyoto schools, the two intellectual centers for Buddhist studies in modern Japan. In 1877, Tokyo University was established by combining what were formerly the Tokyo Kaisei Academy and the Tokyo Medical School. The new university had four faculties: Law, Physical Science, Letters, and Medicine. The Faculty of Letters was subdivided into two parts, the first dealing with history, philosophy, and political science, the second dealing with Japanese and Chinese literature.

Under the influence of the modernist philosopher, Katō Hiroyuki, president of the university during the crucial period from 1881 to 1900, philosophy was stressed as the backbone of the Faculty of Letters. At first, philosophy meant Western philosophy, and the use of English for teaching may account for the popularity of English empiricism and utilitarianism during the initial period. Among the early foreign professors of philosophy was Ernest F. Fenollosa, a follower of Herbert Spencer. Soon, Ludwig Busse, a disciple of Lotze, joined the faculty and initiated a trend toward German, or more precisely, Anglo-German, idealism. In 1893 Busse was succeeded by Raphael

[8] *Studies of Buddhism in Japan*, vol. 4 (Tokyo: The International Buddhist Society, 1942), pp. 131-155.

von Koeber (1848-1923), who was appointed on the recommendation of E. von Hartmann. Koeber, a Russian of German and Swedish extraction, was born in what is present-day Gorki. He had studied under Tchaikovsky at the Moscow Academy of Music before going to Germany to study philosophy. He taught German philosophy—mainly Schopenhauer and Hartmann—but also introduced Greek philosophy and medieval thought to Japan. Concurrently, he taught piano at the Ueno School of Arts. Throughout his long tenure at Tokyo, Koeber influenced many future Japanese philosophers.

In 1879, a learned Sōtō Zen priest, Hara Tanzan, was invited by President Katō—who himself had no appreciation of any religion *as* religion—to serve as a lecturer and to offer a course on Indian (Buddhist) philosophy. In 1882, Inouye Tetsujirō was appointed assistant professor; he offered courses on the history of Oriental philosophy (mostly Confucian and other Chinese systems of thought). In 1885, Nanjō Bunyū, the pupil of Max Müller, became a lecturer and initiated instruction in Sanskrit. In 1890, Murakami Senshō, first as a lecturer and later as a professor, started teaching Indian (Buddhist) philosophy. He replaced Hara Tanzan, who had resigned two years earlier. Later, Murakami's critical-historical study of Buddhist philosophy, especially his negative stance toward Mahāyāna, made him a controversial figure. In 1891, Karl Florenz, who had been teaching German at Tokyo University, took over the Sanskrit courses from the retiring Nanjō. In 1897, Takakusu Junjirō, as a new lecturer, started teaching Pali and Sanskrit, and in the following year, Anesaki Masaharu, another new lecturer, started offering a course entitled "Introduction to the Science of Religion." In 1905, Anesaki was appointed to the newly created Chair of the Science of Religion (*Shūkyō-gaku*). In 1907, Katō Genchi and Hatano Seiichi were appointed lecturers; Katō was advanced to the newly created Chair in Shinto Studies in 1921. In 1908, Tokiwa Daijō became a lecturer and offered courses on Buddhist texts. In 1918, the first Chair of Indian (Buddhist) Philosophy was finally established in Tokyo University. Since then, such eminent scholars as Kimura Taiken, Ui Hakujū, Nagai Makin, Tsuji Naoshirō, Miyamoto Shōson, Hanayama Shinshō, and Nakamura Hajime have promoted philological, textual, historical, and philosophical scholarship in Buddhist studies.

In many ways, Kyoto University contrasts remarkably with Tokyo University. In 1897, Kyoto Imperial University was established to avoid too heavy a concentration of scholarship in Tokyo. It was the second of a series of imperial universities established by the Japanese government. A talented ethicist-philosopher, Ōnishi Hajime (1864-

1900), often called "the Japanese Kant," was slated to become the head of the soon-to-be-reorganized College (later Faculty) of Letters at Kyoto University, but he died before reorganization took place in 1906. Nevertheless, Kyoto soon became an important center of Kantian philosophy in Japan. On its faculty were Kuwaki Gen'yoku (1874-1946), who, however, left for Tokyo University later; Tomonaga Sanjurō (1871-1951); the aestheticist, Fukada Yasukazu (1878-1927); and the ethicist, Fujii Kenjirō (1872-1931). Fukada and Fujii had been heavily influenced by Neo-Kantianism.

When Nishida Kitarō (1870-1945) was appointed to replace Kuwaki in 1910, Kyoto University's destiny as the unrivalled center of philosophy in Japan was secured. After his retirement in 1928, Nishida continued to publish important works. His younger colleagues and successors, such as Tanabe Hajime (1885-1962), Nishitani Keiji (1900-), and Takeuchi Yoshinori (1913-), each in his own way carried on serious philosophical inquiry.

The scholars usually identified with the so-called Kyoto School are primarily philosophers who attempt to formulate their own systems rather than to interpret Western philosophical works. The degree to which Buddhism informs their creative reflection also varies. I should also say that, unlike Frederick Franck, who includes D. T. Suzuki, Hisamatsu Shin'ichi, Kobori Sōhaku Nanrei, Soga Ryōjun, and Kiyosawa Manshi—Buddhist thinkers interested in philosophy—in the Kyoto School,[9] I include only those modern thinkers who are philosophers also inspired or informed by Buddhism. Kyoto University has also had many distinguished scholars in Indian and Buddhist studies— Tsukamoto Zenryū, Nagao Gadjin, Yanagida Seizan, Kajiyama Yūichi, Ojibara Yutaka, and Hattori Masaaki, among others—who have contributed much to linguistic, historical, textual, and doctrinal scholarship. I will focus, however, on the tradition of Kitarō Nishida, which shows a marked contrast to the tradition of Buddhist philosophy in the usual sense of the term.

As far as I can ascertain, there was nothing spectacular about Nishida's life. He was born in Kanazawa and studied at a local high school, where he met another not-so-spectacular fellow student, Suzuki D. Teitarō. They became lifelong friends, mutually helping and stimulating each other. During his study at Tokyo University, no one took particular notice of Nishida. In fact, he was destined to become an obscure high school teacher of German and philosophy. But his

---

[9] See Frederick Franck, ed., *The Buddha Eye: An Anthology of the Kyoto School* (New York: Crossroad, 1982).

first book, *A Study of Good* (*Zen no Kenkyū*), begun in 1906 and published in 1911, put his name on the map. In Nishida, as Takeuchi states, "Japan found its first philosophical genius, a man who built a system permeated with the spirit of Oriental tradition, especially that of Buddhist [Zen] meditation, by employing the Western method of thinking."[10]

When Nishida was appointed to Kyoto University in 1910, he started lecturing on Bolzano, Brentano, Meinong, Husserl, Richert, Fichte, and Bergson. His friend, D. T. Suzuki, who was then in La Salle, Illinois, introduced him to William James. According to Gino K. Piovesana, Nishida attempted to formulate a "logic of place" (*topos*) which could be used as a basis upon which to found Oriental culture, as Greek logic had been the basis for Western culture. Nishida incorporated into his logic a Mahāyāna emphasis on the contradictory aspect of phenomenological reality as ultimately "nothingness."[11] Although he was influenced by the Neo-Kantian school, he opposed its sharp distinction between value and being, between meaning and fact. Instead, he projected an overall unity of value and being and of meaning and fact from a position of "self-consciousness" which, in his view, was an internal union of intuition and reflection. Unlike Fichte's notion of "Act" (*Tathandlung*), Nishida took seriously the self-generation and self-development of concrete experience. As he once said in a revealing statement:

> By intuition (or seeing) I mean our way of seeing the being of things in the world, through which we see a being and also our own act of seeing, as a shadow of the Self-reflection of Nothingness—I mean the shadow of Self-reflection of Nothingness which performs its function by projecting itself on one point within its *topos*.[12]

In order to clarify the *topos* character of Nothingness philosophy, Nishida introduced three key ideas: (1) action-intuition, the reciprocity of which characterizes the structure and dynamics of all creative activity; (2) the Eternal Now, which is reflected in the past-present-future time; and (3) Absolute Nothingness, the principle of the historical world in its identity of contradictions as well as of religion.[13]

Nishida's notion of religion is based on his view of "disjunction-

---

[10] Yoshinori Takeuchi, "Japanese Philosophy," *Encyclopaedia Britannica*, 1968 ed., 12:959. In the following discussion of Nishida and Tanabe, I am greatly indebted to Professor Takeuchi's analysis.

[11] Gino K. Piovesana, *Recent Japanese Philosophical Thought, 1862-1962* (Tokyo: Enderle Bookstore, 1963), p. 89.

[12] Quoted in Takeuchi, "Japanese Philosophy," p. 959.

[13] Discussed in greater detail in ibid., pp. 960-961.

conjunction" between God (Absolute) and man (relative). According to Nishida, God is "Absolute Being and Absolute Nothingness in his true identity of contradiction."[14] In this respect, Nishida was fond of quoting Daitō Kokushi, a Zen master of the fourteenth century:

> From eternity to eternity Buddha [the Absolute] and I [the relative] are separated from each other, yet, at the same time he and I do not fall apart even for a single moment. All day long Buddha and I live facing each other, yet he and I have never a chance to meet each other.[15]

Some of Nishida's books now available in English include: V. H. Viglielmo, trans., *A Study of Good* (Tokyo, 1960); R. Schinzinger, trans., *Intelligibility and the Philosophy of Nothingness* (Honolulu, 1966); D. Dilworth, trans., *Fundamental Problems of Philosophy* (Tokyo, 1970); and D. Dilworth and V. H. Viglielmo, trans., *Art and Morality* (Honolulu, 1973).

Together with Nishida, Tanabe Hajime (1885-1962) is regarded as the "cofounder" of the Kyoto School. Originally trained in science and mathematics, Tanabe switched to philosophy and taught it in the Faculty of Science at Tohoku University, Sendai, the third of the imperial universities. In 1919, he joined the faculty of Kyoto University and eventually became Nishida's successor. Unlike Nishida, who never studied abroad, Tanabe studied two years (1922-24) in Berlin, Leipzig, and Freiburg (where Husserl was teaching). His major book, *A Study of the Philosophy of Mathematics* (*Sūri tetsugaku kenkyū*), was inspired by Cohen and others in the Marburg School of Neo-Kantianism, as well as by Nishida. He was both Nishida's good friend and his critic.

Takeuchi, probably the closest disciple of Tanabe, points out three areas of difference and three areas of agreement between Nishida and Tanabe.[16] The differences may be seen in these areas:

1. In contrast to the action-intuition of Nishida, Tanabe accentuates the "significance of action-faith in religious existence."
2. Nishida's action-intuition presumes our existence as a "creative element" in the historical world. He takes a viewpoint in the historical world itself, where the "perspective of the whole" is visible simultaneously from every outlook. To Tanabe, however, the "road" in the historical world is fraught with obstacles which must constantly be boldly and resolutely overcome.
3. Because of Tanabe's preoccupation with the "ethical viewpoint," he

---

[14] Ibid., p. 961.
[15] Quoted in ibid.
[16] Summarized from Takeuchi's analysis in ibid., p. 962.

surveys the various religious traditions from an ethical perspective. In so doing, he attempts to reconcile the disparate truths of Zen, the Pure Land School, and even Christianity. Nishida's philosophical goal of the "immediate realization of Absolute Nothingness," however, is inspired singularly by Zen, thus reflecting the philosophical influence of Dōgen.

Despite these differences, the following similarities may be noted between Tanabe and Nishida:

1. Both maintain the conviction that "the absolute must be considered . . . Absolute Nothingness."
2. Both believe that the greatest expression of philosophy is to be found in "religious action."
3. Both are convinced of the concept of the "Eternal Now."

According to Tanabe's philosophy of *metanoetics*,[17] one must undergo a "*metanoia* in the 'death-and-resurrection' [conversion] experience" in order to transcend *noetics* ("metaphysics as speculative philosophy in the realm of the subject-object relationship"). Therefore, he rejects both the 'as well as' of Hegel's "speculative synthesis" and the 'either/or' of Kierkegaard's ethical commitment as the "true dialectic." To Tanabe, the true dialectic is 'neither/nor', "a thorough-going negation of our immediacy (repentance of one's radical sin) by the mercy of the Absolute [God or Buddha]," who "for the sake of [the] love and mercy" of "absolute self-surrender" empties Himself (Absolute Nothingness). According to Tanabe's philosophical stance, it is through the mediating function of Christ or the Bodhisattva that the love of Absolute Nothingness can be realized in this world.

The tradition of the Kyoto School is by no means a static and fixed orthodoxy. Some of Nishida's heirs, such as Keiji Nishitani, author of *Religion and Nothingness*,[18] and Tanabe's disciple, Takeuchi Yoshinori,[19] have developed their own philosophical stances, even though they are greatly indebted to their mentors. Granted, their perspectives, objectives, and methods are different from those of "Buddhist philosophers." Still, in the long run, through their philosophical agenda, inspired as it is by Buddhism, these modern Japanese thinkers will advance the cause of Buddhist philosophy because of their dedication to the search for truth wherever it may be unfolded.

[17] Soon to be published by the University of California Press, Berkeley. The following examination of Tanabe's philosophy of *metanoetics* is based largely on Takeuchi's discussion in ibid., p. 961.

[18] Berkeley: University of California Press, 1982.

[19] See his *Heart of Buddhism*, ed. and trans. James W. Heisig (New York: Crossroad, 1983).

310

Appendix: Buddhism in America

A FEW YEARS ago, during my travels in various parts of Asia, I was struck by a widespread impression that existed among the Buddhists that the West is spiritually bankrupt today and is eagerly awaiting the Gospel of Buddha. At the conference of the World Fellowship of Buddhists (WFB) held in Phnom Penh, Cambodia in the fall of 1961, I listened to many impassioned speakers who urged Asian Buddhists to go out as missionaries to the West. In fact, I was overwhelmed by the number of volunteers who offered to teach courses on Buddhism in American colleges and universities. Undoubtedly the presence of delegates from every continent and the pious testimonies of Western Buddhists at the WFB Conference gave much encouragement to the somewhat romantic and wishful thinking of the Asian Buddhists that the time was ripe for a worldwide spiritual crusade by the Buddhists.[1] On the other hand, some of the perceptive Asian Buddhists who have visited the West in recent years have expressed great disappointment in what they observed regarding the actual state of Buddhism in the West. A Japanese Buddhist scholar who spent one year as a Fellow of Union Theological Seminary, New York candidly states: "Before coming here I was told about the 'Zen Boom' and of the great interest in Buddhism that existed in America. That some people have considerable knowledge of Buddhism is obvious. But, for the most part Americans barely recognize the name of Buddhism just as most Japanese people barely know the names of Sikhism and Zoroastrianism. . . ."[2] We can also cite many other contradictory views and impressions of Buddhism in the West, more particularly in America.

[1] The enthusiasm of Western converts to Buddhism is taken seriously by Asian Buddhists, often to a disproportionate degree. Professor King recalls how a Buddhist convert from Catholicism sought to make a Buddhist of him on the spot, "encouraging him by the counsel that if *he* had given up his Catholicism to Buddhism, how much less had a mere Protestant to give up!" See Winston L. King, *A Thousand Lives Away: Buddhism in Contemporary Burma* (Cambridge: Harvard University Press, 1964), p. 76, n. 1.

[2] See Dr. Hanayama Shōyū, "Amerika-jin no Bukkyō," in *Zaike Bukkyō*, no. 106 (January 1963), p. 64.

It goes without saying that Buddhism in the West is a complex phenomenon which has many facets and components. And if one should look at such a phenomenon from a certain perspective, however distorted, diverse factors somehow fall into a discernable pattern, at least to one's own satisfaction. For example, from the perspective of many Asian Buddhists, Buddhism has been destined to spread eastward (*Bukkyō tōzen*) from the land of its origin: first to Central and Southeast Asia, then to China, Korea, and Japan, and finally to North America. Thus, the fact that a few Buddhist delegates happened to be invited to the World's Parliament of Religions (held in Chicago in 1893) was held to be more than a historic accident; for the Gospel of the Lord Buddha, being the "most excellent of all teachings,"[3] was bound to reach the shores of all continents sooner or later anyway. This conclusion is shared by many Western Buddhists, who, however, arrive at it from different perspectives. With the exception of those who have renounced their Western background and now identify themselves with the East, many have been led to Buddhism because of their dissatisfaction with certain aspects of their own religious traditions, such as institutionalization and the loss of spiritual vitality. Notwithstanding, they readily acknowledge the indebtedness of Western civilization as well as themselves to Judaism and Christianity. Thus, an English Buddhist, Mr. Ronald Fussell, considers the Buddhist movement in the West as a return to its own inner source made possible by the know-how of the spiritual life which has been transmitted by Buddhism. In his own words:

In the past Christianity also had its techniques but today, with a few notable exceptions, it is content to remain at the level of exhortation. I am tempted sometimes to say: "I know it is good to love one's enemies, but if, in fact, I hate them, what am I to do about it?" This is where Buddhism comes in for it brings to bear an understanding of just this orientation and of others like it.[4]

Informative and suggestive though these views may be, they do not adequately assess the significance of Buddhism in the wider religious context of the West, especially when we concentrate on the American scene. While there is no single vantage point from which to view objectively all the pertinent factors involved in the development of Bud-

[3] Quoted from the statement of Syöng-myöng, King of Paekche, presented to the court of the Emperor Kimmei in A.D. 552 (according to *Nihon-shoki*).

[4] Ronald Fussell, "The Buddhist Movement and the Revival of Spiritual Life in England," in *The Middle Way* 34, no. 4 (February 1960), p. 156.

dhism in America, we should at least make every effort to view it as one of the important trends and movements that constitute contemporary religious life in America.

AMERICA'S RELIGIOUS HERITAGE

It is a common belief among Americans today that "the New World, from the time of Columbus, has stood midway between Europe and Asia. It is the laboratory in which many values are tested, the field in which everything from Oriental flora and fauna to exotic modes of life and thought is being domesticated."[5] However, the main core of the American cultural tradition was initially molded by Anglo-Saxon culture, so that the men of letters in the American colonies considered themselves members of the European intellectual class, more particularly of England. Understandably, colleges and private academies established in the new continent turned to England and Western Europe for cultural inspiration. There was a small minority of colonials who were not of British stock, but their cultural influence on colonial life was negligible. Religiously, too, the American colonies inherited the spirit of Protestantism from England and Western Europe, so that among the "free white persons" who constituted American society, Jews and Catholics were subjected to discriminatory treatment.[6] However, in the course of time new religious principles developed out of the historic experience of the American people.

We might recall the famous letter of President Fillmore, transmitted to the Japanese government through Commodore Matthew Perry in 1853, in which he stated that "the United States was not like other Christian countries, since it did not interfere in religion at home, much less abroad."[7] Fillmore was no doubt aware of the Japanese hatred of Christianity, and tried to stress in this letter the fact that the United States wanted trade with Japan, not the opportunity for Christian evangelism. Nevertheless, his statement revealed more truth than he realized about the religious ethos of the United States. We learn from church historians that as early as 1700 almost all the major church groups found in America today were represented on American soil. During the colonial period each religious group hoped for the freedom

[5] Arthur E. Christy, ed., *The Asian Legacy and American Life* (New York: The John Day Co., 1942), p. 1.

[6] See Joseph M. Kitagawa, "Convergence and Prejudice in the United States," in *The Graduate Journal* (University of Texas) 7 (1966), Supplement, pp. 131-155.

[7] Cited in George B. Sansom, *Western World and Japan* (New York: Alfred A. Knopf, rev. ed., 1962), p. 488.

to continue to press its absolute religious claims. "But," according to Professor Mead, "what had become obvious to all by the end of the Revolution was that the only way to insure such freedom for itself [each group] was to grant it to others."[8] What developed gradually out of this background was the nebulous principle of "religious liberty," which means, according to Professor Wilhelm Pauck, that each religious group "is enabled to act as if there were no other churches in existence, but in so doing it concedes to other churches, which *do* actually exist as its neighbors and rivals, the right to practice the same kind of isolationism."[9] The result was the adoption of the famous wording of the First Amendment, that is: "Congress shall make no law representing an establishment of religion, or prohibiting the free exercise thereof." This, indeed, was a sound, and probably the only feasible, solution to the problem of religious pluralism in America.

The acceptance of the principle of religious liberty by the Protestant, Catholic, and Jewish groups, however, had far-reaching implications for their subsequent development. All religious groups that have been characterized by Ernst Troeltsch as "Church type" or "Sect type" in Europe became "denominations" on the American scene. Even Roman Catholicism, which claims (at least theologically) to be the only true church on earth, is no exception in this respect. Furthermore, the principle of religious liberty tends to undercut the very basis of monotheism. Thus, despite their affirmation of the doctrine of monotheism, all religious groups in America are compelled in practice to accept the basic tenet of monolatry, and recognize the existence of other deities, or deities of other religious groups, even though each group adheres to its deity as the only true one. In this connection, it might be pointed out that there has never been any clear-cut agreement as to the precise meaning of the "establishment of religion" clause in the Constitution: whether it should be interpreted as "absolute separation of church and state" or "the state's neutrality and equal protection of all religious groups." The ambiguity of this principle has resulted in a series of controversies, such as those concerning the state support of parochial schools, the use of prayer in public schools, and the teaching of reli-

[8] Sidney E. Mead, "The American People: Their Space, Time and Religion," in *The Journal of Religion* 34 (1954), p. 253.

[9] Quoted in ibid. This reminds us of the Japanese situation during the Meiji era when some of the Buddhist leaders fought for the principle of religious freedom ostensibly to emancipate Buddhism from the Shinto-dominated *Daikyō* (Great Teaching) movement. In so doing, they were, grudgingly to be sure, compelled to apply the same principle to other groups, including Christianity.

gion in state-supported educational institutions. These issues are still debated in America today.

America's religious heritage, which appears in one sense to be chaotic because of religious pluralism, communalism, interfaith rivalry, and bigotry, has in another sense developed a uniquely American religious ethos shared by the diverse religious groups. From the time of the founding fathers, Americans have had an overwhelming sense of the drama of a history in which free men, guided by the infinite wisdom of the Almighty, had the task of establishing a novel form of society. This type of optimistic activism also characterizes the thinking of religious leaders, who from the Great Awakening of the 1740s have consistently preached the coming of the new era and free society in the new continent, where Americans—the "new chosen people"—are called upon to work for the redemption of the world.[10] Thus, in spite of the legal controversies regarding the church-state relationship and petty ecclesiastical bickerings, the majority of Americans have taken for granted the internal unity of religion and society to the extent that some scholars suggest the existence of a "subterranean religion of democracy" which underlies the three major religious traditions in America, namely, Judaism, Protestantism, and Catholicism.

What is significant in this respect is that today both the internal religious ethos as well as external ecclesiastical institutional forms do not seem to be viable to a considerable number of Americans. For one thing, democracy is losing its religious underpinning, so that, as one writer succinctly states: "It makes no fundamental difference whether [God] exists or not. It is useful to Western society to believe in Him, and such belief is to be commended; on the other hand, the basic activities of our democracies must be constructed to get along without Him."[11] On the other hand, the loosening of the internal tie that has traditionally bound American society and Judeo-Christian religious faith has tended to encourage the search for novelty in art, philosophy, morality, and religion. And, since World War II, which effectively destroyed the last vestige of isolationism, an increasing number of Americans have become aware of America's global responsibility as well as the fascination, challenge, and stimulation of non-American, non-Western, and non-Christian cultures and religions. That is to say, East-

[10] On this question, see Alan Heimert, *Religion and the American Mind: From the Great Awakening to the Revolution* (Cambridge: Harvard University Press, 1965).

[11] Stephen F. Bayne, Jr., *The Optional God* (New York: Oxford University Press, 1953), p. vii.

ern cultures and religions—including Buddhism—are taken more seriously today than ever before in many quarters of America.

LEARNING AND PIETY

Any attempt to understand the religious situation in America must take into account the historic tension that existed between religious groups and institutions of higher learning. It is well known that a religious controversy delayed the founding of Columbia University for over fifty years. One source of the incompatibility of religion and higher education goes back to the origin of the American university. Most of the nation's leading colleges were originally established by religious groups at a time when American religious life was strongly influenced by emotional revivalism. As a result, educated people until recently tended to choose between being intellectual or pious, but found it difficult to be both. Most of them had nothing but disdain for revivalism and confessional churches. Their religion, if any, had a quality of what Professor Heimert characterizes as Charles Chauncy's heaven: "a sort of glorified Harvard graduate school," which "appealed to Chauncy because he fully expected to serve as its dean, to his colleagues because they had already received their doctorates on earth, and to other Liberals because such a heaven would be an extension—not a reorganization—of the best of all possible worlds: the Boston of the mid-eighteenth century."[12]

It is important to note that both the educated and the pious in America drew their inspiration from Europe—the latter from the tradition of Pietism. Indeed, many of the churches in America were originally transplanted by the missionary society movement created by the Pietists in Western Europe and the British Isles during the eighteenth century. This may account for the strong evangelical temper of American denominations from their inceptions. Convinced as they were that "From Greenland's icy mountains/From India's coral strand/Where Africa's sunny foundations/Roll down their golden sand/From many an ancient river/From many a palmy plain/They call us to deliver/Their land from error's chain," the missionary-minded Pietists viewed all non-Christians as "heathens" and non-Christian religions as "error's chain." Thus, Hudson Taylor, founder of the China Inland Mission, boldly stated: "The Gospel must be preached to these people in a very short time, for they are passing away. There is a great Niagara of souls passing into the dark in China. Every day, every week, every month

[12] Heimert, *Religion and the American Mind*, p. 47.

they are passing away! A million a month in China they are dying without God!"[13]

In sharp contrast to the pious people, educated Americans—the spiritual heirs of the Enlightenment—shared the European intellectuals' enthusiasm for Eastern cultures and religions. If Hudson Taylor thought of China as a kingdom of darkness, Voltaire praised it as the only country where the pure religion of Nature was preserved: "Worship God and practise justice—this is the sole religion of the Chinese literati. . . . O Thomas Aquinas, Scotus, Bonaventure, Francis, Dominic, Luther, Calvin, canons of Westminster, have you anything better?"[14] While such rhapsodic utterances regarding the exotic traditions were not based on serious inquiries into Eastern religions, the tradition of the Enlightenment prepared the ground for the subsequent development of Indology, Buddhology, Sinology, and Japanology in Europe. The influence of the Enlightenment also left distinct marks among the intellectuals in America, from Massachusetts to Virginia. Many of the creative thinkers and artists, including Ralph Waldo Emerson, Henry David Thoreau, William Sturgis Bigelow, Percival Lowell, John La Farge, and Henry Adams, shared their European counterparts' idealization of Eastern cultures and religions.[15] The fact that Edwin Arnold's *Light of Asia*, published in 1879 in England, soon went into eighty editions in America indicates a rather widespread interest in Indian religion and Buddhism among the American reading public in the latter half of the nineteenth century.

The scholarly study of Eastern religions and cultures, however, developed only gradually in America by the combination of several factors. One was the disillusionment of intellectuals in the Judeo-Christian tradition. On this point, Christy writes:

The Nirvana which the disillusioned of New England sought is best defined in the Ingersoll Lecture which Bigelow gave at Harvard in 1908 on *Buddhism and Immortality*. That book, with La Farge's *An Artist's Letters from Japan*, Percival Lowell's *The Soul of the Far East*, Lafcadio Hearn's pages of spiritual autobiography, and the less historical passages of Fenollosa's *Epochs of Chinese and Japanese Art*, expresses the mood of the generation for whom the Western spiritual tradition had lost its force.[16]

[13] Hymn no. 254 from *The Hymnal of the Protestant Episcopal Church* (New York: The Church Pension Fund, 1940). Taylor's statement was made to the Convention of Student Volunteers, who met in Detroit in 1894.

[14] Quoted in Christy, *Asian Legacy and American Life*, p. 22.

[15] On some of these American thinkers, see Van Meter Ames, *Zen and American Thought* (Honolulu: The University of Hawaii Press, 1962).

[16] Christy, *Asian Legacy in American Life*, p. 44.

Equally significant was the influence on America of European work in Oriental studies as well as in the comparative study of religions, languages, and mythologies. Among the scholars of Oriental religions and philosophies, there were a number of missionaries, such as R. E. Hume, John Batchelor, and James Legge.[17] Some of these missionaries, who had developed profound appreciation of Eastern religions, made serious efforts to ameliorate the simple 'either/or' attitude of churches both in Europe and America toward other religions, so that there were at least a sufficient number of church people by 1893 to support a World's Parliament of Religions. While the Parliament itself was not a scholarly gathering, it nevertheless aroused wide interest in the comparative study of religions both in academic and lay circles. Even the conference of the Foreign Mission Boards of the Christian Churches of the United States and Canada recommended in 1904 that theological schools of all denominations provide courses of instruction in comparative religions for missionary candidates.

The comparative study of religions in America, ardently supported by the combined forces of secularized intellectuals and Christian liberals during the first two decades of the present century, had two obvious weaknesses. First was the lack of coherent methodology in the study of religious data. Second was the lack of support from such disciplines as Indology, Buddhology, and Sinology, which were supposed to provide technical knowledge regarding their respective religions.[18] It took another decade or so before significant improvement took place in this area. As to the first, namely the development of a disciplined methodology in the comparative study of religions, I have already discussed it in my article, "The History of Religions in America."[19] We might simply mention that Joachim Wach, who started his

[17] According to George B. Sansom, who considered Legge to be one of the greatest Sinologists, Legge (b. 1815) was educated at Aberdeen and in 1837 began the study of Chinese in the Reading Room of the British Museum. He held a job to support himself and, in order to insure the complete solitude needed for his study, used to rise and commence his Chinese studies at 3 A.M. His great work, *The Chinese Classics*, with text, translation, exegetical notes, prolegomena, and copious indexes, which was the fruit of more than 25 years of assiduous labor, appeared in Hong Kong from 1861 to 1872 in eight volumes. Legge never received any government subsidy, but he never neglected his duties as a minister of religion. (See "Address Delivered by Sir George B. Sansom at the Annual Ceremony of 1956," *The Journal of Asian Studies* 24, no. 4 [August 1965], pp. 564-565.)

[18] We might recall the statement of Max Müller: "Before we compare, we must thoroughly know what we compare." (In his letter to Renan, 1883, quoted in Joachim Wach, *Types of Religious Experience—Christian and Non-Christian* [Chicago: University of Chicago Press, 1951], p. vii.)

[19] It appeared in *The History of Religions: Essays in Methodology*, ed. Mircea Eliade and Joseph M. Kitagawa (Chicago: University of Chicago Press, 1959), pp. 1-30.

scholarly career in Leipzig, Germany, but later taught at Brown University and the University of Chicago, made probably the greatest contribution in this respect to American scholarship.[20] As to the second, space allows us only to touch briefly upon the development of Buddhology in America.

BUDDHIST STUDIES IN AMERICA

According to Professor Edward Conze, up to about 1935 Buddhist study was divided into three distinct schools. The first was the "Older Anglo-German school," represented by T. W. Rhys Davids, H. Oldenberg, and E. J. Thomas, which dominated the scene until about 1914. They concentrated on the Pali tradition of Buddhism. The Pali Text Society was founded in 1881, and its publication series made a great scholarly contribution. The second school, which became influential after 1916, was the "Leningrad school," represented by Stcherbatsky, Rosenberg, and Obermiller; this school died out in the 1940s. The third is the "Franco-Belgian school," represented by de La Vallée Poussin, Jean Przyluski, Sylvain Lévi, Paul Demiéville, and Etienne Lamotte. In the words of Dr. Conze: "While the 'Older Anglo-German school' has died out from inanition, and the Leningrad school has perished through unfavorable conditions, the principles of the Franco-Belgian school have now been universally adopted by all scholars working in this field, whatever the country they may live in."[21] As far as American Buddhological study is concerned, it was greatly influenced by the "Older Anglo-German school" from the latter half of the nineteenth century but the impact of the "Leningrad school" was negligible; today, the "Franco-Belgian school" is beginning to make its influence felt. Through it all, though, America has not produced Buddhological giants comparable in stature to Rhys Davids, Stcherbatsky, or de La Vallée Poussin.

The first significant figure in American Buddhist study was Henry Clarke Warren (1854-1899), one of the cofounders of the Harvard Oriental Series, whose *Buddhism in Translations* (Passages Selected from the Buddhist Sacred Books, and Translated from the Original Pali into English) was first published in 1896. Afflicted by a spinal ailment throughout his life, Warren first studied the history of philos-

[20] See my Introduction ("The Life and Thought of Joachim Wach") to *The Comparative Study of Religions* by Joachim Wach, ed. Joseph M. Kitagawa (New York: Columbia University Press, 1958), pp. xiii-xlviii.

[21] Edward Conze, "Recent Progress in Buddhist Studies," in *The Middle Way* 34, no. 1 (May 1959), p. 7.

ophy and became interested in Oriental philosophy, especially Buddhism. Thus, he studied Sanskrit under Greenough, Lanman, and Bloomfield, both at Johns Hopkins and at Harvard. By chance he visited his brother who was then studying at Oxford, and there he met Rhys Davids under whose influence Warren became a student of Southern Buddhism. Later he wrote: "After long bothering my head over Sanskrit, I found much more satisfaction when I took up the study of Pali. For Sanskrit literature is a chaos; Pali, a cosmos." He became convinced that "these Pali writings furnish the most authoritative account of The Buddha and his Doctrine that we have." Above all, Warren was fascinated by the "dramatic persona" of the Buddha: "We have volumes and volumes of sermons, discourses, and moral tales credited to him, and hundreds of incidents related, apropos of which he pronounced some dictum."[22] Through Warren and others like him, the initial tendency of American Buddhist studies was to view Buddhism primarily as one form of Indian religion, thus equating Buddhology with Indology. The following quotation from the statement of purpose of establishing the Harvard Oriental Series may indicate the spirit of the time. It says, in part:

The central interest in the history of India is the long development of the religious thought and life of the Hindus,—a race akin, by ties of blood and language, to the Anglo-Saxon Stock. The value of the study of non-Christian religions is coming to be recognized by the best friends of Christianity more and more every day. The study tends to broaden and strengthen and universalize the base of religion,—a result of practical and immediate benefit. Works which promote this study stand first in the plans of the Oriental Series; and they are especially timely now, when so much of the widespread interest in Buddhism and other Oriental systems is misdirected by half-knowledge, or by downright error concerning them.[23]

Another important figure in the development of American Buddhist studies was Paul Carus (1852-1919), a freelance German philosopher who settled in La Salle, Illinois and devoted his life to the publication of books and two journals which he founded with the help of his father-in-law, E. C. Hegeler: *The Monist* and the *Open Court*. Dr. Carus was not a Buddhologist per se. Rather, he was interested in promoting religion and philosophy based on scientific foundations. From this viewpoint, he considered that Christianity was unscientific and mythological, whereas Buddhism was singularly free from myth-

[22] Henry Clarke Warren, "General Introduction" to *Buddhism in Translations* (Harvard Oriental Series, Vol. 3) (Cambridge: Harvard University Press, 1896), p. xxvi.
[23] Ibid., p. 388.

ological elements. His enthusiasm for Buddhism led him to comb through the available works on the subject in Western languages and to publish *The Gospel of Buddha* toward the end of the nineteenth century. Hegeler and Carus strongly supported the World's Parliament of Religions in 1893; in fact, Carus served as the Secretary of the Parliament. The Parliament's planners—scholars and liberal religious leaders—invited delegates from all the major religions of the world. They issued invitations to two Japanese Buddhists, Shimaji Mokurai and Nanjō Bunyū, to represent Mahāyāna Buddhism, which was scarcely known in America at that time. Although neither Shimaji nor Nanjō could accept the invitation, several Japanese religious leaders attended the Parliament. One of them was Shaku Sōen, who greatly impressed Hegeler and Carus. It was through this chance encounter between Shaku Sōen and Carus that Suzuki Daisetsu (Dr. D. T. Suzuki), a young disciple of Shaku Sōen, was later invited to come to La Salle, Illinois, where he spent twelve years (1897-1908) assisting the work of Paul Carus.[24] During his stay at La Salle, Dr. Suzuki translated *Asvaghosha's Discourse on the Awakening of Faith in the Mahayana* (1900) and *Sermons of a Buddhist Abbot* (1906). He also published *Outlines of Mahayana Buddhism* (1907). During this period, however, Suzuki, like his mentor Paul Carus, had no contact with academic circles in America.

Following the Russo-Japanese War (1904-1905), America began to take notice of Japan, but with mixed feelings. On the West Coast, emotional anti-Japanese feeling, stimulated by the increase of Japanese immigration, began to take hold. We will discuss the Buddhist activities among the Japanese, and to a lesser degree among the Chinese, immigrants on the West Coast and Hawaii presently. In sharp contrast to the West Coast, the East Coast welcomed Japanese intellectuals and scholars, including Okakura Kakuzō, who spent many years at the Museum of Fine Arts in Boston; Takamine Jōkichi, who made adrenalin and diastase (*Taka-diastase*) available; and Noguchi Hideyo, who made a great contribution to yellow fever prevention.[25] The growing interest in Japanese art, culture, and religion among the East Coast intellectuals was greatly aided by the writings of Ernest Fenollosa, Lafcadio Hearn, and Okakura Kakuzō. In this favorable atmosphere, Ane-

[24] See Daisetz Teitarō Suzuki, "A Glimpse of Paul Carus," in *Modern Trends in World Religions*, ed. Joseph M. Kitagawa (La Salle, Ill.: The Open Court Co., 1959), pp. ix-xiv.

[25] There were some notable exceptions too. For instance, the poet Noguchi Yone (-jirō), who was a close personal friend of Rabindranath Tagore, insisted on living on the West Coast.

saki Masaharu was invited to be Professor of Japanese Literature and Life at Harvard from 1913 to 1915. His Harvard lectures were later published under the titles of *Buddhist Art* (1915), *Nichiren the Buddhist Saint* (1916), and *History of Japanese Religion* (1930). Dr. Anesaki also lectured at some of the other leading universities in America and contributed learned articles to journals and to Hasting's *Encyclopaedia of Religion and Ethics*, which was influential in the scholarly world. Anesaki was fortunate, as he readily acknowledged, in developing warm personal friendships at Harvard with James H. Woods, the Indologist, Josiah Royce, the philosopher, and George F. Moore, the historian of religions. They played no small part in making Mahāyāna Buddhism an important feature of the American tradition of Buddhist studies, which for historic reasons received little impetus from the so-called "Leningrad school."

Meanwhile, the financial crisis of the late 1920s and the rise of Hitler in the early 1930s coincided with a change in the philosophical and religious climate of America. The strong influence of Barthianism in Christian circles was an indication that people were not satisfied to hear what had been believed; rather they asked what ought to be believed. Philosophy, hitherto preoccupied with epistemological questions, began to be concerned with the question of world-view. Buddhist studies, too, began to inquire into the meaning of Buddhist faith. This concern was shared even by those intellectuals who were not professional Buddhologists. For example, Paul Elmer Moore considered Mahāyāna Buddhism as the only viable option to Christian faith,[26] while James B. Pratt attempted to understand "how it feels to be a Buddhist." To do this, according to Pratt, it is not enough to know the history and doctrines of Buddhism. "One must catch its emotional undertone, enter sympathetically into its sentiments, feel one's way into its symbols, its cult, its art, and then ask to impart these things not merely by scientific exposition but in all sorts of indirect ways."[27]

The effort to gain fuller understanding of the meaning of Buddhism—and other religions for that matter—found its expression in a series of scholarly conferences on religions, notably the Conference on Modern Trends in World-Religions, held in Chicago in 1933, and the first East-West Philosophers' Conference, held in Honolulu in 1939. The former invited Kishimoto Hideo, while the latter invited Takakusu Junjirō from Japan. It was also the concern with the meaning of

[26] See his *The Catholic Faith* (Princeton: Princeton University Press, 1931).

[27] James Bissett Pratt, *The Pilgrimage of Buddhism* (New York: Macmillan, 1928), p. viii.

living Buddhism which brought the name of Dr. Suzuki to the attention of American intellectuals; it was with him and through him that America discovered Zen. Although Suzuki toured America in 1936-37, his impact on America was made primarily by his writings, especially *Essays in Zen Buddhism* (3 vols., 1927-1934), *Studies in the Lankavatara Sutra* (1930), *The Training of the Zen Buddhist Monk* (1934), *An Introduction to Zen Buddhism* (1934), *Manual of Zen Buddhism* (1935), and *Zen Buddhism and Its Influence on Japanese Culture* (1938).

World War II, though tragic in so many ways, brought Asia and its cultures and religions close to America. The language training and area studies which developed during the war have greatly expanded since its end. The History of Religions and the Comparative Study of Religions as well as Indology, Buddhology, Sinology, and Japanology have become important ingredients of American university curricula.[28] Notable among the centers of learning for non-Christian religions are such universities as Chicago (History of Religions), Harvard (World Religions), McGill (Islamic Studies), and Wisconsin and Washington (Buddhist Studies). Postwar American Buddhist studies have been greatly enriched by the coming of a number of Buddhologists from abroad: Paul Mus from France, Edward Conze from England, U Thittila from Burma, G. P. Malalasekera from Ceylon, and Miyamoto Shōson, Nakamura Hajime, Takeuchi Yoshinori, and others from Japan. Unique among them was Dr. Suzuki who in 1950 came to America at the age of 80 and spent eight years teaching, writing, and lecturing. If through his writings *Zen, satori,* and *kōan* became the "OK lingo" among the beatniks, it was far from Dr. Suzuki's intention. Undoubtedly, American Buddhist studies found in him the embodiment of Buddhism at its best—the blending of life and religion, knowledge and transcendental knowledge, learning, wisdom, and compassion.[29]

INSTITUTIONALIZED BUDDHISM

Space allows us to say little about institutionalized Buddhism, which has been prevalent primarily among people of Oriental descent. In this sense, the Buddhists are not dissimilar to other ethnic religious groups

[28] For the overall view on Indological and Buddhological studies in America, see Nakamura Hajime, "Amerika gakkai hōkoku," in *Indogaku Bukkyōgaku Kenkyū* 10, no. 1 (January 1962), pp. 308-313, and idem, "Ōbei ni okeru Indogaku Bukkyōgaku no ugoki," in *Indogaku Bukkyōgaku Kenkyū* 12, no. 2 (March 1964), pp. 282-292.

[29] See my tribute to "Daisetz Teitarō Suzuki," in *History of Religions* 6, no. 3 (February 1967), pp. 265-269.

in America, such as Scandinavian Lutheran or Dutch Reformed groups.

The Kingdom of Hawaii, before its annexation by the United States in 1900, attracted Chinese, Koreans, South Sea Islanders, Filipinos, and Japanese, as well as Europeans. In 1879, the total population of Hawaii was only 57,985. In that same year, the United States won the right to import sugar through a reciprocity treaty, and American sugar interests began to actively recruit Oriental labor, particularly from Japan. The census of 1900, made after the annexation, reported the population of Hawaii as approximately 154,000, including 37,000 Hawaiians and part-Hawaiians, 28,000 Caucasians, 5,000 Chinese, and 61,000 Japanese. Among the Japanese and Chinese were practicing Buddhists. The first visitation by a Buddhist priest to Hawaii, however, did not take place until 1887. And only in the 1890s did the Jōdo-shū (1894), Jōdo-shin-shū Honganji-ha (1897), and Jōdo-shin-shū Ōtani-ha (1899) initiate systematic activities; they were followed by the Nichiren-shū (1900), Sōtō-Zen-shū (1903), and Kōya-san Shingon-shū (1914). In the main, Buddhism is not very strong among people of Chinese descent, although there are two active temples which in recent years have invited a few emigré priests from Mainland China via Hong Kong and Taiwan. Among people of Japanese descent, Buddhism, as well as the Buddhist-related "new religions" of Japan, are active. According to the statistics cited in *World Buddhism* (February 1962 issue), the total number of Buddhists in Hawaii is estimated at roughly 100,000. Incidentally, in 1963 the Governor of Hawaii signed a bill establishing April 18 as "Buddha Day" for the state.

The situation of the West Coast of the United States is somewhat different from that of Hawaii, although here too institutionalized Buddhism is a phenomenon predominantly among people of Japanese ancestry and, to a far lesser degree, among people of Chinese and other descents. Records show that there were less than 100 Orientals (mostly Chinese) before the middle of the nineteenth century. With the beginning of the gold rush in California in 1849, railroad builders and gold prospectors recruited Chinese immigrants. But, as soon as business waned, the Burlington Treaty of 1868, which gave Chinese subjects in America the rights of citizens of the most-favored nation, was abrogated. In 1882, Congress suspended Chinese immigration for ten years; this policy was later extended for another ten years. In 1902, this exclusionary policy became permanent. As for the Japanese, there were only about 2,000 of them in America in 1890. The number increased steadily during the 1890s, and a sizable number of the Japanese in Hawaii moved to the West Coast at the time of annexation. West Coast politicians lost no time in demanding a Japanese exclusion act in Congress. Fearing such a drastic measure would strain the relations between the United States and Japan, Theodore Roosevelt concluded a "Gentleman's Agreement" with the Japanese government in 1907, which virtually stopped Japanese immigration without resorting to statutory exclusion. The persistent pressures of West Coast politicians, however, led ultimately to a Supreme Court decision in 1922 that Japanese were ineligible for American citizenship, and to the passage of the 1924 Quota Act, which terminated Japanese immigration altogether.

Religious activities among Orientals on the West Coast were initiated by the evangelistic Christian groups. Only in 1898 did the Jōdo-shin-shū Honganji-ha send two priests to San Francisco, and under their leadership the *Young Buddhist Association* was formed there. In 1900, the first group of Caucasian Buddhists, the *Dharma Sangha of Buddha*, was formed in San Francisco. It was through the invitation of these American Buddhists that Shaku Sōen, who had earlier attended the World's Parliament of Religions in Chicago, toured America in 1905, accompanied by Suzuki Daisetsu. In the following year, another Master of the Rinzai Zen School, Shaku Sōkatsu, accompanied by more than ten disciples, was invited by the American Buddhists in San Francisco. Later, one of his disciples, Sasaki Shigetsu, a sculptor by training, settled in New York;[30] another disciple, Senzaki Nyogen, carried on Zen activities on the West Coast. Both Sasaki and Senzaki had a number of non-Japanese followers. As for the Sōtō Zen School, its activity was initiated by the visit of Nukariya Kaiten to America in 1911; its adherents are mostly people of Japanese descent, however. Other Buddhist groups also started their activities among people of Japanese descent—the Kōya-san Shingon-shū (1912), the Nichiren-shū (1914), the Jōdo-shin-shū Ōtani-ha (1920), the Jōdo-shū (1938), etc. The total number of Buddhists among people of Japanese descent in America in 1940 was estimated to be about 55,000.[31] Of this number, nearly 80 per cent belonged to the Jōdo-shin-shū Honganji-ha which is called the *Hoku-bei Bukkyō-dan* (Buddhist

---

[30] Sasaki's widow, Mrs. Ruth Fuller Sasaki, was instrumental in establishing the *First Zen Institute of America* in New York. She also built a Zen training center for Westerners at Daitoku-ji, Kyoto. Incidentally, Mrs. Sasaki's daughter by her first marriage married (and later divorced) Alan Watts, the author of many popular books on Zen and related subjects.

[31] These figures are taken from Robert Spencer, *Japanese Buddhism in the United States, 1940-46: A Study of Acculturation* (Ph.D. Thesis, University of California, Berkeley, 1946).

Churches of America). Today, it boasts a membership of 100,000 with 68 active and 30 inactive priests under the leadership of their Bishop, Hanayama Shinshō.[32] It also operates the BCA Study Center in Berkeley, California, which conducts annual seminars in English on the Pacific Coast and in Chicago and New York. In 1933, the Buddhist Churches of Canada, which had been under American jurisdiction, became an independent diocese; its membership is estimated to be around 12,000.

In retrospect, it becomes evident that institutional Buddhism, which initially was established primarily among Japanese-speaking immigrants on the West Coast, has undergone many significant changes.[33] Nevertheless, it has retained strong ethnic, cultural, and religious ties with Buddhism in Japan. There are many reasons for this. In this connection, we may recall that after the outbreak of World War I the realization that some Americans still maintained cultural and emotional affiliations with the countries of their ancestors prompted the government and civic and church groups to start the so-called "Americanization" movement in order to transform peoples of different background into "typical Americans." This movement was promoted by Christian groups working among Orientals; their attempts were stymied, however, by the decision of the Supreme Court that Japanese were ineligible for American citizenship. Besides, the pattern of rigid segregation which developed on the West Coast made it virtually impossible for Buddhism, the symbol of Oriental culture, to develop free and natural contacts with the cultural and religious climate of the larger American society.

Ironically, the quick shift of public opinion in America from the wartime hatred to the postwar vogue for things Japanese—including flower arrangement, Jūjitsu, and Zen Buddhism—encouraged institutional Buddhism to retain, rather than shake off, cultural as well as religious vestiges of Asia in general and of Japan in particular. In this situation, institutional Buddhism in America now faces many difficult problems. The late Dr. Tsunoda, who for many years taught at Columbia University, suggested the importance of "indigenizing" Buddhism in America.[34] This is far easier said than done. In 1962, when a group of Japanese delegates visited Chicago on the occasion of the

[32] Dr. Hanayama was formerly Professor at Tokyo University.

[33] For a brief sociological analysis of the Buddhist Churches of America, see Morioka Kiyomi, *Shinshū-kyōdan to "ie" seido* (Tokyo: Sōgen-sha, 1962), pp. 629-639.

[34] Tsunoda Ryūsaku, "Bukkyōto to Amerika," in *Bukkyō to Bunka* (Dedicated to Dr. Daisetz Teitarō Suzuki in Commemoration of his Ninetieth Birthday) (Kyoto: Suzuki-gakujutsu-zaidan, 1960), pp. 239-247.

seventieth anniversary of the introduction of Buddhism to America, a conference was held regarding the future of Buddhism in America. The participants pointed out the inadequacy of Buddhist education for children, the lack of good English books on various aspects of Buddhism, the lack of proper understanding and support from ecclesiastical leaders in Japan, and the fact that Buddhism tends to attract those Caucasian-Americans who do not fit into their own society and religious tradition or those who try to use Buddhism for non-religious ends.[35] This last problem is especially acute in reference to Zen Buddhism, which has fascinated many young nonconformists in America.

There are, of course, a number of groups of sincere American and Canadian Buddhists scattered in various parts of North America. While their number is not impressive, their faith is enriched by that intellectual understanding of both the philosophical and religious dimensions of Buddhism; nonetheless, they too are not altogether free from the temptation to consider Buddhism as a sort of escape from workaday reality. On the other hand, there are some bizarre groups which appropriate the marginal features of Buddhist doctrines and symbols. One of the most extreme examples is the LSD cult, which recently had its "religious celebration" in Chicago. It began with two men on stage, one playing a guitar and the other a bongo drum. Huge figures of Buddha and swirling galaxies were projected from slides onto a large screen. Then, Timothy Leary led the group in prayer and told them he hoped to reproduce "some of the beauty, some of the meaning, some of the terror, of the LSD experience." The celebration was "designed to dramatize the mind of Buddha when he attained spiritual enlightenment five centuries before Christ."[36] It might be pertinent to add that even such unemotional Buddhists as those in England are also susceptible—most likely the residual qualities of their Theosophist background—to fortune-telling, palmistry, and astrology.[37]

In my assessment, there is no question that Buddhism is here in the West to stay. However, the Western religious tradition is not collapsing, as some Hindus and Buddhists in Asia think, nor is the West ready to welcome a wholesale "spiritual colonization by the East."[38] Yet, the religious leaders in the East tend to overlook the complexity

[35] See Tsunemitsu Kōzen, *Nihon-Bukkyō-tobei-shi* (Tokyo: Bukkyō Shuppan-kyoku, 1964), pp. 215-216.

[36] Reported by William Braden in *Chicago Sun-Times*, 8 January 1967, p. 2.

[37] See "Obei no naka no Bukkyo," in *Zaike Bukkyō*, no. 99 (June 1962), pp. 38-49.

[38] Henri de Lubac, *La Rencontre du Bouddhisme et de l'Occident* (Paris: Aubier, 1952), p. 274, n. 46.

of the religious situation in the West. For instance, among the Theravāda Buddhist leaders, according to Dr. King: "There is no real appreciation of the depth of cultural and intellectual difference between
Theravāda East and Christian-secular West, nor of the fact that the
Theravāda tradition will need to re-think and re-present its message in
radically different fashion from that of the traditional past if it is to
receive more than a polite and scholarly hearing on the part of those
it hopes to convert."[39] The problem is no less complicated for Mahāyāna Buddhism on this score. Buddhism in America, and in other parts
of the West for that matter, despite its promises, faces serious problems, the solutions for which are not easy to find. Without succumbing
to rigid gradualism, we must recognize that the solutions of some
problems must ultimately depend on the passage of time—in the
words of Professor Shils, "of time which resolves problems through
supplanting them by new problems, and through the gradual generation of new traditions which only the passage of time can nurture."[40]
Buddhism in the West is no exception.

[39] Winston King, *Buddhism in Contemporary Burma*, p. 79.
[40] Edward Shils, "The Culture of the Indian Intellectual," in *The Sewanee Review*
(April and July 1959), pp. 45-46.

Glossary

Words within the entries set in SMALL CAPITAL letters are defined elsewhere in the Glossary.

AINU. Their identity is not absolutely certain but is most likely Caucasoid. They have preserved many arctic religious beliefs and practices, including the Bear Festival. They live on Hokkaido, Sakhalin, and the Kurile Islands.

AMATERASU Ō-MIKAMI. The tutelary KAMI of the imperial (TENNŌ) clan. Also known as Ō-hirume-no-kami, she is portrayed in mythologies as the central figure in the heavenly domain. Her grandson, Ninigi, was dispatched to rule Japan, and Ninigi's great-grandson, Jimmu, is regarded as the first legendary emperor. Amaterasu is enshrined in the Grand Shrine of ISE.

AMIDA. Amitābha (the Buddha of Infinite Light) or Amitāyus (the Buddha of Infinite Life), whose abode is the Pure Land (Sukhāvatī).

BAKUFU. The feudal regime; the shogunate government.

BOSATSU. Bodhisattva; beings destined for enlightenment and believed to have vowed to save all beings out of their compassion.

BUMMEI-KAIKA. Civilization and enlightenment.

BUNREI. Dividing the spirit of the KAMI. Branch shrines may be established from the original shrine of a certain kami to house his spirit as well; thus the new shrines participate in the power of the original.

BUPPŌ. *See* ŌBŌ.

BUSHIDŌ. The code of the warrior (*bushi*).

CHINGO-KOKKA. Protection of the nation. An important motif of Buddhism in early Japan.

CHINJU. A protecting deity in Shinto belief.

DAINICHI. The Great Sun Buddha (Mahāvairocana), believed to be the essence of the cosmos in Esoteric Buddhism.

DAISHI. Great teacher, e.g. Dengyō Daishi (Saichō) or Kōbō Daishi (Kūkai).

DAJŌKAN. Great Council of State which, together with the JINGIKAN, constituted the government according to the RITSURYŌ system.

DANKA. A household which supports a Buddhist temple; a Buddhist parishioner.

DO-IKKI. A peasant uprising.

DŌZOKU. Traditional Japanese kinship system that includes all the branch families (*bunke*) of a certain main family (*honke*).

ENGI-SHIKI. *Procedures of the Engi Era* (A.D. 901-922), a body of rules supplementing previously promulgated edicts and ceremonial codes. It was completed in 927 and put into effect in 967. Also called the *Institutes of the Engi Era.*

FUDOKI. *Records of Local Surveys*, compiled during the Nara period.

FUJI-KŌ. Devotional confraternity of Mount Fuji.

FUJIWARA. Family name of the descendants of Fujiwara Kamatari (A.D. 614-669). The Fujiwara were the *de facto* dictators of medieval Japan.

FUJU-FUSE. Principle of "not receiving from, and not giving to, nonbelievers." Advocated by Nichiō (1565-1630), one of the leaders of the Nichiren school of Buddhism (NICHIREN-SHŪ).

FUKKO-GAKU. *See* KOGAKU.

FUKKO-SHINTO. The Neo-Shinto movement, advocated by Motoori Norinaga (1730-1801), Hirata Atsutane (1776-1843), and others, which aimed at a "return to antiquity."

FUSŌ-KYŌ. Sect Shinto denomination which venerates Fuso, the classical name of Mount Fuji.

GONGEN. A temporary manifestation of the Buddha.

GORYŌ. Spirits of those who suffered a violent death; believed to curse the living by either haunting them or inflicting a calamity on them.

GORYŌ-YE. Rituals for the purpose of pacifying the vengeful spirits (GORYŌ). Such rituals developed in the ninth century A.D. in Kyoto and gradually spread to the provinces. Significantly, the *goryō-ye* was quite different in form and ethos from the earlier Shinto rituals centering on the KAMI of the clan.

HAIBUTSU KISHAKU. Literally, "elimination of Buddha." It refers to the anti-Buddhist movement that arose in the early MEIJI era.

HAKKŌ-ICHIU. Literally, "the whole world under one roof." This phrase was used by the Japanese militarists during the 1930s and 1940s as a slogan for their expansionist program.

HARAYE or HARAI. The purification ceremonies of Shinto.

HIJIRI. Literally, "holy man," a monk who excels in pious learning. Often used to refer to religious persons with charismatic qualities in contradistinction to leaders of institutionalized religions. Frequently, these are monks who became recluses.

HIMOROGI. An ancient form of Shinto shrine, identified as a piece of unpolluted land surrounded by evergreens. In its center is a sacred tree. Cf. IWA-SAKA.

HOKKE-IKKI. An armed uprising of the adherents of the Nichiren school. *See* NICHIREN-SHŪ.

HOKKE-SHŪ. A school of Buddhism founded by Nichiren (1222-1282) and based on the teaching of the *Lotus* (*Sad-dharma pundarīka*) *Sūtra*; also known as the NICHIREN-SHŪ.

HONGAN. Literally, "original vow." Refers to the eighteenth vow (among forty-eight) of Amida recorded in the *Sukhāvatībyūha* (Sutra of the Pure Land), according to which a devotee who relies on the Amida Buddha and repeats his name is assured of rebirth in the Pure Land.

HONGAN-JI. The Temple of the Original Vow; the name of the main temple of the JŌDO-SHIN-SHŪ (the True Pure Land School). Following the divi-

330

sion of this school into two branches in the seventeenth century, both branches adopted this designation for their respective main temples: the Higashi (Eastern) and Nishi (Western) Hongan-ji.

HONJI. Original or metaphysical nature of the Buddha. According to the theory of *honji suijaku*, the Shinto KAMI were manifestations (or incarnations, *suijaku*) of the original nature of the Buddha. This theory was advanced to justify the Shinto-Buddhist coexistence pattern known as the RYŌBU-SHINTO or *Sannō-ichijitsu-Shintō*.

HOSSHIN. Awakening.

HOSSHIN (*Dharmakaya*). The highest aspect of the Threefold Body of the Buddha. The absolute nature of the Buddha. The other two bodies are the Nirmanakaya (earthly body; in Mahāyāna belief, Śākyamuni and other buddhas) and Sambhogakaya (Supreme Enlightened Mind of the Buddha). Esoteric Buddhism in Japan considers the Hosshin to be active; the Mahāyāna tradition does not.

HOSSŌ. The Vijnaptimatrata or Yogācāra school of Buddhism. It was one of the six schools established in Japan during the Nara period.

HŌTOKU. Literally, "repay the indebtedness." The name of the semireligious movement initiated by Ninomiya Sontoku (1787-1856).

HŌZA. Literally, "teaching circle." A form of discussion group utilized by some of the new religions for the purpose of religious instruction.

IKKI. An uprising, insurrection, or revolt; e.g., DO-IKKI, HOKKE-IKKI, and IKKŌ-IKKI.

IKKŌ-IKKI. An insurrection of the adherents of the IKKŌ-SHŪ.

IKKŌ-SHŪ. Literally, "single-minded or single-directed sect." The name given to the followers of the True Pure Land School (JŌDO-SHIN-SHŪ).

INSEI or INZEI. The rule of the cloistered ex-emperors who usually permitted only ceremonial functions to the nominally reigning monarchs.

ISE. The seat of the great imperial shrine (Kōtai jingū) which enshrines AMATERASU, the tutelary KAMI of the imperial clan.

ISE-KŌ. A devotional association of the faithful of ISE, which usually has a village or hamlet as its local unit, and sends representatives to worship at the Grand Shrine of Ise from time to time. The popularity of Ise was such, however, that sometimes even those who did not belong to *Ise-kō* participated in spontaneous mass pilgrimages to give thanks (*okage mairi*).

ISHIN. Renovation, renewal, or restoration; e.g., MEIJI *ishin*.

IWASAKA. A spot of unpolluted land surrounded by holy rocks which was chosen for the worship of a KAMI. Cf. HIMOROGI.

JINEN. Spontaneity.

JINEN-HŌNI. Things (realities) as they are. In Sanskrit, *tathatā*; also *shinnyo*.

JINGIKAN. Bureau of Shinto (KAMI) Affairs which, together with the DAJŌKAN, constituted the government according to the RITSURYŌ system.

JINGŪ-JI. A Buddhist chapel established within the compound of a Shinto shrine.

JINJA. A Shinto shrine.

331

JINJA HONCHŌ. The Association of Shrine Shinto organized in 1945.

JINJA SHINTO. Shrine Shinto, the post–Second World War name for the disestablished State Shinto. The heir of the shrines and organization previously known as State (*Kokka*) Shinto. Now it is recognized as a religion like any other. There are about 100,000 Shinto shrines, and most of them belong to JINJA HONCHŌ.

JIRIKI. The attempt to attain enlightenment through one's own power.

JI-SHŪ. A school of Amida pietism founded by Ippen (1239-1289). It is called the *Ji* (literally, "time") sect because it follows the custom of singing hymns six times a day.

JIZŌ. Bodhisattva Kṣitigarbha, called Ti-tsang in Chinese. He is believed to stand between this world and the next and to save those on their way to hell.

JŌDO. The Pure Land (*sukhāvatī*), which is Amida's paradise.

JŌDO-SHIN-SHŪ. The True Pure Land School of Buddhism founded by Shinran (1173-1262); also known as the IKKŌ-SHŪ.

JŌDO-SHŪ. The Pure Land school of Buddhism founded by Hōnen (1133-1212).

JŌJITSU. The Satyasiddhi school. It was one of the six Buddhist schools established in Japan during the Nara period.

JŌMON. The name of the earliest period of prehistoric Japan (ca. 2500 B.C.-250 B.C.).

JUKYŌ. Confucianism.

JUNREI. Any religious pilgrimage.

JUSHA. A scholar of Confucianism.

KAIDAN. A Buddhist ordination hall.

KAJI-KITŌ. Magico-religious rites and prayers.

KAMI. Although there are many etymological theories regarding this term, there is none that is acceptable to everybody, nor is there an appropriate Western equivalent. It is often translated as god, spirit, or anything that commands the awe and reverence of man. It refers to both the sacred nature of the cosmos in general and the specific objects of worship in Shinto.

KAMI-DANA. Miniature Shinto shrines, usually kept at home.

KAMI-GAKARI. The state of KAMI-possession.

KANNAGARA. "True Shinto," as it was of old. An adverb that modifies actions of the KAMI. Orthodox Shinto claims to be *kannagara-no-michi* (the way which is in accordance with the will of the *kami*).

KANNUSHI. A head priest of a Shinto shrine.

KEGON. The Avatamsaka school. One of the six Buddhist sects established in Japan during the Nara period.

KIKA-JIN. A person who has become naturalized. Formerly referred specifically to Koreans or Chinese who had become Japanese.

KIRISHITAN. Premodern name for Roman Catholicism and Roman Catholics.

KŌ or KŌSHA. These terms refer to both a devotional association—frequently of laymen and laywomen—and its meetings for the purpose of religious instruction. Many of these associations, which were either Shinto or Buddhist, became new religions after World War II.

KŌAN. Literally, a "public theme." A paradoxical statement utilized by ZEN masters to dispel ordinary logic for the spiritual illumination of disciples.

KŌDŌ. The "Imperial Way" that was advocated by Neo-Shintoists as the ideal principle of polity in Japan.

KOFUN. Ancient mound. Also, the transitional period between prehistoric and early historic Japan (ca. A.D. 250-550), so called because of the large tumuli constructed during this period.

KOGAKU. Also known as *Fukko-gaku*. A long-dead branch of Japanese Confucianism that stressed the study of antiquity, that is, the teachings of Confucius and Mencius.

KOJIKI. *Records of Ancient Matters*, a Japanese classic compiled during the Nara period. Regarded as a semisacred scripture of Shinto, it contains myths, legends, and historical accounts centering on the imperial clan.

KOKUBUNJI. A state-supported official Buddhist temple built during the Nara period. There was one in each province.

KOKUBUNNIJI. A state-supported Buddhist nunnery built in the Nara period.

KOKUGAKU. National Japanese learning, in contradistinction to *Kangaku* (Chinese or Confucian learning) and *Yōgaku* (Western learning).

KOKUTAI. National polity.

KONKŌ-KYŌ. One of the native, premodern (pre-1868) religions, founded by Kawate Bunjirō (1813-1883).

KUROZUMI-KYŌ. One of the native, premodern religions, founded by Kurozumi Munetada (1780-1850).

KUSHA. The Abhidharmakośa school. One of the sixth Buddhist schools established in Japan during the Nara period.

KYŌDAN. Abbreviation of *Nihon Kirisuto Kyōdan* (The Church of Christ in Japan).

KYŌHA SHINTO. Sect Shinto denominations, in contrast to State Shinto.

KYŌKAI. A term used both by Christian and Sect Shinto groups to refer to the church (building and religious community).

MAITREYA. *See* MIROKU.

MAJINAI. A spell or incantation.

MAN'YŌSHŪ. *A Collection of Myriad Leaves*, an anthology of poetry compiled toward the end of the eighth century.

MAPPŌ. According to a Buddhist view of cosmic history, there were three periods. The first thousand years was the period of the "perfect law" (*Saddharma, shōbō*); the second thousand years was that of the "copied law" (*Pratirūpa-dharma, zōbō*); and the third thousand years was the period of the "degeneration of Buddha's law" (*Paschima-dharma, mappō*). Many leaders of Japanese Buddhism during the Kamakura period took this view of cosmic history seriously and believed they were entering the *mappō* period.

MATSURI. Religious ceremonies, rituals, and rites. In popular usage, this term also denotes festivals of various kinds which have lost their religious significance.

MATSURI-GOTO. The affairs of state, government, or political administration. It derives from the word MATSURI, which demonstrates the extent to which political and religious institutions were regarded as interdependent and interpenetrating in ancient Japan. *See also* SAISEI-ITCHI.

MEIJI. The era (1867-1912) which saw the restoration of the emperor and the modernization of Japan; it also signifies the prewar religious-cultural-political-social synthesis.

MIKKYŌ. Literally, "esoteric doctrines." It refers to the esoteric tradition of Buddhism, known variously as *Mantrayāna*, *Tantrayāna*, or *Vajrayāna*. In Japan, there are two main schools of *Mikkyō*: the Shingon school, usually known as the *Tō-Mitsu* (meaning the esoteric tradition of a Shingon temple in Kyoto known as Tō-ji), and the Tendai school, known as the *Tai-Mitsu*. *See also* SHINGON-SHŪ and TENDAI-SHŪ.

MIKO. Although there were various kinds of *Miko* in ancient Japan, they were for the most part charismatic female shamanic diviners. Even today, this type of *Miko* exists in many parts of Japan. The term is also used to designate a supplementary priestess in Shinto shrines today. These women perform sacred dances and assist priests in Shinto rituals.

MIROKU. Maitreya, the future, messianic Buddha.

MONO. Spirits of animals and other "lower" beings. Cf. TAMA.

MUJŌ. Transience or transitoriness, uncertainty, mutability.

MUKYŌKAI. The Non-Church Movement, founded by Uchimura Kanzō (1861-1930), a leading Japanese Christian.

NAORAI. The feast phase of Shinto ceremony in which the rice wine and food offered to deities is consumed.

NEHAN. Nirvana.

NEMBUTSU. Invocation of the holy name of AMIDA.

NICHIREN-SHŪ. A school of Buddhism founded by Nichiren (1222-1282); also known as the HOKKE-SHŪ.

NIHONGI or NIHON-SHOKI. *Chronicles of Japan*, compiled during the Nara period.

NIRMANAKAYA. *See* HOSSHIN (*Dharmakaya*).

NŌ. A highly symbolic form of Japanese drama that has flourished since the fourteenth century.

NORITO. Words addressed to the KAMI in Shinto ceremonies. More specifically, it refers to the ritual passages collected in the tenth-century *Procedures of the Engi Era* (ENGI-SHIKI).

ŌBAKU-SHŪ. A sect of ZEN Buddhism that was transmitted to Japan from China during the TOKUGAWA period.

ŌBŌ. The Emperor's law (usually in relation to *Buppō*, the Buddha's law).

O-FURIKAYE. The belief in a divine mediation that transfers suffering from people to a savior or to the savior's human agent(s). Used mostly by KONKŌ-KYŌ, a Sect Shinto denomination.

334

ONMYŌDŌ. Yin-Yang and Taoist magic.

ONTAKE-KYŌ. Sect Shinto denomination which venerates the KAMI of Mount Ontake.

ŌYŌMEI-GAKU. A branch of Neo-Confucianism that follows the tradition of Wang Yang-ming (in Japanese, Ōyōmei, 1471-1529).

REIGEN. Marvelous efficacy of the KAMI or the Buddha.

REIYUKAI. Literally, "the Association of the Friends of the Spirit." A lay Buddhist organization based on the teachings of the thirteenth-century Buddhist leader, Nichiren. Reiyukai was founded by Kubo Kakutaro (1890-1944) and Kotani Kimi (1901-1971).

RI. Japanese pronunciation of the Chinese word *li*, which means "reason" or "principle."

RINZAI-SHŪ. One of the ZEN Buddhist schools; transmitted to Japan from China by Eisai (or Yosai, 1141-1215).

RISSHŌ KŌSEIKAI. The "Society for the Establishment of Righteousness and Friendly Intercourse," originally an offshoot of REIYUKAI. Founded jointly by Niwano Nikkyo (1906-) and Naganuma Myoko (1899-1957), it is one of the most active new religions (SHINKŌ SHŪKYŌ), devoted especially to the cause of world peace.

RITSURYŌ. The first religious-political-cultural-social synthesis, developed in the seventh and eighth centuries.

RITSU. The Vinaya school, one of the six schools of Buddhism established in Japan during the Nara period.

RUIJI-SHŪKYŌ. Also known as *Shūkyō-ruiji-dantai*; a pseudo or quasi religion.

RYŌBU-SHINTO. As a general term, it refers to the pattern of Shinto-Buddhist coexistence that developed in Japan. Specifically, it is the designation of Shingon-Shinto, which interprets Shinto in accordance with the doctrines of the Shingon school of Buddhism (*see* SHINGON-SHŪ). A similar attempt by the Tendai school of Buddhism is called the *Sannō-ichijitsu-Shinto* (*see* TENDAI-SHŪ).

SAISEI-ITCHI. The ancient Japanese idea that religion (*sai*) and government (*sei*) are inextricably connected and interdependent. *See also* MATSURI-GOTO.

SAMBHOGAKAYA. *See* HOSSHIN (*Dharmakaya*).

SANRON. The Mādhyamika or Sarvasūnyavāda school. One of the six schools of Buddhism established in Japan during the Nara period.

SESSHŌ. The regent for the emperor.

SHIKKEN. The regent for the SHOGUN.

SHIN-BUTSU HANZEN. Separation of Shinto from Buddhism. This measure was taken by the MEIJI regime in order to reestablish Shinto as the *de facto* state religion.

SHIN-BUTSU SHŪGO. The pattern of Shinto-Buddhist amalgamation.

SHINGAKU. Literally, "Mind-Learning." A semireligious movement founded by Ishida Baigan (1685-1744).

SHINGON-SHŪ. *Shingon* is the Japanese pronunciation of the Chinese *Chên-yen*, meaning "true word" (*mantra*). It is a form of Esoteric Buddhism (MIKKYŌ) which was transmitted to China from India by Subhakarasinha (637-735), Vajrabodhi (663-723), and Amoghavajra (705-774). A Japanese monk, Kūkai, better known as Kōbō Daishi (774-835), introduced the esoteric doctrine to Japan in 806 and established the Shingon-shū. Unlike other schools of Buddhism, Esoteric Buddhism is a form of cosmotheism in that DAINICHI is considered the essence of the cosmos (*dharmakaya*). *See also* HOSSHIN.

SHINKŌ SHŪKYŌ. The new religions that have arisen in Japan since the end of the Second World War.

SHIN-SHŪ-REN. Abbreviation of *Shin-Nihon-Shūkyō-dantai-rengōkai* (The Association of New Religions in Japan).

SHŌBŌ. The period of the "perfect law" in Buddhist cosmic history. *See also* MAPPŌ.

SHŌGUN. A warrior-ruler or generalissimo.

SHŌNIN. A holy man who combines pious learning and holy virtues. Often attached as a suffix to a holy man's name, for example, Shinran-shōnin.

SHUGEN. Mastery of magical power.

SHUGEN-DŌ. The method of acquiring magical power by undergoing austere disciplines in the mountains. It refers specifically to the Order of Mountain Ascetics, which is founded on a peculiar blend of folk beliefs, Shinto, and Buddhism with some elements of Yin-Yang and Taoist belief.

SHUSHI-GAKU. A branch of Neo-Confucianism which follows the tradition of Chu Hsi (in Japanese, Shushi; 1130-1200). The TOKUGAWA regime adopted Shushi-gaku as its official doctrine.

SHUSHĪN. Morality or ethics.

SŌKA GAKKAI. Literally, "the Value-Creating Society." A lay Buddhist organization associated with the Nichiren Shoshu sect, it is by far the most active new religion in Japan. Affiliated with this group is a political party known as the Kōmei-tō.

SOKUSHIN JŌBUTSU. To become a Buddha during one's earthly existence. (This is the goal of the Shingon Buddhist.)

SŌTŌ-SHŪ. A branch of ZEN Buddhism transmitted to Japan by Dōgen (1200-1253).

TAI-MITSU. Tendai esoterism. *See also* MIKKYŌ.

TAMA. Spirit or soul of the KAMI and of man. *Ara-mi-tama* is a violent spirit or a spirit that coerces men with power, while *nigimi-tama* is a gentle spirit that pacifies men. *Mi-tama-shiro* (the representation of a spirit) and *shintai* (the *kami* body) are sacred objects through which a certain *kami* is worshipped. *Tama-shizume* or *chinkon* is a ceremony to prevent the soul from leaving the body. *Tama-yori-hime* is a woman or maiden (*hime*) in whom the *tama* of the *kami* dwells. *Kuni-tama* is the spirit of the land (earth). Somewhat different is the use of this term as a synonym for "principle," for example, *yamato-damashii* (the *tama-shii* of *Yamato*), which simply means *Nippon seishin* (the Japanese spirit).

TARIKI. The power of the Other, i.e., AMIDA. Seeking rebirth in the Pure Land (JŌDO) by relying on the compassion of Amida.

336

TENDAI-SHŪ. The Japanese pronunciation of the Chinese T'ien T'ai sect, which was founded by Chih-i or Chih-k'ai (531-597). He advocated the unity of three truths: (1) all things have no self-nature; (2) all things have a provisional existence; and (3) the nature of all realities (*dharmas*) is thus both void (empty) and transitory. Chih-i developed his system based on the *Lotus Sūtra*, which he considered the culmination of all Buddhist doctrines. The Tendai system was introduced to Japan in 805 by Saichō, better known as Dengyō Daishi (767-822). He attempted to incorporate and integrate monastic discipline, esoteric cults, and ZEN (Ch'an) practices into the new system in a synthesis of Shinto and Buddhism called the *Sannō-ichijitsu-Shinto*. Shortly after Saichō's death, the "esoteric tradition" (*Tai-Mitsu*) became paramount in the Tendai school. *See also* MIKKYŌ.

TENNŌ. Emperor.

TERA. A Buddhist temple, pronounced *ji* in compound words, e.g., Hōryū-ji, Tō-ji, and Tōdai-ji.

TERA-KOYA or TERA GOYA. A Buddhist temple school for children.

TERA-UKE. A temple certificate required by the TOKUGAWA regime for every Japanese family in order to prove that its members were Buddhists and not adherents of Roman Catholicism (KIRISHITAN).

TOKUGAWA. Family name of the descendants of Tokugawa Iyeyasu (1542-1616). Also the name of the shogunate or BAKUFU (1603-1867) that witnessed the second great synthesis of religion-polity-culture-society in Japanese history.

TŌ-MITSU. The esoteric tradition of the Shingon school. *See also* MIKKYŌ.

TORII. A sacred gateway formed of two upright and two horizontal beams which is erected in front of a Shinto shrine.

TSUMI. Usually translated as "sin," but connotes sickness, error, and disaster as well as mental and physical defilements. According to Shinto, *tsumi* are removed by ceremonial cleansing (HARAYE).

UBASOKU. The Japanese pronunciation of the Sanskrit *upāsaka* (feminine, *upāsikā*), which means one who is not a *bhikku* (a member of a monastic order) but who follows the law of the Buddha; in other words, a lay ascetic. In Japan, however, the term *ubasoku* often refers to a charismatic leader who practices semi-Buddhist and semi-shamanist austerities. As early as the Nara period, there were many *ubasoku* who claimed to have attained magical power by undergoing austere training at certain mountains. Their tradition developed into the SHUGEN-DŌ. Later, many *ubasoku* became itinerant preachers, healers, and magicians.

UJI. The clan.

UJI-BITO. Member(s) of an UJI.

UJI-GAMI. The ancestral or tutelary KAMI of a particular clan.

UJI-KO. Literally, "a child of the clan." But since everyone within the parish of a Shinto shrine is regarded as a child of the UJI-GAMI, it means simply a parishioner.

UJI-NO-KAMI. The clan chieftain.

URUWASHI. Beautiful.

YAKUSHI. Commonly referred to as the healing Buddha.

YAMA-BUSHI. Literally, "one who sleeps in the mountain": the mountain ascetic of the SHUGEN-DŌ tradition.

YAMATAI. Sometimes pronounced "Yabatai." One of the principalities in Japan during its early historic period.

YAMATO. An early kingdom in Japan, hence the old name of Japan. Also the name of the district now known as the Nara prefecture.

YAYOI. The name of a section of Tokyo where prehistoric pottery was unearthed in 1884. The name Yayoi was thus given to the period ca. 250 B.C.-A.D. 250 by archaeologists.

YOSHI. Good, desirable.

YUIITSU-SHINTO. Also known as Yoshida or Urabe Shinto. A monastic school of Shinto sustained since the Heian period by the priestly family called Yoshida. It was systematized by Yoshida Kanetomo (1435-1511), whose goal was the integration of Shinto, Buddhism, and Confucianism within the framework of Shinto. Thus it is also referred to as *Gempon-sōgen-Shinto* (fundamental and original Shinto).

ZA. Trade guilds that were frequently affiliated with Shinto or Buddhist institutions. Prosperous during the TOKUGAWA period, *za* have disappeared.

ZAZEN. Meditation with crossed legs.

ZEN. *Ch'an* in Chinese, *Zen* in Japanese. The *Dhyana* or meditation school of Buddhism that developed in China and was introducued to Japan by Eisai and Dōgen in the early twelfth century. *See also* ŌBAKU-SHŪ, RINZAI-SHŪ, and SŌTŌ-SHŪ.

ZŌBŌ. The period of the "copied law" in Buddhist cosmic history. *See also* MAPPŌ.

Index

LIBRARY OF CONGRESS CATALOGING-IN-PUBLICATION DATA

Kitagawa, Joseph Mitsuo, 1915-
On understanding Japanese religion.

Includes bibliographical references and index. 1. Japan—Religion. I. Title.

BL2202.K49 1987 291'.0952 87-2795
ISBN 0-691-07313-9 (alk. paper) ISBN 0-691-10229-5 (pbk.)